I always have tried to keep my spiritual ears open for important, new things that the Holy Spirit is saying to the Churches, and through the years I have been permitted to focus in on several of them. As soon as I began hearing Robert Henderson speak on the courts of Heaven I thought that this might be another one of those divine words. Now that he has put his thoughts in writing with Operating in the Courts of Heaven, I am convinced that this revelation is truly a game-changer for those of us intent on advancing God's kingdom. This is one of the most important books you can read for moving ahead in this present season!

C. Peter Wagner, Vice-President
Global Spheres, Inc.

Operating in the Courts of Heaven is an exciting treatise on the legal protocols of presenting a case in front of the Judge of Heaven and the entire legal systemic procedures therein. Robert's ability to provide language and description to the supernatural administration of prayer, allows the process to seem easily explainable to the lay person as well as the legally trained. For those looking for answers to their prayer - the goal posts have been widened and the possibilities for victory assured! I have watched Robert grow and develop his understanding of the heavenly court system and rejoice to see it in black and white.

Natasha Grbich, Director
Ariel Gate International House of Strategy

Robert Henderson has a passion and love for the Body of Christ that is awakening God's people everywhere he ministers. Now Robert has a revelation that we need to seriously consider for unlocking God's will for the world. Here is a key that could change your life and set you free.

Harold R. Eberle
Worldcast Ministries

From the first time I heard Robert teach on the Courtroom of Heaven, the paradigms of my ministry have been shaking and shifting. I was fully aware, with our apostolic intercessory work in Texas, of the authority that we carry as kings and priests of the Most High God, but this material ushered me into a whole new realm of understanding and impartation. Whether we are grandpas, pastors, CEOs, mothers, students or a prayer leader over Texas, it is a powerful revelation to know that your destiny (and the destiny of states and nations) has been inscribed on the books that are set before the Judge and King of all of creation. And He has invited us into that courtroom in order to release and decree that destiny into the earth. This book, Operating in the Courts of Heaven, is not just a "must" read, it is a "must" mindset!

Dr. Thomas Schlueter, Coordinator
Texas Apostolic Prayer Network

OPERATING IN THE

COURTS OF

HEAVEN

Granting God the Legal Right to Fulfill
His Passion and Answer Our Prayers

ROBERT
HENDERSON

It is with profound gratitude that I dedicate this book to God my Father who is Judge of all. To Jesus my High Priest, Mediator and Intercessor whose sacrifice provides all I need to operate before the Throne of Heaven. To Holy Spirit who is my friend and takes all that Jesus did and helps me execute it into place until the verdicts of the cross are seen on the Earth.

I also dedicate this book to my wife Mary and her relentless support and belief in me for all these years. May the Lord greatly reward your faithfulness with years of "being kept busy with the joy of your heart." (Ecclesiastes 5:20)

I also dedicate this book to the Ariel Gate team who has been at the forefront of pioneering these truths for decades. Thanks to Natasha Grbich for your sacrifice and commitment to the Lord and your apostolic intercession. Without you, these truths might still be hidden Thank you so much for creating a model that allowed me to see these principles operate on such a high level. May all your dreams for His Kingdom come true as well as your dreams. He loves you much. Thanks Beverley Watkins for being so passionate and believing in me and working tirelessly to see this book edited and prepared to have its impact. You provided the necessary encouragement in the moments when it would have been more convenient for me to quit and take the easier path. Your prophetic encouragement drove me on and made me feel valuable to the kingdom and believe that I had something to say that was worthwhile. Thanks to all the intercessors of Ariel Gate who have prayed countless prayers for my family and me. Our lives changed when we met you. You guys are the greatest.

Contents

Introduction

Most people I know believe intensely in prayer. Even those who would not consider themselves Christians, actually believe in prayer - especially in times of trouble, trauma and tribulation. Yet, even with this strong belief in prayer there is still a great deal of frustration concerning how it operates and what we need to do to see our prayers answered. We have all found this frustration at the lack of answers to our prayers to be real and at times confusing.

Some, in an attempt to put a positive spin on the whole issue of God's response to it, have said that God answers all prayers. Sometimes His answer is 'Yes', and we get what we are petitioning Him for. Sometimes His answer is 'No', because He knows better than we do what we need. At other times, His answer is 'Wait', because it is a timing issue. As much as I believe that this is at times correct, I believe it to be too trite and simple an answer. I have watched people pray prayers that I knew were in agreement with God's will, heart and timing, and yet the desired answer did not come. I watched these unanswered prayers result in relationships being destroyed, businesses going under and even premature deaths occurring. Devastating consequences took place because there appeared to be no answer from Heaven.

So what is the problem, or better yet what is the solution? Why does Heaven sometimes remain silent when we pray from the earnestness of our hearts? I believe that the Lord has unveiled, at the very least, a partial answer to this dilemma. The answer is found in where the spiritual activity called prayer is actually taking place.

Prayer, at its very core, is where we insert ourselves into a spiritual conflict. Prayer is not just an asking or petitioning of God for some things. When we pray, we engage the Lord Himself, but we are also engaging powers of darkness that want to resist us in our prayer activity. We see this in the book of Daniel. Daniel is interceding, asking God for understanding regarding the Scriptures. Satan does not want this knowledge released to Daniel and high powers of darkness seek to stop him receiving the answer to his prayers. After 21 days, Daniel finally receives the answer to his prayer and also gains understanding of why the answer took so long to come through. Daniel 10:12-14

> Then he said to me, "Do not fear, Daniel, for from the first day that you set your heart to understand, and to humble yourself before your God, your words were heard; and I have come because of your words. But the prince of the kingdom of Persia withstood me twenty-one days; and behold, Michael, one of the chief princes, came to help me, for I had been left alone there with the kings of Persia. Now I have come to make you understand what will happen to your people in the latter days, for the vision refers to many days yet to come." (Daniel 10:12-14)

Daniel's prayer engaged God but also engaged the devil and his forces. My point is simply that prayer is almost always about a conflict. Daniel's words stirred Heaven, but also stirred up hell. When we pray we are entering a conflict. We are moving the powers of heaven for God's kingdom will to be done, but we are also engaging the forces of darkness that are resisting that will from being done. This is the power of our words that are directed toward the Lord.

The Apostle Paul talks about this conflict in many of his writings. In 1 Corinthians 9:26 Paul speaks of "one who beats the air" but doesn't land the blows.

> Therefore I run thus: not with uncertainty. Thus I
> fight: not as one who beats the air (1 Cor. 9:26).

Paul says he doesn't run with uncertainty, yet we certainly have. We participate in spiritual activities wondering if any of it is doing anything in the unseen realm. He then goes on to say that he doesn't fight as one who beats the air. This is a reference to 'shadow boxing'. Shadow boxing is a training method to build stamina and perfect the art of punching. Shadow boxing is for the gym, for training. It is not something you do in the ring with a real opponent opposite you! When there is a real opponent, real blows need to be landed and damage done to the adversary that is trying to knock you out. If you shadow box in a real match, you will simply wear yourself out and not do any real damage to your opponent. You can be sure he will take advantage of your weakened position, knock you out and win the match.

I speak about this from experience. I was a Junior High student in Texas, and our PE teacher decided that we would have a boxing lesson. I remember the mats being put down and each student taking his turn against an opponent on the mats. I found myself matched up against one of the worst athletes in the school. I was an average athlete, definitely better than my opponent. (That's my assessment of it anyway and I'm sticking to it.) We took our position on the mats, facing each other with our gloves in their right position, as we had been instructed, and we began to punch. I don't really remember what happened, other than as I punched, I threw a wild 'haymaker' of a punch that left my jaw completely exposed. My opponent (the non-athlete) saw it and delivered a left hook that landed perfectly. The next thing I knew, I was lying on my back with all the other guys commenting very vocally on what had just happened to me (the better athlete). I was extremely embarrassed and ashamed. This happened because I was wild in my boxing approach and I didn't know how to land my blows.

This is what many Christians are experiencing. They are throwing punch after punch at an unseen opponent, but landing none of them. The problem is that we are discouraged, faint-hearted and would like to just quit. We are wearing ourselves out. But please don't quit. There are answers to the whole realm of unanswered prayers. Let me give you a clue concerning this mystery before we move on in this book.

If we are to get unanswered prayers answered, we must first rightly discern where the conflict is in which we find ourselves. Most teachers on prayer and spiritual warfare teach that we are on a battlefield. I have come to believe deeply that, at the least, initially our prayers are in the courtroom of Heaven and we need to learn how to operate there if we are to get answers released and unlocked.

The protocol of a battlefield will not work in a courtroom and neither will the protocol of a courtroom work on a battlefield. These are two different arenas and we must discover where we are in prayer if we are to be effective. When we come off the battlefield and get into the courtroom and learn to function there, verdicts come out of the realms of God's throne that put in place the cry of our hearts. We must know how to be a part of the legal process of Heaven that grants God the legal right to fulfill His passion on our behalf and in the Earth. This is what this book is about. Don't be faint-hearted, answers are on the way!

1

Where is the Conflict?

Several years ago I was chosen for jury duty. The case was an armed robbery of a convenience store. The young man on trial was one who supposedly was the 'look out' for this robbery. The deciding factor for us as the jury, was his actions, movements and countenance as he was caught on the surveillance camera. He was definitely guilty even though he claimed that he didn't know that the man he was with was going to rob the store when they went in. The problem was that the camera showed a different story. We placed the young man on probation for the sake of his young wife and children so he could have another chance and not go to prison.

All this activity took place in a courtroom where a verdict was rendered. There was no yelling, screaming or physical wrestling. That would have been completely out of order in these proceedings. Everything that was done was about presenting evidence, making a request, answering accusations and other legal processes. The result was a verdict rendered that was consistent with the petitions that were being offered. Justice was served.

I am convinced that prayer is an activity that takes place in the courtroom of Heaven. There are petitions, accusations, arguments and evidence presented in the courts of Heaven just as there are in the courts on Earth. And just as there is protocol in a natural courtroom, there is protocol in the courtroom of Heaven. As a member of that jury, it would have been illegal and against the protocol of the courtroom if I were to have pulled out a sword and begun to shout out my opinion about the case. Everyone would have thought I was crazy and I probably would have been arrested because I had not observed the protocol of the court. In the same way, Heaven's courts also have a spiritual protocol that should be observed.

I believe, through Scripture, that the place of the initial conflict is in a courtroom and not on a battlefield. The first place of intercession should be in the courtroom of Heaven. It is there that we must first win our verdicts before going out to win on the battlefield.

The problem is that most Christians believe that when they pray they are on a battlefield. They rush into a conflict without securing a verdict from Heaven. This is a critical mistake that has caused us to experience defeat, chaos, backlash from satanic forces and even destruction in our lives. We rush into places of prayer only to see things get worse rather than better. This is because we stir things up on a battlefield without first having established a legal precedent to be there. I have heard people say that the worsened situation is a sign that something is moving. It's moving alright, just in the wrong direction. Imagine if military leaders applied this 'wisdom'. When experiencing defeat at the hands of the enemy, we just keep on fighting, keep sending our soldiers onto the battlefield to sacrifice their lives in a war we are hoping to win. It is a ridiculous strategy.

Many times it seems prayer and what is called spiritual warfare, is approached with the mindset of General George Custer, who led his troops into a massacre by Native Americans. As a result of his ignorance, arrogance and disregard for proper military strategy, a large part of the United States Calvary was ambushed and destroyed at Little Big Horn. As sad an event as this is in

American history, Christians repeat it over and over in their own prayer lives. They keep rushing in and yelling at the devil, making decrees and offering up prayers that do more to stir up demonic forces than dismantle them. All of this happens because no legal precedent has been gained from the Throne of God. As a result no answers come from Heaven and we experience casualties rather than victories. What absurdity! Isn't there a better way to do this with the right results? I say 'Yes!' The answer is to move off the battlefield and into the courtroom of Heaven.

In Revelation 19:11 we see how Jesus Himself approaches this.

> Now I saw Heaven opened, and behold, a white horse. And He who sat on him was called Faithful and True, and in righteousness He judges and makes war (Rev. 19:11).

The first thing we must see is that Heaven is open. This means that there is revelation and things that we need to discern in the Heavenly realm. Prayer and warfare should not be a shot in the dark. We should be able to pinpoint the things that need to be dealt with and touch them with accuracy. We must be able to pray within the will of God. We CAN find the needle in the haystack when Heaven is open and revelation is flowing. John the Apostle said if we ask anything according to His will then we have the petition that we are asking of Him. (1 John 5:14-15) One of the critical steps to effective prayer is understanding the will of God and praying in agreement with that will. I will deal more extensively about how this is done in a later chapter.

The main thing I want to point out in Revelation 19:11 is that Jesus, Who is faithful and true, judges in righteousness and makes war. Notice the order of this wording. This is very important. Jesus judges, then makes war. When the Bible speaks of 'judging', it is speaking of judicial activity. There is a decision and a verdict being rendered concerning a situation, petition and/or request. That activity is being judged and there is a legal precedent that is being established concerning it. Out of that judicial activity which is flowing from the courts of Heaven, war is made. We must learn to only make war based on judgments, decisions and verdicts that are received out of the courts of Heaven. To try to make war without a verdict and judgment from the court of Heaven is to suffer defeat and even satanic backlash because we have no legal footing to be there or be engaging in such activity. On the other hand, if we can get legal renderings concerning a situation in place, then we can march onto the battlefield and win every time. The problem has been that we have tried to win on the battlefield without legal verdicts from Heaven backing us up. We must learn how to get these verdicts and judgments in place so answers can come to our prayers and the Kingdom cause of Christ can land on the Earth.

Jesus and the Courts of Heaven

Jesus set prayer in a courtroom setting. In Scripture we see references made to warfare and the battlefield. Yet in Jesus' teaching on prayer in Matthew 6 and Luke 11, Jesus never placed prayer on a battlefield. He spoke of prayer as flowing from the relationship to a father. He spoke of prayer as a friend approaching a friend. Yet when dealing with the question of how to pray, Jesus never said we were on a battlefield. He did however place prayer in a courtroom or judicial setting. In Luke 18:1-8, Jesus speaks of a widow who is seeking justice from a courtroom.

> Then He spoke a parable to them, that men always ought to pray and not lose heart, saying: "There was in a certain city a judge who did not fear God nor

regard man. Now there was a widow in that city; and she came to him, saying, 'Get justice for me from my adversary.' And he would not for a while; but afterward he said within himself, 'Though I do not fear God nor regard man, yet because this widow troubles me I will avenge her, lest by her continual coming she weary me.'" Then the Lord said, "Hear what the unjust judge said. And shall God not avenge His own elect who cry out day and night to Him, though He bears long with them? I tell you that He will avenge them speedily. Nevertheless, when the Son of Man comes, will He really find faith on the earth?" (Luke 18:1-8)

Clearly Jesus is declaring that when we pray, we are entering a courtroom. If this widow could get an answer and a verdict from an unjust judge through her persistent activity in a court, how much more shall we gain answers as the elect of God before the Righteous Judge of all. I think it is very interesting that Jesus spoke this parable so people would not give up on prayer. We must realize that a lack of results does not mean we need to put more effort into something. More effort without additional wisdom usually produces tiredness, fatigue and weariness. What we need is not more effort necessarily, but to learn secrets. Striving produces frustration while the revelation of secrets produces fruit. The mindset that we have had in the Church is flawed. What we are doing is not producing results, but we think that if we can just keep doing it long enough, loud enough or hard enough, then somehow, magically, something different will happen.

Before I entered the ministry, I worked at a meat packing plant where there were many illegal workers. This was before the government began to crack down on this practice. I was in the maintenance crew and was responsible for helping to keep the machines running and production at its maximum. The problem was that some of these workers didn't care what they damaged in the process of doing their job. For instance, one day as a piece of equipment was being moved from one place to another, it had to go through a door. As they were pushing this machinery through the door, it became jammed and wouldn't move. Instead of going around on the other side and seeing why it was stuck, they just called for more people to come and push harder. The result was they 'broke' it free, but damaged other things that were in the way. Their philosophy was the same as many in the Church. Why check and see why something is not working and stuck, when you can just use more effort? More effort is not always the answer. Many times the answer is the discovering of secrets through revelation that actually brings about a breakthrough with less effort and produces greater results. If we have done the same thing for years and it hasn't improved, but in fact it has become even worse, maybe we should investigate. Someone once defined this as the definition of insanity. They said insanity is doing the same thing over and over and expecting something different to happen. We do not need more effort and striving, we need to discover secrets that unlock new dimensions that produce new results.

This is why Jesus was speaking this parable. He was unlocking a secret that prayer is activity in a courtroom. When the widow wanted justice, she went to the courtroom and not the battlefield. She realized she didn't need to march onto a battlefield and yell at her adversary. She simply needed a verdict from the court. In fact she didn't even address her adversary. This parable never mentions her even speaking to him. She spoke only to the judge. When this widow kept on with her pleas before the unjust judge, he finally gave in and granted her request and she received a just verdict in her situation. She understood that if the Judge rendered a legal verdict, any power of the adversary was demolished and she won. Once this was in place her adversary had to bow the knee to the rendering of the court.

This is so for us as well. Any adversary in the spirit realm that is resisting God's Kingdom purpose for us will bow the knee to verdicts from the court of Heaven. We have no need to yell, scream or even curse our foe. All we need is a legal precedent based on a verdict from Heaven and the fight is over. We then simply put into place the verdict that has been set down. This is where decrees come, but only after legality has been established. I will get into this more in a later chapter.

I want us to notice specifically Luke 18:8.

I tell you that He will avenge them speedily (Luke 18:8)

I have watched and witnessed that when I moved off the battlefield and into the courtroom of Heaven, answers came for me that I had prayed years for. All my warring, crying, yelling and petitioning had not brought answers from Heaven. But, when I began to learn how to navigate the courts of Heaven what had never happened before, happened immediately and quickly. My adversaries were silenced and I was avenged 'speedily'.

As with most families, my family does not live in a perfect world. I hope yours does, but mine doesn't. Mary and I have raised six children. I have said often that while they were growing up, we were never bored! We were confused at times, but never bored! There was definitely plenty of activity and life in our home. We have watched all of the children transition into great adults. They all love God, fear Him and honor Mary and I greatly.

This has not been without periods of wrong choices as they struggled to discover their identities. In fact, one of our daughters went through a very short period of rebellious activity. That period was long enough however to end with her being pregnant without being married. I love what a prophet friend of mine says. He declares, "It is not a sin to be pregnant without being married." This statement usually stuns people. After all, how could any legitimate man or woman of God say such a thing? He then continues, "The sin was the fornication that led to the pregnancy. The baby in the womb is not a sin." I love it. Not because of any justification in our own personal circumstance, but because it strikes at the malicious judgment that is so often in the Church concerning such situations. God is a God of forgiveness and mercy. Whether it was our daughter or someone else's, there is forgiveness and redemption for whoever will repent for the activity that brought on the pregnancy outside of marriage. After the repentance then there is a joyous expectation of the child that will be born into the Earth completely blessed by our loving God who is our Father. This is what has happened in our family. Our grandson is a joy to our lives and the whole clan. We cannot imagine life without him.

One of the first places where I saw activity in the courts of Heaven bring a verdict was concerning this grandson. The biological father in the situation decided after five years that he wanted to be back in this child's life. There had been no support of any kind from him up until then. The character of the father was not one which we felt would be a good influence on our grandson. He had a criminal record, several DUI's, plus a couple of assault convictions. It was not a good situation. Yet here he was, wanting visitation rights and the right to take our grandson out of State for extended visitations with his family. Our daughter was greatly perplexed and worried about what the natural courts would do.

It came time for the case to go before a judge. The attorney for my daughter was guarded because he didn't know which way the judge would go. We lived in Colorado Springs and it is a military town. Cases such as these go before the courts regularly because of people who are in the military. They get divorced and one party will be transferred to other regions around the world. It is not uncommon for the courts to allow visitation rights, so a child can be taken out of State and be with the other parent. This is what my daughter thought would happen and this was of great concern to her. But she didn't know her dad (me) had discovered a higher court that could be appealed to.

On the day of the earthly court date, I went into the courts of Heaven, silenced the accuser (we will get to that later) and petitioned the court of Heaven for a verdict and judgment in our daughter and ultimately our grandson's favor. I had some other prophetic people helping me sense what was going on. I very clearly heard and discerned that the court of Heaven had rendered the verdict we were looking for.

My daughter went to the earthly court later that morning. As the judge listened to the evidence, he prepared to render his judgment. He then spoke to the biological father and said these words, "Young man, here's what we are going to do. Whatever the mother wants us to do is what we are going to do. Are you fine with this?" My daughter, her attorney and the biological father were flabbergasted. My daughter's attorney actually took her outside and asked her if she realized what had just happened. He said that this never happens and he was beside himself at the turn of events.

The reason for this activity and verdict was because a higher court, the court of Heaven had already rendered a verdict and the earthly court simply played it out. I have watched this happen in several actual court cases. I have also seen results like this over and over as we have asked Heaven to render verdicts to set Kingdom purposes in place. This principle and awareness is a very powerful thing. The more we learn to present our case in the courts of Heaven, the more we get legal precedents in place that allow us victory on the battlefield every time. Without it we lose and suffer the consequences. Let's learn to go to court!

2

The Books of Heaven

If we really want to get results from the courts of Heaven, we need to know how to operate within these courts. Lawyers go to school for years to learn how to operate within our judicial systems. They learn to speak the language of the courts. Just as they must know how to address the court, present cases and briefs, so we too must learn how to present things before Heaven's court. One of the greatest mysteries to this process is understanding the books or scrolls that are in Heaven.

Daniel 7:10 tells us that there are books or scrolls in Heaven that must be opened before the court of Heaven goes into session. Once the courts of Heaven are seated the books are opened and the court appears to come to session.

> A fiery stream issued
> And came forth from before Him.
> A thousand thousands ministered to Him;
> Ten thousand times ten thousand stood before Him.
> The court was seated,
> And the books were opened (Daniel 7:10).

From this Scripture, we can clearly see that an understanding of 'the books' is foundational to court activity that allows God's

Kingdom purposes to be done. But what are these books and what is written in them?

Types of Books

Psalm 139:16 tells us that each person has a book in Heaven.

> Your eyes saw my substance, being yet unformed.
> And in Your book they all were written,
> The days fashioned for me,
> When as yet there were none of them (Psalm 139:16).

God wrote down in a book the destiny and Kingdom purpose for each of our lives. God 'saw' us in our fleshly form in the Earth, before we ever existed. He saw our days. Not just the number of them, but He saw the activities in them and what we would accomplish in our life. Our individual book is a written record of all that God planned for us and the Kingdom impact He has destined for our lives. Every person ever born has a book written about them. The battle is to get what is in the book to manifest on the Earth.

Even Jesus had a book. Hebrews 10:5-7 tells us that Jesus had a volume of the book that He came into the Earth to fulfill.

> Therefore, when He came into the world, He said:
> "Sacrifice and offering You did not desire,
> But a body You have prepared for Me. In burnt offerings and sacrifices for sin You had no pleasure.
> Then I said, 'Behold, I have come—

In the volume of the book it is written of Me To do
Your will, O God.'" (Heb. 10:5-7)

There is a book in Heaven that chronicled what Kingdom purpose
Jesus would fulfill in the Earth. Jesus came with a passion and a
commitment to complete what had been written in the books of
Heaven about Him. This is interesting because John 1:14 says that
Jesus is the Word made flesh.

> And the Word became flesh and dwelt among us,
> and we beheld His glory, the glory as of the only
> begotten of the Father, full of grace and truth (John
> 1:14).

In other words, Jesus was the Word sent out of Heaven to be born
in the flesh. His physical birth allowed what was written in the
book of Heaven to be made manifest in the flesh. He then spent the
next thirty three and a half years of His life fulfilling what had been
written in His book.

Anything God-ordained is first written in a book or scroll in
Heaven. It must be sent out of Heaven and birthed into the Earth
realm before it can become flesh. This is what happened to Jesus,
but also to us and anything else that is ever 'born' into the Earth
realm. So it could be said that before we came into the Earth, we
were a word written in a scroll. When we were born into the Earth,
we began the process of living out our Kingdom purpose as it was
written in Heaven in our book. This is why Ephesians 2:10 says
that we are His workmanship.

> For we are His workmanship, created in Christ Jesus
> for good works, which God prepared beforehand
> that we should walk in them (Eph. 2:10).

The word workmanship in the Greek means a poem. We are God's poem that was written down in Heaven that has now entered Earth. We are a poem with a point. Our lives carry a message that is creative and life giving. Notice that this poem was written down and the works we are to do were planned beforehand. We were a 'scroll' in Heaven with poetic power that has now entered the Earth to cause the writings of Heaven to become flesh.

There are not just books about individuals. There are also books about churches, apostolic networks, businesses, ministries, cities, states, regions and nations. Heaven is full of books. Anything that is purposed of the Lord will begin as a book in Heaven. The Apostle John while in Heaven was given a book that he was commanded to eat. This book was about nations. Revelation 10:8-11 shows an angel with a little book that had the destinies of nations in it.

> Then the voice which I heard from Heaven spoke to me again and said, "Go, take the little book which is open in the hand of the angel who stands on the sea and on the earth." So I went to the angel and said to him, "Give me the little book." And he said to me, "Take and eat it; and it will make your stomach bitter, but it will be as sweet as honey in your mouth." Then I took the little book out of the angel's hand and ate it, and it was as sweet as honey in my mouth. But when I had eaten it, my stomach became bitter. And he said to me, "You must prophesy again about many peoples, nations, tongues, and kings." (Rev. 10:8-11)

John was instructed to take the book and eat it. This book was from Heaven and was about the future and Kingdom purpose of nations.

We know this because the result of John eating the book was the ability to prophesy to peoples, nations, tongues and kings. It was going to become the job of the Apostle John to prophesy out of the books what God had said about these nations. When John would prophesy from the books, it allowed court sessions to begin. Revelation 19:10 tells us the "testimony of Jesus is the spirit of prophecy."

> And I fell at his feet to worship him. But he said to me, "See that you do not do that! I am your fellow servant, and of your brethren who have the testimony of Jesus. Worship God! For the testimony of Jesus is the spirit of prophecy." (Rev. 19:10)

The word testimony means to give judicial witness. Jesus, from His position as our High Priest and Mediator, is testifying in our behalf in the courts. Notice that this testimony becomes a spirit of prophecy in our mouths. When we prophesy, we are not just speaking to the earthly realm, but we are in fact picking up and discerning the present testimony of Jesus in the courts of Heaven.

We are agreeing with and echoing the testimony of Jesus. This grants Heaven the right testimony to render verdicts in our behalf and the Kingdom purposes of God even in nations.

Where do the Books Come From?

These books that are in Heaven came into being from the 'counsel' of the Lord. Jeremiah 23:18 says there was a 'counsel' of the Lord.

> For who has stood in the counsel of the Lord,
> And has perceived and heard His word?

Who has marked His word and heard it? (Jer. 23:18)

This word counsel in Hebrew is sod. It means a company of persons in session, to consult, or a secret. It comes from the Hebrew word yasad which means to sit down together, to settle and consult. Clearly God has counsels that are held in Heaven for the purpose of planning future Kingdom events. Genesis1:26 says that the Godhead had a counsel about the creating and forming of man.

> Then God said, "Let Us make man in Our image, according to Our likeness; let them have dominion over the fish of the sea, over the birds of the air, and over the cattle, over all the earth and over every creeping thing that creeps on the earth." (Gen. 1:26)

Notice that God said Let Us. In other words there was discussion in the counsel of Heaven concerning the formation of man in the image and likeness of God. From this counsel, books were written about the destiny of Earth, man and God's creation. What was written in these books from the counsel of the Lord is what we are seeking to birth into a flesh demonstration.

In 2 Timothy 1:9 Paul is exhorting Timothy to fulfill what was planned before time began.

> "...who has saved us and called us with a holy calling, not according to our works, but according to His own purpose and grace which was given to us in Christ Jesus before time began," (2 Tim. 1:9)

Notice that purpose and grace were given to Paul and Timothy before time began. This is really interesting. How can something be given to something that doesn't yet exist. Purpose is what is written in the books of Heaven about them and grace was the empowerment to bring it into the realities of the Earth realm. This was given to them before time began or in the counsel of the Lord.

The Hebrew people believe that before we were on Earth we were with God in Heaven. We were spirit beings with God and a part of the counsel of Heaven. They believe that as a part of this counsel, we 'agreed' to the plan that God needed us to fulfill. We accepted the assignment to be born in the time we were born and fulfill what we had committed to. Once we accepted this as a part of the counsel of the Lord, it was written in a scroll or book and we have now come to Earth to be the 'word' of that scroll made flesh. I tend to lean toward this idea based on three things. First of all, this is compatible to what Jesus as our forerunner said in John 13:3.

> Jesus, knowing that the Father had given all things
> into His hands, and that He had come from God and
> was going to God, (John 13:3).

Jesus came as a spirit and entered the body that was prepared for Him. He then fulfilled what was written in the books about Him and returned to Heaven. If Jesus is the forerunner in all things, then it would be consistent with the pattern to assume this is true of us as well. Jesus came as God into the Earth. We came as human spirits into the Earth. But we potentially were all spirits in the presence of the Lord first.

The second thing that has me leaning toward this is something that happened while I was ministering in a certain city. A prophet friend of mine was in attendance and as I spoke of this concept, he suddenly waved to get my attention and wanted to say something. This was abnormal, but I acknowledged him and let him share. As he spoke he said that during worship before I got up to speak he kept hearing, "Back to the future, back to the future."

He said that he didn't say anything because it didn't make sense to him until I began to speak. He then realized that God was confirming what I was going to say, even before I said it. When we live our lives out here in the Earth realm we are actually producing in time what was preordained in the counsels of the Lord eons ago. This is quite fascinating and should grant to us a deep sense of purpose.

Not everyone lives out what was established in the counsels of the Lord and then written in the books. We don't have to, but it is our job to discover and fulfill what is there and bring it to Earth in natural forms. This is what we will be judged on in the hereafter. Our judgment will not be so much about this sin or that sin. Our judgment will be based on how closely we lived our lives to what is written in the books of Heaven. Not to live our lives out in agreement with the books of Heaven is to waste our time here. We may get to spend eternity in Heaven, but we will not have fulfilled His Kingdom agenda for our life and times here on Earth.

The third thing that allows me to lean toward this understanding is a very personal life situation. Mary and I have six children. They are all grown now. Well let's just say they are all of legal age and are all over 20 years old. That would be more truthful. When we had four children and the youngest, Hope, was five, Mary was especially happy because Hope was about to start kindergarten. This would mean that for the first time in many years she would be able to have several hours a day when kids were not at home. We were approaching that wonderful time when this would happen. I will never forget Mary and I going on a trip to a borrowed condo on a golf course. We had ditched the kids somewhere and were going to get some time alone for the first time in a long time. There were several other couples that were on this trip. The condo that we were in didn't have enough bedrooms therefore Mary and I were sleeping on a mattress on the floor. I remember waking up the first morning and lying beside Mary. She looked at me and said, "I need to tell you something." I thought in this wonderful moment of peace and quiet, when it was just the two of us, that she was going to tell me how wonderful I was and how much she loved me and loved our life together. She then blurted out the words I had heard before, "I'm pregnant." I don't know what I said, but it was probably something like, "You're kidding, right?"

But no! It was absolutely true. There went our plans down the drain and at least five more years of kids at home before this one would get into school. The truth is that Micah and his brother Mark, the sixth one (yes, we even had another one after this), have been great blessings in our life. But the event I want to tell you about happened when Micah, this fifth one that we were not expecting, was ten years old.

One night Mary had a dream. In the dream she was told that Micah was supposed to have been born to another couple named Mike and Carol (not the Brady Bunch). Carol had been killed in a car wreck and therefore what God intended to do through them could not occur. Micah couldn't be born into the Earth. The problem was that God needed Micah born so he could fulfill his Kingdom purpose for God's will to be done in the Earth. God chose Mary and I to have Micah instead of the other couple, because Micah had to be born. Isn't that wild? Yet I believe it with every fiber of my being.

It was foreordained in the counsels of Heaven; a book was written as a result of this counsel about and for Micah and God chose us as a second option to get Micah into the Earth. When we received this understanding about Micah's birth, I jokingly said, "God must have been scraping the bottom of the barrel on this one to have to entrust Micah to us!" Actually, I am quite honored that the Lord would entrust one that He needed in the Earth to us. His grace is sufficient for us to impact Micah in the way that is necessary for him to fulfill his book from Heaven.

All of us are a product of the counsel of the Lord. The Lord thought about each one of us and wrote a book about our lives out of that counsel. Each of us has been birthed into the Earth so that His word can be made flesh and what was written in our scrolls can be fulfilled. When this is done, Kingdom influence comes to the Earth and Kingdom cultures that look like Heaven are revealed.

Manifesting the Books

To really understand the "counsel of the Lord" and the books of Heaven we must look at Romans 8:29-30. This passage unveils a five-step process of how to identify and birth the intentions of God into the Earth.

> For whom He foreknew, He also predestined to be conformed to the image of His Son, that He might be the firstborn among many brethren. Moreover whom He predestined, these He also called; whom He called, these He also justified; and whom He justified, these He also glorified. (Romans 8:29-30)

In this Scripture, Paul lists the 5 steps - *foreknew, predestined, called, justified and glorified*. To operate in the courts of Heaven and get what is in Heaven into the Earth, we must understand these stages.

Foreknowledge speaks of that which occurred in the counsel of the Lord. In this counsel decisions were made about destinies in the Earth. This includes individuals, cities, states, businesses and all the way up to nations. There were conclusions that were arrived at concerning what part of God's Kingdom agenda each would fulfill. From the counsel of the Lord, there was a foreknowing of us. This all occurred *before time began*. Once these decisions were made, they were then written down in a book. Once they were written in a book in Heaven, it became a predestined thing. This is the next stage that Paul spoke of.

From the counsel of the Lord (foreknowledge), God then wrote in a book the decisions made that would be our Kingdom reason for existence on the planet. Anything that has a Kingdom purpose has a book in Heaven about it. The books of Heaven contain the Kingdom purposes of God. I like to say that if there isn't a book about it in Heaven, don't waste your time on it. We should only involve ourselves in that which is important to Heaven. If it is important in Heaven, there is a book about it.

Being **predestined** has nothing to do with us not having a choice or a will. In fact we can have a predestined plan for our lives and not fulfill it. Each person born into the Earth arrived with a predestined plan concerning their life. They have a book in Heaven about them. We can either choose to discover what is in the books about us or disregard it and go our own way. It is each ones individual responsibility to discover what was predestined about them and written in the books of Heaven.

Remember that Paul told Timothy in 2 Timothy 1:9 that purpose and grace were given to them before time began. This means that when we find our purpose we will also discover grace that has been apportioned to us for that purpose. This is the chief way we know we have discovered purpose. We realize that in this activity and life ambition there is grace. In other words, you enjoy it, you are good at it, you have success in doing it and others are influenced by your doing of it. It is much like Eric Liddel in the movie "Chariots of Fire" where he chose to honor God by not running on the Sabbath. He said, "When I run, I feel the pleasure of

God." This statement reveals that he had discovered, for this season of his life, the purpose for which he was graced. The two stages of foreknowledge and predestination all occurred before time began. They happened in the eternal realm of God and outside the time realm.

The next stage is the **called** stage. This is the stage where we begin to get glimpses of what we were made for. We begin to discover what is written in the books of heaven about us. This is the biggest question that people have. What is written in my book? What is the predestined plan of God for my life? Psalm 40:6-8 gives us some understanding.

> Sacrifice and offering You did not desire; My ears You have opened. Burnt offering and sin offering You did not require. Then I said, "Behold, I come; In the scroll of the book it is written of me. I delight to do Your will, O my God, And Your law is within my heart." (Psalm 40:6-8)

These verses are actually Jesus prophesying over Himself before He came into the planet. This verse is later picked up and repeated with some minor changes in Hebrews 10:5-7. This is Jesus saying that He has a book in Heaven that He is coming to flesh out in the Earth. Remember that this is our job. We are to flesh out in the Earth what is written in the books of Heaven. Again, John 1:14 says that Jesus was the Word made flesh. In other words, what was written about Him in Heaven in the books, He has come to bring to reality in the Earth.

Notice that Jesus said that in the scroll or volume of the book it was written of Him. He had come to do the will of the Father contained in that book. But then He makes a very powerful statement. In connection to fulfilling what is in the His book, He says, *"And Your law is within my heart"*. So whatever is written in your book in Heaven is also written in your heart. If you want to discover what is in your book, look in your heart. What are your interests, desires, aspirations, longings and passions? These are clues to what is in your book in Heaven. Many times our lives become so cluttered and busy that we need the Holy Spirit to come and unveil for us what is in our hearts. When we discover the passion of our heart, we will begin to discover what is written in our books in Heaven. We will start to have glimpses of what our Kingdom purposes are.

The next stage is the being **justified**. Justified has legal implications. The word means *to be rendered just or innocent*. In other words there are no accusations that can stick. Remember that the devil is the accuser of the brethren who accuses us before God day and night. (Revelation 12:10) The justified stage is where we have been into the courtroom of Heaven and every accusation the devil is using against us is silenced.

Accusations are what the devil uses to keep us from what is written in the books of Heaven about us. This is why so many people are frustrated today. They have a intuitive awareness that they were created for something more than they have become. They sense that something is resisting them from stepping into all they were made for. That which is resisting them is the accusation of the accuser against them in the courts of Heaven. The accuser is presenting evidence to God the Judge of all as to why He cannot legally grant to you what is written in your book. Satan knows that if we get what is in our book, then we will do massive damage to his devilish empire in the Earth. He uses accusations against us to stop us from stepping into all that Heaven has ordained.

He did this to Peter. We will see this clearly as we talk about it in later chapters. Suffice it to say that if we want what is in our books fleshed out in the Earth, the accusations of Satan must be answered. Once this is done then God as Judge of all is free to fulfill His Father's passion toward us and grant what is in the book so heaven's will concerning us can be done.

The fifth and final stage mentioned is being **glorified**. Being glorified is not talking about going to Heaven. It is speaking about us fully stepping into all that is written in the books of Heaven about us. We begin to "live the dream." We live the dream that God had about us before time begin. This has been called the convergence point. It is where everything we have gone through, good or bad, works together to propel us into our ultimate destiny.

We see this in the life of Joseph where he was in his father's house, but then sold into slavery by jealous brothers. He ended up ruling over the household of Potiphar. Then he was cast into prison unjustly, after which he was promoted from this most unlikely place to Prime Minister of Egypt. He became the preserver of life that God had destined him to be as it was written in the books of Heaven. All of these things worked together and converged together to prepare and get Joseph to his appointed place. He then, from his glorified position, had the Kingdom impact that was predestined by God that he was to have. The reaching of the convergence point of our lives can be costly and expensive but worth it. Not only do we find the ultimate satisfaction that we were built for, but God gets His Kingdom purpose fulfilled through us.

The most critical stage of this process for individuals all the way to nations, is being justified. Once we maneuver our ways through the courts of Heaven and get legal things arranged, God can freely then grant to us the passion of His heart.

In the next chapter we will talk about the court activity of Heaven that allows what is written in the books of Heaven to come into the Earth realm. There is a great contention regarding this, but when we know how to function in the courts we grant God the legal rights for the word to be made flesh.

3

Contending for the Books

On a trip to Germany I found myself operating in a Heavenly courtroom setting. The folks that I was ministering with are very skilled at going into the courts of Heaven and getting things legally in place so God's will can be done on the Earth. As we were functioning in this sphere and contending with the powers of darkness over Germany, one of the seer prophets became aware that there was a 'book' that had come into the courtroom. It was tattered, worn and had been through a destructive process. Something had tried to destroy this book. We recognized that this was the book that contained the kingdom purpose of God for Germany. We navigated through the courtroom procedures until we were able to secure the book of Germany that had been taken captive by the demonic principalities. This was good news for the nation of Germany.

Germany, just like any other nation, has a book in Heaven that chronicles what its kingdom purpose is in God's economy. Germany cannot be redeemed to its kingdom purpose until its book is secured, then opened and read into being. When we were able to secure the book legally out of the hands of principalities and powers, we began the journey of accomplishing things in the Heavens. By the way, there was no yelling and screaming at the devil. There was only legal wrangling in the court that allowed us to possess the book of Germany and take it back from satanic powers. This was necessary for Germany to come to a place of redemption and begin the process of becoming a sheep nation.

This is the heart of God for every nation - that they fulfill their destiny as it is written in their book. But in order to fulfill it, they must first lay hold of their book. This is why John was told to eat the scroll or book in Revelation 10:9-11. When he ate the book that had the destinies of nations written in it, he was empowered to prophesy those destinies and reveal them to the nations. And more than that, he could petition for them in the courts of Heaven.

The books in Heaven are absolutely central to the operation of the courts of Heaven. Again, Daniel 7:10 shows us that the court cannot operate until the books are open.

> A fiery stream issued
> And came forth from before Him.
> A thousand thousands ministered to Him;
> Ten thousand times ten thousand stood before Him.
> The court was seated,
> And the books were opened (Dan. 7:10).

Once the court is in session and the books are open, cases can be presented, legal precedents set and the dominion rights of principalities removed from nations. This occurs when we begin to present cases from the revelation we are seeing and understanding out of the books of Heaven. This is why it was so important to get the book of Germany back from the powers of darkness that had taken it captive. Now that we have received the book back, we are able to read prophetically the blueprint of God for the nation. What is written in the book concerning Germany is now closer to being realized than before. There will need to be much more operation in the courts of Heaven, but Germany like any other nation can see its Kingdom purpose fulfilled when we dismantle the legal arguments that allow the powers of darkness to rule. Step by step and piece by piece we take away these legalities and grant God the legal right to fulfill His Kingdom will.

The Word Becomes Flesh

I wanted to use this illustration of what happened in Germany to emphasize that there is a contending for what is in the books. Whether it is on a national level or a personal level, the devil does not want what is in the books to come into reality on the Earth. This is why there were such extreme attempts by satanic powers to keep Jesus out of the Earth. Remember that the devil tried to exterminate the Jewish race several times. This was to remove from the planet the race of people through which Jesus would be born.

Then after He was born, Herod sent out a decree to kill all the babies within Jesus' age range. This was to try to destroy Him. Why was this done and many other things done? What was the purpose? It was to keep the Word from being made flesh (John 1:14). It was to keep what was written about Jesus in the books of Heaven from entering the Earth.

This is true for anything that is written in Heaven. Whether it is nations, churches, businesses, individuals or any other thing, there will be attempts to keep what is in the books from coming into the Earth realm. Satan does not want the word made flesh on any level. Everything that is written in the books about you, nations, Kingdom purposes and God's desires will be contested. The devil does not want what is written in the books to be born into the Earth and be made flesh. It is our job to see this accomplished.

A primary thing I want us to realize is that the conflict for what is in the books is in a courtroom and not on a battlefield. That is why when the court is seated in Daniel 7 the books are then opened. We are not on a battlefield. We are in a courtroom to get

God's Kingdom purposes into the Earth. I know I have already said this, but I must continue to emphasize it because we must make this shift in our thinking. The protocol and manner of operation in a courtroom is different from that on a battlefield. We are seeking to get legal things in place for ultimate victory.

Another very important thing we must know about contending for books to come into the Earth realm is that there are varying levels of courts in Heaven. Zechariah 3:7 shows us that the Lord promised Joshua, the High Priest, that if he walked in holiness, he would have a place to walk in the courts of Heaven.

> "Thus says the Lord of hosts: 'If you will walk in
> My ways,
> And if you will keep My command,
> Then you shall also judge My house,
> And likewise have charge of My courts;
> I will give you places to walk
> Among these who stand here (Zech. 3:7).

This says several very important things to us. First, Joshua was a mortal man that was being granted access and function in the courts of Heaven. I will touch on this more later, but suffice it to say now that what Heaven wants done cannot happen without our involvement. Even though we are physically on Earth, in the spirit we can function in the courts of Heaven and have authority there.

Another thing is that our walk is very important. From our walk or conduct in holiness before the Lord, we gain authority in the courts of Heaven. When we walk in a manner worthy of Him, Heaven recognizes us. So many folks have a misconstrued concept of grace. I thank God for His grace. His grace saves me from my sin, but it also empowers me to live above sin. Titus 1:11-12 tells us that God's real grace not only saves us, but instructs us in forsaking ungodliness and lustful things.

> For the grace of God that brings salvation has appeared to all men, teaching us that, denying ungodliness and worldly lusts, we should live soberly, righteously, and godly in the present age, (Titus 1:11-12)

God's grace will empower me to live in a godly manner in this present age. When I appropriate His grace into my life to live in holiness, I gain authority before the courts of Heaven.

Levels of Courts

The other important thing is that Joshua the High Priest is told that he will have charge of the courts of Heaven. Notice that it is courts plural. This is significant. Even on Earth there are varying levels and types of courts that decide issues. There are small claims courts, criminal courts, civil courts, divorce courts, city courts, district courts, all the way up to the Supreme Court within my nation of America. All these courts have a different function and jurisdiction. These courts function within the sphere that has been granted to them.

In Heaven there are many different courts that operate. Everyone is not recognized or allowed to operate in all courts. Our operation in the courts of Heaven is determined by the measurement of rule or jurisdiction we have been given. For instance, there are only a handful of attorneys that can present cases in the Supreme Court of the United States. If an attorney that is not recognized comes before the Supreme Court he or she will not be allowed to function there. They will be escorted out or not even allowed in. We must realize this or we can get ourselves into major trouble by trying to operate in a jurisdiction of Heaven that we have not been granted. When we do this, we open ourselves up to satanic assault and backlash. We have stepped outside our realm and our lives and the lives of those joined to us could be put in jeopardy. I will talk more about this in another chapter.

The Throne of Grace

The good news is that there is a court we can operate in, as believers, that is accessible for us all. It is called the Throne of grace. Hebrews 4:16 tells us about this court.

> Let us therefore come boldly to the throne of grace,
> that we may obtain mercy and find grace to help in
> time of need (Heb. 4:16).

Everything we deal with on a personal or family level can be brought to the throne of grace. At this throne or in this court we can obtain mercy and find grace to help in our time of need. I function in this court setting on a regular basis.

The first time I functioned in this court was on behalf of my son, Adam. Adam had gone through a very difficult time. He had been married and had a baby with a girl that decided she didn't want to be in ministry with him. They were youth pastors in the Northwest part of our nation and were very effective in this ministry. Through a series of events they moved back to where they had both grown up. She became involved with her 'old friends' and her family. The result was she left Adam and took the baby with her. Adam was not without fault or blame, but nothing warranted this kind of decision being made. The result was a divorce that separated Adam from everything he loved. He didn't want the divorce, but was powerless to stop it. This caused Adam to go into a place of deep depression. I tried everything over the course of the next couple of years to get him out of it. Nothing worked. He would go to work from 3 p.m. until 11 p.m. every day then come home, go to his room and play online video games all night. This was his way of dealing with the pain and loss that he had suffered. I would try and talk to him, encourage him and motivate him to come out of this place. There would be no response from him. He wasn't mean or nasty, he was just lifeless.

In addition to everything I have mentioned, I prayed vigilantly for Adam every day. My attitude towards him and this situation was that brute force in prayer would get the job done. This was my attitude in prayer about everything. I figured if it didn't move, it just needed more effort and time put into it. I didn't understand that if something hasn't moved after much prayer there is a legal reason for it. The devil has a legal right to withstand me. The only thing that will bring an answer is removing the legal right that the devil has to resist us. Please understand that I do believe in persevering prayer. I also have come to believe that revealed strategies will make us more effective than just praying with more force and 'doing time' in prayer. After two years of praying and seeing absolutely no results, I began to get an understanding of operating in the courts of Heaven and coming before His throne of grace.

One morning as I was seeking the Lord and spending time with Him, the Lord said, "Take Adam before My courts." I had never done anything like that before, but I was very open to try. I wasn't dealing with a national issue or a global concern. I was dealing with a personal issue, my own son. I didn't need to be before a court in Heaven that had jurisdiction over what would happen to nations. All I needed to do was be before His throne of grace and find mercy and grace for Adam in this time.

I began by simply approaching His throne of grace with boldness. We are told that because of who Jesus is and what He has done we can approach this throne with absolute confidence. Hebrews 4:14-16 tells us just some of the things that are working on our behalf before this throne of grace.

> Seeing then that we have a great High Priest who has passed through the Heavens, Jesus the Son of God, let us hold fast our confession. For we do not have a High Priest who cannot sympathize with our weaknesses, but was in all points tempted as we are, yet without sin. Let us therefore come boldly to the throne of grace, that we may obtain mercy and find grace to help in time of need (Heb. 4:14-16).

We are told that we have a *Great High Priest* who is Jesus that is before this throne of grace on our behalf. The position of *High Priest* is a legal position before the throne. All we have to do is look at Aaron the High Priest during the Exodus adventures of the Jews to see that his job was to provide the Lord with the legal right to bless Israel. Priests give God the legal privilege to bless instead of curse a person or a thing. Aaron did this through all the sacrifices that he offered and every function of his priesthood.

This is what Jesus is doing as our High Priest now. He is before this throne of grace offering His own blood so God has a legal right to bless us instead of curse us. We don't have to be afraid to come before this throne, because of the position Jesus has won as our High Priest. Notice also that Jesus as High Priest has passed through the Heavens. This is significant. The powers of darkness that occupy these spiritual dimensions called the heavens could not stop Jesus from taking His legal place as High Priest. Because of His absolute obedience to the Father and the blood that He shed, they had no power to keep Him from His place. The result is that these principalities have now lost their legal right to rule.

Jesus has legally overthrown these powers of darkness. It is our job as the Church to execute and administrate this judgment on the Earth. Colossians 2:13-15 shows us the legal position the Lord has granted us. It also clearly articulates the undoing of the previous position of the powers of darkness. We have now been granted, by the work of Jesus on the cross, a legal position in Heaven from which we can operate.

> And you, being dead in your trespasses and the uncircumcision of your flesh, He has made alive together with Him, having forgiven you all trespasses, having wiped out the handwriting of requirements that was against us, which was contrary to us. And He has taken it out of the way, having nailed it to the cross. Having disarmed principalities and powers, He made a public spectacle of them, triumphing over them in it (Col. 2:13-15).

We must understand that the cross of Jesus was a legal transaction. We are here to execute the legalities that this transaction put into place. A legal transaction has no power if it is not executed. For instance, a judge can issue a decree of judgment in a court, but if there is no one to enforce that judgment, it will have no power. When someone is saved, it is because the legalities of what Jesus did on the cross are legally put into place in their lives. When Jesus died on the cross, He legally provided atonement for all of mankind for all ages. 2 Corinthians 5:18-19 declare to us that God in Jesus has reconciled Himself back to the world.

> Now all things are of God, who has reconciled us to Himself through Jesus Christ, and has given us the

> ministry of reconciliation, that is, that God was in Christ reconciling the world to Himself, not imputing their trespasses to them, and has committed to us the word of reconciliation (2 Cor. 5:18-19).

When Jesus died on the cross, God reconciled Himself back to the world legally. Every legal issue that separated God and man was taken out of the way through the cross. Notice though that people that are saved have to 'be reconciled back to God'. They have to legally grab hold of what Jesus did and make it their own. 2 Corinthians 5:20 illustrates this.

> Now then, we are ambassadors for Christ, as though God were pleading through us: we implore you on Christ's behalf, be reconciled to God (2 Cor. 5:20).

In response to God reconciling Himself back to us, we must be reconciled back to Him. Just because Jesus fulfilled every legal issue separating us from God doesn't mean we are automatically saved. We must legally apprehend, for ourselves, what Jesus legally provided for us.

> 1 John 1:9 displays this fact.

> If we confess our sins, He is faithful and just to forgive us our sins and to cleanse us from all unrighteousness (1 John 1:9).

God is faithful and just. Faithful speaks of His covenant keeping nature. He will be true to the covenant He made with us through the blood and body of Jesus. A covenant is a legal entity. This

Scripture also says God is just. This means He administers justice into place. God loves justice and hates injustice. Please notice that nowhere in this Scripture is mercy mentioned. We are not forgiven and cleansed on the basis of God's mercy. We are forgiven and cleansed on the basis of His covenant keeping nature and His justice. In other words, God can legally show us mercy because a legal precedent has been set from the cross that allows the Lord from His covenant and justice to be merciful. His mercy is a result of His justice.

When we meet the legal requirements of confession, God is freed to legally forgive us of our sins. But the forgiveness released to us is found in the just nature of God. Because of what Jesus did for us on the cross, God can now legally forgive and cleanse us when we meet the legal requirement of confession. The cross of Jesus grants God the legal and just right to forgive and cleanse. We are, in essence, executing what Jesus legally purchased for us. But without our confession and repentance that legally puts forgiveness, cleansing and restoration in place, the work of Jesus is for nothing, even though He completed His job. Having a legal decree and executing it into place are two different things.

This is why repentance is so important. Our repentance grants God the legal right to display and show His mercy. Otherwise we live far below what Jesus purchased at the cross. Even though it is legally ours, we can only get it when we execute into place the verdicts of the cross.

Now, back to the story concerning my son, Adam. As Adam languished in his depressed state, the Lord told me to "take Adam to court." As I said before, I had never done this. I simply began by declaring that I intended and wanted to present Adam before God's throne of grace. As I did this, I began to repent for what Adam had allowed in his life. I repented for his lack of faith, his lying down under depression, his giving up and anything else I felt at that moment. I was endeavoring to 'silence' the accuser that was using legal things to resist Adam and his destiny. (Revelation 12: 10) I will get into this in a greater dimension in a later chapter.

Just suffice it to say for the moment that the only weapon the devil has against us and our destiny in the books of Heaven is accusation. I had a right to repent on Adam's behalf as an intercessor until Adam could do it for himself and silence the accuser. This is what an 'intercessor' does. They take a legal position on behalf of another until the other can and will take it for themselves. As I repented for Adam I was getting legal things in place that had been opposing Adam. As soon as I felt that I had answered every legal thing the accuser was using against Adam, I felt a release of the Lord.

Suddenly I heard the Lord say, "Now you repent for all the negative things you have said about Adam in your frustration." I realized at that moment that when I had spoken negative things about Adam, I had actually empowered the accuser against Him. When I had said, "I don't understand why he won't stand up and fight", or "Why won't he get up and move forward?", I had inadvertently empowered the accuser with my 'testimony' concerning Adam. The Lord showed me that the accuser before the throne was actually saying, "Even his own father says these things about him." When people in authority over us speak against us or for us, it becomes testimony before Heaven. Jesus said in Matthew 12:36-37 that our words set legal things in place.

> But I say to you that for every idle word men may speak, they will give account of it in the day of judgment. For by your words you will be justified, and by your words you will be condemned." (Matt. 12:36-37)

The word *idle* actually means something *unemployed*. In other words, we don't mean it, but we say it anyway. These words become testimony before the courts of Heaven that can justify or condemn.

I was being used of the devil to empower his accusations against Adam in the court of Heaven. I then repented of that which I had spoken against Adam from my place of frustration. I immediately felt a release come as legalities began to be put into place in Heaven concerning Adam. I was answering the accusation in the court of Heaven that was legally being used to hold Adam captive in depression. Everything is a legal matter when it comes to Heaven and the spirit realm. We must learn to get things legally in place before we march onto any battlefield.

As soon as I had repented for both Adam and myself, I then began to '*prophesy*' and '*decree*' what was written in Adam's book in Heaven. Remember that each one of us has a book in Heaven with our destinies and days written in it (Psalm 139:15-16). As I had removed everything that was working against Adam legally, I now could prophesy from his book what God had said about him. I began to prophesy the portions of his destiny that I felt were in his book. I broke the spirit of depression and told it to leave. I immediately felt things shift.

A week and a half later I received a call from Adam. This is what he said. "Dad, I don't know what happened. But a week and a half ago all the depression suddenly was gone. I am free from it and am ready to pursue what God made me for." What I had not been able to accomplish in two years of praying, warring, yelling, crying and every other emotional appeal before God, was done in about a fifteen minute period of being before the throne of grace and getting legal things in place.

Adam is back in fulltime ministry as an associate pastor in the Northwest part of our nation. Once legal things were dealt with in the courts of Heaven, the power of depression was broken. The Father's heart was free to come into operation over Adam. He is presently living out his dream of ministry and the dream that God has for him. He is apprehending what is in his book that is written in Heaven.

There is a very real court of Heaven that we have been granted entrance into. From this court we are to get legal things in place so destinies written in the book of Heaven can be fulfilled. In the next chapter I will show us some more of the things I have learned about this process.

4

Books and Destinies

Everything in the spirit realm is about legalities. God has given mankind freedom of choice and therefore He can do nothing unless we give him the legal right. The devil, also, can do nothing unless it is legally allowed. We, as people of the Earth, grant the legal permission for either the devil to work or God to work. Matthew 16:18-19 tells us that we as the Church or Ecclesia of God have been given the right to bind and loose.

> And I also say to you that you are Peter, and on this rock I will build My church, and the gates of Hades shall not prevail against it. And I will give you the keys of the kingdom of Heaven, and whatever you bind on earth will be bound in Heaven, and whatever you loose on earth will be loosed in Heaven." (Matt. 16:18-19)

The word Ecclesia is the word translated church from the Greek. This word means the judicial, legislative and governmental people of God. It speaks of a people that have been granted legal positions on Earth and before the Lord. We have been given the right and authority to get things legally in place so that God's will can come into the Earth realm.

The words bind and loose are actually legal terms at their root. The word bind speaks of getting a binding contract into place, while the word loose speaks of dissolving an existing contract. Jesus was saying that the Ecclesia has a judicial responsibility to establish binding contracts with Heaven that allow God the legal right to invade and impact the planet. The Ecclesia also has the job of legally dissolving contracts with the devil that allow him to operate in the Earth. When we learn to get legal things in place, we can then see the devil expelled and God's will established. This is our job individually and corporately.

Answering the Accuser

This happened in Peter's life. Jesus went into the courts of Heaven on behalf of Peter and secured the destiny written in the books of Heaven for him. Luke 22:31-32 tell us that Satan desired to have Peter.

> And the Lord said, "Simon, Simon! Indeed, Satan
> has asked for you, that he may sift you as wheat. But
> I have prayed for you, that your faith should not fail;
> and when you have returned to Me, strengthen your
> brethren." (Luke 22:31-32)

The words **asked for** in the Greek actually says **demanded for trial**. Satan came and demanded that Peter be put on trial in the courts of Heaven. Satan had developed evidence against Peter to try and thwart what was written in the books of Heaven about him. Remember that when the court is seated, the books are opened (Daniel 7:10). The devil understood something of what was in Peter's book. He understood the significant purpose Peter was to play in the Kingdom of God. He knew that Peter was destined by Heaven to have a radical and dramatic effect. If the devil didn't stop him, Peter would do massive damage to his empire and establish the Kingdom of God. Satan, therefore, had to have a scheme to stop Peter if he could. His plan was to bring him to court and put him on trial. The reason for this was to disqualify Peter legally from what was written in his book. If Satan could disqualify Peter through accusation in court, he could stop the agenda of God for the Earth.

We must realize that Satan is an accuser. Revelation 12:10-11 shows that Satan is accusing us day and night.

> Then I heard a loud voice saying in Heaven, "Now salvation, and strength, and the kingdom of our God, and the power of His Christ have come, for the accuser of our brethren, who accused them before our God day and night, has been cast down. And they overcame him by the blood of the Lamb and by the word of their testimony, and they did not love their lives to the death (Rev. 12:10-11).

Satan is before the throne of God seeking to present evidence in the courts as to why we are disqualified from what is in our books. He wants to stop us, at any cost, from stepping into the destinies written about us in our books. It is our job to answer these accusations and silence them so that God has the legal right to grant us what is written in our books. When this occurs we fulfill our life's destiny and God's Kingdom purposes are done.

The only way the devil can stop us from fulfilling what is in the books, is through accusation. This was the tactic he used against Peter. It is the tactic that he used against Job. Job 1:6-12 shows us activity in the courts of Heaven.

Now there was a day when the sons of God came to present themselves before the Lord, and Satan also came among them. And the Lord said to Satan, "From where do you come?" So Satan answered the Lord and said, "From going to and fro on the Earth, and from walking back and forth on it."

Then the Lord said to Satan, "Have you considered My servant Job, that there is none like him on the Earth, a blameless and upright man, one who fears God and shuns evil?"

So Satan answered the Lord and said, "Does Job fear God for nothing? Have You not made a hedge around him, around his household, and around all that he has on every side? You have blessed the work of his hands, and his possessions have increased in the land. But now, stretch out Your hand and touch all that he has, and he will surely curse You to Your face!"

And the Lord said to Satan, "Behold, all that he has is in your power; only do not lay a hand on his person." So Satan went out from the presence of the Lord (Job 1:6-12).

Satan brings accusations against Job. He accuses Job of serving God with impure motives. As a result of this accusation, Job is thrown into devastation. The Lord as judge allows the devil to operate against Job. I don't have all the answers as to why this was allowed by God, but clearly the devil brought enough accusations against Job that God legally allowed the persecution to occur. Perhaps, there was no-one to answer the accusations brought against Job. This was prior to the cross of Jesus and there was not yet an intercessor or one to stand on Job's behalf. Regardless, it is clear that the tribulation of Job was a result of the accusation of Satan.

It is interesting that the accusation that Satan brought against Job was concerning his motives for serving God. It wasn't about a personal sin or a sin in his lineage or family line. The accusation was that Job only served God because God had a hedge about him and he couldn't be touched. Satan's lambasting of Job was that if life wasn't so good, Job wouldn't serve God. Wow! The accusation was concerning impure motives. In other words, we must not just do the right things; we must do the right things for the right reasons. This is why we must consistently allow the Lord to judge the motives and intents of our hearts. We must cry out with the Psalmist, *"Search me O God and see if their be any wicked ways in me"*. (Psalm 139:23-24) When we do, we take away from the devil any potential realms of accusation he could use against us.

What we must also realize is Job was rewarded in the end with a double portion. Job 42:10 shows that God in His justice restored Job's fortunes.

> And the Lord restored Job's losses when he prayed for his friends. Indeed the Lord gave Job twice as much as he had before (Job 42:10).

Restoration is always a result of legal activity in the courts of Heaven. God decreed a double portion restoration for all Job had suffered. Job had to first pray for the friends who had accused him during his troubles rather than stand with him. It is interesting that when Job prayed for his friends, it granted the courts of Heaven the legal right to restore his fortunes. How often are we not getting our restoration because we will not forgive and release? When Job followed through with prayer and forgiveness, the court rendered verdicts in his behalf of restitution and restoration of all that had been lost. Job qualified himself for this through his faithfulness toward God. The judicial system of Heaven ruled in his favor.

Standing in Holiness

Joshua the High Priest in Zechariah 3:1-7 is being accused of uncleanness and resisted by Satan.

> Then he showed me Joshua the high priest standing before the Angel of the Lord, and Satan standing at his right hand to oppose him. And the Lord said to Satan, "The Lord rebuke you, Satan! The Lord who has chosen Jerusalem rebuke you! Is this not a brand plucked from the fire?"
>
> Now Joshua was clothed with filthy garments, and was standing before the Angel.
> Then He answered and spoke to those who stood before Him, saying, "Take away the filthy garments from him." And to him He said, "See, I have removed your iniquity from you, and I will clothe you with rich robes."
>
> And I said, "Let them put a clean turban on his head."
>
> So they put a clean turban on his head, and they put the clothes on him. And the Angel of the Lord stood by.
>
> Then the Angel of the Lord admonished Joshua, saying, "Thus says the Lord of hosts:
> 'If you will walk in My ways,
> And if you will keep My command, Then you shall also judge My house, And likewise have charge of My courts; I will give you places to walk

Among these who stand here (Zech. 3:1-7).

Satan comes to resist and accuse Joshua of uncleanness. He is resisting him because of what God needed to do through him. The purpose of God through Joshua the High Priest was to rebuild and re-establish Jerusalem. The devil's tactic to stop this from happening was to bring accusation against the one that God would do it through. Our cleanness and holiness is essential to God's will being done. Without it, Satan can stop what God will do through us with accusations.

The Lord's answer to the uncleanness of Joshua was to rebuke Satan. Notice He didn't rebuke Satan for Joshua's sake. He rebuked Satan for the sake of Jerusalem being rebuilt. Sometimes our greatest asset is what God has called us to do. Once Satan was rebuked, Joshua needed to be cleaned up or Satan would have come back and legally resisted him again. Joshua's uncleanness granted Satan the legal right to resist him and what God was doing through him. The result was that the angels began to clean him up. Then the prophet began to cleanse him as well. Notice that the angels are putting clean garments on Joshua in this spiritual atmosphere. But Zechariah the prophet then proclaims a clean turban on his head. In order to be free from any place the devil can accuse us, we need angelic and prophetic input. With these things working on Joshua's behalf, he was cleansed.

Notice the result. If he would stay clean and walk righteously, he would be granted charge of the courts of the Lord and he would judge the house of the Lord. In other words, he would be given authority in the courts of Heaven to be able to render judgments that set things in order. If we are to operate in the judicial place God has for us, we must be cleansed and purified for that operation. We are then granted authority because we have overcome the accusations of the devil and can access what is written in our book.

Before we move into what happened with Peter, we need to understand the way the devil accuses us. Before Satan was cast out of Heaven, he was a part of the judicial operation. Ezekiel 28:14 says that Satan, when he was Lucifer in Heaven, walked on the fiery stones. This is a reference to the courts of the Lord and His Throne.

> "You were the anointed cherub who covers;
> I established you; You were on the holy mountain of
> God; You walked back and forth in the midst of
> fiery stones (Ezek. 28:14).

This was before his fall. He was a part of the legal system of Heaven. One of his jobs was to gather evidence through his walking so God could render verdicts based on it. We then see him after his being cast out still walking. Job 1:7 shows that, as Satan, he was still walking .

> And the Lord said to Satan, "From where do you
> come?"
> So Satan answered the Lord and said, "From going
> to and fro on the earth, and from walking back and
> forth on it." (Job 1:7)

Now Satan is walking about on the Earth during Job's days. But when we get to 1 Peter 5:8 we see why he is walking.

> Be sober, be vigilant; because your adversary the
> devil walks about like a roaring lion, seeking whom
> he may devour (1 Peter 5:8).

Satan is walking about to seek whom he may devour. Remember, Satan can only devour when he has a legal reason. His walking about is for the purpose of gathering evidence so he can accuse and be granted legal rights to destroy. This could explain why we see bad things happen to good people. Somewhere in their lives or history and ancestry the devil finds a legal right to bring destruction. The devil can do nothing unless he finds a legal place he can exploit through his walking about.

When Satan comes before the Throne of God regarding Job, the Lord asked him where he had been. His response was, "From going to and fro on the Earth and walking back and forth on it". The Lord then says to Satan, "Have you considered my servant Job?" in other words, "Have you gathered any evidence against Him"? This is when Satan brings up the whole motive issue. The Lord knew that Satan's walking back and forth was a searching out of people who had Kingdom destinies.

This is exactly what he had done with Peter. He targeted Peter because of the tremendous things in his book. He had gathered evidence against Peter to disqualify him from what was in his book. He had presented it to Heaven and demanded a court date concerning Peter. But Jesus said, "I have prayed for you." Through the prayers of Jesus, Peter was not disqualified, he was qualified for his destiny. I want to look at what happened in the courts of Heaven that allowed Peter to be secured for his future and fulfill what was in the books of Heaven about him.

The Power and Authority Granted Us in the Courts of Heaven

The first thing that allowed Peter's destiny to be secured was Jesus' prayers. Luke 22:31-32 shows that Satan demanded

Peter be put on trial, but Jesus stood for him in the courts of Heaven.

> And the Lord said, "Simon, Simon! Indeed, Satan has asked for you, that he may sift you as wheat. But I have prayed for you, that your faith should not fail; and when you have returned to Me, strengthen your brethren." (Luke 22:31-32)

Everyone would probably think, "Well of course it worked, Jesus prayed for him." What we must realize is that this was BEFORE Jesus died, was buried, resurrected and ascended. In other words this was before He won His position in the courts of Heaven. What Jesus did for Peter, he did as a mortal man. This is important otherwise we disqualify ourselves from what we have been called to do. When Jesus prayed for Peter, he didn't do it as God. He did it as a mortal man.

Philippians 2:5-11 shows us that Jesus lived on Earth as a mortal man. He never once touched His God-powers while here. Everything He did, he did as a man filled with God, not as God.

> Let this mind be in you which was also in Christ Jesus, who, being in the form of God, did not consider it robbery to be equal with God, but made Himself of no reputation, taking the form of a bondservant, and coming in the likeness of men. And being found in appearance as a man, He humbled Himself and became obedient to the point of death, even the death of the cross. Therefore God also has highly exalted Him and given Him the name which is above every name, that at the name of Jesus every knee should bow, of those in Heaven,

and of those on Earth, and of those under the Earth, and that every tongue should confess that Jesus Christ is Lord, to the glory of God the Father (Phil. 2:5-11).

We are told in these Scriptures that Jesus laid aside all of His God-powers and functioned here totally as a human being. Because of His obedience to the Father to do this, He won for Himself a Name greater than all other names. This speaks of the position Jesus holds in Heaven. If Jesus had touched His God-powers while living on the Earth, He would have forfeited the right to be our Savior. Adam, a human being, lost creation. Jesus, the second and last Adam, had to live totally as a human being to win it back.

This is why Satan tempted Jesus in the wilderness with, "If you are the Son of God, turn these stones into bread" (Matthew 4: 3). Satan knew that if Jesus ever touched His God-powers while living on the Earth, He would lose the right to redeem it back to God. The temptation was to use His powers as God to turn the stones into bread.

How did Jesus do what He did while on Earth, if He didn't touch His God-powers? He lived not as God on the planet but rather as a man filled with God. This is what happened at the river Jordan when the Holy Spirit descended on Him. This is why the term *Incarnate One* is used to describe Jesus. Incarnate means a *body filled with a spirit*. This is the way Jesus lived. He never did one recorded miracle until the Holy Spirit filled Him. He lived the exact same way that we are to live. Not as God, but as people filled with God. This means everything He did is legal for us to do as well. If Jesus had performed miracles as God, then we would be excluded from such activity. We are not God, but part of humanity.

This is important concerning Jesus' prayer for Peter. He did not intercede in the courts of Heaven as High Priest or even as God. He had not yet won that position. His prayer for Peter was as a man filled with God and under the unction of the Holy Spirit.

In other words what He did for Peter we can also do. Just like Jesus went into the courts of Heaven and secured Peter's destiny, we too can go into the courts of Heaven and secure our destinies that are in the books. We can secure the destinies of others that are joined to us as well. The main thing is that we should not disqualify ourselves from the power and authority we have in Heaven and its court system.

Closing Doors Opened Through Sin

Another necessary thing that must be done to secure our futures from the books is to realize that Satan will exploit anything possible. Most of us have enough personal issues that supply the devil with accusations to last a lifetime. As big of an issue as this is, there can be an even larger one. We must realize that anything in our bloodline can be legal fodder with which Satan can accuse us. In other words, if people in our bloodline have sexual sins, perversions, covenant breaking, innocent bloodshed, thievery, allegiance to other gods and idols, demonic worship and other things, the devil can exploit this in the courts of Heaven to resist what is written in the books about us. I am not talking about deliverance from personal demons. I am referring to sins in the bloodline from perhaps centuries or millenniums before, where someone opened a legal door that Satan can use to stop destinies. This is seen in Isaiah, chapter 43:25-28.

> "I, even I, am He who blots out your transgressions
> for My own sake;

And I will not remember your sins. Put Me in
remembrance;
Let us contend together;
State your case, that you may be acquitted. Your
first father sinned,
And your mediators have transgressed against Me.
Therefore I will profane the princes of the sanctuary;
I will give Jacob to the curse,
And Israel to reproaches (Isaiah 43:25-28).

There are several issues in this Scripture. Notice that God is
speaking from a courtroom perspective. When He says, "State your
case and be acquitted," this is the language of court settings. The
word acquitted actually means to be justified. All the accusations
against us have been silenced and God is free to deliver to us our
destinies. Also notice that in this scenario, the destiny of a nation
hangs in the balance. God is saying that because there is improper
activity or inadequate operations in the court of Heaven, Jacob is
given over to a curse and Israel to reproaches. Operation in the
courts of Heaven can be on a personal level but it can go all the
way up to the destinies of nations being fulfilled. In this Scripture
the reason a nation was being afflicted was because of the first
father's sin. It goes on to say that the transgressions of a mediator
can also prohibit the destiny of a nation from being realized. Before
I go into these two things, I need to point out some other realities
concerning operations in the courts of Heaven.

The Lord says that He blots out our transgressions for His
own sake. This means that God needs us. The saving of nations is
not a sovereign act. The Lord needs our co-operation in the courts
of Heaven. We need to accept His forgiveness and walk in it. I
usually tell people, "For God's sake, forgive yourself." He needs us

to embrace the grace of His forgiveness so we can stand in the courts and work with Him to get his will done in nations.

Then the Lord says, "Put Me in remembrance." Remember we are in court. When He says, "Put Me in remembrance," He is saying that we should remind Him of what He wrote in the books of Heaven. Call God into remembrance concerning what He said about you or a church or a business or a family or even a nation. God is saying, "Give Me a legal reason to fulfill what I previously ordained." This is our job. We are to grant God the legal reason to show mercy and fulfill what is written in the books of Heaven. Then the Lord says, "Let us contend together." Remember that this is from a courtroom setting. This Scripture does not mean that we should contend with **Him**, but rather that we are going to contend **with Him** against the accuser. Together we will answer every accusation until God legally can grant what was written in the books. God is not our enemy. We are together with Him as individuals and also as the Ecclesia granting God the legal right to fulfill His passions. Once this is in place the Kingdom rule of God legally comes into Earth spheres.

The Transgressions of the Mediators

Notice that there are two things that can hinder us from getting verdicts for nations and ourselves. They are the mediator's transgressions and first fathers' sins. The word mediator in the Hebrew means one who is attempting to speak a foreign language. A court system has its own language. If you are not educated in speaking the language of the court you will not be effective. Attorneys go to school for many years learning the law and how to speak the language of the courts. They learn the protocol of the judicial system so they can be heard. Without a proper knowledge of this system and an adherence to it they cannot function nor gain verdicts from the courts. Neither can we in the courts of Heaven.

Proper behavior and protocol is necessary if we are to be effective in this ultimate court system.

God said through Isaiah that these mediators (which is a legal term and function) had sinned. In other words their sin had caused them to lose their place and authority in the courts of Heaven. We may be able to bluff our way through things on Earth, but if there is sin in our lives, the spirit realm knows it. When we have undealt with sin in our lives, we forfeit any and all authority in the courts of Heaven. In Isaiah 43, the result was a nation coming under curses, reproaches and judgment. Could it be that the reason we have not been effective in turning nations to their Kingdom purpose is because those of us who were to have authority in Heaven have forfeited it because of our sin? May we repent, and the Lord forgive us. Nations hang in the balance. We must learn to operate in the courts of Heaven and grant the Lord His legal right to bless the nations and us again. It is His heart to bless us, but we must grant Him the legal right to do so.

The First Fathers' Sins

The other issue that was causing nations to fall short of the destiny written in the books concerning them, was the first fathers' sin. This speaks of not my personal sin, but the sin connected to my bloodline. If there are sins that have contaminated my bloodline from even thousands of years gone by, this grants the accuser the legal right to resist me in the courts of Heaven. This is why we see Nehemiah, Daniel and others repenting for the sins of their forefathers. They understood that until these sins that had allowed the devil to bring them into captivity were dealt with legally, there would be no deliverance. The devil would have a legal reason to afflict and hold them until that legal reason was taken away. Nehemiah, for instance, repented for himself, his nation and its history so that in the courts of Heaven the accuser would be silenced. We see this in Nehemiah 1:5-7.

> And I said: "I pray, Lord God of Heaven, O great and awesome God, You who keep Your covenant and mercy with those who love You and observe Your commandments, please let Your ear be attentive and Your eyes open, that You may hear the prayer of Your servant which I pray before You now, day and night, for the children of Israel Your servants, and confess the sins of the children of Israel which we have sinned against You. Both my father's house and I have sinned. We have acted very corruptly against You, and have not kept the commandments, the statutes, nor the ordinances which You commanded Your servant Moses (Neh. 1:5-7).

Nehemiah repented for himself, his nation, his fathers' sins and his history that granted the devil legal rights to afflict him. This is a picture of the first fathers' sin. If the devil cannot find a legal reason in my own personal life to stop what is in the books about me, he will search my bloodline. We see him doing this with Jesus. John 14:30 shows that the devil came and searched Jesus out, but found no place to accuse Him.

> I will no longer talk much with you, for the ruler of this world is coming, and he has nothing in Me (John 14:30).

The reason the devil could find nothing in Jesus was because He lived a perfect life but also had a perfect bloodline. His bloodline was from God the Father through the Holy Spirit. Our bloodline though is not perfect. There are all sorts of things the devil can unveil as he searches us out. When he finds something that is not dealt with in our bloodline, it gives him a legal right to resist us with that thing. The truth is that the devil will not bother with our bloodline until we become a governmental threat against him. We see this same strategy in the political arena all the time. When someone begins to rise on the political scene during election periods they always become a target. Their attempt to take a high governmental position causes their adversaries to search them out and their history. They are seeking to find a place of accusation that will damage them and disqualify them from the office they seek. This is very similar to what happens in the spirit realm when we begin to step into governmental places of authority to shift things.

The more we become ones that can step into the courts of Heaven and get things legally in place, the more he will seek a way to stop us. Remember, his only weapon against us is accusation in the courts. Every other attack flows from accusations made.

I personally experienced this. I was privileged to develop and lead an apostolic center that was a strong display of God's grace in the Earth. We had the supernatural flowing, healing occurring, prosperity in place and we were impacting the region for the Kingdom. The Lord then spoke to my wife, Mary, and I to hand this ministry off and begin to launch into a bigger Kingdom sphere. We obeyed and did what we were told to do. What I didn't understand was that when I transitioned from a local sphere of ministry to a national and even international one, I became a bigger threat to the devil. I had no known sin in my life. I sought to live a holy lifestyle before the Lord. We had blessings in every dimension in our home and family. Life was good. When we stepped out of the local ministry and into a bigger Kingdom effect, everything changed. One of the main things that occurred was that literally millions of dollars were stolen from us. I had very diligently sought to have things properly ordered so that we would have plenty of finances to do the ministry God had assigned to us. As I was no longer leading a local work, I had spent years getting things financially in place so Mary and I could do whatever we were called to do. I was sure everything was properly ordered. What I didn't understand was legal fight I was engaging.

I don't want to bore you with details. Just suffice it to say that people whom I trusted implicitly turned against me and incited others to do the same. This resulted in personal and financial devastation. We went from a very secure future to having to wonder how we could pay the bills from month to month, week to week and even day to day. Even though the Lord was faithful, I still wondered how this had happened. We had faithfully obeyed in every area and had always practiced the principles of honor. We had obeyed the Lord in all forms of giving. We had shown mercy to people many times. We had always taken care of our leaders and others as well. Now it seemed that everything we had done to secure our future hadn't worked. I really wondered why this had happened as I sought to navigate through those very difficult days.

Then I began to learn about bloodlines and the courts of Heaven. As I was preparing to minister for a particular group, the leader said they would like to cleanse my bloodline. This group is highly apostolic and prophetic. I agreed for this to be done. As we began to go into the courts of the Lord one of the seer prophets suddenly said that someone in my bloodline and history had made a covenant with a demonic god named Parax. Someone pulled out the computer and googled Parax. To my astonishment there was a demonic god named Parax and its chief characteristic was to 'suck dry'. Instantly a light came on for me. I realized that as I became a bigger threat in the spirit realm, the devil and his forces had searched out my bloodline and found that an ancestor connected to me had made a covenant with this demonic entity. This gave the devil the legal right to go after all that Mary and I had built and steal it away. I knew that what we had experienced was not a result of our own personal sin, but the result of a sin in my bloodline that granted the devil a legal right to resist and attack me. Finally, I understood what had stood against me. I repented for the ones in my ancestry that had made this covenant and then renounced and broke that covenant off my family line. The result was that a new realm of blessing began to break through in my life.

The devil will search our bloodlines and find ways to accuse us legally. We must know how to cleanse our bloodlines consistently so that we can take up our authority in the courts of Heaven without fear of backlash.

This is why before every restoration that occurred in Bible times, there was not just repentance for personal sin, but also for "Fathers' sins." For instance when Nehemiah began to cry out for the restoration of Israel and especially Jerusalem, he repented for his own sins and the sins of his fathers. Nehemiah 1:4 - 6 show the prayers that Nehemiah prayed to begin the restoration process.

> So it was, when I heard these words, that I sat down and wept, and mourned for many days; I was fasting and praying before the God of heaven. And I said: "I pray, LORD God of heaven, O great and awesome God, You who keep Your covenant and mercy with those who love You and observe Your commandments, please let Your ear be attentive and Your eyes open, that You may hear the prayer of Your servant which I pray before You now, day and night, for the children of Israel Your servants, and confess the sins of the children of Israel which we

have sinned against You. Both my father's house
and I have sinned (Neh. 1:4-6).

When Nehemiah repented for his fathers' sin, he was not
endeavoring to alter their eternal state.   Their own life had
established what that status would be.   The purpose of his
repentance was to snatch from the devil the legal right to keep
Israel in a place of captivity and oppression. It was the "fathers'
sins" that had legally allowed this to occur. To get Israel free and
Jerusalem restored, something legal had to shift in the spirit
realm. Someone had to ask for and receive mercy from the Lord.
Once the mercy of God against their sin was received, legal issues
in the heavenly realm were altered. God could now have a legal
right to undo the captivity of the Jews and bring restoration to them
and their land. But without dealing with the "fathers' sins" that had
allowed it, nothing would be able to shift. Sin does not just
disappear over time. It only disappears when someone grabs hold
of the blood of Jesus and appropriates it into place against that sin.
When this is done, legal things come into order and heaven moves
as a result.

This is what was happening with Peter. My suspicion is that
Peter had plenty of personal issues the devil could use against him,
but I am sure that the devil had searched Peter's bloodline and had
found reasons to accuse him before Heaven. Jesus went into that
trial setting, interceded for Peter and answered those accusations.
The result was that Peter did step into his destiny. The devil was
not successful in causing Peter to be disqualified. Peter shook the
Earth and nations and fulfilled what was written in his book.

We will, too, when we learn to operate in the courts of
Heaven and answer the accusations of the enemy. Not only do our
individual destinies hang in the balance, but the destinies of nations

as well. Let's grant God the legal right to fulfill the passion of His heart and what He wrote in the books before time began.

5

Voices in the Courts

There are many different voices in a court. There is the voice of the judge, the voice of the attorneys, the voice of witnesses, the voice of bailiffs, the voice of recorders, the voice of the jury and others as well. There are also many different voices in the courts of Heaven. Our job is to understand these voices and come into agreement with them. As we join with these voices and release our faith and agreement with them, God's Kingdom will on Earth is then free to be accomplished.

Any lack of the Kingdom being manifest is because of a legal issue. The Father's heart is very clear. God is not withholding from us. If there is a lack of manifestation of Kingdom purpose, it is because we have yet to grant the Father the legal right to fulfill His passion toward us. If we are praying according to the will of God and have prayed for an extended time without results, something legal is standing in the way of the answer. Somewhere in the spirit realm the demonic powers have found a legal right to resist the answer from coming to us. The accuser of the brethren is speaking against us. The answer to this is to learn and agree with the voices in the court of Heaven. When we do, the accuser is silenced and we set in motion Heaven to be manifest in the Earth.

You Have Come to Mount Zion

In order to understand the different voices operating in the courts of Heaven we have to understand 'Zion'. Hebrews 12:22-24 tells us where we have been positioned as New Testament believers.

> But you have come to Mount Zion and to the city of the living God, the Heavenly Jerusalem, to an innumerable company of angels, to the general assembly and church of the firstborn who are registered in Heaven, to God the Judge of all, to the spirits of just men made perfect, to Jesus the Mediator of the new covenant, and to the blood of sprinkling that speaks better things than that of Abel (Heb. 12:22-24).

In the preceding verses we are told that we haven't come to Mount Sinai, which was the place where the Law was given. We have not come to the place of legalism and of death. In that place the children of Israel were afraid to approach God and did not even want to hear His voice. This place was necessary in that it was where the Law was given. The Law served to bring us to Christ, but it was not to be the place where we stayed. It was to be a part of the journey, but not the destination. The destination was to be Mount Zion. The earthly manifestation of Mount Zion was established by King David as a place where perpetual worship was offered. It is where David set up the ark of the covenant and had 24-hour worship every day. This was one of the first orders of business that David performed once he became king of all of Israel.

People think that Zion is therefore about worship. But Zion is not about worship. It is about the purpose of worship. King David commissioned worship to cultivate and host the presence of the Lord so that from that presence, he could govern a nation. This is the purpose of worship. Out of worship is to flow the governing authority of God through His church. When we worship there is to be a rearranging of the heavenly or spiritual realm until Heaven is allowed to enter Earth. This is what Psalm 110:1-2 declares.

> The Lord said to my Lord, "Sit at My right hand,
> Till I make Your enemies Your footstool."
> The Lord shall send the rod of Your strength out of
> Zion. Rule in the midst of Your enemies!
> (Psa. 110:1-2)

Notice what is declared about Zion. The rod of the strength of the Lord will flow out of Zion and cause the enemies of God to be subdued. The purpose of the activity of Zion is rulership and governmental authority. The activity of Zion is worship that allows the Lord's rod of strength to be wielded against His enemies.

When the Word of the Lord says that we have come to Zion, it is saying we have come to this governmental place in God. We have been privileged out of a place of intimate worship with the Lord to govern with Him. We are no longer at Mount Sinai but now at Mount Zion, the place of His governing power.

Also, please be aware, that we are not trying to get to Zion. We have been granted as New Testament believers to be there already. One of the problems with us as the Church, is that we are still trying to get to a place that we have already been positioned in. If we could simply understand the divine placement of the Lord in our life, we would begin to function in faith and see things we have been waiting on begin to happen. Yet so often we are striving to get positioned when we have already been positioned by the Lord and His grace. If we can by revelation understand this and begin to function from that place, we will begin to exercise Kingdom rule. *We have come to Mount Zion.*

The Mountain of the Lord's House

To further understand what we have come to, we should consider Isaiah 2:1-4.

> The word that Isaiah the son of Amoz saw concerning Judah and Jerusalem.
> Now it shall come to pass in the latter days
> That the mountain of the Lord's house
> Shall be established on the top of the mountains,
> And shall be exalted above the hills;
> And all nations shall flow to it.
> Many people shall come and say,
> "Come, and let us go up to the mountain of the Lord, To the house of the God of Jacob;
> He will teach us His ways,
> And we shall walk in His paths."
> For out of Zion shall go forth the law,
> And the word of the Lord from Jerusalem.
> He shall judge between the nations,
> And rebuke many people;
> They shall beat their swords into plowshares,
> And their spears into pruning hooks;
> Nation shall not lift up sword against nation,
> Neither shall they learn war anymore. (Isaiah 2:1-4)

We see that the mountain of the Lord's House will be established in the top of the mountains. The word top is the Hebrew word *rosh* and it means *head*. It is saying that the mountain of the Lord's house will be the *head* of all other mountains. Anytime we read about mountains in Scripture they are speaking of governments, seen and unseen.

We see this in Jesus speaking with His disciples after their unsuccessful attempt to cast the demon out of the boy. This story is found in Matthew 17:19-21. Jesus informs them that if they have faith as a grain of mustard seed, they can speak to *this mountain* and it would move. Jesus was informing them that one of the reasons why they could not help the boy was because they were dealing with a *demonic mountain* in the spirit. This was no ordinary demonic situation. For whatever reason, this boy had become a place of a demonic government. The power and authority required to deal with this was greater than a normal circumstance. Because they hadn't recognized this, they had been unsuccessful. There are times when we encounter not just demonic imps that need to be cast out, but demonic mountains that have become governmental in nature and function. This requires a greater realm of authority to move them out of the way.

When it says the mountain of the Lord's house is in the top of the mountains, it is saying that the government of God will rule over all other governments. This reference to the mountain of the Lord's house is very interesting. The best way I know how to relate what I believe the Lord is saying here is through a dream that a prophet's wife had about me. In her dream her husband, the prophet, and I had identical garages standing next to each other. The moment I heard there were garages in the dream, I knew it spoke of a ministry center. Garages house vehicles. Vehicles almost always speak of ministry, business and anything that is being led or directed. When I dream about driving a car, flying a plane or anything like that, I know God is speaking about the ministry I direct and lead. When she told me about the garages, I knew it spoke of that which housed the ministry.

She went on to relay that as she entered her husband's garage it looked like a normal garage. But as she entered my garage, it had a mountain in it although you couldn't tell it from the outside. When she told me the dream, I wondered if there was a mountain in my garage because I lived in Colorado. I didn't yet understand that mountains spoke of government. As I became aware of this concept I knew that God was saying that He was raising a ministry center that would have a mountain in it. He was raising a House with a Mountain in it. It would look like a normal house from the outside, but it would be a governmental people that would exercise governmental authority from the mountain in the house.

This is what God is doing today. He is causing to arise Houses with Mountains in them. They may look like normal churches from the outside, but they are governmental on the inside. They are not interested in just having good activities and service and being blessed. They want to see the Kingdom of God come to the Earth. They want to see life reflect a Kingdom culture in the planet. They are houses with mountains in them.

We see this same concept echoed in Isaiah 56:7.

> Even them I will bring to My holy mountain, And make them joyful in My house of prayer. Their burnt offerings and their sacrifices Will be accepted on My altar;
> For My house shall be called a house of prayer for all nations." (Isaiah 56:7)

Notice the words *house* and *mountain* are used interchangeably here. God brings these people to the holy mountain and makes them joyful in the house of prayer. So the house is in the mountain and the mountain is in the house. God's intention has always been to have a house that had a mountain in it. His desire is a house that is governmental and has influence and authority over all other forms of government in the spirit realm. From this mountain of the Lord's house the other mountains begin to reflect a Kingdom culture. This is an Old Testament picture of what Jesus said He would build in Matthew 16:18-19.

> And I also say to you that you are Peter, and on this rock I will build My church, and the gates of Hades shall not prevail against it. And I will give you the keys of the kingdom of Heaven, and whatever you bind on earth will be bound in Heaven, and whatever you loose on earth will be loosed in Heaven." (Matt. 16:18-19)

The Church that Jesus said He would build is from the Greek word Ecclesia. An *Ecclesia* within the Greek and Roman culture of Jesus' day spoke of a governmental, legislative and judicial body that made decisions and judgments that determined how society functioned. When Jesus said He would build this kind of people, He was speaking of building a house with a mountain in it. It is very important that we understand this.

This means that as the Ecclesia of God we have been given the right to stand in the courts of Heaven which are found inside the mountain of the Lord's House. From there we are to exercise our authority as the Ecclesia that will allow what is in the books of Heaven to come to Earth. As we take up our place in the courts of Heaven inside the mountain, we become a part of God's government in the Earth. This is the place we have been given as those who have 'Come to Mount Zion'.

To further understand this, let's go back to Isaiah 2. In these verses we see that the mountain of the Lord's house is in the top of the mountains. As we continue to read about this house with a mountain in it, we discover that God actually identifies this mountain and it has a name. Isaiah chapter 2:3 tells us this mountain's name.

> Many people shall come and say,
> "Come, and let us go up to the mountain of the
> Lord, To the house of the God of Jacob;
> He will teach us His ways,
> And we shall walk in His paths."
> For out of Zion shall go forth the law,
> And the word of the Lord from Jerusalem.
> (Isaiah 2:3)

This verse says that people will come and inspire each other to go up to this mountain/house. They then identify the mountains name. They say it is Zion. From Mount Zion the law will go forth. When Hebrews 12: 22 says we have come to Mount Zion, it is saying we have arrived at the governmental and judicial authority of the Lord and have become the house with a mountain in it. When we come to Mount Zion, we are commissioned and authorized to operate in the court system of Heaven. From this position we can begin to read what is written in the books of Heaven and legally administrate them into the Earth. The Word, through our function of faith, will become flesh in the Earth.

Discipling Nations from Mount Zion

Notice also in Isaiah 2:4 that through the operation in the mountain of the Lord's house, nations are judged and set in order.

> He shall judge between the nations,
> And rebuke many people;

They shall beat their swords into plowshares,
And their spears into pruning hooks;
Nation shall not lift up sword against nation,
Neither shall they learn war anymore.
(Isaiah 2:4)

From the mountain of the Lord's house He (Jesus) will judge nations. Jesus will judge nations from the house with the mountain in it, which is us. We as the Ecclesia will take our rightful place and through governing with Jesus set Kingdom rule in order over nations. This is what Jesus said we would do in Matthew 28:19-20.

Go therefore and make disciples of all the nations, baptizing them in the name of the Father and of the Son and of the Holy Spirit, teaching them to observe all things that I have commanded you; and lo, I am with you always, even to the end of the age." Amen (Matt. 28:19-20).

We are commissioned to disciple nations. We are not just to make disciples **in** nations, we are to disciple the nations themselves until they reflect a Kingdom culture. We are here to make nations look more like Heaven than like hell. We are here to turn nations from goat nations to sheep nations. (Matthew 25:31)

The way this is done is through the Church or house with a mountain in it operating with Jesus to judge nations. The word judge always speaks of judicial activity. Through judicial activity in the court of Heaven we set in place legal precedents that take away every right of demonic principalities to rule and influence nations. Once this is done we are then able to remove these powers and their influence over nations. These nations are freed to respond to the Gospel of the Kingdom and become expressions of His love, kindness and mercy. Justice will prevail and the people of these nations will be blessed because the cruelty of the devil and his forces is legally and then functionally removed.

This all happens from the Mountain named Zion. We have come to Mount Zion. In Mount Zion is the court/judicial system of Heaven. When you read Hebrews 12:22-24, everything mentioned is of legal nature.

> But you have come to Mount Zion and to the city of the living God, the Heavenly Jerusalem, to an innumerable company of angels, to the general assembly and church of the firstborn who are registered in Heaven, to God the Judge of all, to the spirits of just men made perfect, to Jesus the Mediator of the new covenant, and to the blood of sprinkling that speaks better things than that of Abel (Heb. 12:22-24).

God is revealed as the Judge, Jesus is the Mediator, the blood is speaking and testifying because everything here is part of the court system of Heaven. When we come to Mount Zion, we come to the legal system of Heaven where nations are judged. In this place God is granted the legal right to fulfill His passion. We, the Ecclesia, are to be the house with the mountain in it. We are a part of this system and function.

Hebrews 12:22-24 lists the voices within the court system of Heaven. There are eight voices mentioned that we can encounter in the courts of Heaven and are to come into agreement with. There is one more voice in the courts mentioned elsewhere. There are a total of nine voices we are to learn to function within the court system. When we come into agreement with these voices, we become a part of granting God the legal right to fulfill His passion.

A dear apostolic friend said to me recently that God had spoken to him to agree with the intercession of Heaven. I believe that these voices represent the intercession of Heaven and it is with these, that we need to come into agreement. When we do, we grant God the evidence to render verdicts and judgments in agreement with His Kingdom will. We have been given a great privilege as His Ecclesia to function in the courts and win verdicts from Heaven that free nations to come under Kingdom domain.

We will study these voices in a reverse order from how they are spoken of in Scripture. The nine voices in the courts of Heaven include:

1.   **The voice of the blood of Jesus.** The blood of Jesus releases testimony before the Throne of God that allows the Lord legal right to fulfill His passion.

2.   **The Mediator of the new covenant.** Mediators are officers of a legal system sent to resolve conflict.

3.   **The spirit of just men made perfect.** This speaks of those who are a part of the Church who have died and are in Heaven. They still have a viable and necessary function in the court system of Heaven.

4.   **God, the Judge of all.** Isn't it interesting that God is revealed not as Father or Lord but as Judge in this Scripture. It is because the Holy Spirit desires us to recognize the legal position God holds as Judge of all.

5.   **The Church of the firstborn registered in Heaven.** We as the Ecclesia have a tremendous place in the courts when we have been authorized and recognized.

6.   **The general assembly.** The word in the Greek is universal companionship and it speaks of the multitudes worshipping the Lord about His throne. Their function of worship is essential to the operation of the courts.

7. **An innumerable company of angels.** There are varying ranks of angels that are a part of the court of Heaven's operations.

8. **The city of the living God, Heavenly Jerusalem.** This is actually the wife of the Lamb as is mentioned in the book of Revelation. The wife or Bride of the Lamb's voice has a tremendous impact in the courts of Heaven.

9. **The voice of finance.** Our giving of finances has great weight and authority when they come into agreement with Heaven's desire and intent.

We will look at each of these voices and their effect in the courts of Heaven in the next chapters. When we learn how to come into agreement with these voices, verdicts are rendered from the court so God's will is done in the Earth. There is nothing that cannot be accomplished when we get legal things in place. Once the legal issues are resolved and the devil's rights revoked, God is free to functionally take back the planet through His church. When we as the Church have come to Mount Zion and are ready to agree with the voices of Heaven, the result will be unprecedented breakthrough and victory.

6

The Testimony of the Blood

A lady told me a story of her daughter, living in another State, who was charged with attempted murder. It seemed that she and her husband had had a fight one evening. He left in one car while she jumped in the other family car and pursued him. She eventually rammed his car with her car. The police were called and because of the circumstances surrounding the incident, she was arrested and charged with attempted murder. As time progressed the husband and wife reconciled, but the District Attorney in the county where they lived, persisted in keeping the charges alive and pushing toward the court date. As the date loomed for the beginning of the trial, this mother approached me and asked if we could take this situation before the court of Heaven. I agreed and we set a date to meet and do this the day before the jury selection began.

As we began the process of coming before the court of Heaven, I led the lady in submitting herself to the Lord and His authority. We then brought her daughter and the entire situation before the court. I had a couple of seer prophets working with me to help discern what was going on in the courts of Heaven. As we began to pray I asked the lady to take her place as mother and intercessor and repent for her daughter. We began to sense very distinctly what the accuser was using against this young lady that was about to go on trial. The mom repented, with tears, as specifically as she could for her daughter's disobedience and rebellion. It wasn't very long before we felt the accusations had been dealt with before the court of Heaven. The accuser had been silenced and we were now free to ask the Lord for mercy. As we did this, the seers clearly heard and saw that the judge in the case would dismiss the case and it wouldn't even go to trial. We believed that the court of Heaven had made a ruling in favor of this lady's daughter.

The next afternoon I got a call from a very excited mom who reported that when the jury selection was about to begin, the judge in the case looked at the evidence and abruptly dismissed the case. The young woman was released from all charges and was free to resume her life after months of torment and uncertainty.

The court of Heaven had ruled and it was played out on Earth in a natural court. This all happened because of the testimony of the blood of Jesus on behalf of this lady's daughter. The blood had answered every accusation against this daughter and silenced the accuser that had demanded destruction. The accuser has no answer for the blood of Jesus. Therefore God the judge of all was granted the legal right to show mercy because of the blood.

A judge can only render verdicts on the basis of testimony given. Even though he may want to find in favor of another, he, from his position of justice, can only render verdicts based on what is testified. So it is in the courts of Heaven with God as the Supreme Judge of all. The judgments that come from the throne are always just and in agreement with the testimony presented in the courts. The nine voices that I have listed in the last chapter are voices that are testifying in the court of Heaven and are giving the Lord the legal right to fulfill His desire and passion. I believe that the blood of Jesus is the major voice in the court that testifies and has audience before God.

Revelation 12:10-11 tells us the accuser is overcome by the blood of Jesus.

> Then I heard a loud voice saying in heaven, "Now salvation, and strength, and the kingdom of our God, and the power of His Christ have come, for the accuser of our brethren, who accused them before our God day and night, has been cast down. And they overcame him by the blood of the Lamb and by the word of their testimony, and they did not love their lives to the death (Rev. 12:10-11).

When we learn how to come into agreement with the testimony of the blood of Jesus we find great power for redemption. The blood is not only testifying for our forgiveness and redemption but also for the redemption of the whole Earth. Nations will be redeemed because of the blood of Jesus. Agreement with the blood allows us to sense the passion that God has for nations. But it is the blood of Jesus that gets Kingdom verdicts from God's throne.

Blood has a Voice

All blood has a voice and speaks. We see this in the case of Cain killing Abel. In Genesis 4:8-12 we see Abel's blood getting a verdict from the Throne of God.

> Now Cain talked with Abel his brother; and it came to pass, when they were in the field, that Cain rose up against Abel his brother and killed him
> Then the Lord said to Cain, "Where is Abel your brother?"
> He said, "I do not know. Am I my brother's keeper?"

> And He said, "What have you done? The voice of your brother's blood cries out to Me from the ground. So now you are cursed from the earth, which has opened its mouth to receive your brother's blood from your hand. When you till the ground, it shall no longer yield its strength to you. A fugitive and a vagabond you shall be on the earth." (Gen. 4:8-12)

The Lord said that the blood of Abel was crying out to Him from the ground. Based on what Abel's blood was testifying, God renders judgment and a sentence against Cain. He was sentenced to be a vagabond and wanderer for the remainder of his days. The sentence was on the basis of the blood of Abel's testimony. The testimony of blood is very powerful before God's throne.

The High Priest would go behind the veil once a year on the Day of Atonement. He would sprinkle and pour out the blood of the Passover lamb. On the basis of the testimony of that blood, God would render a verdict that the sins of a nation were rolled back for one more year. The animal's blood could only release testimony that allowed God to be merciful for one year at a time. But when Jesus spilt His blood and poured and sprinkled it at the real altar in Heaven, the testimony of that blood allows God the legal right to forgive sins forever. Based on the testimony of Jesus' blood God now has legal right to be merciful and forgive sins and secure destinies forever.

To further help us understand the voice of blood, let me share a very personal story that happened when I was seeking to cleanse my bloodline. Everyone needs to have their bloodline cleansed. If the devil/accuser cannot find grounds to accuse us based on our behavior, he will search our bloodline to discover something to use against us in the heavenly court. This search is all the more diligent as we become an increasing threat to the powers of darkness. I have previously shared some of my experiences of how this affected my family and me personally. It is imperative to cleanse the bloodline so we can win victories in the court, but also not suffer a backlash from the devil and his forces.

We must realize that the cleansing of our bloodline should be done on a regular basis. If you were to look at your family tree you would discover that, as one person said to me, "It actually looks more like a jungle than a tree." Your history and ancestry have many branches and offshoots to it. Satan will search everything out to find any legal place to resist you in the courts of Heaven. Consistent cleansing of your bloodline keeps the devil from exploiting the sins of your forefathers against you and His Kingdom will.

As my bloodline was being cleansed another time, the seer prophets helping in this process saw that an ancestor of mine had been burned at the stake by Native American Indians. This ancestor cursed the Indians as he died. It was discerned by those who were seeing this, that the reason for this occurrence was my ancestor had stolen the Indian's land. As this was revealed I began to repent for what my forefathers had done. I repented for all the maliciousness and thievery against this Indian nation.

As I was doing this a prophet friend of mine was in the room. He was sitting next to me on the couch. I was aware that as I was walking through this scenario, he got up and moved away from me. As we concluded the session of repentance and the cleansing of my bloodline, I asked my prophet friend why he moved during the process. His response startled me. He said, "I could feel the violence coming from your blood." My blood was speaking a violent thing as it was being cleansed. My literal blood in my veins had a voice of violence.

As this was said, I realized at least one of the reasons why I had struggled against anger in my life, especially in my earlier years. The anger that was in me had its roots in my blood that was defiled by the sins of my past generations. My blood had anger in it. Through the cleansing of my bloodline, not only was the legal right removed that the devil was using to resist me, but my blood was cleansed from the improper voice that it had.

The Cry of Jesus' Blood

All blood has a voice. Jesus' blood in the courts of Heaven has the greatest voice. His blood cries out for our forgiveness and redemption. We know this because as He was dying on the cross, He spoke forgiveness to all who would receive it. Luke 24:33-34 shows Jesus releasing forgiveness even as He is being crucified.

> And when they had come to the place called Calvary, there they crucified Him, and the criminals, one on the right hand and the other on the left. Then Jesus said, "Father, forgive them, for they do not know what they do." (Luke 24:33-34)

This is the cry of Jesus' blood. He is crying and testifying and granting the evidence of His blood before the courts of Heaven as the reason for our redemption. But Jesus blood also is testifying for more than just our salvation. The sacrifice of Jesus' blood also purchased all of creation back to God. Jesus blood is also crying out and granting God the legal right as Judge to secure all the Earth back under His Kingdom rule. We need to understand how large a sacrifice Jesus made on the cross and what it legally did. His sacrifice has legally secured nations back to the rule of God. Isaiah 49:6 says that the Father prophesied to Jesus that He would be salvation to the ends of the Earth.

"Indeed He says,
'It is too small a thing that You should be My
Servant To raise up the tribes of Jacob,
And to restore the preserved ones of Israel;
I will also give You as a light to the Gentiles,
That You should be My salvation to the ends of the
earth.'" (Isaiah 49:6)

The Father said that Jesus' sacrifice was too great for just Israel's salvation. His sacrifice demanded that all the nations of the Earth would be redeemed. The blood of Jesus before the Throne of God is crying for nations to be redeemed. His blood is not just crying for the people in nations, but also the government of nations to function in a Kingdom culture.

Jesus' blood will not be silent until all that He bought at the cross is legally appropriated and set in place as a reality in the Earth. It is our job to agree with the testimony of the blood of Jesus until nations reflect His passion. His blood is legal testimony in the courts of Heaven for this.

The Church/Ecclesia must engage in and agree with the testimony of Jesus' blood. We are the stewards of His sacrifice in the Earth. We are to agree and add our testimony before the courts of Heaven for nations to be redeemed. Anything less than discipling nations, is an insult to the cross of Jesus. His blood is crying for this and we must set ourselves in agreement. The same passion that is carried in His blood must be in us.

The Moravians of centuries ago were a people sold out to the Lord. Many of them would sell themselves into slavery in foreign lands. Travelling as slaves, on slave ships, they headed to their new destination. They did this so that they could reach unevangelized people groups. They had a passion to reach the world with the gospel of Jesus Christ. What a commitment to the

Lord and His Kingdom. As they were loading themselves on these ships they would sing a song. The words to this song are:

> I lay my life down
> I lay my self down
> I lay my crowns down at Your feet
>
> To win for the Lamb the rewards of His suffering
> To win for the Lamb the lost
> To win for the Lamb the rewards of His suffering
> And take up the cross

What a pure view of a people who had been possessed by the passion of the Lord. They had been overtaken by a passion and voice contained in the blood of Jesus. His blood is crying out for nations and all people groups to know Him in His power and glory.

The Blood of the Martyrs

There is one other aspect of the testimony of blood. As I have said, Jesus' blood is the predominant voice in the courts. But there is the voice of other people's blood that is also crying out and giving testimony in the courts of Heaven. Revelation 6:9-11 tells of the voice of the martyrs who gave their blood for a Kingdom cause while alive in the Earth.

> When He opened the fifth seal, I saw under the altar the souls of those who had been slain for the word of God and for the testimony which they held. And they cried with a loud voice, saying, "How long, O Lord, holy and true, until You judge and avenge our blood on those who dwell on the earth?" Then a white robe was given to each of them; and it was

said to them that they should rest a little while
longer, until both the number of their fellow
servants and their brethren, who would be killed as
they were, was completed (Rev. 6:9-11).

These martyrs are crying out for the 'avenging' of their blood. We
could look at this and think they are crying out for someone to be
punished for the spilling of their blood. Perhaps this is so, but I
believe that what they are really desiring and communicating is
their desire for what they spilt their blood for, to matter. In other
words if they laid down their lives before the Lord so people and
nations could be redeemed, their blood is still crying in the courts
of Heaven for this. Blood never stops crying. Remember it has the
power to get verdicts from the throne of Heaven. This is shown in
Revelation 12:11.

And they overcame him by the blood of the Lamb
and by the word of their testimony, and they did not
love their lives to the death (Rev. 12:11).

When someone doesn't love their lives unto death, the accuser has
no power against them. The accusations of the accuser have no
power against this person and their testimony. They have now won
a great testimony before the courts of heaven. This is what
Hebrews, chapter 11:1-2 declares.

Now faith is the substance of things hoped for, the
evidence of things not seen. For by it the elders
obtained a good testimony (Heb. 11:1-2).

Through living in faith and laying their lives down, the elders
obtained a good testimony. This means they are still speaking

before the courts of Heaven because they loved not their lives unto death, but laid them down for the sake of the Kingdom. When anyone does this, their blood has a voice in the courts of Heaven. It is crying out and testifying for what it was spilt for, to become a reality in the Earth. These under the Throne in Revelation 6 want what they gave their life for, to matter. Their blood is still speaking in the courts of Heaven to this end.

It is our job as individuals to come into agreement with the blood of Jesus in the courts. We must use the blood for our justification, we must agree with the blood for the nations it was given for and we must let the passion of the blood's voice impact and empower us. When we do, we become qualified to operate in the courts of Heaven and see verdicts rendered that grants God the legal right to fulfill His will.

The Lord is looking for the ones who will stand in their place and grant Him legal precedents to put in place the legalities of the cross. When this occurs, principalities are silenced and legal things come to order.

The reason nations are not being won to the Lord is because principalities and powers have a legal right through the sins of generations to hold them. They give witness in the courts of Heaven based on this legal right God, as Judge of all, cannot violate His own law and just take from these demonic powers their hold. The reason they have the domination must legally be removed. The legal removal of their rights is when our sins and the sins of the fathers are cleansed away by the blood of Jesus. When we repent of these sins and ask for the blood to cleanse, the legal right of principalities that are ruling nations is revoked from the courts of Heaven. Once their legal right is annulled, we can them rebuke them and they will flee. No amount of binding, loosing, rebuking or decreeing will work until the legal reason they are dominating is taken way. This is what the blood of Jesus does for us and the Kingdom purpose of God. Our requests, which up to now have been resisted, can then be granted and nations can come under Kingdom influence. The blood of Jesus is powerful. Let's use it and agree with it until Heaven invades Earth.

7

The Mediator's Testimony

I have a friend who found himself being sued for the fulfillment of a contract his company had signed. The company had agreed to pay this person a salary of $42,000. The problem was that the company that had been started, floundered and went out of business. This person, who was demanding payment, had been the person responsible for making the startup company a success. He obviously didn't do his job but was still demanding payment. As the day of the court date approached the judge in the matter ordered that both parties had to go before a 'mediator' to see if something could be worked out before they appeared in his courtroom. This was done and a solution was agreed upon by both parties. They then appeared before the judge for him simply to put his stamp on it and authorize it as legal.

The purpose of a mediator is to bring parties together into a place of agreement. Mediators and mediation is a legal function. The Bible says in Hebrews 12:24 that we have a mediator of the New Covenant.

> To Jesus the Mediator of the new covenant, and to the blood of sprinkling that speaks better things than that of Abel (Heb. 12:24).

We have come to Jesus as the Mediator of the New Covenant. Jesus is the One who is standing in the courts of Heaven as the Heavenly Mediator bringing God the Father and man together in agreement. The Scripture says the Man, Jesus, is the mediator. 1 Timothy 2:5 says that Jesus in His humanity and His Godhood stands as the mediator between God and us.

> For there is one God and one Mediator between God
> and men, the Man Christ Jesus (1 Tim. 2:5).

The thing that makes one a mediator is that he or she is 'fair' with both parties. A mediator has to be able to see where each party stands. As God, Jesus understands the demands of holiness, purity and righteousness. These standards cannot be compromised and are non-negotiable. God as God can never allow His righteousness to be compromised. The demand of God upon man is be holy as I am holy. 1 Peter 1:1-16 shows us this demand.

> But as He who called you is holy, you also be holy
> in all your conduct, because it is written, "Be holy,
> for I am holy." (1 Pet. 1:1-16)

God has never lessened His demands on Man. He just answered them in and through Jesus Christ. In addition, He grants us the grace that empowers us to live holy lives as He is holy. If and when we fail, there is forgiveness for us through Jesus Christ. I John 2:1 tells us that we are to strive not to sin, but should we sin, what Jesus accomplished on the cross grants God the legal right to forgive us.

> My little children, these things I write to you, so that
> you may not sin. And if anyone sins, we have an

Advocate with the Father, Jesus Christ the righteous
(1 John 2:1).

Jesus is in the courts of Heaven as our Mediator bringing God and
us together so what legally needs to happen can. Not only does
Jesus as Mediator stand for the demands of God in holiness, but He
also stands as Man understanding our frailty. He lived as a man and
understands the pressures and temptations of our humanity.
Scripture says, Jesus was tempted and yet did not sin. Hebrews
4:15-16 encourages us with the fact that Jesus understands where
we live and what we war against.

> For we do not have a High Priest who cannot
> sympathize with our weaknesses, but was in all
> points tempted as we are, yet without sin. Let us
> therefore come boldly to the throne of grace, that we
> may obtain mercy and find grace to help in time of
> need (Heb. 4:15-16).

When the Bible says Jesus was tempted this means He felt the pull
and enticement of sin. It was real. Yet from the power of the Holy
Spirit and the grace He supplied, Jesus said "No" to sin every time.
Because of this He has won a place in the courts of Heaven greater
than any other place. It also means He understands the limits on our
humanity. Because of this He is qualified to stand as our Mediator
with God and as God's Mediator with us.

Notice the reason for Jesus' mediation is concerning the
New Covenant. He is the mediator of the New Covenant. The term
'covenant' is a legal term as well. Anytime God made covenant
with man, he came into a legal agreement. He was promising on the
basis of covenant that He would fulfill His Word and promises
connected to that covenant. Jesus as our Mediator and God's

Mediator is working to remove every hindrance from our getting the promises of the New Covenant. There are many promises connected to the New Covenant. This covenant is based on better promises and a better sacrifice. Hebrews 8:6 says that the covenant Jesus is mediating is based on better promises.

> But now He has obtained a more excellent ministry, inasmuch as He is also Mediator of a better covenant, which was established on better promises (Heb. 8:6).

Jesus is here to mediate into place everything that is legally ours by virtue of His cross and sacrifice. God made promises based on Jesus' blood and sacrifice. These promises are ours in Jesus. They belong to us. But our own weakness and humanity work against us from getting these promises.

The accuser will resist us from getting the promises contained in the New Covenant. Jesus by His blood and sacrifice as our Mediator is working to answer every accusation so we can legally have what was legally bought and paid for at the cross. Anything that we have yet to get from the sacrifice of the cross is because something legal is being used by the devil to resist it. Jesus, as Mediator, is working to remove this so we can have all that Jesus paid for us to have. If we have prayed and have yet to get what is legally ours from the cross, we must operate in discernment before the courts of Heaven to remove what hinders us. Our Mediator is operating on our behalf as well.

Our Mediator, Jesus, is presenting before the courts of Heaven our legal claims based on what He accomplished on the cross. The accuser of the brethren is pointing out in the courts why God cannot legally grant what Jesus bought and paid for. The accuser bases his accusation out of the holiness of the Lord. Before

God can legally grant what Jesus purchased for us and is ours by covenant, the Mediator must answer these accusations in the courts. This usually requires our repentance and a putting into place of the blood of Jesus for our sins. Remember the devil has no answer for the blood. When we truly repent of our sins the blood cleanses them away and also takes away the right of the devil to resist us. We are now free to receive of the promises of the New Covenant.

One of the ways the mediator operates in the courts of Heaven in our behalf is through His testimony. Revelation 19:10 gives us a very interesting insight into Jesus releasing testimony as our Mediator.

> And I fell at his feet to worship him. But he said to me, "See that you do not do that! I am your fellow servant, and of your brethren who have the testimony of Jesus. Worship God! For the testimony of Jesus is the spirit of prophecy." (Rev. 19:10)

John the Apostle makes a mistake in worshipping someone sent with a message. This was not an angel because he says he is his fellow servant and of his brothers. This one was of the Great Cloud of witnesses I assume. We will touch this later. This man then grants John revelation. He says the testimony of Jesus is the spirit of prophecy. When Jesus as Mediator is testifying in the courts of Heaven, it can become prophecy in the mouth of us here on Earth. As we prophesy, we are agreeing and releasing the same testimony that Jesus is releasing in the courts of Heaven.

Prophecy isn't just information in the Earth realm. Prophecy is agreeing with the testimony of Jesus in the courts of Heaven. This is why every word will be established in the mouth of two or three witnesses. 2 Corinthians 13:1 says that things are established and considered to be true where more than one witness has said the same thing.

> This will be the third time I am coming to you. "By the mouth of two or three witnesses every word shall be established." (2 Cor. 13:1)

This Scripture refers to court proceedings. When we prophesy we should be speaking what Jesus is testifying. Our voice in the courts agreeing with the voice of the Mediator grants God evidence to release verdicts in our behalf. The promises of the New Covenant are then free to come into the Earth realm.

To understand Jesus as the Mediator we need to know that *mediator* is an all-inclusive term of Jesus' function in the courts of Heaven. I have briefly explained what a mediator is. There are others terms associated with this term of mediator. Jesus is called High Priest, Intercessor and Advocate as our Mediator.

Jesus the High Priest

As High Priest, it is Jesus' responsibility to present an offering that grants God the legal right to show mercy and not judgment. This is the basic function of the High Priest. This is what Aaron did as High Priest. Through the offerings he presented, God was then free to be merciful to a people He would otherwise have had to judge. The good news is that not only is Jesus the High Priest, he is also the offering that He as High Priest offers. His sacrifice and offering is sufficient for God legally to forgive, save and redeem us into our destinies. Hebrews 9:11-12 show us that Jesus' sacrifice gave Him something as High Priest to offer.

> But Christ came as High Priest of the good things to come, with the greater and more perfect tabernacle not made with hands, that is, not of this creation. Not with the blood of goats and calves, but with His own blood He entered the Most Holy Place once for all, having obtained eternal redemption (Heb. 9:11-12).

Jesus as High Priest offered His own blood in the Most Holy Place to grant God the legal right to bless us, save us and redeem us into our destinies. This is the function of the High Priest. Even though Jesus as High Priest operates here, we have to appropriate this activity as believers. This requires faith and repentance in what Jesus has, and is, doing. We must understand that Jesus has finished the work of redemption but is still active in the courts of Heaven until all He has done becomes reality in our lives. Jesus, from a place of rest, is now waiting until we, the Ecclesia, embrace and activate all He has done. Hebrews 10:12-13 show us that Jesus' present activity is from a place of rest.

> But this Man, after He had offered one sacrifice for sins forever, sat down at the right hand of God, from that time waiting till His enemies are made His footstool (Heb. 10:12-13).

When Scripture says that Jesus has sat down, it doesn't imply inactivity. Sitting down speaks of a place of absolute dominion and rulership. From this place He is waiting for His people, the Ecclesia to work with Him to put into place all that He legally purchased and paid for. He is still active from this place of dominion. When the Bible speaks of 'rest' it is not speaking just of peace. It is speaking of a position of dominion and rulership. This is what

Hebrews 4:9 says that *"There remains therefore a rest for the people of God"*, even though it has been spoken of since creation. God is not waiting on a people just to have peace. He is waiting on a people to enter His position of dominion and rule from that place. He is waiting on us to discover and find the place of rulership with Him that He always desired.

When God made Adam on the sixth day, Adam arose on the seventh day and said to God, "What are we going to do today?" God responded, "Nothing. I want you to learn immediately that everything we are going to do, we are going to do from rest."

We do not accomplish the will of God from striving. We accomplish the will of God through resting in Him. Remember 'rest' is not inactivity. Rest is working from a position of dominion and absolute authority. This is what Jesus is doing. He is still operating as Mediator, High Priest, Intercessor and Advocate. All of these things He is doing are from a position of rest and rulership.

Jesus - The Intercessor

As our High Priest, Jesus is functioning in the courts of Heaven as our Intercessor. Hebrews 7:25 shows that Jesus is interceding for us.

> Therefore He is also able to save to the uttermost those who come to God through Him, since He always lives to make intercession for them (Heb. 7:25).

Jesus ever lives to make intercession for us. Intercession is a legal activity. When we intercede, we are granting God the legal right to intervene in a situation. Through our intercession we are putting things legally into place for God to win. If God loses, it is because something legal has not been dealt with by us. Intercession is always made on the basis of an offering. If there is no offering then there is no basis for intercession. But where there is an offering, God remembers us. Psalm 20:1-4 shows us that God blessed and remembered them on the basis of their offerings.

> May the Lord answer you in the day of trouble;
> May the name of the God of Jacob defend you;
> May He send you help from the sanctuary,
> And strengthen you out of Zion;
> May He remember all your offerings,
> And accept your burnt sacrifice.
>   Selah
> May He grant you according to your heart's desire,
> And fulfill all your purpose. (Psalm 20:1-4)

The Psalmist is speaking of how God will defend, help and strengthen us. Then he says, *"May He remember all your offerings and burnt sacrifices."* It is offerings that create the basis by which we are heard.

Jesus as our Intercessor also needs an offering to form the basis on which His prayer is heard. His body and His blood which He offered on the Cross are His offering. If Jesus didn't give His body and blood as an offering, He could not be our Intercessor. Hebrews 7:25-27 shows us that Jesus' function as Intercessor is connected to the offering of Himself that He made. Because of this sacrifice that is on the altar, His intercession has power and is legally accepted.

> Therefore He is also able to save to the uttermost
> those who come to God through Him, since He
> always lives to make intercession for them. For such
> a High Priest was fitting for us, who is holy,

harmless, undefiled, separate from sinners, and has become higher than the Heavens; who does not need daily, as those high priests, to offer up sacrifices, first for His own sins and then for the people's, for this He did once for all when He offered up Himself (Heb. 7:25-27).

This is good news for us. We should also have gifts on the altar. Our financial giving, sacrifices and offerings of ourselves create a basis for us to pray and intercede. Even if all that we have is the offering of Jesus' blood and body, we have a legal right to stand in the courts of the Lord. The truth is that Jesus as Intercessor has a right to be heard in Heaven because of His offering. This is true for us as well. Abel was heard and accepted because of his offering. Hebrews 11:4 says that God testified of Abel's offering.

By faith Abel offered to God a more excellent sacrifice than Cain, through which he obtained witness that he was righteous, God testifying of his gifts; and through it he being dead still speaks (Heb. 11:4).

God gave witness that Abel was righteous because He testified of his gifts. In other words, the Lord from His throne, deemed Abel righteous based on the faith gifts he brought to the Lord. The Scripture goes on to say that he is still speaking today. I personally believe that his extravagant giving and offerings granted him a place of intercession still being heard today.

Jesus as our Intercessor is interceding on the basis of His sacrifice for us. His intercession is in agreement with what His blood is speaking. It has great power in the courts of Heaven as we agree.

Jesus - Our Advocate

The last thing that Jesus being our Mediator means is He is our Advocate. 1 John 2:1-2 show us that we have an advocate with the Father, Jesus Christ the Righteous.

> My little children, these things I write to you, so that you may not sin. And if anyone sins, we have an Advocate with the Father, Jesus Christ the righteous. And He Himself is the propitiation for our sins, and not for ours only but also for the whole world (1 John 2:1-2).

As our Advocate, Jesus is our intercessor, comforter and consoler. From His righteous position in the courts of Heaven, we have imputed righteousness. When we fail or sin, God will forgive us for Jesus' sake and impute His righteousness to us so we can stand legally in the courts of Heaven. This only occurs if we repent. We must really repent and turn away from sin. Once this is done, we are positioned in the courts of Heaven to be a part of the process. This is what 2 Corinthians 5:21 says,

> For He made Him who knew no sin to be sin for us, that we might become the righteousness of God in Him (2 Cor. 5:21).

We are the righteousness of God in Christ Jesus. We, by faith, repent and receive the imputed righteousness that comes from the Lord Jesus Christ and His sacrifice. This is what allows us to stand in the courts of the Lord. Again, the accuser has no answer for the blood.

Jesus is our Advocate and will comfort and console us when we fail. He will also chasten us and press us to greater holiness. His grace doesn't just forgive us; His grace empowers us to overcome sin.

To illustrate this, let me share an event from my own personal life. Several years ago Mary and I took our 6 children on a vacation to a resort in Mexico. It was one of the resorts where you paid a price and then all the food, lodging and some activities were then available to you. This was a big thing for our family of 8. We did not have a lot of money and felt privileged to be able to do this as a family. I think it was the second night that I had a dream. In my dream Jesus came to me. He didn't look like Jesus. In fact He looked like a well-known actor, yet I knew it was Jesus without question. Jesus said to me, "You have grieved the Father". The moment He said this I knew exactly what I had been doing that had grieved the Lord. I began to weep in the dream. Jesus turned to go back to the Father and I reached out to touch Him as He was leaving. He stopped and turned back to me. I then said to Him, "Is this going to cause me to lose my destiny". I was very broken over what I had been told. Jesus then looked at me and said, "I did not come to tell you this so you would be overcome, I came to tell you this so you would overcome". I then awoke.

When I woke up everything in me wanted to discard this dream as not being the Lord because of who Jesus looked like. I didn't want to hear the message Jesus had brought me. But I knew it was the Lord. I believe the reason Jesus chose to look like someone that I didn't think He would look like, was to see if I would hear truth from Him in whatever form He brought it. Mark 16:12 says Jesus appeared to them in another form. They wouldn't recognize Him except by the Spirit. We have to be able to hear Him and receive from Him even when we would like to disregard the message. I did however embrace the message He brought. I knew this was in agreement with the Word of God. Jesus was acting as my Advocate with the Father. He came to tell me what the Father's posture was toward me at that present moment, but also how to correct it. I did get past the pain of the chastisement and overcome what could have destroyed my future and destiny. It was because of Jesus' operation and function as my Advocate that empowered me to do this. As Advocate, He not only brought comfort, but also pressed me to overcome and go to new realms of holiness.

The longer we walk with Jesus, the more we learn to say no to sin. Even on our best days of walking before Him and with Him, I still need His righteousness imputed to me. This is what grants me authority and place in the courts of Heaven. I do not come on my own merit, but on the merit of who He is and what He has done for me. The Father will receive us for Jesus sake, if we repent and grab hold of His provisions for forgiveness and His power to walk in holiness. We cannot excuse our sin. Everything that is necessary for us to overcome has been provided. May we not grieve the Father, but please Him and His heart. Our Advocate waits to help us into this life of empowerment and overcoming.

Jesus' voice as Mediator is speaking in the courts of Heaven. From this voice and agreement with this voice there is testimony released that grants God the legal right to fulfill His passion. When we understand this, we do not have to pull back in shame. We walk forward in true repentance receiving the forgiveness of the Lord, taking our place before His throne of grace. When we do, judicial activity comes from the court that grants God the legal right to invade the planet. May we be a part of this process.

8

The Testimony of Just Men Made Perfect

A young man who is a close friend of our family found himself in legal trouble. He became involved in a fight (started by the other person) and during the fight, he broke the man's jaw. The long and short of it was that this young man was found guilty of a misdemeanor assault charge and placed on probation. Instead of being diligent to take care of the things required concerning his probation, he left the State.

About two years later, his wife took a teaching job that required them to live in this State again. The problem was that he had violated the terms of his parole in this State and there was now a warrant out for his arrest. The young man wanted to set things in order. He did not want this hanging over his head as he knew it would be only a matter of time until he was stopped for a traffic violation or some other incident and he would be off to jail.

His lawyer therefore arranged a meeting with the District Attorney and they agreed to recommend to the judge that this young man should pay all the fines and penalties and spend 10 days in county jail. The judge could accept the recommendation or he could disregard it and set his own penalty.

On hearing of his situation, I began to tell him about the court of Heaven. I explained that he could appeal to the Lord who sits on the throne of grace to find mercy in his time of need. We had a 'court session' on behalf of his situation. I remember leading this young man through the process of answering accusations in the court of Heaven that were standing against him. The Spirit of the Lord came upon that time of prayer and the young man began to weep in repentance at the choices he had made and even the violence and anger that had been a part of his life. I sensed very clearly that a verdict came from the court that justified this young man and forgiveness and redemption flowed out of the courts of Heaven.

On the day of the actual court proceedings, the young man and his lawyer stood before a judge who had a reputation for being business-like and not given to extending mercy. As the lawyer presented the facts before the judge and the judge read the DA's recommendation, his countenance changed. The judge said that this seemed like a 'slap on the wrist' for two years of parole violation. It wasn't looking good for the young man.

The judge could sentence him to two years of jail time if he chose. Then suddenly with no input from anyone in the court, the judge looked at the young man and said, "Here's what I am going to do. I am going to suspend ALL jail time. I am going to let you continue your education. I am going to re-institute your driver's license, (it had been suspended) and I am going to allow you another chance to get this behind you." The judge granted more than was requested!

The court of Heaven had answered the plea of the young man and the verdict of Heaven manifested in a natural court. This happened because we went into the court of Heaven, silenced the accusations of the devil and received a sentence of mercy from

God. If we can learn to function in the courts of Heaven and stop yelling at the devil, we will see life altered on the planet.

Thrones and the Court System

There is a very real court system in Heaven. Every time we read about the Throne of God in Heaven, we must understand that it is not simply referring to a place of worship, but also to the Judge's seat in the court system. The Throne of God is where the courts of Heaven operate. There is no clearer place we see this than in Daniel 7:9-10.

> I watched till thrones were put in place,
> And the Ancient of Days was seated;
> His garment was white as snow,
> And the hair of His head was like pure wool.
> His throne was a fiery flame,
> Its wheels a burning fire;
> A fiery stream issued
> And came forth from before Him.
> A thousand thousands ministered to Him;
> Ten thousand times ten thousand stood before Him.
> The court was seated,
> And the books were opened. (Dan. 7:9-10)

What a powerful description of the throne of God. Notice that the throne of God is central to the court of Heaven and it is surrounded by many other thrones. The book of Revelation tells us that, apart from God's throne, there are at least 24 other thrones that also form part of the court system.

> Around the throne were twenty-four thrones, and on
> the thrones I saw twenty-four elders sitting, clothed

> in white robes; and they had crowns of gold on their
> heads (Rev. 4:4).

We see here that those who occupy these thrones have a crown on their heads and play a part in the court system of Heaven. They are humans that have overcome and won the right to take these thrones. We know this because of the crowns that they wear.

Crowns are for humans who have faithfully served the Lord and gained a place of authority in the Lord. This includes not only those who are presently in Heaven, but also those of us who are still alive in the Earth. You can be alive on Earth and still be a part of the court system of Heaven. In fact if we do not take our place in the courts of Heaven, God's plans for the planet cannot come to fruition. I often say that, in the natural, my feet may be on the floor, but in the spirit, I am standing in the courts of the Lord playing a vital purpose to His Kingdom cause.

2 Timothy 4:8 says that the Apostle Paul would wear a crown as well as others who loved the coming and appearing of the Lord.

> Finally, there is laid up for me the crown of
> righteousness, which the Lord, the righteous Judge,
> will give to me on that Day, and not to me only, but
> also to all who have loved His appearing (2 Tim.
> 4:8).

James 1:12 promises that a crown of life will be given to those who endure temptation and love the Lord.

> Blessed is the man who endures temptation; for
> when he has been approved, he will receive the

crown of life which the Lord has promised to those
who love Him (James. 1:12).

My point is that those who overcome in this life win for themselves
crowns and places in the court system of Heaven. Even Jesus won
His place as High Priest and His other functions in the courts by
virtue of His obedience to the Father.

I think it is clear that 12 of the 24 who are the elders that are
wearing crowns in the courts of Heaven and occupying thrones are
the original apostles. Jesus spoke to them in Luke 22:28-30.

> "But you are those who have continued with Me in
> My trials. And I bestow upon you a kingdom, just as
> My Father bestowed one upon Me, that you may eat
> and drink at My table in My kingdom, and sit on
> thrones judging the twelve tribes of Israel." (Luke
> 22:28-30)

Jesus promised these apostles that they would sit on twelve thrones
judging the twelve tribes of Israel. Remember that judging is a
judicial act. Notice also that these positions that Jesus refers to, are
given as a result of their faithfulness to continue with Him in His
tribulation. Again, positions within the courts are won not given.

The other 12 thrones that are mentioned in Revelation are
probably occupied by representatives of the twelve tribes of Israel.
This would be consistent with the order and language of Scripture.
These 24 elders that occupy 24 thrones make up some of the
thrones that are a part of the courts of Heaven.

The Great Cloud of Witnesses

I know that many people believe that Heaven is a place
where we go to sit on clouds and play golden harps all day. This is

absolutely untrue! Revelation 6:9-11 gives us a picture of some of the activity going on in Heaven.

> When He opened the fifth seal, I saw under the altar the souls of those who had been slain for the word of God and for the testimony which they held. And they cried with a loud voice, saying, "How long, O Lord, holy and true, until You judge and avenge our blood on those who dwell on the earth?" Then a white robe was given to each of them; and it was said to them that they should rest a little while longer, until both the number of their fellow servants and their brethren, who would be killed as they were, was completed (Rev. 6:9-11).

These martyrs (people who laid down their lives for the sake of the Gospel) are still praying and interceding. They are crying out for justice concerning their own blood that was spilled. They are requesting that the reason for their sacrifice would become a reality. There are many in the Heavenly realm who are still crying and praying for what they spilt their blood for, to be realized on the Earth. They are a part of the great cloud of witnesses. Hebrews 11:39-40 and Hebrews 12:1-2 speak of this great cloud of witnesses.

> And all these, having obtained a good testimony through faith, did not receive the promise, God having provided something better for us, that they should not be made perfect apart from us. Therefore we also, since we are surrounded by so great a cloud of witnesses, let us lay aside every weight, and the sin which so easily ensnares us, and let us run with

endurance the race that is set before us (Heb. 12:1-2).

This great cloud of witnesses has a role in the courts of Heaven. The word witness in Hebrews 12:1 speaks of those who give judicial testimony. The cloud of witnesses has a voice in the courts of the Lord concerning the Kingdom purposes for which they laid down their lives. Notice that they have a right to speak in the courts because they have won for themselves a good testimony, which is about judicial approval.

We need to understand that the saints of old are still invested in the causes for which they gave their lives. They are not just cheering us on from some celestial grand stand. They are actually in the courts releasing their voice and testimony on behalf of those of us who must now complete the work for which they gave their lives.

This is what the term spirits of just men made perfect refers to in Hebrews 12:23.

> To the general assembly and church of the firstborn who are registered in Heaven, to God the Judge of all, to the spirits of just men made perfect (Heb. 12:23).

These saints of old still have a voice and are releasing testimony in the courts of Heaven. They have won a place in the courts because of their obedience to the Lord while on Earth.

The Church in Heaven and on Earth

As we function in the courts from the earthly realm, we are to come into agreement with the intercession of these witnesses. Our agreement with them produces the legal right for Heaven to fulfill the reason for which they laid down their lives. Whatever the reason was—spheres of society being won to the Lord, geographical locations brought under Kingdom domain or nations discipled into a Kingdom culture—there must be legal precedents in place before it can be fulfilled. This will only happen when the Church that is on Earth and the Church that is in Heaven come into agreement for His Kingdom will to be done. Ephesians 3:14-15 shows us that there is one church, whether we are in Earth or already in Heaven.

> For this reason I bow my knees to the Father of our
> Lord Jesus Christ, from whom the whole family in
> Heaven and Earth is named (Eph. 3:14-15).

Whether we are in Heaven or on Earth, we are one church. Together we are striving for one purpose and that is, to see Heaven invade the Earth and God's ultimate Kingdom agenda manifest. This church (in Heaven and Earth) must take its place in the court system of Heaven.

As I was about to teach on the great cloud of witnesses and their function in the courts of the Lord, my wife, Mary, had a dream. I had not told her what I was about to teach. I was actually afraid that she wouldn't be able to embrace it and, quite honestly, I was a little unsure of what I was about to share. When she had this dream with no knowledge of what I was about to teach, it got my attention.

In the dream my natural father (who had passed away 16 years before) came to her and communicated that he had not cared for the funeral service that we had held for him. He told Mary, in the dream, that he wanted another service. He explained that since he had been in Heaven, he had heard an African children's choir singing "O Happy Day". He now wanted another funeral service in which an African children's choir would sing "O Happy Day". In the dream, plans were being made to 'redo' his funeral service to honor him appropriately.

When she told me this dream, I knew it was the Lord confirming to me what I was about to teach. I taught the lesson on the great cloud of witnesses. I told those who were present that the cloud of witnesses that were functioning in the courts of the Lord were to be honored for the sacrifice they had made for the Kingdom of God. I knew this was what was being communicated through Mary's dream about my Dad.

As the service ended, I played a clip of an African children's choir singing "O Happy Day." I did this in honor of my Dad and his life. Without his influence I would not be in the ministry today. I was honoring the legacy of my natural father and his place in the great cloud of witnesses. As we did this, a tremendous presence of the Lord filled the room and I knew it was the Lord bearing witness to the understanding that had been brought.

They Cannot Be Made Perfect Without Us

The great cloud of witnesses stand before the Throne of Heaven testifying and witnessing concerning God's Kingdom purposes still to be accomplished. The Bible clearly says that they, without us, cannot be made perfect. Hebrews 11:39-40 tells us that their ultimate passion cannot be fulfilled without us finishing and joining with their sacrifice to see God's agenda done.

> And all these, having obtained a good testimony through faith, did not receive the promise, God having provided something better for us, that they

should not be made perfect apart from us (Heb. 11:39-40).

The great cloud of witnesses, obtained a good testimony and the right to speak in the courts of Heaven. Through their testimony, judgments can now be released from the throne that are instrumental in establishing God's will on Earth. The cloud of witnesses laid down their lives to see the Kingdom come on Earth and they remain invested in this mission until it becomes a reality. They, without us, cannot be made perfect.

Several years ago I had a dream that I was sitting at breakfast with Smith Wigglesworth, the great apostle of faith who had a tremendous healing ministry. I remember in the dream thinking that this man is dead, but yet here I am speaking with him as if he were alive. The thought I had was that I wanted him to pray for me before the 'meeting' was over. The dream ended before this could happen.

For years this dream intrigued me. What was the significance, if any, of me speaking with Smith Wigglesworth? A man who had already died and gone to Heaven? I now believe that Smith Wigglesworth is part of the great cloud of witnesses. My 'meeting' with him concerned something he carried in his ministry that I was to carry in mine. Could it be that he was actually interceding for me to come into the anointing that he carried for healing? Could it be that he was petitioning the courts of Heaven for a verdict that would allow me to walk in the same authority that he walked in as 'the apostle of faith'?

Many years later when I was in a meeting where seer prophets were present who saw into Heaven and the court system, one of them began to declare that Smith Wigglesworth was present and wanted to give me his anointing. I was flabbergasted! First, the dream and now a prophetic word. However, I am very careful with this kind of thing. I know that it is really easy to wander off into realms of delusion and even witchcraft. Yet I didn't want to miss anything that the Lord had for me.

The seer prophet, who is very humble, wanted to take her scarf that she had around her neck and place it as a mantle on my neck to symbolize the anointing of Smith Wigglesworth coming upon me. I submitted to this and to my amazement when the scarf was place around my neck an intense heat and fire went into my neck and down my back. I definitely received something from the Lord and have begun to walk in it. The cloud of witnesses is committed to helping us fulfill our assignments in our generations because without us, they will not be made perfect.

Here is a final story to illustrate the operation of the great cloud of witnesses in the courts of Heaven. A young man was terribly injured in a car accident. The doctors said that he should have died. Instead he was in a coma for an extended period of time. When he came out of this coma he told a very intriguing story. While in the coma, he found himself in the courtroom of Heaven. The issue being debated in the courts of Heaven was whether this young man should come on to Heaven or stay on Earth and fulfill what was written in the books of Heaven about him. He said there were several people that were giving their opinions and testimonies in the matter.

Suddenly a man walked into the courtroom. He had a long white beard, was very humble and began to testify as to why this young man should be allowed to stay on Earth and fulfill his destiny. On the basis of this man's testimony the court rendered a verdict that allowed the young man to live and finish his course. Now, remember, the young man in his comatose state is witnessing this whole process.

As the man with the long white beard turned to leave, the young man called to him, "Sir, Sir, please stop, Sir." The man stopped and looked at this young man whose destiny on Earth had just been secured. As the man stopped, the young man said, "Sir, what is your name." The man responded, "My name is Noah." Wow! Some would have a real problem with this for various reasons. It does however align with the fact that there are spirits of just men made perfect that function in the courts of Heaven.

Even the Lord Himself spoke of Noah as one of three that were extreme intercessors that had won a place in the courts of Heaven. Ezekiel 14:14 lists Noah, Daniel and Job as ones that hold great authority as intercessors.

> Even if these three men, Noah, Daniel, and Job, were in it, they would deliver only themselves by their righteousness," says the Lord GOD (Ezek. 14:14).

When God spoke these words, all of them were already dead and in Heaven, yet God refers to them as still functioning in intercession. Do they still hold place of function in the courts of Heaven as a part of the just men made perfect? I believe so. They are still a part of the activities of the court to help grant God the legal right to fulfill His Father's passion.

There is a very real cloud of witnesses in Heaven. They are a part of the court system of Heaven. They have a strategic function as witnesses in this judicial process. They cannot be made perfect without us. May we learn to flow in agreement with them for God's purposes to manifest on Earth.

9

The Voice of the Judge

The O. J. Simpson trial was hailed as The Trial of the Century. He was charged with the murder of his ex-wife, Nicole Simpson, and Ron Goldman. The outcome of the trial was that O. J. was found innocent of the crime and set free. This was a surprising verdict that is debated to this day. What I remember most clearly was the drama that surrounded the trial as evidence was presented by both prosecution and defense attorneys.

The Judge in that case was Lance Ito. Many have criticized his overseeing of the trial. They complain that he allowed into evidence things that should never have been allowed and that he was swayed by the publicity generated by this high profile trial. Regardless of all this, the fact remains that during the trial, Judge Ito had the final word.

The same is true in the courts of Heaven. The Judge who sits on the throne of the courts of Heaven has the final say. In the courts of Heaven there can be a multitude of witnesses, evidence being presented and cases being petitioned, but only the Judge of Righteousness determines the verdict. His verdicts are always just and true. We see this in 1 Kings 22:19-23 when Micaiah begins to reveal what he saw in the courts of Heaven concerning Ahab and his destruction.

Then Micaiah said, "Therefore hear the word of the
Lord: I saw the Lord sitting on His throne, and all
the host of Heaven standing by, on His right hand
and on His left. And the Lord said, 'Who will
persuade Ahab to go up, that he may fall at Ramoth
Gilead?' So one spoke in this manner, and another
spoke in that manner. Then a spirit came forward
and stood before the Lord, and said, 'I will persuade
him.' The Lord said to him, 'In what way?' So he
said, 'I will go out and be a lying spirit in the mouth
of all his prophets.' And the Lord said, 'You shall
persuade him, and also prevail. Go out and do so.'
Therefore look! The Lord has put a lying spirit in
the mouth of all these prophets of yours, and the
Lord has declared disaster against you." (1 Kings
22:19-23)

As the Lord was hearing from the host of Heaven around the
throne, there was a debate on how they could make Ahab fall. Ahab
had led Israel into wickedness and the Lord was ready to judge
him. The Scripture says that one said they could do it this way and
another could do it that way. Then a spirit came forward during the
proceedings and declared that he would go and be a lying spirit in
the mouth of Ahab's prophets. The Lord on the throne passed a
sentence. He said, "Go and prevail."

What an awesome glimpse into the court system of Heaven.
In this Scripture, there are many voices in the court giving ideas
and testimonies concerning what should be done. But when the
Lord was ready to make the decision and pass judgment, it was The
Lord who sits on the Throne as Judge Who rendered it. The Lord is
the Righteous Judge Who does all things well.

Father and Judge

It is quite interesting in Hebrews 12:23 that the Lord is revealed as "The Judge of All."

> To the general assembly and church of the firstborn who are registered in Heaven, to God the Judge of all, to the spirits of just men made perfect (Heb. 12:23).

He is not revealed as our Father, our Savior or our King. He is revealed as the Judge. The reason for this is that these Scriptures are revealing the court system of Heaven and He as Judge has the final word and place. He is in fact all the things previously mentioned and much more, but He is the Judge of All because He renders verdicts, judgments and sentences that bring order and justice.

I want to make a statement here that is at the core of this book. It is our job as individuals and the Ecclesia to grant God, as the Judge of all, the legal right to fulfill His fatherly passion. We should remember that God is a Father. In his heart, he carries dreams, desires and longings for His family, just as earthly fathers do. He longs to see these desires of His heart towards His family come to pass. God is also the Judge of all who must render legal judgments in righteousness and holiness. As we have discovered, there can be legal issues that hinder His fatherly desires being fulfilled. God will never compromise Himself as Judge in order to fulfill His fatherly desires. To do so would make Him less than God. Therefore, it is our job as His people, His Ecclesia, to put in place the legal precedents needed for God to legally fulfill His desires as a Father.

Removing the Legal Right of the Enemy

One of the best ways for me to explain this is through a personal experience. There was a lady very close to our family that was diagnosed with breast cancer. When this lady was 13 years old, her own mother had been diagnosed with breast cancer and she died at just 43 years of age. The disease had spread in her body just as it was now spreading in her daughter's body. This friend of ours was 43 when she was diagnosed and also had a 13 year old daughter. The parallels were astounding. I knew we were dealing with a generational, family curse.

When she was on her death-bed, her husband called me and asked if I would pray for her. I went to her home where there were already other people gathered at her bedside praying for her. I placed my hand on her head and as I began to pray I felt the Father's passion to heal this woman. It was unmistakable. I had felt this many times before in many situations and knew it well. I prayed the best prayer I knew how to pray. I prayed with the unction and power of the Spirit of the Lord. It wasn't a natural prayer, it was a supernatural one. Yet, twelve hours later, she died. She died at age 43, leaving behind a 13-year-old daughter - exactly as her mother had done! What a tragedy. It was only much later that I was able to explain why this had happened. At the time of my prayer, I did not know that this lady and her husband had connived to steal resources that belonged to someone else. This activity of dishonor and thievery had opened the door for the family curse to come upon her life.

Proverbs 26:2 says that a curse has to have a **cause** to alight.

> Like a flitting sparrow, like a flying swallow, So a
> curse without cause shall not alight. (Prov. 26:2)

Curses are pictured as sparrows and swallows flying around and looking for a place to land. They cannot land unless a legal right allows them to land. This woman had a curse in her family, that was circling her and looking for a legal opportunity to land and afflict her. She had actually confessed, professed and done everything she knew to do, to keep this away from her and her family for years.

When she and her husband opened the door to this curse through their dishonor and thievery, the curse now had a legal reason to be able to land on her. Micah 2:1-3 shows what happened in this situation.

> Woe to those who devise iniquity,
> And work out evil on their beds!
> At morning light they practice it,
> Because it is in the power of their hand.
> They covet fields and take them by violence,
> Also houses, and seize them.
> So they oppress a man and his house,
> A man and his inheritance.
> Therefore thus says the Lord:
> "Behold, against this family I am devising disaster,
> From which you cannot remove your necks;
> Nor shall you walk haughtily,
> For this is an evil time. (Micah 2:1-3)

God says that if someone who has been granted power through trust, uses that power to steal away inheritances, a disaster can come upon them that they won't be able to escape. This is what happened to this lady and her family. As a result of her participation in these deviant practices, the devil had a legal right to afflict her with a family curse. The devil was legally allowed to take her life even though God's passion was to heal her. The only way that the Lord could have healed her was if she had repented of that which she had done. Then the power of the curse would have been broken and God as Judge could have fulfilled His passion as Father, legally.

Remember, God cannot compromise Himself as Judge to fulfill His fatherly passion. We must grant Him the legal right as Judge to satisfy the desires of His heart as Father. Otherwise the devil wins and God loses, even though His passion is always to do us good. When we grasp this principle, we will stop asking, "Why didn't God do something?" whenever something bad happens. God cannot intervene until we give Him the legal right to do so. His passion is always to bless, heal and show mercy. This is why James 1:16-17 tells us that it is God's passion always to do good.

> Do not be deceived, my beloved brethren. Every good gift and every perfect gift is from above, and comes down from the Father of lights, with whom there is no variation or shadow of turning (James 1:16-17).

When we read in Scripture that something evil was done 'by God', my own personal opinion is that God did not 'do' it, he simply had to 'allow' it legally. When the devil has a legal right to perform evil, God must allow it unless someone comes to the court of Heaven to contest that right.

Let us look at the example of Job. God did not kill Job's children, afflict him with sickness or take away his wealth. Satan did. God did not want this to happen, but Satan presented a case showing his legal right to afflict Job. His accusations against Job concerned the motives of Job's heart. Job 1:9-11 we see Satan telling the Lord that Job was only serving God because God had blessed and secured him so much.

> So Satan answered the LORD and said, "Does Job fear God for nothing? Have You not made a hedge around him, around his household, and around all that he has on every side? You have blessed the work of his hands, and his possessions have increased in the land. But now, stretch out Your hand and touch all that he has, and he will surely curse You to Your face!"(Job 1:9-11)

It appears that everything is judged and evaluated in Heaven. Even when we are doing everything right, the devil can still question our motives. This is what threw Job into his tribulation. This tells me that we need to allow the Holy Spirit to, not only empower us to walk rightly, but also from a pure and clean heart. God had to allow these afflictions until Job set things in order and rescinded Satan's legal rights. Once Job did this, God rendered a judgment that restored to Job twice what he had lost.

When evil occurs, we should always look for the legal right that allows it. When we do, we can confidently go into the court of Heaven, deal with the legalities and shut the door on evil.

This principle explains why intercessors so often feel the passion of God in their prayer and yet nothing seems to change. It is very possible to feel what God feels, experience His desires and be unable to move anything in the spirit realm. Knowing God's heart and being able to administrate it legally are two very different things. If we want to see God's passion manifest on Earth, we must get things legally in place. The devil always resists God and us with legalities. The Lord will not override His own judicial system to grant His passion. He cannot. We must step into that system and grant Him the legal right to fulfill His passion.

Repentance - The Missing Key

In Matthew 16:18-19 Jesus said that the governmental people, His Ecclesia, that He would build, would use keys of authority to set in place legal things and remove legal things so His Kingdom purposes would be done.

> And I also say to you that you are Peter, and on this rock I will build My church, and the gates of Hades shall not prevail against it. And I will give you the keys of the kingdom of Heaven, and whatever you bind on earth will be bound in Heaven, and whatever you loose on earth will be loosed in Heaven." (Matt. 16:18-19)

The Church or Ecclesia has been given keys to bind and loose. As I shared in a previous chapter, the words bind and loose are legal in their nature. We, as God's individual and corporate people, are to go into the courts of Heaven and put binding things in place so God can legally fulfill His Father's passion. We are also to loose or dissolve contracts that the devil has in the Earth realm that allow him the legal right to kill, steal and destroy. He has to have a legal right to do it, our job is to remove that legal right from him. We do this through repentance for ourselves and our history and the history of our nations. Anything that the devil is doing in the nations is because our sins and the sins of our generations have granted him the legal right to do it. When we repent, we are removing his legal right of operation. We are breaking the devil's snare. 2 Timothy 2:25-26 tells us we break the snare and set people free through repentance.

> ... in humility correcting those who are in opposition, if God perhaps will grant them repentance, so that they may know the truth, and that they may come to their senses and escape the snare of the devil, having been taken captive by him to do his will (2 Tim. 2:25-26).

Notice that God grants repentance. Repentance is a legal activity that affects the courts of Heaven. When I repent and come into agreement with the testimony of the blood and the other voices, the accuser is silenced. The snare he has fashioned is broken, and we can escape. We are no longer bound to him to do his will, but are freed from his oppression. He no longer has a legal right to torment and terrorize us. When we repent, we grant God, as the Judge of all the legal right to render verdicts from His throne in agreement with His Kingdom purpose.

The Judge of all is waiting on us to give Him the legal right to manifest His goodness.

The Mandate of the Ecclesia

Genesis 18:20-21 shows us that God Himself went down to Sodom and Gomorrah to examine the cries and evidence before Him that demanded judgment.

> And the Lord said, "Because the outcry against Sodom and Gomorrah is great, and because their sin is very grave, I will go down now and see whether they have done altogether according to the outcry against it that has come to Me; and if not, I will know." (Gen. 18:20-21)

Somehow or other the outcry against Sodom and Gomorrah had reached the throne of God. This cry was presenting evidence that the city was worthy of judgment and destruction. The Lord went down to investigate and validate the evidence that had been given. The Lord does something very interesting. He brings Abraham into the equation. Genesis 18:17-18 shows that God shares with Abraham what is about to happen.

> And the Lord said, "Shall I hide from Abraham what I am doing, since Abraham shall surely become a great and mighty nation, and all the nations of the earth shall be blessed in him? (Gen. 18:17-18)

A casual reading would cause us to think that God is just sharing information with Abraham because he is His friend. This is true, but there is a much deeper reason why God shared this with Abraham. He brought Abraham into the equation because God was seeking a legal reason to show mercy. He knew that Abraham would seek to give God a legal reason to show mercy. Genesis 18:22-26 shows that Abraham is seeking to give God a legal reason to spare this wicked place.

> Then the men turned away from there and went toward Sodom, but Abraham still stood before the Lord. And Abraham came near and said, "Would You also destroy the righteous with the wicked? Suppose there were fifty righteous within the city; would You also destroy the place and not spare it for the fifty righteous that were in it? Far be it from You to do such a thing as this, to slay the righteous with the wicked, so that the righteous should be as the wicked; far be it from You! Shall not the Judge of

all the earth do right?" So the Lord said, "If I find in
Sodom fifty righteous within the city, then I will
spare all the place for their sakes." (Gen. 18:22-26)

Please notice that Abraham petitioned God on the basis of Him
being Judge and judging righteously. God agreed with Abraham
and said He would not destroy it for the sake of fifty righteous.
Abraham continued to petition God as judge and finally had it
reduced to ten righteous men. The Lord said for the sake of ten
righteous men He would spare the city and territory. Genesis
18:32-33 shows this legal exchange taking place.

Then he said, "Let not the Lord be angry, and I will
speak but once more: Suppose ten should be found
there?" And He said, "I will not destroy it for the
sake of ten." So the Lord went His way as soon as
He had finished speaking with Abraham; and
Abraham returned to his place. (Gen. 18:32-33)

God was looking for a reason to be merciful and knew that
Abraham would endeavor to give it to Him legally. I have heard
many people say that Abraham stopped too soon in his
intercession. This is simply not true. In the culture of that day and
in Jewish culture, ten denotes the smallest number that constitutes a
government. God said that if He could find ten righteous men, the
smallest number that could represent government, for the sake of
those ten He would spare the city. We sometimes think we need the
whole of population to repent, or at least the majority, to receive
God's mercy. All we actually need is a governmental
representation of the population to petition the courts of Heaven for
mercy instead of judgment.

This is the job of the Ecclesia. To be that governmental representation who can operate in the court of Heaven to secure blessings from Heaven for a nation and a generation. God will spare nations for the sake of the Ecclesia within it, if we are righteous and carry recognizable, governmental authority in the courts of Heaven. God is looking for a reason to be righteous and show mercy. It is our job as His people to get things legally in place so as Judge He can fulfill His fatherly passion.

The Lord is Judge of all. He is also our Father who desires to bless us and release to us our inheritance. May we become proficient in His courts so He legally has the right as Judge to bless our going out and coming in. This is the passion of the Father's heart.

10

The Testimony of the General Assembly

When a judge enters a courtroom, it is customary that all rise in honor of the judge. There is to be an atmosphere of honor in the courtroom toward the judge and all the happenings of the court. The court holds within its power the ability to pass judgments that can alter lives with its decisions. So it is in the court of Heaven. If a natural, earthly court, has this power, how much more the Heavenly court where the Judge of All is presiding. In the court of Heaven, there is to be an atmosphere of worship and reverence in which all proceedings and verdicts occur.

This is why Scripture says that in this court of Heaven we have come to the General Assembly. Hebrews 12:23 says this.

> To the general assembly and church of the firstborn who are registered in Heaven, to God the Judge of all, to the spirits of just men made perfect (Heb. 12:23).

The term General Assembly means universal companionship or a mass-meeting. This speaks of the multitude that is worshipping about the throne of Heaven from every tribe, tongue, nation and people. Revelation 7:9-12 gives us a glimpse of this mass-meeting of worship about the throne.

> After these things I looked, and behold, a great multitude which no one could number, of all nations, tribes, peoples, and tongues, standing before the throne and before the Lamb, clothed with white robes, with palm branches in their hands, and crying out with a loud voice, saying,
>
> "Salvation belongs to our God who sits on the throne, and to the Lamb!"
>
> All the angels stood around the throne and the elders and the four living creatures, and fell on their faces before the throne and worshipped God, saying:
>
> "Amen! Blessing and glory and wisdom, Thanksgiving and honor and power and might, Be to our God forever and ever.
> Amen." (Rev. 7:9-12)

In the court system of Heaven around the throne there is worship. Worship is a part of the proceedings of the court. Worship at its core is governmental in nature. Worship, in fact, creates the atmosphere that the Court of Heaven operates from. When we worship we take our place in the General Assembly that is in the court system of Heaven. Even though our feet are on the planet, in the spirit we ascend and become part of this worshipping multitude in the courts of Heaven. We often say that God's presence 'came', as we worshipped. I would like to present another concept. Perhaps the presence of the Lord didn't so much 'come' as we 'ascended' or 'went' into the atmosphere of the Throne and the courts of

Heaven. When we worship, we step into the governmental process of the throne room of Heaven. We take our place in the throne room and from there become a part of the process of Heaven in rendering verdicts that touch and change the Earth. From our worship we shouldn't just get goose-bumps and a little teary-eyed. When our worship is joined to Heaven, we will exercise governmental authority out of the courts of Heaven. We can see this somewhat in Revelation 5:8-14. These verses show us that worship starts around the throne and moves from sphere to sphere until all of creation is worshipping.

> Now when He had taken the scroll, the four living creatures and the twenty-four elders fell down before the Lamb, each having a harp, and golden bowls full of incense, which are the prayers of the saints. And they sang a new song, saying:
> "You are worthy to take the scroll, And to open its seals;
> For You were slain,
> And have redeemed us to God by Your blood Out of every tribe and tongue and people and nation,
> And have made us kings and priests to our God; And we shall reign on the earth."
> Then I looked, and I heard the voice of many angels around the throne, the living creatures, and the elders; and the number of them was ten thousand times ten thousand, and thousands of thousands, saying with a loud voice:
> "Worthy is the Lamb who was slain
> To receive power and riches and wisdom,
> And strength and honor and glory and blessing!" And every creature which is in Heaven

and on the earth and under the earth and such as are in the sea, and all that are in them, I heard saying:

"Blessing and honor and glory and power
Be to Him who sits on the throne,
And to the Lamb, forever and ever!"

Then the four living creatures said, "Amen!" And the twenty-four elders fell down and worshipped Him who lives forever and ever. (Rev. 5:8-14)

Worship begins about the Throne with the four living creatures and the multitude of angels and elders - thousands times ten thousands of them. Then it invades every creature in Heaven, on Earth and under the Earth. It impacts those who are in the sea. They were all heard to be worshipping the Lord who sits on the throne. The worship that had its origin with the four living creatures about the Throne touches and involves all the creation of God before it is finished.

This tells me a couple of things. Worship doesn't originate on Earth, it originates in Heaven. The worship that God desires and is necessary to Heavenly judicial activity has, as its source, Heaven itself. The second thing this tells me is we are to become a part of the worship about the Throne and not be separate in our worship here in the Earth.

As we worship we are to enter and stand in the courts of Heaven helping to create the atmosphere from which judicial activity takes place. When we experience His presence in the Earth realm, it is because we have stepped into the realm of Heaven and have become a part of the process. This is why we see in Hebrews 12:22-24 that we have come to certain things. These things haven't come to us, we have come to them. We have moved into the spiritual dimension in Heaven. Though we may be in the natural realm in the Earth, simultaneously we can be in the spirit about the Throne of God in Heaven. This occurs through our interacting with the worship of Heaven and becoming a functional part of the General Assembly or mass-meeting about the throne.

The Tabernacle of David

We see this in the life of David and his establishment of Zion. One of the first things David did when he came to the full rulership of Israel was to establish the place called Zion. He retrieved the Ark of the Covenant from where it had resided and brought it to Jerusalem. He set up what became known as the Tabernacle of David on Mount Zion.

> So they brought the ark of the Lord, and set it in its place in the midst of the tabernacle that David had erected for it. Then David offered burnt offerings and peace offerings before the Lord. (2 Samuel 6:17)

David cultivated and hosted the presence of God on Mount Zion. He established 24-hour worship there so he could effectively govern a nation from the presence of the Lord. The worship of David's tabernacle connected to the worship of Heaven allowing a flow of judicial activity from Heaven to Earth. David did not rule from natural abilities but from supernatural abilities out of Heaven.

If we are to function in the courts of Heaven effectively we must become worshippers. Our worship must be connected and joined to what is happening around the Throne of God. This is why Jesus said God is seeking worshippers. John 4:23-24 shows us the passion of the Father for worshippers to take their place.

> But the hour is coming, and now is, when the true
> worshippers will worship the Father in spirit and
> truth; for the Father is seeking such to worship Him.
> God is Spirit, and those who worship Him must
> worship in spirit and truth (John 4:23-24).

Notice that the Lord is not seeking worship but worshippers. When we worship in spirit and in truth, we qualify to function as God's governmental people. True worship enables us to step into the judicial process of Heaven with great reverence, fear, awe and honor. When we cultivate the heart of a worshipper, we will create an atmosphere in the Earth that can join with Heaven and see verdicts rendered out of the court system.

A story that helps relate this principle concerning worship happened to me after the Lord gave me a dream. In the dream I was shown that 9/11 occurred because of judicial activity in the courts of Heaven. The principalities and powers were granted the legal right to attack America because there was no Ecclesia or governmental people recognized in Heaven at that time to stop it.

As I awoke from the dream I had a distinct sense that if we didn't take our place in the courts of Heaven that another significant attack on American soil was coming. I called together the Ecclesia I apostolically led and shared that, for whatever reason, we had been assigned to stop any potential attack. We met as God's governmental people on 11/11/11. As we began to enter the courts of Heaven, I clearly sensed that we were in for a struggle. In fact, as we began to seek to deal with any legal issue that would allow another attack, I was aware of very strong demonic resistance. I actually wanted to back away and not pursue it any further, but knew I was in too deep. I was past the point of no return.

As the seer/prophet gifts were telling me what they were seeing and sensing, I was doing my best to get it in place in the courts. As the apostle in the matter, I was responsible for administrating what the seers/prophets were seeing and understanding. We were repenting of everything that was empowering the demonic hierarchy in its efforts to bring more destruction to America. Yet as we were doing this, nothing seemed to be changing. It appeared that the principalities had a case and we weren't getting things arranged for God's will to be done.

After quite a long period of time, I suddenly felt very strongly that we were to worship as we were in the courts, with a particular song. I began to lead the song acappella. As we worshipped with this song, I suddenly felt the atmosphere change. The seers/ prophets confirmed that we had in fact got a rendering from the courts and had stopped another attack from occurring. I knew it because of the shift in that atmosphere that took place and the seer/prophets confirmed it by what they were seeing.

We had silenced the accuser and gotten a judgment of mercy from the Throne of Heaven over America. Mercy for America had been secured in whatever the issue was that Heaven needed us to intervene in. This happened because of our worship. Somehow our worship created an atmosphere and released testimony in the courts that granted God the Judge the legal right to fulfill His Father's passion.

Our worship creates atmospheres for the court to operate in, but also releases testimony into the courts that allows the Lord the legal right to implement His passion into the Earth. Worship is a very powerful tool in the courts of Heaven. We must be worshippers who declare His glory, kindness, passion, worthiness and holiness. When we do, our voice as the Ecclesia begins to agree with the other voices in the courts of Heaven. Together we grant the Lord the legal rights to impact the Earth with His will and desire.

It is interesting that after this operation in the courts, the arrest of three terrorist suspects happened. A man named Jose Pimentel was arrested on November 20, 2011, for plans to bomb different places in New York City. On January 7, 2012, Sami Osmakac was arrested for his terrorist plot. In February 2012, Aminie El Khalifi was arrested for the plan he had devised to attack America as well. Whether these were directly related to our operation in the courts of Heaven cannot be proved beyond doubt. But I know that what was done through our operation and worship in the courts of Heaven put some things legally in place for God's will to be done. Our operations in the courts of Heaven are not only necessary for our personal and family lives, but also for nations. The Holy Spirit will guide us through this function to get the necessary legal things in place for the Father's will to be done.

There is no way that any of us would dare to enter a natural court in Earth and not honor the judge on his seat while seeking a favorable verdict from him. We intuitively know that honor is demanded and expected. As we seek to enter the courts of Heaven and see decisions and verdicts rendered on our behalf, may we increasingly become worshippers that please the heart of the Father. May we be a part of the worship of the One Who sits on the Throne Who creates atmospheres for judicial activity. From this atmosphere we are allowing God as Judge of all legally to be able to fulfill His fatherly passion. When this happens Heaven legally invades the Earth and His will is done here as it is in Heaven. What a privilege we have been granted. May all glory, honor, praise and thanksgiving be granted to Him Who sits on the throne.

11

The Testimony of the Ecclesia/Church

Anyone who speaks and gives testimony in a court must first be recognized. Everyone from the judge to the attorneys to the jurors to the witnesses must have been commissioned, assigned, authorized and sworn in. Judges are appointed to their bench by governmental leaders. Attorneys must be recognized by the court for the function they perform. Jurors are chosen and sworn in, as are witnesses who give testimony in the courts. If we are going to have impact in a court setting we must have jurisdiction to operate there. It is the same in the courts of Heaven. We are told that the Church of the firstborn is registered in Heaven for operation in the courts of the Lord. In other words we, as the Church/Ecclesia, have been granted a voice in the court system of Heaven. Hebrews 12:23 shows us this.

> To the general assembly and church of the firstborn who are registered in Heaven, to God the Judge of all, to the spirits of just men made perfect (Heb. 12:23).

We, as the Church of the firstborn, have been registered in the courts of Heaven and therefore have been granted a jurisdiction in the courts. We have a legal right to operate in this court and are a part of the process of Heaven. This is so important and cannot be underestimated.

Knowing Your Jurisdiction

The Apostle Paul spoke of measurement of rule or the sphere he had been granted. 2 Corinthians 10:13 tells us that Paul stayed within his measurement, spheres, limits and jurisdiction.

> We, however, will not boast beyond measure, but within the limits of the sphere which God appointed us—a sphere which especially includes you (2 Cor. 10:13).

If we are to be effective and protected, we must stay within the sphere that has been granted to us by God. The word in the Greek for sphere is metron. It means a measure or a limited portion. We each have been granted a metron to function in. When we function in that metron or limited portion appointed to us, we have success and protection.

As I mentioned in another chapter, there are varying levels of court operations in Heaven. Just as there are criminal courts, small claim courts, civil courts and other expressions in Earth, so in Heaven there are different dimensions of courts. We have to be recognized and registered to operate within a sphere of Heaven. To get outside our God ordained sphere is unproductive and very dangerous. We open ourselves to satanic onslaught, attack and even destruction.

The good news is that we can all operate in the court that the Bible calls the throne of grace. Every one of us as believers has rights, privileges and authorities in this sphere. Hebrews 4:16 tell us we are to come boldly to this court of Heaven.

> Let us therefore come boldly to the throne of grace,
> that we may obtain mercy and find grace to help in
> time of need (Heb. 4:16).

We can come and present our petitions that relate to family and personal issues in this court. It is very easy to get verdicts rendered on our behalf in this court of Heaven. From His throne of grace the Lord will bless us with mercy and grace for our time of need. When we move past that which is personal and family oriented and step into intercession for churches, cities, states, regions and nations, we are entering a conflict which requires another jurisdiction. We must be recognized in Heaven to function in the courts of Heaven concerning these things. It is one thing to pray prayers of blessings over governments, rulers and territories; it is another thing to engage principalities that rule these places. In the courts of Heaven only those who have been granted jurisdiction should engage principalities and ruling powers. Contending with principalities that have been empowered through multiple generations of sin, is a very deadly and dangerous thing to do, if we are not recognized in the courts of Heaven on this level.

This is why the Bible speaks of the *Church registered in Heaven*. The Ecclesia/Church is God's legislative, governmental and judicial people and they have been registered and authorized to operate within the court system of Heaven. When the Church is functioning where it is meant to, we have an authority to get verdicts from the court against powers of darkness. With these verdicts in hand, we win on the battlefield every time. The issue is we must have the jurisdiction to accomplish these things. We cannot fake the spirit realm out. If we haven't been given the jurisdiction from Heaven to operate there, the spirit realm and its forces know it and will exploit it. We are no threat to them if we do not have legitimate authority.

In fact, if we do not carry realms of authority that the spirit dimension recognizes we can be in trouble. We see this in the occasion of the sons of Sceva in Acts 19:13-17. These begin to seek to use the Name of Jesus as a formula for exorcism without the authority associated with it.

> Then some of the itinerant Jewish exorcists took it upon themselves to call the name of the Lord Jesus over those who had evil spirits, saying, "We exorcise you by the Jesus whom Paul preaches." Also there were seven sons of Sceva, a Jewish chief priest, who did so. And the evil spirit answered and said, "Jesus I know, and Paul I know; but who are you?" Then the man in whom the evil spirit was leaped on them, overpowered them, and prevailed against them, so that they fled out of that house naked and wounded. This became known both to all Jews and Greeks dwelling in Ephesus; and fear fell on them all, and the name of the Lord Jesus was magnified (Acts 19:13-17).

These guys got themselves in trouble because they tried to engage the demonic without carrying jurisdiction in the spirit realm to do it. The result was chaotic and treacherous. We cannot fake the spirit realm out. They know whether we have the authority we are seeking to function in, or if we do not. It is imperative that we carry authority and jurisdiction before we seek to uproot and remove powers of darkness.

Apostolic Jurisdiction

The key to an Ecclesia and its jurisdiction is the apostle to which it is joined. Apostles carry the governmental authority that causes an Ecclesia to arise. Every true Ecclesia recognized in Heaven is connected and joined to apostles. 1 Corinthians 12:28 says the Lord has set the apostles first.

> And God has appointed these in the Church: first apostles, second prophets, third teachers, after that miracles, then gifts of healings, helps, administrations, varieties of tongues (1 Cor. 12:28).

When Jesus builds an Ecclesia He begins with an apostle. 1 Corinthians 12:28 shows us the order and ranking of the Lord and His government.

> And God has appointed these in the Church: first apostles, second prophets, third teachers, after that miracles, then gifts of healings, helps, administrations, varieties of tongues (1 Cor. 12:28).

The Lord has set the apostle first. The word "first" is the Greek word "proton" and it means first in rank, importance, preeminence and influence. In other words when the Lord begins something, He starts with an apostle. This is why Jesus spent 3 ½ years calling and fashioning apostles. On the Day of Pentecost in the upper room, the apostle along with the other 120, were empowered with the Holy Spirit. The Church then "came out of the apostles" not the "apostles out of the Church." This is still the divine order of God today. When God gets ready to raise a governmental people recognized in heaven, He begins it with an apostle.

The apostle is first in prominence, authority, and influence. He then joins to that apostle, a people that will carry and function in governmental and judicial authority in the courts of Heaven. Different Ecclesias carry different jurisdictions. The jurisdiction of an Ecclesia is determined by the jurisdiction of the apostle who birthed it and the apostles who are joined to it.

Apostles have varying realms of authority and jurisdiction. Paul spoke of not being less than the greatest of apostles. 2 Corinthians 11:5 speaks to this understanding.

> For I consider that I am not at all inferior to the most eminent apostles (2 Cor. 11:5).

The fact that Paul spoke of great apostles says that there are apostles with different rankings in the spirit realm. Just like there are one star generals all the way up to five star generals in the United States of America military, there are also different levels of authority among apostles. Some apostles have jurisdiction over a small town. Other apostles have jurisdiction in major cities. Still other apostles have jurisdiction in States or territories. God even has apostles that have jurisdiction in nations. The jurisdiction of an apostle will determine the jurisdiction of the Ecclesia which he or she leads.

That Ecclesia can then go with the apostle into the courts of Heaven and be a part of getting verdicts out of Heaven granting God the legal right to fulfill His passion as Father in the Earth. This is a critical key to seeing society changed and nations being discipled. To reclaim society back to a Kingdom culture, it will require the legal reason the devil has resisted us to be removed. Once these legal reasons of resistance are removed we can then implement Kingdom influence back into our culture.

To help understand these ideas let me share with you a personal story. As a result of some very severe backlash against me, I am very careful about how I operate in determining my God ordained jurisdiction. Backlash from the devil occurs for two reasons. One reason is that we do not have authority to do what we are trying to do. We are outside our jurisdiction. We have believed our own press reports and not sought the Lord to determine our true measurement of rule.

The other reason for backlash is where we are within our jurisdiction, but there is something in our history that gives the devil a legal right to attack us. We must learn how to set our personal history in order so that when we step into our jurisdiction, the devil has no legal right to attack us. We do this through repentance. Any personal sin issues in my history or bloodline must be thoroughly repented of and brought under the blood of Jesus. Without this, demonic powers have a legal right to attack us as we seek a legal footing against them.

As I was learning (and continue to learn), how to operate in the courts of Heaven, I invited a ministry from South Africa into Colorado Springs where I lived. They were the first ministry I saw functioning in the courts of Heaven. This ministry is led by Natasha Grbich, who is a seasoned intercessor and apostolic leader. Her words to me as I began to teach on the courts of Heaven were, "You have given us language for what we have been doing for twenty years." I had witnessed how they operated and had recognized a strategy from the Lord that we as the Church knew little about. I know it is a missing key and strategy that will take us as the Church into the next dimension.

As this ministry came into Colorado Springs to be with me for some meetings, the Lord spoke to me before they were to arrive and said, "Declare that Natasha and her team have a right to be in this city because you invited them."

I didn't know how significant this would be. At one of the services, we were in the courts of Heaven seeking judgments and verdicts from the Throne when suddenly a principality came into the court of Heaven and asked Natasha, "Who said you could be here?" This interaction in the court was witnessed by one of the seer prophets that functions with Natasha. This seer prophet then went on to relay how the principality continued asking questions, "Did Steve Bach say you could be here?" and "Did Hickenlooper give you permission to be in this State?"

Here is the amazing thing about this, Bach was the Mayor of Colorado Springs and Hickenlooper was the Governor of Colorado at this time. This little seer prophet from Africa had no way of knowing this naturally, but heard the powers of darkness asking the questions. The powers of darkness wanted to know, "Who, in authority, gave Natasha the right to be in this region of the world and be taking us to court?" These principalities were seeking to resist our function in the courts of Heaven by questioning if Natasha was outside her jurisdiction as a South African.

Natasha looked at me and said, "You must come and answer this." So I stepped forward and said, "I, Robert Henderson as an apostolic leader residing in Colorado Springs, invited and have allowed these to be here." Suddenly I knew why God prompted me to make that declaration a few days before they arrived. The principalities seek to use the issue of jurisdiction to resist us from accomplishing things in the court system of Heaven. The powers of darkness will always question our measurement of rule in the court. They know what your measurement is, but do you?

They now knew that Natasha and the team had a legal right to be in our city and function there because of my invitation. However, the wrangling did not stop there. The powers of darkness that were seeking to diminish and take away our legal jurisdiction then asked of me, "Who are you?" Again, this was being revealed by what the seer prophet was seeing happening in the spirit realm. Obviously it was a natural progression in the wrestling that was going on in the court system of Heaven. If I was the one who had invited Natasha into the city, then the question was, "Who was I?"

Let me say that these powers knew who I was. They wanted to see, did I know who I was. I began to answer before the court of Heaven that I was an apostle sent by the Lord Jesus Christ to the city of Colorado Springs. After several moments before the courts of Heaven it was established by the courts that I had a jurisdiction in the courts of Heaven and had a right to bring Natasha and the team into the city to function there.

All of this was about who had the right and measurement of rule to function in the courts of Heaven concerning Colorado Springs. The powers of darkness will use the issue of jurisdiction to resist and disqualify us from operating in the courts of Heaven. We have to be well established and our realms of authority must be documented in the courts of Heaven for us to operate there. We must be registered in Heaven for the realms in which we are seeking to operate.

Again, we can speak blessings over anything. But if we are going to wrestle with principalities in high places for regions of the Earth we must have a recognized jurisdiction in that realm. Apostles, and the Ecclesias they lead, must be registered in Heaven. We should also know that what the Earth applauds, many times Heaven doesn't recognize. Just because someone has a reputation in Earth does not mean they have a jurisdiction in the spirit realm. Again, we cannot fake the spirit realm out.

Here is one more story that helps us understand being registered in Heaven. During the summer of 2012 a very strong wild fire broke out in Colorado Springs. It made international news for several days as the fire-fighters battled to bring the blaze under control. It was later stated that this fire moved at three football fields per second, destroying 347 homes as it came into the Colorado Springs city limits.

Two months before this fire erupted, one of my sons had a prophetic dream. In his dream he saw Pikes Peak, which is the mountain Colorado Springs is under, spewing out fire like a volcano. The main point of his dream was that while homes were burning all around us, our home had a shield of protection from God around it that would not allow it to burn. This is exactly what happened. The fire raged around us and neighborhoods very close to us were destroyed, while our home and neighborhood were divinely protected. The fire was so close to our home that we were evacuated for five days.

The day after we were evacuated the television reported that the same weather conditions that had driven the fire to consume all these homes would continue and that more of the city was in danger. The fire was only 5% contained and was still burning out of control. There was much trepidation in the city as everything possible was being done to control the fire.

As all this was going on, I heard the Lord say, "You have the authority to stop this fire." I knew He meant that we could go into the courts of Heaven and break what was driving this fire. There are always wild fires in Colorado during the summer, but somehow or other this fire was now being driven by the consuming powers of the devil. When the Lord said, "I had the authority to stop it", I knew this was a part of my jurisdiction. Because I am an apostle and lived in Colorado Springs, this granted me authority in the courts of Heaven to deal with this destroying fire.

I called together a total of ten people that operate in a seer gifting to help me discern what was happening in the spirit realm. As we began to pray and submit ourselves to the Lord, the spirit realm opened up to the seers with me. Whatever dimension of jurisdiction an apostle carries, seer and prophetic gifts will begin to see into that dimension. An apostle's authority will open that realm in the spirit arena. The gifts that are functioning connected to that apostles' call will begin to "see" what is happening in the unseen world.

As I began to pray with these seers, they began to sense and see what was driving this fire. They immediately saw a dragon with his claws in the ground. This dragon, which clearly was a ruling force in the spirit realm over Colorado Springs said, "This is mine because they gave it to me." In other words I have the right to consume this territory with fire and destruction because someone from the past gave this territory to me.

The seers then sensed and saw two things. Somewhere in the history of the region children had been offered in fire. This was the sin of Molech. Molech was a god of the Ammonites that people honored by causing their children to be burned as offerings. (Leviticus 18:21) They would offer their seed as a sacrifice to this demonic god. This most likely occurred when native groups ruled the land. The burning of children in sacrifice to demonic gods and the spilling of blood was empowering this dragon legally to consume the region.

The seers also saw General Palmer repenting for whatever his sins were in the courts of Heaven. The Bible says there is a great cloud of witnesses that are surrounding us and about the Throne of Heaven. We have talked about this in previous chapters. We agreed with Palmer's repentance and also repented for anything General Palmer had done that would allow this fire the legal right to burn. This was our realm of jurisdiction. General Palmer was one of the chief founders of Colorado Springs and was a godly man from all accounts. But founding fathers' sins can have a great effect when devils are looking for legal rights to reign and control.

We repented as the Ecclesia of God in the region and took away the legal right of this dragon to consume the land. We sensed clearly that things were shifting and verdicts were coming from the court of Heaven in our favor and in favor of the region. The seers actually saw the dragon's claws come out of the ground and the dragon leave the court. We had taken away the legal right of the principality to consume and destroy.

Once this was done, I then apostolically began to proclaim and decree that the weather patterns change. The forecast was for low humidity, high winds and dry thunderstorms to drive the fire the next five days. I began to decree high humidity, moisture in the air and everything that made it conducive for the firefighters to extinguish the flames.

This is exactly what happened. Every day the news would forecast unfavorable conditions and every day, they were wrong. The weather changed and favored the fire-fighters! In a matter of days the fire was 100% contained and no longer posed a danger to the city.

I firmly believe this was because we took away the legal right of the devil in the court of Heaven to consume the land. Once this was done we were free, as a representation of the Ecclesia, to make decrees from the courts of Heaven that Heaven backed up. There were many people praying that helped in this matter, but I also know that things shifted because of strategic activity in the courts of Heaven. An Ecclesia, registered and recognized in Heaven's courts, used their authority to grant God the legal right to spare and bless a region. We must walk in the jurisdiction that Heaven grants us.

The Lampstand

There is one final thing that I want to point out concerning the Church that is recognized and registered in Heaven. Jesus spoke to the Church of Ephesus and warned them that if they didn't repent, they could lose their lamp stand. This is found in Revelation 2:4-5.

> Nevertheless I have this against you, that you have left your first love. Remember therefore from where you have fallen; repent and do the first works, or else I will come to you quickly and remove your lampstand from its place—unless you repent (Rev. 2:4-5).

When Jesus threatened to remove the lampstand, He was warning that this church would lose its governmental authority and its right to function in the courts of Heaven. The lampstand spoke about the Church's identity and jurisdiction. To understand this we need to examine the meaning of a lampstand. In Zechariah 4:1-6 we see the prophet having a vision of two olive trees fueling seven lamps.

> Now the angel who talked with me came back and wakened me, as a man who is wakened out of his sleep. And he said to me, "What do you see?"
>
> So I said, "I am looking, and there is a lampstand of solid gold with a bowl on top of it, and on the stand seven lamps with seven pipes to the seven lamps. Two olive trees are by it, one at the right of the bowl and the other at its left." So I answered and spoke to the angel who talked with me, saying, "What are these, my lord?"
>
> Then the angel who talked with me answered and said to me, "Do you not know what these are?"
>
> And I said, "No, my lord." So he answered and said to me:

> "This is the word of the Lord to Zerubbabel: 'Not by
> might nor by power, but by My Spirit,' Says the
> Lord of hosts. (Zech. 4:1-6)

These two olive trees, fuelling the seven lamps with perpetual oil,
speak of the anointing that empowers the Church. I want to focus in
on the source of this anointing which is said to be these two olive
trees. Revelation 11:3-6 tells us that these two trees carry certain
DNA.

> And I will give power to my two witnesses, and they
> will prophesy one thousand two hundred and sixty
> days, clothed in sackcloth." These are the two olive
> trees and the two lampstands standing before the
> God of the earth. And if anyone wants to harm them,
> fire proceeds from their mouth and devours their
> enemies. And if anyone wants to harm them, he
> must be killed in this manner. These have power to
> shut Heaven, so that no rain falls in the days of their
> prophecy; and they have power over waters to turn
> them to blood, and to strike the earth with all
> plagues, as often as they desire (Rev. 11:3-6).

These two witnesses that are the two olive trees feeding the lamps
are of the nature and DNA of Moses and Elijah. Moses turned
water to blood and struck Egypt with plaques while Elijah shut the
Heavens and did not allow it to rain. The purpose of both of these
prophets was to affect nations. Moses delivered a nation through
his ministry while Elijah turned a nation back to God. They each
carried governmental anointing and authority.

This is to be the anointing and authority flowing out of the
olive trees and feeding the lamp stand of the Church. When Jesus

says He is going to remove the lampstand, He is threatening to remove their recognized place in Heaven. If this were to happen, they would still be deemed a church on Earth but not recognized in Heaven.

This is the case of many groups today. They may be called churches on Earth but they are not Ecclesias as far as Heaven is concerned. They are not registered in Heaven. They have either lost their jurisdiction or never had it. We must have Ecclesias that are recognized in Heaven if we are to function there and see verdicts come out of Heaven.

We are looking for true apostles to birth real Ecclesias that Heaven recognizes. When this happens we have the right to take our place and see Earth changed as a result of the verdicts of Heaven.

12

The Voice of Angels in the Court

Evidence is a very important element in any court case. Judgments are rendered on the basis of the evidence presented in court. A judge may know that a decision should go a certain way, but if there is no evidence given to warrant that decision, the judge cannot render it.

A dear Korean friend of mine that translates in a court system of a large American city told me a story that accented this point. It seems that a young lawyer was trying to present a case before a judge. He was having a difficult time in getting everything communicated properly. The judge in the situation actually stopped the young attorney and said, "Young man, I can see what you are trying to do, but you are going to have to help me here". In other words the judge in the situation wanted to render a verdict in favor of the case the young attorney represented, but could not until the evidence was properly presented. So it is in the courts of Heaven. The righteous Judge of All must have proper legal reasons presented to Him for righteous verdicts to come forth.

In the court of Heaven, angels have the important task of gathering and presenting evidence. They release the necessary testimonies and evidence needed for God to render judgments.

A husband and wife I know were involved in a wrongful death suit. One of their daughters had died in a traffic accident and they believed that a trucking company was at fault. The evidence presented in the lawsuit confirmed that the trucking company was indeed at fault and the judge rendered a verdict in their favor. At the conclusion of the trial, the judge approached this couple and expressed his sympathy for their loss. As a father, he empathized with the pain of their situation and wanted to help them. As a judge, there was nothing he could do until the evidence was presented and he could legally render a judgment. The evidence warranted the judgment that the jury delivered and it was very evident that the judge was pleased with the verdict. His years of judicial activity in our court systems caused him to rejoice when justice was done.

The Judge of all also needs evidence presented that warrants the verdicts He desires. This is why I say, it is our job to agree with the voices of Heaven and present our case until we grant God, as Judge, the legal right to fulfill His fatherly passion.

All the voices in Heaven operate for this purpose, but it is our job to agree with them until legal precedents are in place. God will never just render a judgment; He needs the input and agreement from the Church on Earth because man has been given this authority in the Earth realm. Psalm 115:16 says that the children of men have the God ordained authority in the Earth.

> The Heaven, even the Heavens, are the Lord's; But the earth He has given to the children of men. (Psalm 115:16)

The Lord will not normally overstep the authority He has granted us. If we, as humans, are in authority in the Earth realm, then it is up to us to grant God the legal right to accomplish His will here. We must know how to exercise this authority in the courts of Heaven to give God the legal right to intervene on Earth.

Angels are a huge part of this process. Hebrews 12:22 declares that there is an innumerable company of angels that is a part of the court system of Heaven. The term innumerable company in the Greek actually means a ten thousand, myriad and indefinite number. The word angels means a messenger and one who brings tidings. There are innumerable angels in the courts of Heaven that all have different jobs. Some are there to worship, some are there to declare and decree and some are there to run with messages.

There are at least four ranks of angels operating within the court system of Heaven. I have heard teaching that says there are ten ranks, but for our purpose we will deal with four. Colossians 1:16 names the thrones, dominion, principalities and powers as dimensions of ranks.

> For by Him all things were created that are in Heaven and that are on earth, visible and invisible, whether thrones or dominions or principalities or powers. All things were created through Him and for Him (Col 1:16).

People normally think of this as depicting a satanic hierarchy structure. This is, however, a structure in the spirit realm that operates in the satanic realm, but also in the Heavenly realm. Satan is not a creator. Any structure that he uses was copied from what he had seen in Heaven. He was a part of the hierarchy structure of Heaven and knows it well. This structure was first, and still is, the structure of Heaven. Notice that all these things were created through Him and for Him. All these ranks were created to assist this Lord in fulfilling his agenda. Let us look at these ranks of angels in an attempt to understand some of the operations of this innumerable company.

Thrones

The first rank mentioned is thrones. This word in the Greek means to sit, a stately seat, a potentate. Anyone who sits on a throne in Heaven has a voice in the Heavenly court. Remember that there are thrones around The Throne in Heaven. (Daniel 7:9) Scripture records that there are 24 thrones around God's Throne, but there are probably many more. I would suggest that archangels are some who sit on these thrones. The word archangels come from the Greek word archo and means first in rank and political power. If thrones are listed first in the spirit realm this means they must be occupied by archangels. 1 Thessalonians 4:16 says that archangels will accompany Jesus at His return.

> For the Lord Himself will descend from Heaven with a shout, with the voice of an archangel, and with the trumpet of God. And the dead in Christ will rise first (1 Thess. 4:16).

The voice of an archangel has the power to bring dead people back to life. Archangels are very powerful beings. Michael is also said to be an archangel. Jude 8:9 tells us that Michael contended with the devil.

> Likewise also these dreamers defile the flesh, reject authority, and speak evil of dignitaries. Yet Michael the archangel, in contending with the devil, when he disputed about the body of Moses, dared not bring

against him a reviling accusation, but said, "The
Lord rebuke you!" (Jude 8-9)

Michael as an archangel was very careful to stay within his
jurisdiction. He actually invoked the Lord Himself to rebuke the
devil. If Michael, one of the archangels of Heaven, is so careful to
stay within his jurisdiction, how much more should we? Also
please be aware that in John 5:28-29 Jesus said that this voice
would indeed bring people in the graves back to life.

> Do not marvel at this; for the hour is coming in
> which all who are in the graves will hear His voice
> and come forth—those who have done good, to the
> resurrection of life, and those who have done evil, to
> the resurrection of condemnation (John 5:28-29).

It states here that it is Jesus' voice that will bring them from the
grave and yet when Jesus comes back, it is with the voice of the
archangel. If it is in fact the voice of the archangel speaking on
behalf of Jesus, it is as if Jesus Himself is uttering the words.
Suffice it to say that these archangels carry great power and
authority from the Lord. They, therefore, from the position of
thrones have influence in the courts of the Lord.

Dominions

The next rank of angel mentioned is dominions. In my
opinion, the angels known as cherubim are in this rank. Exodus
25:21-22 states there are two cherubs over the mercy seat that
cover the ark of the covenant.

> You shall put the mercy seat on top of the ark, and
> in the ark you shall put the Testimony that I will

> give you. And there I will meet with you, and I will
> speak with you from above the mercy seat, from
> between the two cherubim which are on the ark of
> the Testimony, about everything which I will give
> you in commandment to the children of Israel (Ex.
> 25:21-22).

Moses was taken to Heaven and given a 'tour' of, among other
things, the Tabernacle. Then God commanded him to make a
replica on Earth of what he had seen in Heaven. The above
Scripture shows that he was instructed to place two cherubim (a
type of angel) over the mercy seat, just as it is in Heaven.

From this place, God said, He would meet with Moses and
speak with him from the mercy seat. I am glad that the voice of the
Lord always flows from His mercy. When we hear the Lord's
voice, it is from the mercy seat of Heaven. Hearing His voice is
part of the privilege of being in the courts of the Lord. The real ark
of the covenant is actually in the court system of Heaven. The
Apostle John saw this ark and the real mercy seat. Revelation 11:19
reflects and demonstrates what he saw.

> Then the temple of God was opened in Heaven, and
> the ark of His covenant was seen in His temple. And
> there were lightnings, noises, thunderings, an
> earthquake, and great hail (Rev. 11:19).

There are two cherubim who stand over the real ark and cover it
with their wings. Scripture teaches that, prior to his being cast out
of Heaven, Satan was a covering cherub Ezekiel 28:14 declares
this.

"You were the anointed cherub who covers;

I established you;
You were on the holy mountain of God;
You walked back and forth in the midst of fiery stones." (Ez. 28:14)

There are three things revealed about cherubs here. The first thing is they are anointed. They have a supernatural empowerment to fulfill their function. Secondly, they cover and defend. This is why the two cherubim are seen with their wings over the mercy seat. They guard the presence and mercy of the Lord. The third thing mentioned is that they are on the holy mountain of God. A mountain always speaks of government. This holy mountain's name is Zion. It is the place of government and the court system of Heaven. We have come to this place. (Hebrews 12: 22)

Cherubim have a function in the courts of Heaven to help verdicts come forth that fulfill the Father's passion. We choose to agree with the function of this rank of angels even when we don't fully understand. We, by faith, agree with the order of Heaven to see God's will be done on the Earth.

Principalities

The third rank of angels mentioned is principalities. When we hear this word we normally think of demonic powers. There are demonic principalities, but they originally were principalities in God's order and Kingdom. The demonic principalities fell with Lucifer before time began. They were cast out of Heaven for their rebellion against God. They then ceased to be angelic powers in the Heavenly realm and became demonic entities against the will of God. Principalities were probably seraphim when in Heaven. Isaiah 6:1-3 shows us one of the functions of the seraphim.

> In the year that King Uzziah died, I saw the
> Lord sitting on a throne, high and lifted up, and the
> train of His robe filled the temple. Above it stood
> seraphim; each one had six wings: with two he
> covered his face, with two he covered his feet, and
> with two he flew. And one cried to another and said:
>   "Holy, holy, holy is the Lord of hosts; The
> whole earth is full of His glory!"
> (Isaiah 6:1-3)

The seraphim declare perpetually the holiness of the Lord.
This same scenario that Isaiah saw, the Apostle John saw and
recorded in Revelation 4:8.

> The four living creatures, each having six wings,
> were full of eyes around and within.
> And they do not rest day or night, saying:
> "Holy, holy, holy, Lord God Almighty,
> Who was and is and is to come!" (Rev. 4:8)

The previous verses say that these living creatures had the face of a
lion, a calf, a man and a flying eagle. I believe it is possible that
Isaiah recorded things that John later added to. These were
seraphim that are creatures before the throne and are declaring the
holiness of God in Heaven's courts. The interesting thing about this
is that the term seraphim actually means a flying serpent. We tend
to think that serpents are always evil, yet they had their origin in
the courts of Heaven. Remember that the serpent in the Garden of
Eden was sentenced by God to crawl on its belly after it yielded
itself as Satan's vehicle to deceive Eve. Prior to this, it was
probably a flying creature. This is what made the judgment of God

against the serpent so strong. God again, cast Satan down from his exalted place and made him crawl on his belly in the dust.

Principalities of the demonic sort that now influence regions of the Earth are many times seen as dragons. These are fallen seraphim that have chosen to align with Satan in his transgression against the Lord. I have had several dreams which have helped me understand this better.

After our move to Colorado Springs, I was told by the Lord in a dream, that I had been assigned to the city and the demonic principalities knew it. The result, in this dream, was lightning bolts being thrown at me by these principalities.

As time progressed I had another dream. In this dream I was under a church structure in the city. I was seeking to clean up things that were polluted and defiled in the unseen realms of this church. As I was reaching into a dark, cavernous place I suddenly disrupted and disturbed a creature. When this creature emerged from this dark place, it was a serpent with a dragon's head on it. It stood about 30 feet tall and was very intimidating. I knew it was the prince that influenced the region.

This serpent with a dragon's head was a fallen seraphim that had been assigned by demonic hierarchy to this region of our nation. It was a seraphim that used to fly, but had now lost its glory and was set against the purposes of God. I share this simply to make the point that seraphim are flying serpents with six wings. They function in the courts of Heaven. The fallen seraphim are now principalities that function within regions to resist the will of God.

To underscore the significance of this, let me share one more dream that brought me great understanding. I had a dream where a well-known apostle's wife sent me his response to the 9/11 attacks on the USA. 9/11 was when America was attacked and the twin towers in New York City fell. The world changed forever on that day. In the dream I received his documented response on a piece of paper with a letterhead. At the bottom of the page, there was a handwritten note from his wife. She had noted what she had seen prior to 9/11 in the court system of Heaven that allowed this tragedy to occur. In the courts of Heaven, the four living creatures were crying out, "Holy, Holy, Holy is the Lord God Almighty." They were releasing their testimony before the courts of Heaven. However, there were also their demonic counterparts in the courts of Heaven. These demonic principalities were declaring before the courts of Heaven, "BOC denied, BOC denied, BOC denied."

In my dream, I knew that as a result of these words, destruction had hit America. When I awoke I tried to figure out the significance of "BOC." I googled this word and discovered that it is an acronym for Body of Christ. I understood immediately that the Lord was showing me how the enemy had a legal right to withstand the Body of Christ in the courts of Heaven.

The devil had found a legal right to resist the Body of Christ and its influence in the courts and perpetrate the 9/11 attacks. It wasn't God's will or God's judgment on America. It was a failure for us, as the Body of Christ, to take our place as the Ecclesia and grant God the legal right to thwart the plans of the devil. Because we have not understood this, we are still suffering the consequences of 9/11 until this day.

The demonic powers had a legal right to deny the Body of Christ the necessary influence we should have had in the courts of Heaven. They were therefore able to do the will of Satan rather than the will of God. We must learn how to come into agreement with the voice of the seraphim that cries out, "Holy, Holy, Holy" rather than empower the demonic principalities that are looking for a legal right to destroy. Nations and their destinies hang in the balance. It is our job as the Ecclesia to grant God the legal right to show mercy rather than allow destruction.

Powers

The final rank of angels is powers. This word means jurisdiction or authority. Psalm 103:20 mentions angels as part of the hierarchy of Heaven.

> Bless the Lord, you His angels,
> Who excel in strength, who do His word,
> Heeding the voice of His word (Psalm 103:20).

The word angel here means to dispatch as a deputy. This makes sense since they are the ones who do His word. These are the angels that carry out the verdicts that come from the courts of the Lord. They come to empower us and help us execute any and every judgment from the courts of Heaven.

There are many functions of these angelic beings. One of them is to land scrolls that carry judgment of the Lord against anything that is standing in the way of God's Kingdom purpose. We see this in Zechariah 5:1-4.

> Then I turned and raised my eyes, and saw there a flying scroll.
> And he said to me, "What do you see?"
> So I answered, "I see a flying scroll. Its length is twenty cubits and its width ten cubits."
> Then he said to me, "This is the curse that goes out over the face of the whole earth: 'Every thief shall be expelled,' according to this side of the scroll; and, 'Every perjurer shall be expelled,' according to that side of it."
> "I will send out the curse," says the Lord of hosts; "It shall enter the house of the thief

And the house of the one who swears falsely by My name.

It shall remain in the midst of his house And consume it, with its timber and stones." (Zech. 5:1-4)

Zechariah was a prophet who prophesied during the restoration period of Israel. There were many enemies to this restoration process. Clearly there were thieves and perjurers that were stealing away the assets necessary for restoration. Suddenly, the prophet encounters an angel that is revealing a scroll that carries judgment against these thieves and perjurers.

Judgments or verdicts against what is resisting God's will come from Heaven's court as scrolls in the spirit realm. They are scrolls or judgments that must be landed and made manifest on Earth.

We are in a process of restoration, just like they were in the days of Zechariah. Acts 3:19-21 shows us that everything the prophets spoke of must be restored before Jesus can return.

Repent therefore and be converted, that your sins may be blotted out, so that times of refreshing may come from the presence of the Lord, and that He may send Jesus Christ, who was preached to you before, whom heaven must receive until the times of restoration of all things, which God has spoken by the mouth of all His holy prophets since the world began (Acts 3:19-21).

There is actually a four-step process revealed here. It begins with our *repentance*. The next phase is God's response to our repentance with *refreshing*. Then from refreshing we move to restoration. Then from restoration comes the *return*.

Notice that Heaven is holding Jesus until the restoration of everything that the prophets spoke of becomes a reality in the Church and the world. The knowledge of the glory of the Lord will cover the Earth as the waters cover the sea. (Habakkuk 2: 14)

We have watched the Lord send moves of refreshings as the body of Christ has repented. Part of this was the Toronto Outpouring and the Revival at Pensacola. But now it is time for Restoration to flow out of the refreshings. The restoration is a recovering of apostolic power and authority that sets the Church into a new dimension of operation. As this occurs, the Earth will experience a new level of Kingdom power being administrated and experienced. The devil is resisting this restoration on a corporate and even personal level. We need scrolls/books released from the Heavenly courts to remove every hindrance holding back restoration. The Ecclesia has two jobs. The first is to get verdicts from the courts of Heaven. The second job of the Ecclesia is to land these verdicts/scrolls until everything functionally that is standing in the way of restoration is removed.

I use the word landed, because, just as an airplane needs to find a landing strip in order to land on Earth and release its cargo, so it is with scrolls. Scrolls/Books are Heavenly instructions that should produce a tangible result in the Earth realm. Just like an airplane, they need to find a landing strip where they can touch Earth and release the verdict so that the will of Heaven can be done on Earth.

Zechariah sees the scroll as a result of an angel showing it to him. When he sees it, he can read it, receive the instruction and carry it out on Earth. I am convinced that our prayers and activities in the court of Heaven have resulted in many scrolls/ books being released. The problem is we haven't seen them to land them. This has hindered Kingdom order coming into the planet.

The job of the Ecclesia is to grant God the legal right to fulfill His Kingdom passion. Once this is granted, we must land the scrolls/verdicts/judgments that come from the courts of Heaven. This requires angelic help. We need the angelic powers that have been deputized from Heaven to open our eyes and help us land the scrolls. Until these scrolls/books from Heaven are landed that which is standing in the way of God's will being done, will continue to resist. We need angelic and prophetic help to be able to move out of the way all that is resisting God's will from being done.

May the Lord open our eyes to the angelic powers that operate out of the courts of Heaven. I am convinced that much has already been released and simply needs to be landed. Once this occurs we will see Kingdom order and justice come to the Earth. Nations will shift and come into Kingdom destiny because we as the Ecclesia are accomplishing our mandates from Heaven. We are granting God the legal right to fulfill His passions and then with angelic help we are landing His righteous judgments in the Earth. "Come Your Kingdom, be done Your will, on Earth as it is in Heaven!"

13

The Testimony of the Bride

Without exception, Mary, my wife of 35 plus years, has the greatest influence over me. We have been together since we were 16 years old and in High School. That history alone grants her great influence in my life. Add to this, my profound respect for her wisdom and prophetic gifting and I pay very close attention to her and what she thinks.

Why am I sharing this? The next voice that gives testimony in the courts of Heaven is listed as the city of the living God, Heavenly Jerusalem. It doesn't take a great Bible scholar to realize this term refers to the Lamb's wife. Revelation 21:9-10 shows us the connection between this city and the bride of the Lord.

> Then one of the seven angels who had the seven bowls filled with the seven last plagues came to me and talked with me, saying, "Come, I will show you the bride, the Lamb's wife." And he carried me away in the Spirit to a great and high mountain, and showed me the great city, the holy Jerusalem, descending out of Heaven from God (Rev. 21:9-10).

John is taken to a high mountain which I believe is Mount Zion. The angel wants John to see the Bride from the place of governmental and judicial activity. He doesn't want John to simply see the Bride as the lover of the Lord, but rather as the governmental entity that brings Heaven into Earth.

Much has been written about this city, but to me, it is a clear depiction of Heaven invading Earth. It is a picture of a Heavenly influence that can be invoked over natural cities until they reflect the glory of God and His Kingdom culture. The Bride's voice and testimony give God the legal right to invade Earth. The Bride is the lover of the Lord and her voice has great impact in the courts of Heaven.

One of the best places we see the power of a bride influencing the verdicts of Judges, Kings and Potentates is in the life and relationship of David and Bathsheba. David had promised that the child of his union with Bathsheba, Solomon, would be King by the mandates of the Lord. However, when David was weak and close to death, another son tried to arise and take the throne. Bathsheba went to David at the urging of the prophet Nathan and made an appeal to the king. Remember now, appeals happen in courtrooms. The result of the appeal is that David calls Bathsheba to him to declare that Solomon will be king. Her appeal as the Bride was heard. 1 Kings 1:28-31 records this.

> Then King David answered and said, "Call Bathsheba to me." So she came into the king's presence and stood before the king. And the king took an oath and said, "As the Lord lives, who has redeemed my life from every distress, just as I swore to you by the Lord God of Israel, saying, 'Assuredly Solomon your son shall be king after me, and he shall sit on my throne in my place,' so I certainly

will do this day." Then Bathsheba bowed with her face to the earth, and paid homage to the king, and said, "Let my lord King David live forever!" (1 Kings 1:28-31)

King David made a judgment and rendered a verdict based on the appeal of Bathsheba. Her history as his lover and wife gave her an influence that resulted in this judgment.

We must realize that when we are the Lord's bride and have a history of loving and worshipping Him, we have great influence in the courts of Heaven. For our sake the Lord will render judgments that allow Heaven to invade Earth. The Bride of Christ within any city can get verdicts out of Heaven that allow reformation of the city. Charles Finney made a profound statement that resonates to this day. He said, "Revival is no more a miracle than a crop of wheat. Any city can obtain revival from Heaven when valiant souls enter the conflict determined to win or die or if necessary to win and die."

This statement says to me that when we as the Bride of Christ position ourselves in prayer in the courts of Heaven, we grant God the legal right to invade the Earth. The result will be Heaven's influence coming to Earth until cities reflect His glory and Kingdom culture.

God is Doing a New Thing

Isaiah 43:18-20 shows what God will do for the sake of His people and the aftermath of that.

"Do not remember the former things,
Nor consider the things of old.
Behold, I will do a new thing,

> Now it shall spring forth;
> Shall you not know it?
> I will even make a road in the wilderness
> And rivers in the desert.
> The beast of the field will honor Me,
> The jackals and the ostriches,
> Because I give waters in the wilderness
> And rivers in the desert,
> To give drink to My people, My chosen.
> (Isaiah 43:18-20)

The Lord promises a new thing that will be done. Notice that He says He will do it. The question is, will we know it and recognize it when it happens? It seems unfathomable, yet it is quite possible for the Lord to do something new and we, His people, completely miss it and stay stuck in the old. We must ask the Lord to make us sensitive and aware of His new thing so we don't persecute and dismiss the new thing of the Lord.

The Lord promises to bring rivers in the desert and roads in the wilderness. **He** will do this for the purpose of giving His people drink. He does this for His chosen. And notice that when He does this, even the animals will be affected. Scripture says that the beasts will honor Him. This means that when God responds to His Chosen people, even unredeemed people and societies will be affected, reformed and transformed. My point is, it all begins out of the love of the Bridegroom for His Bride. He will do for the Bride what would not otherwise be done. The result will be rivers flowing in the desert, Heaven invading Earth.

The Authority of the Bride

We have to realize the authority and influence we have in Heaven as the Bride. Song of Solomon 4:9 shows the passion that erupts in the heart of Jesus toward His bride.

> You have ravished my heart, My sister, my spouse;
> You have ravished my heart With one look of your
> eyes, With one link of your necklace.
> (Song of Solomon 4:9)

The Bridegroom wants the Bride to understand the effect she has on Him. His heart becomes ravished and greatly moved with passion when she looks at Him. When we worship, yearn and long for the Lord, His heart is moved. In these moments of intimacy great things can be asked for and received. The term *pillow talk* is used sometimes to express the secrets and longings exchanged between two lovers. During times of intimacy hearts are unlocked and things are expressed that would not be expressed at other times.

In a sense we can have pillow talk with the Lord. During times of intimate exchange we can ask for things and see the Lord respond because we have ravished His heart. We can actually inaugurate activity in the courtroom from the bedroom of intimacy with the Lord. From this place of great influence we can see cities saved and Heaven touch Earth.

When the Heavenly city begins to invade natural cities through the Bride's governmental and judicial administration, we will see real transformation in our cities. Kingdom culture will develop within the city as the Heavenly city becomes super-imposed upon it. Let us examine some of the changes one can expect when the Heavenly city descends to Earth.

The Government of God Over Cities

Natural cities can begin to have the government of God operating within it that will result in peace and tranquility coming to that city. There will also be prosperity and blessing wherever the government of God is established. The city of the living God is Heavenly Jerusalem. Jerusalem always speaks of the government of God. Jerusalem is the seat from which the Lord would govern the Earth. Jeremiah 3:17 shows that Jerusalem is the Throne of God.

> At that time Jerusalem shall be called The Throne of the Lord, and all the nations shall be gathered to it, to the name of the Lord, to Jerusalem. No more shall they follow the dictates of their evil hearts (Jer. 3:17).

The reason there has always been such a battle for natural Jerusalem is because it is destined to be the seat of God's government. This is why it was attacked and even destroyed. This is why when people were sent back to restore it, there was always contention. In Ezra 4:16, King Artaxerxes was cautioned that if he allowed Jerusalem to be rebuilt that he would have no more dominion within that region.

> We inform the king that if this city is rebuilt and its walls are completed, the result will be that you will have no dominion beyond the River (Ezra 4:16).

When we get Heavenly Jerusalem out of Heaven and over cities in the Earth, these cities begin to take on governmental qualities. The government of God invades the Earth. Not only does that city experience the blessings of living under God's Kingdom rule, but from that city, Kingdom rule can go forth. This is the result of the Bride loving the Bridegroom and seeing verdicts come from Heaven because of her influence.

The Beauty of the Bride in Our Cities

Another thing that happens as a result of the Bride's influence in Heaven is that the beauty of the Lord is seen within natural cities. Revelation 21:2 shows this affect of Heaven invading Earth.

> Then I, John, saw the holy city, New Jerusalem,
> coming down out of Heaven from God, prepared as
> a bride adorned for her husband (Rev. 21:2).

The beauty of the Bride prepared for her husband will begin to determine what a city looks like. As the Bride becomes more and more prepared for her husband, the Lord, she begins to dictate the atmosphere of a city. Right now principalities and powers of the demonic realm are determining what cities look like. As the Bride is prepared, she will win judgments in the court of Heaven that will dethrone these demonic powers and take the seat of dominion in the spirit realm from which they once ruled. When this occurs the beauty of the Bride of Christ will create an atmosphere within cities where His splendor is known. The beauty, purity and holiness of the Bride will prevail in the atmospheres of cities.

Revelation 21:3 tells us that God will begin to dwell in the Earth realm as a result of the Bride and this city coming down.

> And I heard a loud voice from Heaven saying,
> "Behold, the tabernacle of God is with men, and He
> will dwell with them, and they shall be His people.

God Himself will be with them and be their God"
(Rev. 21:3).

Whole cities can become the dwelling place of God. If the Bride
within a city can wield her influence in the courts of Heaven, that
city can host the presence of the Lord. We talk about the presence
of the Lord being in a service or among His people, what would
happen if the presence of the Lord tabernacled in a city?

Everything would be blessed in that city. People would
drive into that city and get saved. Is it possible for the Bride to be
so influential in the courts of Heaven that the rule of principalities
is broken and the presence of the Lord replaces it? I believe that it
is not only possible, but it is our portion. We don't have to yell and
scream at the devil, we simply take up our place as the Bride of
Christ. Using our God-ordained influence in the courts, we can
unlock what is in the books of Heaven about a city and see His
Kingdom culture established.

Healing Our Cities
When Heaven invades Earth, wounds are healed and tears
dry up. Revelation 21:4 says,

And God will wipe away every tear from their eyes;
there shall be no more death, nor sorrow, nor crying.
There shall be no more pain, for the former things
have passed away." (Rev. 21:4)

Our cities can become a place of healing instead of a place of
wounding. We see this in the book of Acts 8:6-8 where Philip
preaches the Gospel of Kingdom rule and a whole city comes to
joy.

And the multitudes with one accord heeded the things spoken by Philip, hearing and seeing the miracles which he did. For unclean spirits, crying with a loud voice, came out of many who were possessed; and many who were paralyzed and lame were healed. And there was great joy in that city (Acts 8:6-8).

Great joy came to the city of Samaria because the rule of the Kingdom impacted and brought Heaven to Earth. There is so much pain, hatred, animosity and disillusionment in our cities today. Imagine what it will be like when the Bride takes her place in the courts and grants the Lord the legal right to establish Kingdom rule?

We see this in the days of Elisha when Jericho was a pleasant city but the waters in the city were poisoned. The prophet knew what to do to heal the waters so the pleasantness of the city could be restored. 2 Kings 2:19-22 shows that God healed the waters so there was no more barrenness.

Then the men of the city said to Elisha, "Please notice, the situation of this city is pleasant, as my lord sees; but the water is bad, and the ground barren."

And he said, "Bring me a new bowl, and put salt in it." So they brought it to him. Then he went out to the source of the water, and cast in the salt there, and said,

"Thus says the Lord: 'I have healed this water; from it there shall be no more death or barrenness.'"

> So the water remains healed to this day,
> according to the word of Elisha which he spoke (2
> Kings 2:19-22).

This happened right after Elijah was taken away and Elisha had received his mantle. It is interesting to me that the men came to Elisha and made their request. I am sure the water had been bad for a long time and, for whatever reason, the water had not been healed during Elijah's tenure. When the 'leadership' changed, they came to Elisha and asked him if he could solve the problem of the city. He took a new bowl and put salt in it. He then went to the source and poured the salt in the water and healed the waters. With that, healing came to the city.

Let me point out several things here. First of all Elisha asked for a new bowl. He, in fact, was the new bowl. He was in essence saying that what the old administration had not done, he, as the new administration, would do. He was making a distinction between the old and the new. He wasn't tearing down the old, he was establishing himself as the new. This is important. If we are to see cities healed we must accept the new administration that God is establishing. Elisha would carry the mantle in a different way than Elijah did and would bring healing to cities.

Secondly, he placed salt in the bowl. We are the salt of the Earth as the body of Christ. We are to be the answer for cities that are crying out for healing.

And Thirdly, they went to the source. The source of the problem is what is ruling the cities. The principalities and powers that rule our cities must be summoned to and legislated against in the court of Heaven. Yelling, screaming and cursing will not get the job done. We must have verdicts from the courts that remove these powers and allow us as the salt of the Earth to take our place.

Having followed this protocol, Elisha's proclamation could then bring lasting results. The waters stayed healed. When we establish legal precedents, our decrees settle affairs permanently. This is the job of the Bride within a city. Our influence as the Bride of Christ gives God the legal right for Heaven to invade Earth. Cities can be healed and God's Kingdom culture established. May the Lord grant us the wisdom, understanding and enlightenment to function as His Bride, agree with the other voices of testimony and see cities reformed for the glory of God.

14

The Testimony of Finances

During my tenure of leading an apostolic center in Texas, a lady came to me after one of the services and put a sum of money in my hand. She told me that she was sowing this for her alcoholic husband who had been on a drinking binge and was now in a rehabilitation centre. The doctors had told her that the damage of this last binge was permanent and he would never be the same. In fact he could be incapacitated for the rest of his life. They actually used the term, 'a vegetable'.

At the time that she gave me the money, I did not understand what she was doing. I am not sure she understood except that the Lord had told her she was to sow this money for her husband's restoration. Two days later, the Lord told me to go to the rehabilitation center and pray for this man. I contacted the lady and arranged to travel to the center with her. When we walked into the room, the gentleman was slouched in a wheelchair with drool dribbling out of his mouth. He seemed completely unaware of our presence.

I knelt in front of him, put my hands on his knees and prayed a very simple prayer for complete restoration. To my amazement, this man began to revive. In a few short minutes he and his wife were dancing the Texas Two step right in front of me!

It was absolutely one of the most significant miracles I have ever witnessed, simply because of the way it happened.

It would be many years before I understood at least some of the spiritual things that occurred to produce this miracle. This man was completely delivered, healed, restored and spent the remainder of his days in complete service to the Lord. He had spent the major part of his life as an alcoholic, but from that day he never drank again because of what Jesus did for him. The courts rendered a verdict of healing for him because of the testimony of the finances his wife sowed.

Finances have a Voice

Your finances and money have a voice that is heard in the courts of Heaven. When we sow we are not just supporting a worthy cause or ministry. When we sow, we are releasing and amplifying our voice in the courts of Heaven. Hebrews 7:8 declares a very powerful truth.

> Here mortal men receive tithes, but there he receives them, of whom it is witnessed that he lives (Heb. 7:8).

This Scripture is speaking of our tithes and offerings. We are not bringing them to a Levitical priesthood. We are bringing them to Jesus, our High Priest who belongs to the eternal priesthood of Melchizedek. There in this Scripture speaks of the courts of Heaven where Jesus functions as our High Priest. When we bring these offerings to the Lord, it produces a witness in the courts of Heaven. The word witness means one who gives judicial testimony. Our money has a testimony in the courts of Heaven. It speaks in the court system of God on our behalf.

Raising a Memorial

Our money carries our faith and all that is in our heart and speaks when we sow it into the Kingdom of God. This is what happened to Cornelius in Acts 10:3-4. His prayer mingled with his offerings and created a memorial before the Lord.

> About the ninth hour of the day he saw clearly in a vision an angel of God coming in and saying to him, "Cornelius!"
>
> And when he observed him, he was afraid, and said, "What is it, lord?"
>
> So he said to him, "Your prayers and your alms have come up for a memorial before God.
> (Acts 10:3-4)

We know the result of this was the Gospel entering the Gentile world through this man's house. His diligent seeking of the Lord and his giving created this memorial before the throne of God that resulted in an angelic visitation.

The word memorial simply means a reminder or to bring to memory. This is what happens at memorials. We remember. Memorials speak to us about our heritage, intent, sacrifice and even a sense of responsibility to continue what someone else started. The monuments in our nation are designed to speak to us and cause us to remember what it cost for our nation to exist. These memorials speak to elicit from us actions consistent with the sacrifices of our forefathers.

Every year, in the South where I grew up, my family would go to the country cemetery where portions of our family were buried. The first Saturday of June each year, the whole family would gather at this cemetery. There would be an inter-denominational service where we sang and someone brought a message. Afterwards, we would have lunch under the pavilion that had been specially built for these events.

In its heyday, there were hundreds of people at these gatherings. People would drive for several hours to spend the day with family and friends. People who had grown up in that community (or their parents/grandparents had been raised there) would bring their children and show them off for all to see. It was a tradition that I remember well. I would meet cousins I didn't even know I had. These gatherings were called memorials.

When we were adults, my mom would still ask us, "Are ya'll coming to the memorial." (Remember, I am from the South.) The answer to that question had better be, "Yes." She wanted her family to be a part of this tradition and memorial. I often wondered why this was called a memorial. I now understand it was because there was a need to remember. We needed to get together and allow our heritage to speak to us to remind of us of where we had come from and how we should not forget the values that had brought us this far.

When the angel said to Cornelius that his activities had come before God and created a memorial, he was saying it had caused God to remember him. A memorial is something that speaks and stirs memory and hopefully actions. Part of what stirred God to action was the sound and memorial that Cornelius's offering made in Heaven. It was releasing judicial testimony as a witness before the courts of Heaven.

There are a couple of places in the Old Testament where we see memorials being created so Heaven can respond based on testimony being released. In Numbers 5:26 we are told of the memorial portion of an offering and what the priest was to do with it.

> And the priest shall take a handful of the offering, as
> its memorial portion, burn it on the altar … (Num.
> 5:26)

When someone brought a certain offering prescribed by the law,
the priest would take a handful of the grain and burn it on the altar.
As the smoke from the altar and the offering ascended, it carried
with it the idea that Heaven received this portion and it created a
memorial before God. This is why it was called the memorial
portion. The rest of the offering was for the priest and his
livelihood. The memorial portion was intended to speak in Heaven
and cause God to remember the one who had brought the offering.
This offering had a voice that caused God to remember.

Your Offering Has a Voice
Another place we see this is in Numbers 10:10. As the
people would bring their offerings, Aaron and his sons would blow
trumpets over the offering. The Bible says this created a memorial
before God.

> Also in the day of your gladness, in your appointed
> feasts, and at the beginning of your months, you
> shall blow the trumpets over your burnt offerings
> and over the sacrifices of your peace offerings; and
> they shall be a memorial for you before your God: I
> am the Lord your God." (Num. 10:10)

The blowing of the trumpets over the offering caused a memorial to
be before God. It would release testimony in the courts of Heaven
that granted God legal right to answer the cry of our hearts.
Trumpets speak of the prophetic voice. In 1 Corinthians 14:8-9,

Paul refers to the spiritual gift of prophecy as a trumpet that needs to give a clear sound.

> For if the trumpet makes an uncertain sound, who will prepare for battle? So likewise you, unless you utter by the tongue words easy to understand, how will it be known what is spoken? For you will be speaking into the air (1 Cor. 14:8-9).

When we bring our offerings, we should sound the trumpet or prophesy over our offerings. Whatever we prophesy over our offerings is the sound and testimony they will carry into the courts of Heaven. On the basis of the voice of our offerings, God is free to render judgments and verdicts on our behalf.

We see this in the case of Abel's offering to God. In Hebrews 11:4, God testifies of Abel's offering.

> By faith Abel offered to God a more excellent sacrifice than Cain, through which he obtained witness that he was righteous, God testifying of his gifts; and through it he being dead still speaks (Heb. 11:4).

Notice the wording. Abel obtained a *witness* that he was righteous because God was *testifying* of his gifts. The word witness means to give *evidence*. It comes from the word that means to witness *judicially*. The word testifying is the same Greek word, *martureo*. In both cases the Scripture is implying a courtroom setting. Abel obtained judicial testimony that he was righteous, because God bore witness and testified of his gifts. In other words, God as judge accepted the testimony of Abel's offerings and rendered Abel righteous. This verdict still stands today. Not only is his life still speaking as a testimony, but Abel won for himself a place of influence in the courts of Heaven because of his faithfulness and the testimony of his offerings. Our offerings have a voice in the courts of Heaven.

We see this played out in Deuteronomy 26:16-19. This whole chapter is about the commands God gave concerning offerings. He commanded the people to worship Him with their firstfruits and tithes after they came into the Promise Land. In the verses mentioned, the Lord shows what would happen as they kept the command to worship Him with their offerings.

> This day the Lord your God commands you to observe these statutes and judgments; therefore you shall be careful to observe them with all your heart and with all your soul.
>
> Today you have proclaimed the Lord to be your God, and that you will walk in His ways and keep His statutes, His commandments, and His judgments, and that you will obey His voice.
>
> Also today the Lord has proclaimed you to be His special people, just as He promised you, that you should keep all His commandments,
>
> and that He will set you high above all nations which He has made, in praise, in name, and in honor, and that you may be a holy people to the Lord your God, just as He has spoken." (Deut. 26:16-19)

The Lord commands these ordinances to be kept on *this day*. Then He says that when they keep these ordinances today, they are *proclaiming* their commitment and loyalty to God. In other words, when they brought their offering and kept the command, their offering began to proclaim or testify before the Lord.

Notice the next verse says that on the basis of this testimony, God now proclaimed or rendered a verdict over them. He began to declare them blessed above all nations and that they were set on high. Our offerings have a voice and can create a testimony in Heaven when we know how to bring them.

We should know that our finances carry the present tense statement of our hearts into Heaven. Remember that the judge can only render verdicts based on the evidence presented. If we bring our offerings with uncleanness, bitterness or unforgiveness in our hearts, our offerings will give the 'wrong' testimony in Heaven's court. This is why Jesus in Matthew 5:23-24 says we are to deal with any estrangement before we bring our offering.

> Therefore if you bring your gift to the altar, and there remember that your brother has something against you, leave your gift there before the altar, and go your way. First be reconciled to your brother, and then come and offer your gift (Matt. 5:23-24).

If we bring an offering into the courts of Heaven with unforgiveness in our hearts, it releases the wrong testimony in the courts. We do not want the results of this testimony in our lives. Jesus actually goes on to say that if we bring these gifts while in this state, the court of Heaven can release verdicts that put us in prison. Matthew 5:25-26 chronicles this.

> Agree with your adversary quickly, while you are on the way with him, lest your adversary deliver you to the judge, the judge hand you over to the officer, and you be thrown into prison. Assuredly, I say to

you, you will by no means get out of there till you
have paid the last penny (Matt. 5:25-26).

An offering offered with bitterness releases testimony in the courts
of Heaven that gives our adversary the legal right to have us
delivered to a prison. We must make sure that our offerings carry a
good testimony. This is so very important. If our offerings brought
with problems in our heart have this much power on the negative
side, then how powerful it must be when done with right attitudes
and motives.

We see this in Malachi 3:3-5. The prophet is prophesying
about the coming of the Messiah and His purging effect. He is
declaring that the purpose for this purging is so we can bring an
offering in righteousness. Wow! Offerings must really be important
to God's agenda being carried out if the Messiah's purpose for
coming was to empower us to bring righteous offerings. These
verses help us to understand this.

He will sit as a refiner and a purifier of
silver; He will purify the sons of Levi, And purge
them as gold and silver, That they may offer to the
LORD An offering in righteousness.

"Then the offering of Judah and Jerusalem
Will be pleasant to the LORD, As in the days of old,
As in former years. And I will come near you for
judgment; I will be a swift witness Against
sorcerers, Against adulterers, Against perjurers,
Against those who exploit wage earners and widows
and orphans, And against those who turn away an
alien—Because they do not fear Me," Says the
LORD of hosts (Malachi 3:3-5).

Notice that when we are purged, as priest (which is what the sons of Levi speak of), then we are able to present an offering in righteousness. When every wrong motive is purged and every attitude adjusted, then our offering will be accepted.

Notice that the result of offerings being received and accepted is that God begins to judge. Remember that judgment is courtroom activity. Based on what our offerings, presented in righteousness, are testifying, God begins to be a witness and release judgment against everything afflicting society and His purpose in society. Our offering presented with a pure heart after our purging, releases evidence in the courts of Heaven that allows God as Judge to deal with every destructive thing touching our society. He judges sorcery, adultery, perjurers, inequity, economic oppression and injustice against the needy and poor. When we, as the Ecclesia and people of God, bring our offerings with a right heart, we are releasing testimony against that which is working against society. How powerful is this? Our offerings don't just meet needs; they produce judicial sounds that gives God the right to fulfill His passion in the Earth. When we bring an offering in righteousness, we come into agreement with Heaven and give the Father legal right to render judgments on our behalf.

A Review of the Nine Voices

There are nine voices that are speaking in the courts of Heaven concerning the Lord's Kingdom desire and His passion for us as Father. In review, these nine voices are the blood, the Mediator, spirit of just men made perfect (great cloud of witnesses), The Judge, the general assembly, the Church of firstborn, the innumerable angels, the bride and our offerings.

We must learn to agree with the intercession of Heaven that each brings and establish evidence that grants God the legal right as Judge to fulfill His fatherly passion toward us. This is our job as individuals before His throne of grace and as the Ecclesia. In the last chapter, I will seek to bring it all together and share how to bring cases before the Lord and His court.

15

Presenting Cases in the Courts of Heaven

Now that we a have better understanding of the courts of Heaven, let's learn to present our petitions and cases before the Lord. I want to seek to bring everything together so that at the conclusion, you can step into this dimension and see God's passion toward you fulfilled. The entire purpose for these final thoughts is to empower us to move with boldness and confidence before the Lord.

Get Off the Battlefield

The first thing we must do to step into the courts of Heaven is to get off the battlefield. We have to recognize the need for legal precedents to be set before we run to the battle. We are in a conflict, but it is a legal one. Remember that Jesus never pictures prayer in a battlefield context. He did put prayer however in a courtroom or judicial setting in Luke 18:1-8.

In this parable a widow is seeking a verdict of justice from an unrighteous judge. Among other things, one glaring aspect of this story stands out. This woman, in her efforts to deal with her adversary, never spoke to her adversary, but only to the judge. She understood that when a rendering could be obtained from the judge, then her adversary became of no consequence. The adversary's legal footing for hurting, harming, stealing or otherwise tormenting her would be removed. The adversary would have to bend the knee to the verdict of the court. Once the court rendered a verdict then it could be executed into place. The verdict from the court is the legal wrestling, the executing it into place is the battlefield part. We have tried to run to the battlefield without verdicts from the court. We have found ourselves ineffective or even soundly defeated. Those days are over as we get off the battlefield and into the courtroom.

This is what the Apostle Paul was referring to in Ephesians 6:12.

> For we do not wrestle against flesh and blood, but against principalities, against powers, against the rulers of the darkness of this age, against spiritual hosts of wickedness in the Heavenly places (Eph. 6:12).

The term wrestle is a very apt term for what goes on in the courts of the Lord. Through our maneuvering in the courts we actually put into place the legalities necessary for God's Kingdom will to be done. If you have ever been in a natural court setting you will attest to this. Attorneys maneuver, operate and wrestle with each other to get the legal upper hand. The same is true in the court of Heaven, especially when dealing with principalities over regions. It is our job to enforce the legal judgment that Jesus won at the cross, on the powers of darkness, stripping them of all illegitimate authority that they hold over us individually and corporately. It takes some legal wrangling to set this in place. Once it is done, we can then march onto the battlefield and win every time. The battle in the courtroom always precedes the victory on the battlefield. This whole book is about learning to win in the courtroom so we can win on the battlefield. Once we have had a change of perspective and see the primary place of conflict as a courtroom, we are ready to present our case.

Presenting Our Case

We can only present our case once we have read from the books in Heaven. Daniel 7:10 sets the scene.

> A fiery stream issued
> And came forth from before Him.
> A thousand thousands ministered to Him;
> Ten thousand times ten thousand stood before Him.
> The court was seated,
> And the books were opened. (Dan. 7:10)

The good news is that the books are open. The books are not closed, locked, or sealed. This means we can discern and understand by revelation what is in the books. On a personal level, the books reveal our Kingdom purpose and destiny. This is not a once-off revelation, but rather an ongoing journey of discovery.

When we are dealing with cities, states, or nations, prophets will help us understand God's Kingdom will as it is written in the books. When a prophet prophesies, they are simply reading out of the books of Heaven. They are unveiling the secrets contained in the books.

Once this is done, apostles with jurisdiction in the given sphere can begin to present the case before the courts. We present the city, state, or nation in the court and remind the Lord of what He wrote about it in the books. We are presenting our case and putting God into remembrance. (Isaiah 43:26-27)

This operation sets the court in motion. Just as in a natural court, the proceedings start with the prosecution presenting its case. It is a powerful thought that we as mortal people have the authority to set in motion the courts of Heaven, but it is true.

When we present from the books what has been written before time began, court comes to session. This is why in Daniel 7, the court is seated, and the books are open. The court is going to make decisions based on what is presented from the books of Heaven by us as individuals and as the Ecclesia. It is an awesome place God has given us.

Agreeing with Our Accuser

Once we have presented the case for what has been written in the books, we will almost always encounter the accuser seeking to deny us what is in the books. (Revelation 12:10) Any and all accusations that he brings to seek to disqualify us from getting what is in the books must be answered. This will require us to repent and humble ourselves before the Lord for nations and ourselves.

It is interesting that right after the Lord speaks the parable in Luke 18:1-8, that His next teaching launches into two men who went up to pray. The one was a Pharisee and the other a tax collector. This parable is in Luke 18:9-14. Jesus contrasts how the Pharisee was self-righteous and very arrogant, while the tax collector was very humble and surrendered. The end of the parable was that the tax collector went down to his house "justified" rather than the religious Pharisee.

> Also He spoke this parable to some who trusted in themselves that they were righteous, and despised others: "Two men went up to the temple to pray, one a Pharisee and the other a tax collector. The Pharisee

stood and prayed thus with himself, 'God, I thank You that I am not like other men—extortioners, unjust, adulterers, or even as this tax collector. I fast twice a week; I give tithes of all that I possess.' And the tax collector, standing afar off, would not so much as raise his eyes to heaven, but beat his breast, saying, 'God, be merciful to me a sinner!' I tell you, this man went down to his house justified rather than the other; for everyone who exalts himself will be humbled, and he who humbles himself will be exalted" (Luke 18:9-14).

Jesus spoke this parable in connection to or as an extension of His teaching on praying from a judicial place. To be justified means to render as just or innocent. To be justified is a legal position of being found not guilty and innocent. One of the things Jesus is teaching in connection to operating in the courts of Heaven, is that God responds to humility and surrender. I have found that humility and surrender carry great weight in the courts of Heaven. If we want to have an audience in the courts, we must appear there with a humble spirit and a broken and contrite heart. These sacrifices, God will not despise. (Psalm 51:17)

Through repentance we set in place the voice of the blood of Jesus and every other voice releasing testimony. Remember that there are nine voices that can speak in the court system of Heaven. We can agree with these voices in several ways. One of the primary ways we can agree is through our repentance. When we sense accusations being used against us, we should simply agree with them. Matthew 5:25 says we are to agree with our adversary quickly.

> Agree with your adversary quickly, while you are on
> the way with him, lest your adversary deliver you to
> the judge, the judge hand you over to the officer,
> and you be thrown into prison (Matt. 5:25).

To agree with our adversary simply means that we are quick to repent of anything being used against us in the courts. I have no need to answer for myself. I don't justify myself. I allow the blood of Jesus to justify me. I also draw from any/or all of the other voices in the courts that would speak as well. They will speak on my behalf when I have repented and accessed the blood.

My attitude is that I can never go wrong with repentance. Self- justification can destroy me, but repentance will cause me to be accepted. My experience has been that as I repent for anything in my history or even bloodline issues, the Holy Spirit will grant me repentance. (2 Timothy 2:25) As I began to repent for things in my bloodline that I was not even aware of, it isn't uncommon for me to begin to feel real remorse. I have been moved to tears, as the Holy Spirit brought conviction and sorrow into my heart, so that my repentance was real. This took away the accusations of the devil and silenced his ability to disqualify me.

Confessing Our Sin

Our words before the throne of God are very powerful. In Hosea 14:1-2 the prophet is urging the people to use 'words' to return to the Lord.

> O Israel, return to the Lord your God,
> For you have stumbled because of your iniquity;
> Take words with you,
> And return to the Lord. Say to Him,
> "Take away all iniquity; Receive us graciously,

For we will offer the sacrifices of our lips. (Hosea 14:1-2)

Right words before the courts of the Lord are very powerful. Because of our words, God will forgive us. The sacrifices of our lips in departing from iniquity and returning to the Lord, give God the legal right to forgive us. This is why John told us to confess our sins. 1 John 1:9 declares that our confession, or saying what God says about something, grants the Lord legal right to forgive and cleanse us.

> If we confess our sins, He is faithful and just to forgive us our sins and to cleanse us from all unrighteousness (1 John 1:9).

Our words set legal things in motion. Our words become testimony and agreements with the courts of Heaven. Our words grant the Lord the legal right to fulfill His passion toward us, which is always mercy and goodness. This is a part of what overcomes the accuser of the brethren, the word of our testimony. Revelation 12:10-11 declares that the word of our testimony in agreement with God's purposes overcomes and silences accusation.

> Then I heard a loud voice saying in Heaven, "Now salvation, and strength, and the kingdom of our God, and the power of His Christ have come, for the accuser of our brethren, who accused them before our God day and night, has been cast down. And they overcame him by the blood of the Lamb and by the word of their testimony, and they did not love their lives to the death (Rev. 12:10-11).

Part of the word of our testimony is to 'confess' and use words to grant God the legal right to be merciful to us.

Another thing that allows us to come into concert and agreement with the voices of Heaven and silence the accuser is our offerings. As I shared in the previous chapter, our finances have a voice. When we bring finances with a clean heart and full of passion toward the Lord, these finances add a voice of agreement with Heaven. It is appropriate to offer finances and then prophesy over them and with them into the courts of Heaven. When we do, we are becoming a part of the operation of Heaven to see His will done on Earth.

Resisting the Devil

Once the accuser has been silenced and the wrestling match in the courts is finished, we are now set to rebuke any and all demonic forces. This may include the rebuking and renouncing of any and every demonic activity. It is amazing how quickly the operation of the devil is stopped and removed once his legal rights are thwarted. When we have put in place through our repentance the legalities of Heaven, the devil will have to stop and desist any and all operations. The legal right has been removed and the rights of his operation are broken. If we have rebuked the devil and it hasn't moved, it is because he still has a legal right to be there. Colossians 2:13-14 shows us that Jesus set in place every legal thing necessary to break satanic holds.

> And you, being dead in your trespasses and the uncircumcision of your flesh, He has made alive together with Him, having forgiven you all trespasses, having wiped out the handwriting of requirements that was against us, which was

> contrary to us. And He has taken it out of the way,
> having nailed it to the cross (Colossians 2:13-14).

Every bit of 'paperwork' against us in Heaven, Jesus nailed it to His cross and took it out of the way. The words handwriting of requirements actually means a legal document and/or a law, ordinance or decree. In other words, positionally Jesus dealt with every accusation or bit of 'paperwork' that the accuser can use to resist us in the courts of Heaven. It has been removed. This doesn't mean that the devil will not try to use it. Whether it is our sin or the sin of our bloodline. Just as we had to appropriate what Jesus did for us when we were born again (and it wasn't just automatic), there are times where, in specifics, we must appropriate or execute it into place. The devil will seek to use things against us. We must take the blood of Jesus and with our repentance and faith put what Jesus did for us in place in that given area. We verbally and with faith accept and forcibly put into place the work of Jesus on the cross in our behalf. When we do, we have taken away any legal footing the devil tries to use.

The word contrary in these verses means covertly. The sacrifice of Jesus deals with even the 'hidden' things in our bloodline that are standing against us. When, by the Spirit revelation, these bloodline issues come to light, we repent of these things, apply the blood of Jesus and break any place the devil might be trying to exploit. When we do, we become positioned to functionally get verdicts from the courts of Heaven. The accuser has been silenced and God is now free to answer our prayer from His Father's heart. Any legal place Satan has been using against us is taken away.

I have found that once the legal right is broken, he will go when he is resisted. James 4:7 is very clear.

> Therefore submit to God. Resist the devil and he
> will flee from you (James 4:7).

Submitting to God involves humility, surrender, repentance and submission to the Lord. Once this is in place and any and every place of rebellion is out of us, we will resist and he will flee. The devil no longer has a legal right to stay. Our rebuke now carries power and he will flee.

Making Decrees

The last thing we do as legal things have now been ordered is we are free to make decrees that carry the authority of the court of Heaven. Our decrees are based on what is written in the books. Every objection has been removed and the Judge is now free to fulfill His fatherly passion and release His kingdom will in our lives. Nothing is resisting us legally and the decrees now have power.

To get the full effect of this understanding we should look at our position as kings and priests. We are told that we are kings and priests to our God. (Revelation 1:6; Revelation 5:10) This speaks of our spiritual positioning in heaven. These are places given to us by and through the work of Jesus on the cross. The job of a priest is to intercede. The job of a king is to decree. When priests intercede, they grant God the legal right to show mercy. This is most clearly seen in the priest taking the blood into the Holy of Holies on the Day of Atonement. The priest would offer the blood of the Passover lamb in that holy place as prescribed by the Lord. The offering of that blood would grant God the legal right to roll the sins of the people and a nation back for one more year. The Lord by His own mandate needed the function of the priest administrating the blood so He was granted the legalities He needed to bless and show mercy. The job of priest is to strategically intercede so that legal things are in place. Once legal positioning is obtained, then kings, from that place in the spirit, can make decrees. This is why we are to be priests and kings to our God. This is best seen in Jesus coming to Lazarus' tomb in John 11:41-44.

> Then they took away the stone from the place where the dead man was lying. And Jesus lifted up His eyes and said, "Father, I thank You that You have heard Me. And I know that You always hear Me, but because of the people who are standing by I said this, that they may believe that You sent Me." Now when He had said these things, He cried with a loud voice, "Lazarus, come forth!" And he who had died came out bound hand and foot with grave clothes, and his face was wrapped with a cloth. Jesus said to them, "Loose him, and let him go" (John 11:41-44).

Jesus comes to the tomb of Lazarus and says to the Father that He has already prayed. Jesus has been functioning in His priesthood on the journey to Lazarus' tomb. He has dealt with every legal reason why Lazarus has died prematurely. He has been in the courts of Heaven and dealt with the accusations of the devil that allowed Lazarus to die in an untimely fashion. He knows everything is in place legally for what He is about to do. As a result when Jesus comes to Lazarus' tomb, He steps from His priesthood into His kingship. Now He is no longer interceding, now He is decreeing. With authority, He simply decrees, "Lazarus come forth." The dead man rises and comes out of the grave full of life and resurrection power. This is a perfect picture of our function as priest and kings in the courts of Heaven. Once we, from our priesthood, have things legally in place, we can then step into our kingship and make decrees the courts of Heaven back up. Things shift and change in these times by executed verdicts from Heaven put into place.

As we utter the words of governmental decrees, the Heavenly realm is reordered and things come into place for Heaven to invade Earth. There is now a contract and verdict in place from the courts that allows Heaven to manifest on Earth. What a powerful thing! The Holy Spirit will help us in our weakness to maneuver in the courts of Heaven. As we do, we become a part of God's agenda in the planet.

My heart's cry is that this book will help to deal with all the frustration and even skepticism among God's people regarding prayer. I pray that all the prayers that have been prayed in true sincerity but seem to have been unanswered will fade into history as we learn the secrets of the courts. He has not been an uncaring God, or One that is distant. The problem has been that we haven't understood that we must grant God the legal right as Judge to fulfill His fatherly passion. He longs to answer and bless.

We must grant Him the legal right to do so by operating in the courts of Heaven, agreeing with the voices that speak on our behalf and see verdicts rendered from His Throne that establish Kingdom order. When this is done, Heaven will truly invade Earth. Our lives will come to new levels of living, nations will be discipled and Kingdom cultures put into place. There will be an escaping of the destructive schemes of the devil as his legal rights of operation will cease and desist. He will flee at our rebuke because his legal footing has been taken away in the courts of Heaven. Let's move forward and see God's will done. Let's go to court! The verdicts of Heaven are waiting for us.

Recommended   Reading

repentance
natasha grbich

cleansing your
generational
bloodline

restoring the first estate
volume 1

Jesus Christ bought us with His blood and we do not belong to ourselves. He paid the price on Calvary for us to come into the fullness of our destiny, but it remains our responsibility to deliver ourselves to God. We must CHOOSE to repent and break all of the agreements / contracts / covenants that we have entered into through personal sin or inherited from our forefathers. This process of cleansing our bloodlines is a long one that requires diligence and perseverance. He has already done it at the cross, but we must work out our salvation with fear and trembling.

Apostle Natasha draws on more than 20 years of experience in bloodline deliverance prayer to give us guidelines to do this. This is not just a book to read, but rather a manual to work and pray through, together with the Holy Spirit. If you want to go to a new level in God, this manual will be invaluable to you!

More great resources from

Robert   Henderson

Voice of Reformation

My definition of reformation is the tangible expression of the Kingdom of God in society. One of the greatest challenges facing the Body of Christ is producing the reformers that are necessary to see these mountains re-claimed. When vision is created - intercessors are empowered and reformers are produced and commissioned into their function in these mountains - we will see a living demonstration of the Kingdom of God in Planet Earth through reformation.

The Caused Blessing

When we function in firstfruits, our influence is felt for generations to come, especially throughout our lineage. I always say that if a man's influence only lasts for the span of his natural life, then he is a failure. God intends for our influence to far outlive our natural days. One way this occurs is through the act of firstfruits.

Consecrated Business

Through the principal of firstfruits, businesses can become Kingdom in nature because they are consecrated to the Lord and become holy unto Him. This book will teach you how to birth a Kingdom Business and propel you into a new level of prosperity and influence.

Such dangerous angels walk through Lent.
Their walls creak *Anne! Convert! Convert!*
My desk moves. Its cave murmurs Boo
and I am taken and beguiled.

Or wrong. For all the way I've come
I'll have to go again. Instead, I must convert
to love as reasonable
as Latin, as solid as earthenware:
an equilibrium
I never knew. And Lent will keep its hurt
for someone else. Christ knows enough
staunch guys have hitched on him in trouble,
thinking his sticks were badges to wear.

4.

Spring rusts on its skinny branch
and last summer's lawn
is soggy and brown.
Yesterday is just a number.
All of its winters avalanche
out of sight. What was, is gone.
Mother, last night I slept
in your Bonwit Teller nightgown.
Divided, you climbed into my head.
There in my jabbering dream
I heard my own angry cries
and I cursed you, *Dame*
keep out of my slumber.
My good Dame, you are dead.
And Mother, three stones
slipped from your glittering eyes.

Now it is Friday's noon
and I would still curse
you with my rhyming words
and bring you flapping back, old love,

old circus knitting, god-in-her-moon,
all fairest in my lang syne verse,
the gauzy bride among the children,
the fancy amid the absurd
and awkward, that horn for hounds
that skipper homeward, that museum
keeper of stiff starfish, that blaze
within the pilgrim woman,
a clown mender, a dove's
cheek among the stones,
my Lady of my first words,
this is the division of ways.

And now, while Christ stays
fastened to his Crucifix
so that love may praise
his sacrifice
and not the grotesque metaphor,
you come, a brave ghost, to fix
in my mind without praise
or paradise
to make me your inheritor.

All My Pretty Ones

(1962)

> All my pretty ones?
> Did you say all? O hell-kite! All?
> What! all my pretty chickens and their dam
> At one fell swoop? . . .
> I cannot but remember such things were,
> That were most precious to me.

Macbeth

*all my Pretty ones
* The abortion
* young

... the books we need are the kind that act upon us like a misfortune, that make us suffer like the death of someone we love more than ourselves, that make us feel as though we were on the verge of suicide, or lost in a forest remote from all human habitation — a book should serve as the ax for the frozen sea within us.

from a letter of Franz Kafka
to Oskar Pollak

I

THE TRUTH THE DEAD KNOW

For my mother, born March 1902, died March 1959
and my father, born February 1900, died June 1959

Gone, I say and walk from church,
refusing the stiff procession to the grave,
letting the dead ride alone in the hearse.
It is June. I am tired of being brave.

We drive to the Cape. I cultivate
myself where the sun gutters from the sky,
where the sea swings in like an iron gate
and we touch. In another country people die.

My darling, the wind falls in like stones
from the whitehearted water and when we touch
we enter touch entirely. No one's alone.
Men kill for this, or for as much.

And what of the dead? They lie without shoes
in their stone boats. They are more like stone
than the sea would be if it stopped. They refuse
to be blessed, throat, eye and knucklebone.

ALL MY PRETTY ONES

Father, this year's jinx rides us apart
where you followed our mother to her cold slumber;

a second shock boiling its stone to your heart,
leaving me here to shuffle and disencumber
you from the residence you could not afford:
a gold key, your half of a woolen mill,
twenty suits from Dunne's, an English Ford,
the love and legal verbiage of another will,
boxes of pictures of people I do not know.
I touch their cardboard faces. They must go.

But the eyes, as thick as wood in this album,
hold me. I stop here, where a small boy
waits in a ruffled dress for someone to come . . .
for this soldier who holds his bugle like a toy
or for this velvet lady who cannot smile.
Is this your father's father, this commodore
in a mailman suit? My father, time meanwhile
has made it unimportant who you are looking for.
I'll never know what these faces are all about.
I lock them into their book and throw them out.

This is the yellow scrapbook that you began
the year I was born; as crackling now and wrinkly
as tobacco leaves: clippings where Hoover outran
the Democrats, wiggling his dry finger at me
and Prohibition; news where the *Hindenburg* went
down and recent years where you went flush
on war. This year, solvent but sick, you meant
to marry that pretty widow in a one-month rush.
But before you had that second chance, I cried
on your fat shoulder. Three days later you died.

These are the snapshots of marriage, stopped in places.
Side by side at the rail toward Nassau now;
here, with the winner's cup at the speedboat races,
here, in tails at the Cotillion, you take a bow,

here, by our kennel of dogs with their pink eyes,
running like show-bred pigs in their chain-link pen;
here, at the horseshow where my sister wins a prize;
and here, standing like a duke among groups of men.
Now I fold you down, my drunkard, my navigator,
my first lost keeper, to love or look at later.

I hold a five-year diary that my mother kept
for three years, telling all she does not say
of your alcoholic tendency. You overslept,
she writes. My God, father, each Christmas Day
with your blood, will I drink down your glass
of wine? The diary of your hurly-burly years
goes to my shelf to wait for my age to pass.
Only in this hoarded span will love persevere.
Whether you are pretty or not, I outlive you,
bend down my strange face to yours and forgive you.

YOUNG

A thousand doors ago
when I was a lonely kid
in a big house with four
garages and it was summer
as long as I could remember,
I lay on the lawn at night,
clover wrinkling under me,
the wise stars bedding over me,
my mother's window a funnel
of yellow heat running out,
my father's window, half shut,
an eye where sleepers pass,
and the boards of the house
were smooth and white as wax
and probably a million leaves

sailed on their strange stalks
as the crickets ticked together
and I, in my brand new body,
which was not a woman's yet,
told the stars my questions
and thought God could really see
the heat and the painted light,
elbows, knees, dreams, goodnight.

LAMENT

Someone is dead.
Even the trees know it,
those poor old dancers who come on lewdly,
all pea-green scarfs and spine pole.
I think . . .
I think I could have stopped it,
if I'd been as firm as a nurse
or noticed the neck of the driver
as he cheated the crosstown lights;
or later in the evening,
if I'd held my napkin over my mouth.
I think I could . . .
if I'd been different, or wise, or calm,
I think I could have charmed the table,
the stained dish or the hand of the dealer.
But it's done.
It's all used up.
There's no doubt about the trees
spreading their thin feet into the dry grass.
A Canada goose rides up,
spread out like a gray suede shirt,
honking his nose into the March wind.
In the entryway a cat breathes calmly
into her watery blue fur.

The supper dishes are over and the sun
unaccustomed to anything else
goes all the way down.

TO A FRIEND WHOSE WORK HAS COME TO TRIUMPH

Consider Icarus, pasting those sticky wings on,
testing that strange little tug at his shoulder blade,
and think of that first flawless moment over the lawn
of the labyrinth. Think of the difference it made!
There below are the trees, as awkward as camels;
and here are the shocked starlings pumping past
and think of innocent Icarus who is doing quite well:
larger than a sail, over the fog and the blast
of the plushy ocean, he goes. Admire his wings!
Feel the fire at his neck and see how casually
he glances up and is caught, wondrously tunneling
into that hot eye. Who cares that he fell back to the sea?
See him acclaiming the sun and come plunging down
while his sensible daddy goes straight into town.

THE STARRY NIGHT

That does not keep me from having a terrible need
of — shall I say the word — religion. Then I go
out at night to paint the stars.
     VINCENT VAN GOGH in a letter to his brother

The town does not exist
except where one black-haired tree slips
up like a drowned woman into the hot sky.
The town is silent. The night boils with eleven stars.
Oh starry starry night! This is how
I want to die.

It moves. They are all alive.
Even the moon bulges in its orange irons
to push children, like a god, from its eye.
The old unseen serpent swallows up the stars.
Oh starry starry night! This is how
I want to die:

into that rushing beast of the night,
sucked up by that great dragon, to split
from my life with no flag,
no belly,
no cry.

OLD DWARF HEART

True. All too true. I have never been at home in
life. All my decay has taken place upon a child.
    Henderson the Rain King, by SAUL BELLOW

When I lie down to love,
old dwarf heart shakes her head.
Like an imbecile she was born old.
Her eyes wobble as thirty-one thick folds
of skin open to glare at me on my flickering bed.
She knows the decay we're made of.

When hurt she is abrupt.
Now she is solid, like fat,
breathing in loops like a green hen
in the dust. But if I dream of loving, then
my dreams are of snarling strangers. *She* dreams that . . .
strange, strange, and corrupt.

Good God, the things she knows!
And worse, the sores she holds
in her hands, gathered in like a nest
from an abandoned field. At her best

54

she is all red muscle, humming in and out, cajoled
by time. Where I go, she goes.

Oh now I lay me down to love,
how awkwardly her arms undo,
how patiently I untangle her wrists
like knots. Old ornament, old naked fist,
even if I put on seventy coats I could not cover you . . .
mother, father, I'm made of.

I REMEMBER

By the first of August
the invisible beetles began
to snore and the grass was
as tough as hemp and was
no color — no more than
the sand was a color and
we had worn our bare feet
bare since the twentieth
of June and there were times
we forgot to wind up your
alarm clock and some nights
we took our gin warm and neat
from old jelly glasses while
the sun blew out of sight
like a red picture hat and
one day I tied my hair back
with a ribbon and you said
that I looked almost like
a puritan lady and what
I remember best is that
the door to your room was
the door to mine.

THE OPERATION

After the sweet promise,
the summer's mild retreat
from mother's cancer, the winter months of her death,
I come to this white office, its sterile sheet,
its hard tablet, its stirrups, to hold my breath
while I, who must, allow the glove its oily rape,
to hear the almost mighty doctor over me equate
my ills with hers
and decide to operate.

It grew in her
as simply as a child would grow,
as simply as she housed me once, fat and female.
Always my most gentle house before that embryo
of evil spread in her shelter and she grew frail.
Frail, we say, remembering fear, that face we wear
in the room of the special smells of dying, fear
where the snoring mouth gapes
and is not dear.

There was snow everywhere.
Each day I grueled through
its sloppy peak, its blue-struck days, my boots
slapping into the hospital halls, past the retinue
of nurses at the desk, to murmur in cahoots
with hers outside her door, to enter with the outside
air stuck on my skin, to enter smelling her pride,
her upkeep, and to lie
as all who love have lied.

No reason to be afraid,
my almost mighty doctor reasons.

I nod, thinking that woman's dying
must come in seasons,
thinking that living is worth buying.
I walk out, scuffing a raw leaf,
kicking the clumps of dead straw
that were this summer's lawn.
Automatically I get in my car,
knowing the historic thief
is loose in my house
and must be set upon.

2.

Clean of the body's hair,
I lie smooth from breast to leg.
All that was special, all that was rare
is common here. Fact: death too is in the egg.
Fact: the body is dumb, the body is meat.
And tomorrow the O.R. Only the summer was sweet.

The rooms down the hall are calling
all night long, while the night outside
sucks at the trees. I hear limbs falling
and see yellow eyes flick in the rain. Wide eyed
and still whole I turn in my bin like a shorn lamb.
A nurse's flashlight blinds me to see who I am.

The walls color in a wash
of daylight until the room takes its objects
into itself again. I smoke furtively and squash
the butt and hide it with my watch and other effects.
The halls bustle with legs. I smile at the nurse
who smiles for the morning shift. Day is worse.

Scheduled late, I cannot drink
or eat, except for yellow pills

and a jigger of water. I wait and think
until she brings two mysterious needles: the skills
she knows she knows, promising, soon you'll be out.
But nothing is sure. No one. I wait in doubt.

I wait like a kennel of dogs
jumping against their fence. At ten
she returns, laughs and catalogues
my resistance to drugs. On the stretcher, citizen
and boss of my own body still, I glide down the halls
and rise in the iron cage toward science and pitfalls.

The great green people stand
over me; I roll on the table
under a terrible sun, following their command
to curl, head touching knee if I am able.
Next, I am hung up like a saddle and they begin.
Pale as an angel I float out over my own skin.

I soar in hostile air
over the pure women in labor,
over the crowning heads of babies being born.
I plunge down the backstair
calling *mother* at the dying door,
to rush back to my own skin, tied where it was torn.
Its nerves pull like wires
snapping from the leg to the rib.
Strangers, their faces rolling like hoops, require
my arm. I am lifted into my aluminum crib.

3.

Skull flat, here in my harness,
thick with shock, I call mother
to help myself, call toe of frog,
that woolly bat, that tongue of dog;

call God help and all the rest.
The soul that swam the furious water
sinks now in flies and the brain
flops like a docked fish and the eyes
are flat boat decks riding out the pain.

My nurses, those starchy ghosts,
hover over me for my lame hours
and my lame days. The mechanics
of the body pump for their tricks.
I rest on their needles, am dosed
and snoring amid the orange flowers
and the eyes of visitors. I wear,
like some senile woman, a scarlet
candy package ribbon in my hair.

Four days from home I lurk on my
mechanical parapet with two pillows
at my elbows, as soft as praying cushions.
My knees work with the bed that runs
on power. I grumble to forget the lie
I ought to hear, but don't. God knows
I thought I'd die — but here I am,
recalling mother, the sound of her
good morning, the odor of orange and jam.

All's well, they say. They say I'm better.
I lounge in frills or, picturesque,
I wear bunny pink slippers in the hall.
I read a new book and shuffle past the desk
to mail the author my first fan letter.
Time now to pack this humpty-dumpty
back the frightened way she came
and run along, Anne, and run along now,
my stomach laced up like a football
for the game.

II

I want no pallid humanitarianism — If Christ be not God,
I want none of him; I will hack my way through existence
alone . . .

Guardini

A CURSE AGAINST ELEGIES

Oh, love, why do we argue like this?
I am tired of all your pious talk.
Also, I am tired of all the dead.
They refuse to listen,
so leave them alone.
Take your foot out of the graveyard,
they are busy being dead.

Everyone was always to blame:
the last empty fifth of booze,
the rusty nails and chicken feathers
that stuck in the mud on the back doorstep,
the worms that lived under the cat's ear
and the thin-lipped preacher
who refused to call
except once on a flea-ridden day
when he came scuffing in through the yard
looking for a scapegoat.
I hid in the kitchen under the ragbag.

I refuse to remember the dead.
And the dead are bored with the whole thing.

But you — you go ahead,
go on, go on back down
into the graveyard,
lie down where you think their faces are;
talk back to your old bad dreams.

THE ABORTION

Somebody who should have been born
is gone.

Just as the earth puckered its mouth,
each bud puffing out from its knot,
I changed my shoes, and then drove south.

Up past the Blue Mountains, where
Pennsylvania humps on endlessly,
wearing, like a crayoned cat, its green hair,

its roads sunken in like a gray washboard;
where, in truth, the ground cracks evilly,
a dark socket from which the coal has poured,

Somebody who should have been born
is gone.

the grass as bristly and stout as chives,
and me wondering when the ground would break,
and me wondering how anything fragile survives;

up in Pennsylvania, I met a little man,
not Rumpelstiltskin, at all, at all . . .
he took the fullness that love began.

61

Returning north, even the sky grew thin
like a high window looking nowhere.
The road was as flat as a sheet of tin.

Somebody who should have been born
is gone.

Yes, woman, such logic will lead
to loss without death. Or say what you meant,
you coward . . . this baby that I bleed.

WITH MERCY FOR THE GREEDY

For my friend, Ruth, who urges me to make an
appointment for the Sacrament of Confession

Concerning your letter in which you ask
me to call a priest and in which you ask
me to wear The Cross that you enclose;
your own cross,
your dog-bitten cross,
no larger than a thumb,
small and wooden, no thorns, this rose —

I pray to its shadow,
that gray place
where it lies on your letter . . . deep, deep.
I detest my sins and I try to believe
in The Cross. I touch its tender hips, its dark jawed face,
its solid neck, its brown sleep.

True. There is
a beautiful Jesus.
He is frozen to his bones like a chunk of beef.
How desperately he wanted to pull his arms in!
How desperately I touch his vertical and horizontal axes!
But I can't. Need is not quite belief.

62

All morning long
I have worn
your cross, hung with package string around my throat.
It tapped me lightly as a child's heart might,
tapping secondhand, softly waiting to be born.
Ruth, I cherish the letter you wrote.

My friend, my friend, I was born
doing reference work in sin, and born
confessing it. This is what poems are:
with mercy
for the greedy,
they are the tongue's wrangle,
the world's pottage, the rat's star.

FOR GOD WHILE SLEEPING

Sleeping in fever, I am unfit
to know just who you are:
hung up like a pig on exhibit,
the delicate wrists,
the beard drooling blood and vinegar;
hooked to your own weight,
jolting toward death under your nameplate.

Everyone in this crowd needs a bath.
I am dressed in rags.
The mother wears blue. You grind your teeth
and with each new breath
your jaws gape and your diaper sags.
I am not to blame
for all this. I do not know your name.

Skinny man, you are somebody's fault.
You ride on dark poles —
a wooden bird that a trader built

63

for some fool who felt
that he could make the flight. Now you roll
in your sleep, seasick
on your own breathing, poor old convict.

IN THE DEEP MUSEUM

My God, my God, what queer corner am I in?
Didn't I die, blood running down the post,
lungs gagging for air, die there for the sin
of anyone, my sour mouth giving up the ghost?
Surely my body is done? Surely I died?
And yet, I know, I'm here. What place is this?
Cold and queer, I sting with life. I lied.
Yes, I lied. Or else in some damned cowardice
my body would not give me up. I touch
fine cloth with my hands and my cheeks are cold.
If this is hell, then hell could not be much,
neither as special nor as ugly as I was told.

What's that I hear, snuffling and pawing its way
toward me? Its tongue knocks a pebble out of place
as it slides in, a sovereign. How can I pray?
It is panting; it is an odor with a face
like the skin of a donkey. It laps my sores.
It is hurt, I think, as I touch its little head.
It bleeds. I have forgiven murderers and whores
and now I must wait like old Jonah, not dead
nor alive, stroking a clumsy animal. A rat.
His teeth test me; he waits like a good cook,
knowing his own ground. I forgive him that,
as I forgave my Judas the money he took.

Now I hold his soft red sore to my lips
as his brothers crowd in, hairy angels who take
my gift. My ankles are a flute. I lose hips
and wrists. For three days, for love's sake,

64

I bless this other death. Oh, not in air —
in dirt. Under the rotting veins of its roots,
under the markets, under the sheep bed where
the hill is food, under the slippery fruits
of the vineyard, I go. Unto the bellies and jaws
of rats I commit my prophecy and fear.
Far below The Cross, I correct its flaws.
We have kept the miracle. I will not be here.

GHOSTS

Some ghosts are women,
neither abstract nor pale,
their breasts as limp as killed fish.
Not witches, but ghosts
who come, moving their useless arms
like forsaken servants.

Not all ghosts are women,
I have seen others;
fat, white-bellied men,
wearing their genitals like old rags.
Not devils, but ghosts.
This one thumps barefoot, lurching
above my bed.

But that isn't all.
Some ghosts are children.
Not angels, but ghosts;
curling like pink tea cups
on any pillow, or kicking,
showing their innocent bottoms, wailing
for Lucifer.

III

THE FORTRESS

while taking a nap with Linda

Under the pink quilted covers
I hold the pulse that counts your blood.
I think the woods outdoors
are half asleep,
left over from summer
like a stack of books after a flood,
left over like those promises I never keep.
On the right, the scrub pine tree
waits like a fruit store
holding up bunches of tufted broccoli.

We watch the wind from our square bed.
I press down my index finger —
half in jest, half in dread —
on the brown mole
under your left eye, inherited
from my right cheek: a spot of danger
where a bewitched worm ate its way through our soul
in search of beauty. My child, since July
the leaves have been fed
secretly from a pool of beet-red dye.

And sometimes they are battle green
with trunks as wet as hunters' boots,
smacked hard by the wind, clean

66

as oilskins. No,
the wind's not off the ocean.
Yes, it cried in your room like a wolf
and your pony tail hurt you. That was a long time ago.
The wind rolled the tide like a dying
woman. She wouldn't sleep,
she rolled there all night, grunting and sighing.

Darling, life is not in my hands;
life with its terrible changes
will take you, bombs or glands,
your own child at
your breast, your own house on your own land.
Outside the bittersweet turns orange.
Before she died, my mother and I picked those fat
branches, finding orange nipples
on the gray wire strands.
We weeded the forest, curing trees like cripples.

Your feet thump-thump against my back
and you whisper to yourself. Child,
what are you wishing? What pact
are you making?
What mouse runs between your eyes? What ark
can I fill for you when the world goes wild?
The woods are underwater, their weeds are shaking
in the tide; birches like zebra fish
flash by in a pack.
Child, I cannot promise that you will get your wish.

I cannot promise very much.
I give you the images I know.
Lie still with me and watch.
A pheasant moves
by like a seal, pulled through the mulch
by his thick white collar. He's on show

like a clown. He drags a beige feather that he removed,
one time, from an old lady's hat.
We laugh and we touch.
I promise you love. Time will not take away that.

IV

OLD

I'm afraid of needles.
I'm tired of rubber sheets and tubes.
I'm tired of faces that I don't know
and now I think that death is starting.
Death starts like a dream,
full of objects and my sister's laughter.
We are young and we are walking
and picking wild blueberries
all the way to Damariscotta.
Oh Susan, she cried,
you've stained your new waist.
Sweet taste —
my mouth so full
and the sweet blue running out
all the way to Damariscotta.
What are you doing? Leave me alone!
Can't you see I'm dreaming?
In a dream you are never eighty.

THE HANGMAN

Reasonable, reasonable, reasonable . . . we walked through
ten different homes, they always call them homes,
to find one ward where they like the babies who
look like you. Each time, the eyes that no one owns
watched us silently, these visitors from the street

that moves outside. They watched, but did not know
about time, there in the house where babies never grow.
My boy, though innocent and mild
your brain is obsolete.
Those six times that you almost died
the newest medicine and the family fuss
pulled you back again. Supplied
with air, against my guilty wish,
your clogged pipes cried
like Lazarus.

At first your mother said . . . why me! why me!
But she got over that. Now she enjoys
her dull daily care and her hectic bravery.
You do not love anyone. She is not growing a boy;
she is enlarging a stone to wear around her neck.
Some nights in our bed her mouth snores at me coldly
or when she turns, her kisses walking out of the sea,
I think of the bad stories,
the monster and the wreck.
I think of that Scandinavian tale
that tells of the king who killed nine
sons in turn. Slaughtered wholesale,
they had one life in common
as you have mine,
my son.

WOMAN WITH GIRDLE

Your midriff sags toward your knees;
your breasts lie down in air,
their nipples as uninvolved
as warm starfish.
You stand in your elastic case,

still not giving up the new-born
and the old-born cycle.
Moving, you roll down the garment,
down that pink snapper and hoarder,
as your belly, soft as pudding,
slops into the empty space;
down, over the surgeon's careful mark,
down over hips, those head cushions
and mouth cushions,
slow motion like a rolling pin,
over crisp hairs, that amazing field
that hides your genius from your patron;
over thighs, thick as young pigs,
over knees like saucers,
over calves, polished as leather,
down toward the feet.
You pause for a moment,
tying your ankles into knots.
Now you rise,
a city from the sea,
born long before Alexandria was,
straightway from God you have come
into your redeeming skin.

THE HOUSE

In dreams
the same bad dream goes on.
Like some gigantic German toy
the house has been rebuilt
upon its kelly-green lawn.
The same dreadful set,
the same family of orange and pink faces
carved and dressed up like puppets
who wait for their jaws to open and shut.

Nineteen forty-two,
nineteen forty-three,
nineteen forty-four . . .
it's all the same. We're at war.
They've rationed the gas for all three cars.
The Lincoln Continental breathes in its stall,
a hopped up greyhound waiting to be sprung.

The Irish boy
who dated her
(lace curtain Irish, her mother said)
urges her through the lead-colored garages
to feel the patent-leather fenders
and peek at the mileage.
All that money!
and kisses too.
Kisses that stick in the mouth
like the vinegar candy she used to pull
with her buttery fingers, pull
until it was white like a dog's bone,
white, thick and impossible to chew.

Father,
an exact likeness,
his face bloated and pink
with black market scotch,
sits out his monthly bender
in his custom-made pajamas
and shouts, his tongue as quick as galloping horses,
shouts into the long distance telephone call.
His mouth is as wide as his kiss.

Mother,
with just the right gesture,
kicks her shoes off,
but is made all wrong,

impossibly frumpy as she sits there
in her alabaster dressing room
sorting her diamonds like a bank teller
to see if they add up.

The maid
as thin as a popsicle stick,
holds dinner as usual,
rubs her angry knuckles over the porcelain sink
and grumbles at the gun-shy bird dog.
She knows something is going on.
She pricks a baked potato.

The aunt,
older than all the crooked women
in *The Brothers Grimm*,
leans by a gooseneck lamp in her second floor suite,
turns up her earphone to eavesdrop
and continues to knit,
her needles working like kitchen shears
and her breasts blown out like two
pincushions.

The houseboy,
a quick-eyed Filipino,
slinks by like a Japanese spy
from French Provincial room
to French Provincial room,
emptying the ash trays and plumping up
the down upholstery.
His jacket shines, old shiny black,
a wise undertaker.

The milkman walks in his cartoon
every other day in the snoozy dawn,
rattling his bottles like a piggy bank.
And gardeners come, six at a time,

pulling petunias and hairy angel bells
up through the mulch.

This one again,
made vaguely and cruelly,
one eye green and one eye blue,
has the only major walk-on so far,
has walked from her afternoon date
past the waiting baked potatoes,
past the flashing back of the Japanese spy,
up the cotton batten stairs,
past the clicking and unclicking of the earphone,
turns here at the hall
by the diamonds that she'll never earn
and the bender that she kissed last night
among thick set stars, the floating bed
and the strange white key . . .
up like a skein of yarn,
up another flight into the penthouse,
to slam the door on all the years
she'll have to live through . . .
the sailor who she won't with,
the boys who will walk on
from Andover, Exeter and St. Marks,
the boys who will walk off with pale unlined faces,
to slam the door on all the days she'll stay the same
and never ask why and never think who to ask,
to slam the door and rip off her orange blouse.
   Father, father, I wish I were dead.

At thirty-five
she'll dream she's dead
or else she'll dream she's back.
All day long the house sits
larger than Russia
gleaming like a cured hide in the sun.

All day long the machine waits: rooms,
stairs, carpets, furniture, people —
those people who stand at the open windows like objects
waiting to topple.

WATER

We are fishermen in a flat scene.
All day long we are in love with water.
The fish are naked.
The fish are always awake.
They are the color of old spoons
and caramels.
The sun reaches down
but the floor is not in sight.
Only the rocks are white and green.
Who knows what goes on in the halls below?

It's queer to meet the loon falling in
across the top of the yellow lake
like a checkered hunchback
dragging his big feet.
Only his head and neck can breathe.
He yodels.
He goes under yodeling
like the first mate
who sways all night in his hammock, calling
            I have seen, I have seen.

            Water is worse than woman.
            It calls to a man to empty him.
            Under us
            twelve princesses dance all night,
            exhausting their lovers, then giving them up.
            I have known water.

I have sung all night
for the last cargo of boys.
I have sung all night
for the mouths that float back later,
one by one,
holding a lady's wornout shoe.

WALLFLOWER

Come friend,
I have an old story to tell you —

Listen.
Sit down beside me and listen.
My face is red with sorrow
and my breasts are made of straw.
I sit in the ladder-back chair
in a corner of the polished stage.
I have forgiven all the old actors for dying.
A new one comes on with the same lines,
like large white growths, in his mouth.
The dancers come on from the wings,
perfectly mated.

I look up. The ceiling is pearly.
My thighs press, knotting in their treasure.
Upstage the bride falls in satin to the floor.
Beside her the tall hero in a red wool robe
stirs the fire with his ivory cane.
The string quartet plays for itself,
gently, gently, sleeves and waxy bows.
The legs of the dancers leap and catch.
I myself have little stiff legs,
my back is as straight as a book
and how I came to this place —
the little feverish roses,

the islands of olives and radishes,
the blissful pastimes of the parlor —
I'll never know.

HOUSEWIFE

Some women marry houses.
It's another kind of skin; it has a heart,
a mouth, a liver and bowel movements.
The walls are permanent and pink.
See how she sits on her knees all day,
faithfully washing herself down.
Men enter by force, drawn back like Jonah
into their fleshy mothers.
A woman *is* her mother.
That's the main thing.

DOORS, DOORS, DOORS

1. *Old Man*

Old man, it's four flights up and for what?
Your room is hardly any bigger than your bed.
Puffing as you climb, you are a brown woodcut
stooped over the thin rail and the wornout tread.

The room will do. All that's left of the old life
is jampacked on shelves from floor to ceiling
like a supermarket: your books, your dead wife
generously fat in her polished frame, the congealing

bowl of cornflakes sagging in their instant milk,
your hot plate and your one luxury, a telephone.

You leave your door open, lounging in maroon silk
and smiling at the other roomers who live alone.
Well, almost alone. Through the old-fashioned wall
the fellow next door has a girl who comes to call.

Twice a week at noon during their lunch hour
they pause by your door to peer into your world.
They speak sadly as if the wine they carry would sour
or as if the mattress would not keep them curled

together, extravagantly young in their tight lock.
Old man, you are their father holding court
in the dingy hall until their alarm clock
rings and unwinds them. You unstopper the quart

of brandy you've saved, examining the small print
in the telephone book. The phone in your lap is all
that's left of your family name. Like a Romanoff prince
you stay the same in your small alcove off the hall.
Castaway, your time is a flat sea that doesn't stop,
with no new land to make for and no new stories to swap.

2. *Seamstress*

I'm at pains to know what else I could have done
but move out of his parish, him being my son;

him being the only one at home since his Pa
left us to beat the Japs at Okinawa.

I put the gold star up in the front window
beside the flag. Alterations is what I know

and what I did: hems, gussets and seams.
When my boy had the fever and the bad dreams

I paid for the clinic exam and a pack of lies.
As a youngster his private parts were undersize.

I thought of his Pa, that muscly old laugh he had
and the boy was thin as a moth, but never once bad,

as smart as a rooster! To hear some neighbors tell,
Your kid! He'll go far. He'll marry well.

So when he talked of taking the cloth, I thought
I'd talk him out of it. You're all I got,

I told him. For six years he studied up. I prayed
against God Himself for my boy. But he stayed.

Christ was a hornet inside his head. I guess
I'd better stitch the zipper in this dress.

I guess I'll get along. I always did.
Across the hall from me's an old invalid,

aside of him, a young one — he carries on
with a girl who pretends she comes to use the john.

The old one with bad breath and his bed all mussed,
he smiles and talks to them. He's got some crust.

Sure as hell, what else could I have done
but pack up and move in here, him being my son?

3. *Young Girl*

Dear love, as simple as some distant evil
we walk a little drunk up these three flights
where you tacked a Dufy print above your army cot.

The thin apartment doors on the way up will
not tell on us. We are saying, we have *our* rights
and let them see the sandwiches and wine we bought

for we do not explain my husband's insane abuse
and we do not say why your wild-haired wife has fled
or that my father opened like a walnut and then was dead.
Your palms fold over me like knees. Love is the only use.

Both a little drunk in the middle afternoon
with the forgotten smart of August on our skin
we hold hands as if we still were children who trudge

up the wooden tower, on up past that close platoon
of doors, past the dear old man who always asks us in
and the one who sews like a wasp and will not budge.

Climbing the dark halls, I ignore their papers and pails,
the twelve coats of rubbish of someone else's dim life.
Tell them need is an excuse for love. Tell them need prevails.
Tell them I remake and smooth your bed and am your wife.

V

For Comfort
who was actually my grandfather

LETTER WRITTEN ON A FERRY WHILE CROSSING LONG ISLAND SOUND

I am surprised to see
that the ocean is still going on.
Now I am going back
and I have ripped my hand
from your hand as I said I would
and I have made it this far
as I said I would
and I am on the top deck now
holding my wallet, my cigarettes
and my car keys
at 2 o'clock on a Tuesday
in August of 1960.

Dearest,
although everything has happened,
nothing has happened.
The sea is very old.
The sea is the face of Mary,
without miracles or rage
or unusual hope,
grown rough and wrinkled
with incurable age.

Still,
I have eyes.
These are my eyes:
the orange letters that spell
ORIENT on the life preserver
that hangs by my knees;
the cement lifeboat that wears
its dirty canvas coat;
the faded sign that sits on its shelf
saying KEEP OFF.
Oh, all right, I say,
I'll save myself.

Over my right shoulder
I see four nuns
who sit like a bridge club,
their faces poked out
from under their habits,
as good as good babies who
have sunk into their carriages.
Without discrimination
the wind pulls the skirts
of their arms.
Almost undressed,
I see what remains:
that holy wrist,
that ankle,
that chain.

Oh God,
although I am very sad,
could you please
let these four nuns
loosen from their leather boots

and their wooden chairs
to rise out
over this greasy deck,
out over this iron rail,
nodding their pink heads to one side,
flying four abreast
in the old-fashioned side stroke;
each mouth open and round,
breathing together
as fish do,
singing without sound.

Dearest,
see how my dark girls sally forth,
over the passing lighthouse of Plum Gut,
its shell as rusty
as a camp dish,
as fragile as a pagoda
on a stone;
out over the little lighthouse
that warns me of drowning winds
that rub over its blind bottom
and its blue cover;
winds that will take the toes
and the ears of the rider
or the lover.

There go my dark girls,
their dresses puff
in the leeward air.
Oh, they are lighter than flying dogs
or the breath of dolphins;
each mouth opens gratefully,
wider than a milk cup.

My dark girls sing for this.
They are going up.
See them rise
on black wings, drinking
the sky, without smiles
or hands
or shoes.
They call back to us
from the gauzy edge of paradise,
good news, good news.

FROM THE GARDEN

Come, my beloved,
consider the lilies.
We are of little faith.
We talk too much.
Put your mouthful of words away
and come with me to watch
the lilies open in such a field,
growing there like yachts,
slowly steering their petals
without nurses or clocks.
Let us consider the view:
a house where white clouds
decorate the muddy halls.
Oh, put away your good words
and your bad words. Spit out
your words like stones!
Come here! Come here!
Come eat my pleasant fruits.

LOVE SONG FOR K. OWYNE

When I lay down for death
my love came down to Craigy's Sea
and fished me from the snakes.
He let me use his breath.
He pushed away the mud and lay with me.
And lay with me in sin.

I washed lobster and stale gin
off your shirt. We lived in sin
in too many rooms. Now you live in Ohio
among the hard fields of potatoes,
the gray sticks and the bad breath
of the coal mines. Oh Love, you know
how the waves came running up the stairs
for me, just as the nervous trees
in Birnam wood crept up upon Macbeth
to catch his charmed head turning and well aware.
I was not safe. I heard the army in the sea
move in, again and again, against me.

Shuffled between caring and disgrace
I took up all our closet space.
What luxury we first checked into,
to growl like lawyers until I threw
my diamonds and cash upon the floor.
You'd come for death. I couldn't suit you
until the sun came up as mild as a pear
and the room, having hurt us, was ours.
You sang me a song about bones, dinosaur
bones. Though I was bony you found me fair.
In the bay, the imported swans drank for hours
like pale acrobats or gently drunken flowers.

FLIGHT

Thinking that I would find you,
thinking I would make the plane
that goes hourly out of Boston
I drove into the city.
Thinking that on such a night
every thirsty man would have his jug
and that the Negro women would lie down
on pale sheets and even the river into town
would stretch out naturally on its couch,
I drove into the city.
On such a night, at the end of the river,
the airport would sputter with planes
like ticker-tape.

Foot on the gas
I sang aloud to the front seat,
to the clumps of women in cotton dresses,
to the patches of fog crusting the banks,
and to the sailboats swinging on their expensive hooks.
There was rose and violet on the river
as I drove through the mist into the city.
I was full of letters I hadn't sent you,
a red coat over my shoulders
and new white gloves in my lap.

I dropped through the city
as the river does,
rumbling over and under, as indicated,
past the miles of spotted windows
minding their own business,
through the Sumner Tunnel,
trunk by trunk through its sulphurous walls,
tile by tile like a men's urinal,
slipping through
like somebody else's package.

Parked, at last,
on a dime that would never last,
I ran through the airport.
Wild for love, I ran through the airport,
stockings and skirts and dollars.
The night clerk yawned all night at the public,
his mind on tomorrow's wages.
All flights were grounded.
The planes sat and the gulls sat,
heavy and rigid in a pool of glue.

Knowing I would never find you
I drove out of the city.
At the airport one thousand cripples
sat nursing a sore foot.
There was more fog
and the rain came down when it thought of it.
I drove past the eye and ear infirmaries,
past the office buildings lined up like dentures,
and along Storrow Drive the streetlights
sucked in all the insects who
had nowhere else to go.

FOR ELEANOR BOYLAN TALKING WITH GOD

God has a brown voice,
as soft and full as beer.
Eleanor, who is more beautiful than my mother,
is standing in her kitchen talking
and I am breathing in my cigarettes like poison.
She stands in her lemon-colored sun dress
motioning to God with her wet hands
glossy from the washing of egg plates.
She tells him! She tells him like a drunk
who doesn't need to see to talk.

It's casual but friendly.
God is as close as the ceiling.

Though no one can ever know,
I don't think he has a face.
He had a face when I was six and a half.
Now he is large, covering up the sky
like a great resting jellyfish.
When I was eight I thought the dead people
stayed up there like blimps.
Now my chair is as hard as a scarecrow
and outside the summer flies sing like a choir.
Eleanor, before he leaves tell him . . .
Oh Eleanor, Eleanor,
tell him before death uses you up.

THE BLACK ART

A woman who writes feels too much,
those trances and portents!
As if cycles and children and islands
weren't enough; as if mourners and gossips
and vegetables were never enough.
She thinks she can warn the stars.
A writer is essentially a spy.
Dear love, I am that girl.

A man who writes knows too much,
such spells and fetiches!
As if erections and congresses and products
weren't enough; as if machines and galleons
and wars were never enough.
With used furniture he makes a tree.
A writer is essentially a crook.
Dear love, you are that man.

Never loving ourselves,
hating even our shoes and our hats,
we love each other, *precious, precious.*
Our hands are light blue and gentle.
Our eyes are full of terrible confessions.
But when we marry,
the children leave in disgust.
There is too much food and no one left over
to eat up all the weird abundance.

LETTER WRITTEN DURING A JANUARY NORTHEASTER

Monday

Dearest,
It is snowing, grotesquely snowing,
upon the small faces of the dead.
Those dear loudmouths, gone for over a year,
buried side by side
like little wrens.
But why should I complain?
The dead turn over casually,
thinking . . .
              Good! No visitors today.
My window, which is not a grave,
is dark with my fierce concentration
and too much snowing
and too much silence.
The snow has quietness in it; no songs,
no smells, no shouts or traffic.
When I speak
my own voice shocks me.

Tuesday

I have invented a lie.
There is no other day but Monday.
It seemed reasonable to pretend
that I could change the day
like a pair of socks.
To tell the truth
days are all the same size
and words aren't much company.
If I were sick, I'd be a child,
tucked in under the woolens, sipping my broth.
As it is,
the days are not worth grabbing or lying about.
Nevertheless, you are the only one
that I can bother with this matter.

Monday

It would be pleasant to be drunk:
faithless to my tongue and hands,
giving up the boundaries
for the heroic gin.
Dead drunk
is the term I think of,
insensible,
neither cool nor warm,
without a head or a foot.
To be drunk is to be intimate with a fool.
I will try it shortly.

Monday

Just yesterday,
twenty-eight men aboard a damaged radar tower
foundered down seventy miles off the coast.
Immediately their hearts slammed shut.

The storm would not cough them up.
Today they are whispering over Sonar.
Small voice,
what do you say?
Aside from the going down, the awful wrench,
the pulleys and hooks and the black tongue . . .
What are your headquarters?
Are they kind?

Monday

It must be Friday by now.
I admit I have been lying.
Days don't freeze
and to say that the snow has quietness in it
is to ignore the possibilities of the word.
Only the tree has quietness in it;
quiet as the crucifix,
pounded out years ago
like a handmade shoe.
Someone once
told an elephant to stand still.
That's why trees remain quiet all winter.
They're not going anywhere.

Monday

Dearest,
where are your letters?
The mailman is an impostor.
He is actually my grandfather.
He floats far off in the storm
with his nicotine mustache and a bagful of nickels.
His legs stumble through
baskets of eyelashes.
Like all the dead
he picks up his disguise,

shakes it off and slowly pulls down the shade,
fading out like an old movie.
Now he is gone
as you are gone.
But he belongs to me like lost baggage.

Live or Die

(1966)

For Max and Fred . . .
who made me an honorary landsman.

With one long breath, caught and held
in his chest, he fought his sadness over
his solitary life. Don't cry, you idiot!
Live or die, but don't poison everything . . .

from an early draft of Herzog
by Saul Bellow

AUTHOR'S NOTE

To begin with, I have placed these poems (1962–1966)
in the order in which they were written with all due apol-
ogies for the fact that they read like a fever chart for a
bad case of melancholy. But I thought the order of their
creation might be of interest to some readers, and, as
André Gide wrote in his journal, "Despite every resolution
of optimism, melancholy occasionally wins out: man has
decidedly botched up the planet."

AND ONE FOR MY DAME

A born salesman,
my father made all his dough
by selling wool to Fieldcrest, Woolrich and Faribo.

A born talker,
he could sell one hundred wet-down bales
of that white stuff. He could clock the miles and sales

and make it pay.
At home each sentence he would utter
had first pleased the buyer who'd paid him off in butter.

Each word
had been tried over and over, at any rate,
on the man who was sold by the man who filled my plate.

My father hovered
over the Yorkshire pudding and the beef:
a peddler, a hawker, a merchant and an Indian chief.

Roosevelt! Willkie! and war!
How suddenly gauche I was
with my old-maid heart and my funny teenage applause.

Each night at home
my father was in love with maps
while the radio fought its battles with Nazis and Japs.

Except when he hid
in his bedroom on a three-day drunk,
he typed out complex itineraries, packed his trunk,

his matched luggage
and pocketed a confirmed reservation,
his heart already pushing over the red routes of the nation.

I sit at my desk
each night with no place to go,
opening the wrinkled maps of Milwaukee and Buffalo,

the whole U.S.,
its cemeteries, its arbitrary time zones,
through routes like small veins, capitals like small stones.

He died on the road,
his heart pushed from neck to back,
his white hanky signaling from the window of the Cadillac.

My husband,
as blue-eyed as a picture book, sells wool:
boxes of card waste, laps and rovings he can pull

to the thread
and say *Leicester, Rambouillet, Merino,*
a half-blood, it's greasy and thick, yellow as old snow.

And when you drive off, my darling,
Yes, sir! Yes, sir! It's one for my dame,
your sample cases branded with my father's name,

your itinerary open,
its tolls ticking and greedy,
its highways built up like new loves, raw and speedy.

January 25, 1962

THE SUN

I have heard of fish
coming up for the sun
who stayed forever,
shoulder to shoulder,

avenues of fish that never got back,
all their proud spots and solitudes
sucked out of them.

I think of flies
who come from their foul caves
out into the arena.
They are transparent at first.
Then they are blue with copper wings.
They glitter on the foreheads of men.
Neither bird nor acrobat
they will dry out like small black shoes.

I am an identical being.
Diseased by the cold and the smell of the house
I undress under the burning magnifying glass.
My skin flattens out like sea water.
O yellow eye,
let me be sick with your heat,
let me be feverish and frowning.
Now I am utterly given.
I am your daughter, your sweet-meat,
your priest, your mouth and your bird
and I will tell them all stories of you
until I am laid away forever,
a thin gray banner.

May 1962

FLEE ON YOUR DONKEY

Ma faim, Anne, Anne,
Fuis sur ton âne . . . Rimbaud

Because there was no other place
to flee to,
I came back to the scene of the disordered senses,
came back last night at midnight,
arriving in the thick June night

97

without luggage or defenses,
giving up my car keys and my cash,
keeping only a pack of Salem cigarettes
the way a child holds on to a toy.
I signed myself in where a stranger
puts the inked-in X's —
for this is a mental hospital,
not a child's game.

Today an interne knocks my knees,
testing for reflexes.
Once I would have winked and begged for dope.
Today I am terribly patient.
Today crows play black-jack
on the stethoscope.

Everyone has left me
except my muse,
that good nurse.
She stays in my hand,
a mild white mouse.

The curtains, lazy and delicate,
billow and flutter and drop
like the Victorian skirts
of my two maiden aunts
who kept an antique shop.

Hornets have been sent.
They cluster like floral arrangements on the screen.
Hornets, dragging their thin stingers,
hover outside, all knowing,
hissing: *the hornet knows.*
I heard it as a child
but what was it that he meant?
The hornet knows!
What happened to Jack and Doc and Reggy?

Who remembers what lurks in the heart of man?
What did The Green Hornet mean, *he knows?*
Or have I got it wrong?
Is it The Shadow who had seen
me from my bedside radio?

Now it's *Dinn, Dinn, Dinn!*
while the ladies in the next room argue
and pick their teeth.
Upstairs a girl curls like a snail;
in another room someone tries to eat a shoe;
meanwhile an adolescent pads up and down
the hall in his white tennis socks.
A new doctor makes rounds
advertising tranquilizers, insulin, or shock
to the uninitiated.

Six years of such small preoccupations!
Six years of shuttling in and out of this place!
O my hunger! My hunger!
I could have gone around the world twice
or had new children — all boys.
It was a long trip with little days in it
and no new places.

In here,
it's the same old crowd,
the same ruined scene.
The alcoholic arrives with his golf clubs.
The suicide arrives with extra pills sewn
into the lining of her dress.
The permanent guests have done nothing new.
Their faces are still small
like babies with jaundice.

Meanwhile,
they carried out my mother,

wrapped like somebody's doll, in sheets,
bandaged her jaw and stuffed up her holes.
My father, too. He went out on the rotten blood
he used up on other women in the Middle West.
He went out, a cured old alcoholic
on crooked feet and useless hands.
He went out calling for his father
who died all by himself long ago —
that fat banker who got locked up,
his genes suspended like dollars,
wrapped up in his secret,
tied up securely in a straitjacket.

But you, my doctor, my enthusiast,
were better than Christ;
you promised me another world
to tell me who
I was.

I spent most of my time,
a stranger,
damned and in trance — that little hut,
that naked blue-veined place,
my eyes shut on the confusing office,
eyes circling into my childhood,
eyes newly cut.
Years of hints
strung out — a serialized case history —
thirty-three years of the same dull incest
that sustained us both.
You, my bachelor analyst,
who sat on Marlborough Street,
sharing your office with your mother
and giving up cigarettes each New Year,
were the new God,
the manager of the Gideon Bible.

I was your third-grader
with a blue star on my forehead.
In trance I could be any age,
voice, gesture — all turned backward
like a drugstore clock.
Awake, I memorized dreams.
Dreams came into the ring
like third string fighters,
each one a bad bet
who might win
because there was no other.

I stared at them,
concentrating on the abyss
the way one looks down into a rock quarry,
uncountable miles down,
my hands swinging down like hooks
to pull dreams up out of their cage.
O my hunger! My hunger!

Once,
outside your office,
I collapsed in the old-fashioned swoon
between the illegally parked cars.
I threw myself down,
pretending dead for eight hours.
I thought I had died
into a snowstorm.
Above my head
chains cracked along like teeth
digging their way through the snowy street.
I lay there
like an overcoat
that someone had thrown away.
You carried me back in,
awkwardly, tenderly,
with the help of the red-haired secretary

who was built like a lifeguard.
My shoes,
I remember,
were lost in the snowbank
as if I planned never to walk again.

That was the winter
that my mother died,
half mad on morphine,
blown up, at last,
like a pregnant pig.
I was her dreamy evil eye.
In fact,
I carried a knife in my pocketbook —
my husband's good L. L. Bean hunting knife.
I wasn't sure if I should slash a tire
or scrape the guts out of some dream.

You taught me
to believe in dreams;
thus I was the dredger.
I held them like an old woman with arthritic fingers,
carefully straining the water out —
sweet dark playthings,
and above all, mysterious
until they grew mournful and weak.
O my hunger! My hunger!
I was the one
who opened the warm eyelid
like a surgeon
and brought forth young girls
to grunt like fish.

I told you,
I said —
but I was lying —

that the knife was for my mother . . .
and then I delivered her.

The curtains flutter out
and slump against the bars.
They are my two thin ladies
named Blanche and Rose.
The grounds outside
are pruned like an estate at Newport.
Far off, in the field,
something yellow grows.

Was it last month or last year
that the ambulance ran like a hearse
with its siren blowing on suicide —
Dinn, dinn, dinn! —
a noon whistle that kept insisting on life
all the way through the traffic lights?

I have come back
but disorder is not what it was.
I have lost the trick of it!
The innocence of it!
That fellow-patient in his stovepipe hat
with his fiery joke, his manic smile —
even he seems blurred, small and pale.
I have come back,
recommitted,
fastened to the wall like a bathroom plunger,
held like a prisoner
who was so poor
he fell in love with jail.

I stand at this old window
complaining of the soup,

examining the grounds,
allowing myself the wasted life.
Soon I will raise my face for a white flag,
and when God enters the fort,
I won't spit or gag on his finger.
I will eat it like a white flower.
Is this the old trick, the wasting away,
the skull that waits for its dose
of electric power?

This is madness
but a kind of hunger.
What good are my questions
in this hierarchy of death
where the earth and the stones go
Dinn! Dinn! Dinn!
It is hardly a feast.
It is my stomach that makes me suffer.

Turn, my hungers!
For once make a deliberate decision.
There are brains that rot here
like black bananas.
Hearts have grown as flat as dinner plates.
Anne, Anne,
flee on your donkey,
flee this sad hotel,
ride out on some hairy beast,
gallop backward pressing
your buttocks to his withers,
sit to his clumsy gait somehow.
Ride out
any old way you please!
In this place everyone talks to his own mouth.
That's what it means to be crazy.

Those I loved best died of it —
the fool's disease.

June 1962

THREE GREEN WINDOWS

Half awake in my Sunday nap
I see three green windows
in three different lights —
one west, one south, one east.
I have forgotten that old friends are dying.
I have forgotten that I grow middle-aged.
At each window such rustlings!
The trees persist, yeasty and sensuous,
as thick as saints.
I see three wet gargoyles covered with birds.
Their skins shine in the sun like leather.

I'm on my bed as light as a sponge.
Soon it will be summer.
She is my mother.
She will tell me a story and keep me asleep
against her plump and fruity skin.
I see leaves —
leaves that are washed and innocent,
leaves that never knew a cellar,
born in their own green blood
like the hands of mermaids.

I do not think of the rusty wagon on the walk.
I pay no attention to the red squirrels
that leap like machines beside the house.
I do not remember the real trunks of the trees
that stand beneath the windows

as bulky as artichokes.
I turn like a giant,
secretly watching, secretly knowing,
secretly naming each elegant sea.

I have misplaced the Van Allen belt,
the sewers and the drainage,
the urban renewal and the suburban centers.
I have forgotten the names of the literary critics.
I know what I know.
I am the child I was,
living the life that was mine.
I am young and half asleep.
It is a time of water, a time of trees.

June 1962

SOMEWHERE IN AFRICA

Must you leave, John Holmes, with the prayers and psalms
you never said, said over you? Death with no rage
to weigh you down? Praised by the mild God, his arm
over the pulpit, leaving you timid, with no real age,

whitewashed by belief, as dull as the windy preacher!
Dead of a dark thing, John Holmes, you've been lost
in the college chapel, mourned as father and teacher,
mourned with piety and grace under the University Cross.

Your last book unsung, your last hard words unknown,
abandoned by science, cancer blossomed in your throat,
rooted like bougainvillea into your gray backbone,
ruptured your pores until you wore it like a coat.

The thick petals, the exotic reds, the purples and whites
covered up your nakedness and bore you up with all

106

their blind power. I think of your last June nights
in Boston, your body swollen but light, your eyes small

as you let the nurses carry you into a strange land.
. . . If this is death and God is necessary let him be hidden
from the missionary, the well-wisher and the glad hand.
Let God be some tribal female who is known but forbidden.

Let there be this God who is a woman who will place you
upon her shallow boat, who is a woman naked to the waist,
moist with palm oil and sweat, a woman of some virtue
and wild breasts, her limbs excellent, unbruised and chaste.

Let her take you. She will put twelve strong men at the oars
for you are stronger than mahogany and your bones fill
the boat high as with fruit and bark from the interior.
She will have you now, you whom the funeral cannot kill.

John Holmes, cut from a single tree, lie heavy in her hold
and go down that river with the ivory, the copra and the gold.

July 1, 1962

IMITATIONS OF DROWNING

Fear
of drowning,
fear of being that alone,
kept me busy making a deal
as if I could buy
my way out of it
and it worked for two years
and all of July.

This August I began to dream of drowning. The dying
went on and on in water as white and clear

as the gin I drink each day at half-past five.
Going down for the last time, the last breath lying,
I grapple with eels like ropes — it's ether, it's queer
and then, at last, it's done. Now the scavengers arrive,
the hard crawlers who come to clean up the ocean floor.
And death, that old butcher, will bother me no more.

I
had never
had this dream before
except twice when my parents
clung to rafts
and sat together for death,
frozen
like lewd photographs.

Who listens to dreams? Only symbols for something —
like money for the analyst or your mother's wig,
the arm I almost lost in the washroom wringer,
following fear to its core, tugging the old string.
But real drowning is for someone else. It's too big
to put in your mouth on purpose, it puts hot stingers
in your tongue and vomit in your nose as your lungs break.
Tossed like a wet dog by that juggler, you die awake.

Fear,
a motor,
pumps me around and around
until I fade slowly
and the crowd laughs.
I fade out, an old bicycle rider
whose odds are measured
in actuary graphs.

This weekend the papers were black with the new highway
fatalities and in Boston the strangler found another victim

and we were all in Truro drinking beer and writing checks.
The others rode the surf, commanding rafts like sleighs.
I swam — but the tide came in like ten thousand orgasms.
I swam — but the waves were higher than horses' necks.
I was shut up in that closet, until, biting the door,
they dragged me out, dribbling urine on the gritty shore.

Breathe!
And you'll know . . .
an ant in a pot of chocolate,
it boils
and surrounds you.
There is no news in fear
but in the end it's fear
that drowns you.

September 1962

MOTHER AND JACK AND THE RAIN

I have a room of my own.
Rain drops onto it. Rain drops down like worms
from the trees onto my frontal bone.
Haunted, always haunted by rain, the room affirms
the words that I will make alone.
I come like the blind feeling for shelves,
feeling for wood as hard as an apple,
fingering the pen lightly, my blade.
With this pen I take in hand my selves
and with these dead disciples I will grapple.
Though rain curses the window
let the poem be made.

Rain is a finger on my eyeball.
Rain drills in with its old unnecessary stories . . .

I went to bed like a horse to its stall.
On my damp summer bed I cradled my salty knees
and heard father kiss me through the wall
and heard mother's heart pump like the tides.
The fog horn flattened the sea into leather.
I made no voyages, I owned no passport.
I was the daughter. Whiskey fortified
my father in the next room. He outlasted the weather,
counted his booty and brought
his ship into port.

Rain, rain, at sixteen
where I lay all night with Jack beside a tiny lake
and did nothing at all, lay as straight as a bean.
We played bridge and beer games for their own sake,
filled up the lamp with kerosene,
brushed our teeth, made sandwiches and tea
and lay down on the cabin bed to sleep.
I lay, a blind lake, feigning sleep while Jack
pulled back the wooly covers to see
my body, that invisible body that girls keep.
All that sweet night we rode out
the storm back to back.

Now Jack says the Mass
and mother died using her own bones for crutches.
There is rain on the wood, rain on the glass
and I'm in a room of my own. I think too much.
Fish swim from the eyes of God. Let them pass.
Mother and Jack fill up heaven; they endorse
my womanhood. Near land my ship comes about.
I come to this land to ride my horse,
to try my own guitar, to copy out
their two separate names like sunflowers, to conjure

up my daily bread, to endure,
somehow to endure.

October 1962

CONSORTING WITH ANGELS

.I was tired of being a woman,
 tired of the spoons and the pots,
 tired of my mouth and my breasts,
 tired of the cosmetics and the silks.
There were still men who sat at my table,
circled around the bowl I offered up.
The bowl was filled with purple grapes
and the flies hovered in for the scent
and even my father came with his white bone.
But I was tired of the gender of things.

Last night I had a dream
and I said to it . . .
"You are the answer.
You will outlive my husband and my father."
In that dream there was a city made of chains
where Joan was put to death in man's clothes
and the nature of the angels went unexplained,
no two made in the same species,
one with a nose, one with an ear in its hand,
one chewing a star and recording its orbit,
each one like a poem obeying itself,
performing God's functions,
a people apart.

"You are the answer,"
I said, and entered,
lying down on the gates of the city.

111

Then the chains were fastened around me
and I lost my common gender and my final aspect.
Adam was on the left of me
and Eve was on the right of me,
both thoroughly inconsistent with the world of reason.
We wove our arms together
and rode under the sun.
I was not a woman anymore,
not one thing or the other.

O daughters of Jerusalem,
the king has brought me into his chamber.
I am black and I am beautiful.
I've been opened and undressed.
I have no arms or legs.
I'm all one skin like a fish.
I'm no more a woman
than Christ was a man.

February 1963

THE LEGEND OF THE ONE-EYED MAN

Like Oedipus I am losing my sight.
Like Judas I have done my wrong.
Their punishment is over;
the shame and disgrace of it
are all used up.
But as for me,
look into my face
and you will know that crimes dropped upon me
as from a high building
and although I cannot speak of them
or explain the degrading details
I have remembered much
about Judas —

about Judas, the old and the famous —
that you overlooked.

The story of his life
is the story of mine.
I have one glass eye.
My nerves push against its painted surface
but the other one
waiting for judgment
continues to see . . .

Of course
the New Testament is very small.
Its mouth opens four times —
as out-of-date as a prehistoric monster,
yet somehow man-made,
held together by pullies
like the stone jaw of a back-hoe.
It gouges out the Judaic ground,
taking its own backyard
like a virgin daughter.

And furthermore how did Judas come into it —
that Judas Iscariot,
belonging to the tribe of Reuben?
He should have tried to lift him up there!
His neck like an iron pole,
hard as Newcastle,
his heart as stiff as beeswax,
his legs swollen and unmarked,
his other limbs still growing.
All of it heavy!
That dead weight that would have been his fault.
He should have known!

In the first place who builds up such ugliness?
I think of this man saying . . .

Look! Here's the price to do it
plus the cost of the raw materials
and if it took him three or four days
to do it, then, they'd understand.
They figured the boards in excess
of three hundred pounds.
They figured it weighed enough
to support a man. They said,
fifteen stone is the approximate weight
of a thief.

Its ugliness is a matter of custom.
If there was a mistake made
then the Crucifix was constructed wrong . . .
not from the quality of the pine,
not from hanging a mirror,
not from dropping the studding or the drill
but from having an inspiration.
But Judas was not a genius
or under the auspices of an inspiration.

I don't know whether it was gold or silver.
I don't know why he betrayed him
other than his motives,
other than the avaricious and dishonest man.
And then there were the forbidden crimes,
those that were expressly foretold,
and then overlooked
and then forgotten
except by me . . .
Judas had a mother
just as I had a mother.
Oh! Honor and relish the facts!
Do not think of the intense sensation
I have as I tell you this
but think only. . .

Judas had a mother.
His mother had a dream.
Because of this dream
he was altogether managed by fate
and thus he raped her.
As a crime we hear little of this.
Also he sold his God.

March 1963

LOVE SONG

I was
the girl of the chain letter,
the girl full of talk of coffins and keyholes,
the one of the telephone bills,
the wrinkled photo and the lost connections,
the one who kept saying —
Listen! Listen!
We must never! We must never!
and all those things . . .

the one
with her eyes half under her coat,
with her large gun-metal blue eyes,
with the thin vein at the bend of her neck
that hummed like a tuning fork,
with her shoulders as bare as a building,
with her thin foot and her thin toes,
with an old red hook in her mouth,
the mouth that kept bleeding
into the terrible fields of her soul . . .

the one
who kept dropping off to sleep,

as old as a stone she was,
each hand like a piece of cement,
for hours and hours
and then she'd wake,
after the small death,
and then she'd be as soft as,
as delicate as . . .

as soft and delicate as
an excess of light,
with nothing dangerous at all,
like a beggar who eats
or a mouse on a rooftop
with no trap doors,
with nothing more honest
than your hand in her hand —
with nobody, nobody but you!
and all those things.
nobody, nobody but you!
Oh! There is no translating
that ocean,
that music,
that theater,
that field of ponies.

April 19, 1963

MAN AND WIFE

To speke of wo
    that is in mariage . . .

We are not lovers.
We do not even know each other.
We look alike

but we have nothing to say.
We are like pigeons . . .

that pair who came to the suburbs
by mistake,
forsaking Boston where they bumped
their small heads against a blind wall,
having worn out the fruit stalls in the North End,
the amethyst windows of Louisburg Square,
the seats on the Common
And the traffic that kept stamping
and stamping.

Now there is green rain for everyone
as common as eyewash.
Now they are together
like strangers in a two-seater outhouse,
eating and squatting together.
They have teeth and knees
but they do not speak.
A soldier is forced to stay with a soldier
because they share the same dirt
and the same blows.

They are exiles
soiled by the same sweat and the drunkard's dream.
As it is they can only hang on,
their red claws wound like bracelets
around the same limb.
Even their song is not a sure thing.
It is not a language;
it is a kind of breathing.
They are two asthmatics
whose breath sobs in and out
through a small fuzzy pipe.

Like them
we neither talk nor clear our throats.
Oh darling,
we gasp in unison beside our window pane,
drunk on the drunkard's dream.
Like them
we can only hang on.

But they would pierce our heart
if they could only fly the distance.

May 1963

THOSE TIMES . . .

At six
I lived in a graveyard full of dolls,
avoiding myself,
my body, the suspect
in its grotesque house.
I was locked in my room all day behind a gate,
a prison cell.
I was the exile
who sat all day in a knot.

I will speak of the little childhood cruelties,
being a third child,
the last given
and the last taken —
of the nightly humiliations when Mother undressed me,
of the life of the daytime, locked in my room —
being the unwanted, the mistake
that Mother used to keep Father
from his divorce.
Divorce!
The romantic's friend,

romantics who fly into maps
of other countries,
hips and noses and mountains,
into Asia or the Black Forest,
or caught by 1928,
the year of the *me*,
by mistake,
not for divorce
but instead.

The me who refused to suck on breasts
she couldn't please,
the me whose body grew unsurely,
the me who stepped on the noses of dolls
she couldn't break.
I think of the dolls,
so well made,
so perfectly put together
as I pressed them against me,
kissing their little imaginary mouths.
I remember their smooth skin,
those newly delivered,
the pink skin and the serious China-blue eyes.
They came from a mysterious country
without the pang of birth,
born quietly and well.
When I wanted to visit,
the closet is where I rehearsed my life,
all day among shoes,
away from the glare of the bulb in the ceiling,
away from the bed and the heavy table
and the same terrible rose repeating on the walls.

I did not question it.
I hid in the closet as one hides in a tree.

I grew into it like a root
and yet I planned such plans of flight,
believing I would take my body into the sky,
dragging it with me like a large bed.
And although I was unskilled
I was sure to get there or at least
to move up like an elevator.
With such dreams,
storing their energy like a bull,
I planned my growth and my womanhood
as one choreographs a dance.

I knew that if I waited among shoes
I was sure to outgrow them,
the heavy oxfords, the thick execution reds,
shoes that lay together like partners,
the sneakers thick with Griffin eyewash
and then the dresses swinging above me,
always above me, empty and sensible
with sashes and puffs,
with collars and two-inch hems
and evil fortunes in their belts.

I sat all day
stuffing my heart into a shoe box,
avoiding the precious window
as if it were an ugly eye
through which birds coughed,
chained to the heaving trees;
avoiding the wallpaper of the room
where tongues bloomed over and over,
bursting from lips like sea flowers —
and in this way I waited out the day
until my mother,
the large one,
came to force me to undress.

I lay there silently,
hoarding my small dignity.
I did not ask about the gate or the closet.
I did not question the bedtime ritual
where, on the cold bathroom tiles,
I was spread out daily
and examined for flaws.

I did not know
that my bones,
those solids, those pieces of sculpture
would not splinter.

I did not know the woman I would be
nor that blood would bloom in me
each month like an exotic flower,
nor that children,
two monuments,
would break from between my legs
two cramped girls breathing carelessly,
each asleep in her tiny beauty.
I did not know that my life, in the end,
would run over my mother's like a truck
and all that would remain
from the year I was six
was a small hole in my heart, a deaf spot,
so that I might hear
the unsaid more clearly.

June 1963

TWO SONS

Where and to whom
you are married I can only guess
in my piecemeal fashion. I grow old on my bitterness.

On the unique occasion
of your two sudden wedding days
I open some cheap wine, a tin of lobster and mayonnaise.

I sit in an old lady's room
where families used to feast
where the wind blows in like soot from north-northeast.

Both of you monopolized
with no real forwarding address
except for two silly postcards you bothered to send home,

one of them written in grease
as you undid her dress
in Mexico, the other airmailed to Boston from Rome

just before the small ceremony
at the American Church.
Both of you made of my cooking, those suppers of starch

and beef, and with my library,
my medicine, my bath water,
both sinking into small brown pools like muddy otters!

You make a toast for tomorrow
and smash the cup,
letting your false women lap the dish I had to fatten up.

When you come back I'll buy
a wig of yellow hair;
I'll squat in a new red dress; I'll be playing solitaire

on the kitchen floor.
Yes . . . I'll gather myself in
like cut flowers and ask you how you are and where you've been.

July 22, 1963

TO LOSE THE EARTH

To lose the earth you know, for greater knowing; to lose
the life you have, for greater life; to leave the friends
you loved, for greater loving; to find a land more kind
than home, more large than earth . . . Thomas Wolfe

The wreckage of Europe or the birth of Africa,
the old palaces, the wallets of the tourists,
the Common Market or the smart cafés,
the boulevards in the graceful evening,
the cliff-hangers, the scientists,
and the little shops raising their prices
mean nothing to me.
Each day I think only
of this place, only this place
where the musician works.
He plays his flute in a cave
that a pharaoh built by the sea.
He is blowing on light,
each time for the first time.
His fingers cover the mouths of all the sopranos,
each a princess in an exact position.

If you can find it,
the music takes place in a grotto,
a great hole in the earth.
You must wait outside the mouth hole for hours
while the Egyptian boatman howls the password
and the sea keeps booming and booming.
At that point you will be in a state of terror,
moaning, "How can we?"
for you will see only the unreliable chain
that is meant to drag you in.
It is called *Waiting on the Edge.*

At the moment of entry
your head will be below the gunwales,

123

your shoulders will rock and struggle
as you ship hogsheads of water.
"Here?" you will ask,
looking around for your camera and shoes
and then you will not need to ask
for the flutist is playing.
This is the music that you waited for
in the great concert halls,
season after season,
and never found.
It is called *Being Inside*.

It is close to being dead.
Although you had expected pain
there will be no pain,
only that piper, that midwife
with his unforgettable woman's face.
The left side of the flute cannot be seen.
It grows into the wall like something human.
It is driven into the wall like a pipe
that extends, some say,
into the sun.
The flutist sucks and blows.
He is both a woman
and a man,
abandoned to that great force
and spilling it back out.
He is the undefiled,
the eternal listener
who has cried back into the earth.

In the distance other travelers,
others like you who came out of simple curiosity,
remain for generations.
From all sides of the cave
you will notice the protruding fingernails

of the dead.
From their coffins
as stale as cheap cigars,
through the tons of suffocating dirt,
they heard
and dug down immediately and persistently.
They scratched down for centuries
in order to enter.

At the far right,
rising from an underground sea,
his toes curled on a black wave,
stands the dwarf;
his instrument is an extension of his tongue.
He holds it fast
as if it would get away,
wet and cold and slippery as it is.
He is the other half.
The one you hadn't expected.
You will jump up and point at him
shouting, "It is you!"
but he will not listen.
He plays his own song, cursing the wind
with his enormous misshapen mouth.

And you, having heard,
you will never leave.
At the moment of entry
you were fed —
— and then you knew.

January 1963

SYLVIA'S DEATH

for Sylvia Plath

O Sylvia, Sylvia,
with a dead box of stones and spoons,

with two children, two meteors
wandering loose in the tiny playroom,

with your mouth into the sheet,
into the roofbeam, into the dumb prayer,

(Sylvia, Sylvia,
where did you go
after you wrote me
from Devonshire
about raising potatoes
and keeping bees?)

what did you stand by,
just how did you lie down into?

Thief! —
how did you crawl into,

crawl down alone
into the death I wanted so badly and for so long,

the death we said we both outgrew,
the one we wore on our skinny breasts,

the one we talked of so often each time
we downed three extra dry martinis in Boston,

the death that talked of analysts and cures,
the death that talked like brides with plots,

the death we drank to,
the motives and then the quiet deed?

(In Boston
the dying
ride in cabs,
yes death again,
that ride home
with *our* boy.)

O Sylvia, I remember the sleepy drummer
who beat on our eyes with an old story,

how we wanted to let him come
like a sadist or a New York fairy

to do his job,
a necessity, a window in a wall or a crib,

and since that time he waited
under our heart, our cupboard,

and I see now that we store him up
year after year, old suicides

and I know at the news of your death,
a terrible taste for it, like salt.

(And me,
me too.
And now, Sylvia,
you again
with death again,
that ride home
with *our* boy.)

And I say only
with my arms stretched out into that stone place,

what is your death
but an old belonging,

a mole that fell out
of one of your poems?

(O friend,
while the moon's bad,
and the king's gone,
and the queen's at her wit's end
the bar fly ought to sing!)

O tiny mother,
you too!
O funny duchess!
O blonde thing!

February 17, 1963

PROTESTANT EASTER
eight years old

When he was a little boy
Jesus was good all the time.
No wonder that he grew up to be such a big shot
who could forgive people so much.
When he died everyone was mean.
Later on he rose when no one else was looking.
Either he was hiding or else
he went up.
Maybe he was only hiding?
Maybe he could fly?

Yesterday I found a purple crocus
blowing its way out of the snow.

It was all alone.
It was getting its work done.
Maybe Jesus was only getting his work done
and letting God blow him off the Cross
and maybe he was afraid for a minute
so he hid under the big stones.
He was smart to go to sleep up there
even though his mother got so sad
and let them put him in a cave.
I sat in a tunnel when I was five.
That tunnel, my mother said,
went straight into the big river
and so I never went again.
Maybe Jesus knew my tunnel
and crawled right through to the river
so he could wash all the blood off.
Maybe he only meant to get clean
and then come back again?
Don't tell me that he went up in smoke
like Daddy's cigar!
He didn't blow out like a match!

It is special
being here at Easter
with the Cross they built like a capital T.
The ceiling is an upside-down rowboat.
I usually count its ribs.
Maybe he was drowning?
Or maybe we are all upside down?
I can see the face of a mouse inside
of all that stained-glass window.
Well, it could be a mouse!
Once I thought the Bunny Rabbit was special
and I hunted for eggs.
That's when I was seven.
I'm grownup now. Now it's really Jesus.

I just have to get Him straight.
And right now.

Who are we anyhow?
What do we belong to?
Are we a *we*?
I think that he rose
but I'm not quite sure
and they don't really say
singing their *Alleluia*
in the churchy way.
Jesus was on that Cross.
After that they pounded nails into his hands.
After that, well, after that,
everyone wore hats
and then there was a big stone rolled away
and then almost everyone —
the ones who sit up straight —
looked at the ceiling.

Alleluia they sing.
They don't know.
They don't care if he was hiding or flying.
Well, it doesn't matter how he got there.
It matters where he was going.
The important thing for me
is that I'm wearing white gloves.
I always sit straight.
I keep on looking at the ceiling.
And about Jesus,
they couldn't be sure of it,
not so sure of it anyhow,
so they decided to become Protestants.
Those are the people that sing

when they aren't quite
sure.

Spring 1963

FOR THE YEAR OF THE INSANE
a prayer

O Mary, fragile mother,
hear me, hear me now
although I do not know your words.
The black rosary with its silver Christ
lies unblessed in my hand
for I am the unbeliever.
Each bead is round and hard between my fingers,
a small black angel.
O Mary, permit me this grace,
this crossing over,
although I am ugly,
submerged in my own past
and my own madness.
Although there are chairs
I lie on the floor.
Only my hands are alive,
touching beads.
Word for word, I stumble.
A beginner, I feel your mouth touch mine.

I count beads as waves,
hammering in upon me.
I am ill at their numbers,
sick, sick in the summer heat
and the window above me
is my only listener, my awkward being.
She is a large taker, a soother.

The giver of breath
she murmurs,
exhaling her wide lung like an enormous fish.

Closer and closer
comes the hour of my death
as I rearrange my face, grow back,
grow undeveloped and straight-haired.
All this is death.
In the mind there is a thin alley called death
and I move through it as
through water.
My body is useless.
It lies, curled like a dog on the carpet.
It has given up.
There are no words here except the half-learned,
the *Hail Mary* and the *full of grace*.
Now I have entered the year without words.
I note the queer entrance and the exact voltage.
Without words they exist.
Without words one may touch bread
and be handed bread
and make no sound.

O Mary, tender physician,
come with powders and herbs
for I am in the center.
It is very small and the air is gray
as in a steam house.
I am handed wine as a child is handed milk.
It is presented in a delicate glass
with a round bowl and a thin lip.
The wine itself is pitch-colored, musty and secret.
The glass rises on its own toward my mouth
and I notice this and understand this
only because it has happened.

I have this fear of coughing
but I do not speak,
a fear of rain, a fear of the horseman
who comes riding into my mouth.
The glass tilts in on its own
and I am on fire.
I see two thin streaks burn down my chin.
I see myself as one would see another.
I have been cut in two.

O Mary, open your eyelids.
I am in the domain of silence,
the kingdom of the crazy and the sleeper.
There is blood here
and I have eaten it.
O mother of the womb,
did I come for blood alone?
O little mother,
I am in my own mind.
I am locked in the wrong house.

August 1963

CROSSING THE ATLANTIC

We sail out of season into an oyster-gray wind,
over a terrible hardness.
Where Dickens crossed with *mal de mer*
in twenty weeks or twenty days
I cross toward him in five.
Wrapped in robes —
not like Caesar but like liver with bacon —
I rest on the stern
burning my mouth with a wind-hot ash,
watching my ship

133

bypass the swells
as easily as an old woman reads a palm.
I think, as I look North, that a field of mules
lay down to die.

The ship is 27 hours out.
I have entered her.
She might be a whale,
sleeping 2000 and ship's company,
the last 40¢ martini
and steel staterooms where night goes on forever.
Being inside them is, I think,
the way one would dig into a planet
and forget the word *light*.
I have walked cities,
miles of mole alleys with carpets.
Inside I have been ten girls who speak French.
They languish everywhere like bedsheets.

Oh my Atlantic of the cracked shores,
those blemished gates of Rockport and Boothbay,
those harbor smells like the innards of animals!
Old childish Queen, where did you go,
you bayer at wharfs and Victorian houses?

I have read each page of my mother's voyage.
I have read each page of her mother's voyage.
I have learned their words as they learned Dickens'.
I have swallowed these words like bullets.
But I have forgotten the last guest — terror.
Unlike them, I cannot toss in the cabin
as in childbirth.
Now always leaving me in the West
is the wake,
a ragged bridal veil, unexplained,
seductive, always rushing down the stairs,
never detained, never enough.

The ship goes on
as though nothing else were happening.
Generation after generation,
I go her way.
She will run East, knot by knot, over an old bloodstream,
stripping it clear,
each hour ripping it, pounding, pounding,
forcing through as through a virgin.
Oh she is so quick!
This dead street never stops!

September 1963

WALKING IN PARIS

I come back to your youth, my Nana,
as if I might clean off
the mad woman you became,
withered and constipated,
howling into your own earphone.
I come, in middle age,
to find you at twenty in high hair and long Victorian skirts
trudging shanks' mare fifteen miles a day in Paris
because you could not afford a carriage.
I have walked sixteen miles today.
I have kept up.

I read your Paris letters of 1890.
Each night I take them to my thin bed
and learn them as an actress learns her lines.
"Dear homefolks" you wrote,
not knowing I would be your last home,
not knowing that I'd peel your life back to its start.
What is so real as walking your streets!
I too have the sore toe you tend with cotton.
In Paris 1890 was yesterday

135

and 1940 never happened —
the soiled uniform of the Nazi
has been unravelled and reknit and resold.
To be occupied or conquered is nothing —
to remain is all!

Having come this far
I will go farther.
You are my history (that stealer of children)
and I have entered you.
I have deserted my husband and my children,
the Negro issue, the late news and the hot baths.
My room in Paris, no more than a cell,
is crammed with 58 lbs. of books.
They are all that is American and forgotten.
I read your letters instead,
putting your words into my life.

Come, old woman,
we will be sisters!
We will price the menus in the small cafés, count francs,
observe the tower where Marie Antoinette awaited her beheading,
kneel by the rose window of Notre Dame,
and let cloudy weather bear us home early
to huddle by the weak stove in Madame's kitchen.
We will set out tomorrow in stout shoes
to buy a fur muff for our blue fingers.
I take your arms boldly,
each day a new excursion.
Come, my sister,
we are two virgins,
our lives once more perfected
and unused.

October 1963

MENSTRUATION AT FORTY

I was thinking of a son.
The womb is not a clock
nor a bell tolling,
but in the eleventh month of its life
I feel the November
of the body as well as of the calendar.
In two days it will be my birthday
and as always the earth is done with its harvest.
This time I hunt for death,
the night I lean toward,
the night I want.
Well then —
speak of it!
It was in the womb all along.

I was thinking of a son . . .
You! The never acquired,
the never seeded or unfastened,
you of the genitals I feared,
the stalk and the puppy's breath.
Will I give you my eyes or his?
Will you be the David or the Susan?
(Those two names I picked and listened for.)
Can you be the man your fathers are —
the leg muscles from Michelangelo,
hands from Yugoslavia,
somewhere the peasant, Slavic and determined,
somewhere the survivor, bulging with life —
and could it still be possible,
all this with Susan's eyes?

All this without you —
two days gone in blood.

I myself will die without baptism,
a third daughter they didn't bother.
My death will come on my name day.
What's wrong with the name day?
It's only an angel of the sun.
Woman,
weaving a web over your own,
a thin and tangled poison.
Scorpio,
bad spider —
die!

My death from the wrists,
two name tags,
blood worn like a corsage
to bloom
one on the left and one on the right —
It's a warm room,
the place of the blood.
Leave the door open on its hinges!

Two days for your death
and two days until mine.

Love! That red disease —
year after year, David, you would make me wild!
David! Susan! David! David!
full and disheveled, hissing into the night,
never growing old,
waiting always for you on the porch . . .
year after year,
my carrot, my cabbage,
I would have possessed you before all women,
calling your name,
calling you mine.

November 7, 1963

CHRISTMAS EVE

Oh sharp diamond, my mother!
I could not count the cost
of all your faces, your moods —
that present that I lost.
Sweet girl, my deathbed,
my jewel-fingered lady,
your portrait flickered all night
by the bulbs of the tree.

Your face as calm as the moon
over a mannered sea,
presided at the family reunion,
the twelve grandchildren
you used to wear on your wrist,
a three-months-old baby,
a fat check you never wrote,
the red-haired toddler who danced the twist,
your aging daughters, each one a wife,
each one talking to the family cook,
each one avoiding your portrait,
each one aping your life.

Later, after the party,
after the house went to bed,
I sat up drinking the Christmas brandy,
watching your picture,
letting the tree move in and out of focus.
The bulbs vibrated.
They were a halo over your forehead.
Then they were a beehive,
blue, yellow, green, red;
each with its own juice, each hot and alive
stinging your face. But you did not move.
I continued to watch, forcing myself,
waiting, inexhaustible, thirty-five.

I wanted your eyes, like the shadows
of two small birds, to change.
But they did not age.
The smile that gathered me in, all wit,
all charm, was invincible.
Hour after hour I looked at your face
but I could not pull the roots out of it.
Then I watched how the sun hit
your red sweater, your withered neck,
your badly painted flesh-pink skin.
You who led me by the nose,
I saw you as you were.
Then I thought of your body
as one thinks of murder . . .

Then I said Mary —
Mary, Mary, forgive me
and then I touched a present for the child,
the last I bred before your death;
and then I touched my breast
and then I touched the floor
and then my breast again as if,
somehow, it were one of yours.

December 24, 1963

KE 6–8018

Black lady,
two eyes,
low as tobacco, who inked you in?
The shoemaker could not do it,
nor the sculptor nor the cubist.
Trunk is what you are, with two washbowls.
You are a sweetener, a drawer of blood — that's all,

140

a hot voice, an imminence and then a death.
Why death? Death's in the goodbye.

My love,
when you leave in which crevice will you hide?
What signs will remain?
Black slime will not come of it,
nor backwash from the traveler.
You will rest
Like a drowned bat upon my shoulder.
In one hand I will have to hold that silence.
There will be no track anymore.
There will be only that peculiar waiting.
There will be nothing to pick up.
There will be nothing.

There will have been a house —
a house that I knew,
the center of it,
a tiny heart,
synthetic though it was
making that thin buzz-buzz
like a sly beetle.

Black lady,
what will I do
without your two flowers?
I have inhabited you, number by number.
I have pushed you in and out like a needle.
Funny digits, I have danced upon your trunk
and I have knelt on your torso.
With my words I have perjured my soul.
Take note — there will be an absence.
It will be a cancer, spreading like a white dog
who doubles back, not knowing his name.

Although I will inherit darkness
I will keep dialing left to right.
I will struggle like a surgeon.
I will call quickly for the glare of the moon.
I will even dial milk.
I will hold the thread that was fished through the ceiling
that leads to the roof, the pole, the grass,
that ends in the sea.

I will not wait at the rail
looking upon death,
that single stone.
I will call for the boy-child I never had.
I will call like the Jew at the gate.
I will dial the wound over and over
and you will not yield
and there will be nothing,
black lady, nothing,
although I will wait,
unleashed and unheard.

January 3, 1964

WANTING TO DIE

Since you ask, most days I cannot remember.
I walk in my clothing, unmarked by that voyage.
Then the almost unnameable lust returns.

Even then I have nothing against life.
I know well the grass blades you mention,
the furniture you have placed under the sun.

But suicides have a special language.
Like carpenters they want to know *which tools*.
They never ask *why build*.

Twice I have so simply declared myself,
have possessed the enemy, eaten the enemy,
have taken on his craft, his magic.

In this way, heavy and thoughtful,
warmer than oil or water,
I have rested, drooling at the mouth-hole.

I did not think of my body at needle point.
Even the cornea and the leftover urine were gone.
Suicides have already betrayed the body.

Still-born, they don't always die,
but dazzled, they can't forget a drug so sweet
that even children would look on and smile.

To thrust all that life under your tongue! —
that, all by itself, becomes a passion.
Death's a sad bone; bruised, you'd say,

and yet she waits for me, year after year,
to so delicately undo an old wound,
to empty my breath from its bad prison.

Balanced there, suicides sometimes meet,
raging at the fruit, a pumped-up moon,
leaving the bread they mistook for a kiss,

leaving the page of the book carelessly open,
something unsaid, the phone off the hook
and the love, whatever it was, an infection.

February 3, 1964

THE WEDDING NIGHT

There was this time in Boston
before spring was ready — a short celebration —
and then it was over.
I walked down Marlborough Street the day you left me
under branches as tedious as leather,
under branches as stiff as drivers' gloves.
I said, (but only because you were gone)
"Magnolia blossoms have rather a southern sound,
so unlike Boston anyhow,"
and whatever it was that happened, all that pink,
and for so short a time,
was unbelievable, was pinned on.

The magnolias had sat once, each in a pink dress,
looking, of course, at the ceiling.
For weeks the buds had been as sure-bodied
as the twelve-year-old flower girl I was
at Aunt Edna's wedding.
Will they bend, I had asked,
as I walked under them toward you,
bend two to a branch,
cheek, forehead, shoulder to the floor?
I could see that none were clumsy.
I could see that each was tight and firm.
Not one of them had trickled blood —
waiting as polished as gull beaks,
as closed as all that.

I stood under them for nights, hesitating,
and then drove away in my car.
Yet one night in the April night
someone (someone!) kicked each bud open —
to disprove, to mock, to puncture!
The next day they were all hot-colored,

moist, not flawed in fact.
Then they no longer huddled.
They forgot how to hide.
Tense as they had been,
they were flags, gaudy, chafing in the wind.
There was such abandonment in all that!
Such entertainment
in their flaring up.

After that, well —
like faces in a parade,
I could not tell the difference between losing you
and losing them.
They dropped separately after the celebration,
handpicked,
one after the other like artichoke leaves.
After that I walked to my car awkwardly
over the painful bare remains on the brick sidewalk,
knowing that someone had, in one night,
passed roughly through,
and before it was time.

April 27–May 1, 1964

LITTLE GIRL, MY STRING BEAN,
MY LOVELY WOMAN

My daughter, at eleven
(almost twelve), is like a garden.

Oh, darling! Born in that sweet birthday suit
and having owned it and known it for so long,
now you must watch high noon enter —
noon, that ghost hour.
Oh, funny little girl — this one under a blueberry sky,

this one! How can I say that I've known
just what you know and just where you are?

It's not a strange place, this odd home
where your face sits in my hand
so full of distance,
so full of its immediate fever.
The summer has seized you,
as when, last month in Amalfi, I saw
lemons as large as your desk-side globe —
that miniature map of the world —
and I could mention, too,
the market stalls of mushrooms
and garlic buds all engorged.
Or I think even of the orchard next door,
where the berries are done
and the apples are beginning to swell.
And once, with our first backyard,
I remember I planted an acre of yellow beans
we couldn't eat.

Oh, little girl,
my stringbean,
how do you grow?
You grow this way.
You are too many to eat.

I hear
as in a dream
the conversation of the old wives
speaking of *womanhood.*
I remember that I heard nothing myself.
I was alone.
I waited like a target.

Let high noon enter —
the hour of the ghosts.

146

Once the Romans believed
that noon was the ghost hour,
and I can believe it, too,
under that startling sun,
and someday they will come to you,
someday, men bare to the waist, young Romans
at noon where they belong,
with ladders and hammers
while no one sleeps.

But before they enter
I will have said,
Your bones are lovely,
and before their strange hands
there was always this hand that formed.

Oh, darling, let your body in,
let it tie you in,
in comfort.
What I want to say, Linda,
is that women are born twice.

If I could have watched you grow
as a magical mother might,
if I could have seen through my magical transparent belly,
there would have been such ripening within:
your embryo,
the seed taking on its own,
life clapping the bedpost,
bones from the pond,
thumbs and two mysterious eyes,
the awfully human head,
the heart jumping like a puppy,
the important lungs,
the becoming —
while it becomes!
as it does now,

a world of its own,
a delicate place.

I say hello
to such shakes and knockings and high jinks,
such music, such sprouts,
such dancing-mad-bears of music,
such necessary sugar,
such goings-on!

Oh, little girl,
my stringbean,
how do you grow?
You grow this way.
You are too many to eat.

What I want to say, Linda,
is that there is nothing in your body that lies.
All that is new is telling the truth.
I'm here, that somebody else,
an old tree in the background.

Darling,
stand still at your door,
sure of yourself, a white stone, a good stone —
as exceptional as laughter
you will strike fire,
that new thing!

July 14, 1964

A LITTLE UNCOMPLICATED HYMN
for Joy

is what I wanted to write.
There *was* such a song!

148

A song for your kneebones,
a song for your ribs,
those delicate trees that bury your heart;
a song for your bookshelf
where twenty hand-blown ducks sit in a Venetian row;
a song for your dress-up high heels,
your fire-red skate board,
your twenty grubby fingers,
the pink knitting that you start
and never quite finish;
your poster-paint pictures,
all angels making a face,
a song for your laughter
that keeps wiggling a spoon in my sleep.

Even a song for your night
as during last summer's heat wave
where your fever stuck at 104 for two weeks,
where you slept, head on the window sill,
lips as dry as old erasers, your thirst
shimmering and heavy as I spooned water in,
your eyes shut on the thumping June bugs,
the lips moving, mumbling,
sending letters to the stars.
Dreaming, dreaming,
your body a boat,
rocked by your life and my death.
Your fists wound like a ball,
little fetus, little snail,
carrying a rage, a leftover rage
I cannot undo.

Even a song for your flight
where you fell from the neighbor's tree hut,
where you thought you were walking onto solid blue air,
you thought, *why not?*

and then, you simply left the boards behind
and stepped out into the dust.

O little Icarus,
you chewed on a cloud, you bit the sun
and came tumbling down, head first,
not into the sea, but hard
on the hard packed gravel.
You fell on your eye. You fell on your chin.
What a shiner! What a faint you had
and then crawled home,
a knocked-out humpty dumpty
in my arms.

O humpty-dumpty girl,
I named you Joy.
That's someone's song all by itself.
In the naming of you I named
all things you are . . .
except the ditch
where I left you once,
like an old root that wouldn't take hold,
that ditch where I left you
while I sailed off in madness
over the buildings and under my umbrella,
sailed off for three years
so that the first candle
and the second candle
and the third candle
burned down alone on your birthday cake.
That ditch I want so much to forget
and that you try each day to forget.

Even here in your school portrait
where you repeat third grade,
caught in the need not to grow —
that little prison —

even here you keep up the barrier
with a smile that dies afraid
as it hides your crooked front tooth.
Joy, I call you
and yet your eyes just here
with their shades half-drawn over the gunsights,
over your gigantic knowledge,
over the little blue fish who dart back and forth,
over different streets, the strange rooms,
other people's chairs, other people's food,
ask, "Why was I shut in the cellar?"

And I've got words,
words that dog my heels,
words for sale you might say,
and multiplication cards and cursive writing
that you ignore to teach my fingers
the *cat's cradle* and the *witch's broom.*
Yes! I have instructions before dinner
and hugs after dinner and still those eyes —
away, away,
asking for hymns . . .
without guilt.

And I can only say
a little uncomplicated hymn
is what I wanted to write
and yet I find only your name.
There *was* such a song,
but it's bruised.
It's not mine.

You will jump to it someday
as you will jump out of the pitch of this house.
It will be a holiday, a parade, a fiesta!
Then you'll fly.

You'll really fly.
After that you'll, quite simply, quite calmly
make your own stones, your own floor plan,
your own sound.

I wanted to write such a poem
with such musics, such guitars going;
I tried at the teeth of sound
to draw up such legions of noise;
I tried at the breakwater
to catch the star off each ship;
and at the closing of hands
I looked for their houses
and silences.
I found just one.

> you were mine
> and I lent you out.

I look for uncomplicated hymns
but love has none.

March 1965

YOUR FACE ON THE DOG'S NECK

It is early afternoon.
You sit on the grass
with your rough face on the dog's neck.
Right now
you are both as still as a snapshot.
That infectious dog ought to let a fly bother her,
ought to run out in an immense field,
chasing rabbits and skunks,
mauling the cats, licking insects off her rump,
and stop using you up.

My darling, why do you lean on her so?
I would touch you,
that pulse brooding under your Madras shirt,
each shoulder the most well built house,
the arms, thin birches that do not escape the breeze,
the white teeth that have known me,
that wait at the bottom of the brook
and the tongue, my little fish! . . .
but you are stopped in time.

So I will speak of your eyes
although they are closed.
Tell me, where is each stubborn-colored iris?
Where are the quick pupils that make
the floor tilt under me?
I see only the lids, as tough as riding boots.
Why have your eyes gone into their own room?
Goodnight they are saying
from their little leathery doors.
Or shall I sing of eyes
that have been ruined with mercy and lust
and once with your own death
when you lay bubbling like a caught fish,
sucking on the manufactured oxygen?
Or shall I sing of eyes
that are resting so near the hair
of that hateful animal?
Love twists me, a Spanish flute plays in my blood,
and yet I can see only
your little sleep, an empty place.

But when your eyes open
against the wool stink of her thick hair,
against the faintly sickening neck of that dog,
whom I envy like a thief,
what will I ask?
Will I speak up saying,

there is a hurried song, a certain seizure
from which I gasp?
Or will your eyes lie in wait,
little field mice nestling on their paws?
Perhaps they will say nothing,
perhaps they will be dark and leaden,
having played their own game
somewhere else,
somewhere far off.

Oh, I have learned them and know that
when they open and glance at me
I will turn like a little dancer
and then, quite simply,
and all by myself,
I will fall,
bound to some mother/father,
bound to your sight,
bound for nowhere
and everywhere.
Or, perhaps, my darling,
because it is early afternoon,
I will forget that my voice is full of good people,
forget how my legs could sprawl on the terrace,
forget all that the birds might witness,
the torn dress, the shoes lost in the arbor,
while the neighbor's lawnmower bites and spits out
some new little rows of innocent grass.
Certainly,
I need not speak of it at all.
I will crouch down
and put my cheek near you,
accepting this spayed and flatulent bitch you hold,
letting my face rest in an assembled tenderness
on the old dog's neck.

May 19, 1965

SELF IN 1958

What is reality?
I am a plaster doll; I pose
with eyes that cut open without landfall or nightfall
upon some shellacked and grinning person,
eyes that open, blue, steel, and close.
Am I approximately an I. Magnin transplant?
I have hair, black angel,
black-angel-stuffing to comb,
nylon legs, luminous arms
and some advertised clothes.

I live in a doll's house
with four chairs,
a counterfeit table, a flat roof
and a big front door.
Many have come to such a small crossroad.
There is an iron bed,
(Life enlarges, life takes aim)
a cardboard floor,
windows that flash open on someone's city,
and little more.

Someone plays with me,
plants me in the all-electric kitchen,
Is this what Mrs. Rombauer said?
Someone pretends with me —
I am walled in solid by their noise —
or puts me upon their straight bed.
They think I am me!
Their warmth? Their warmth is not a friend!
They pry my mouth for their cups of gin
and their stale bread.

What is reality
to this synthetic doll

who should smile, who should shift gears,
should spring the doors open in a wholesome disorder,
and have no evidence of ruin or fears?
But I would cry,
rooted into the wall that
was once my mother,
if I could remember how
and if I had the tears.

June 1958–June 1965

SUICIDE NOTE

*You speak to me of narcissism but I reply that it is
a matter of my life . . .* Artaud

*At this time let me somehow bequeath all the leftovers
to my daughters and their daughters . . .* Anonymous

Better,
despite the worms talking to
the mare's hoof in the field;
better,
despite the season of young girls
dropping their blood;
better somehow
to drop myself quickly
into an old room.
Better (someone said)
not to be born
and far better
not to be born twice
at thirteen
where the boardinghouse,
each year a bedroom,
caught fire.

156

Dear friend,
I will have to sink with hundreds of others
on a dumbwaiter into hell.
I will be a light thing.
I will enter death
like someone's lost optical lens.
Life is half enlarged.
The fish and owls are fierce today.
Life tilts backward and forward.
Even the wasps cannot find my eyes.

Yes,
eyes that were immediate once.
Eyes that have been truly awake,
eyes that told the whole story —
poor dumb animals.
Eyes that were pierced,
little nail heads,
light blue gunshots.

And once with
a mouth like a cup,
clay colored or blood colored,
open like the breakwater
for the lost ocean
and open like the noose
for the first head.

Once upon a time
my hunger was for Jesus.
O my hunger! My hunger!
Before he grew old
he rode calmly into Jerusalem
in search of death.

This time
I certainly
do not ask for understanding
and yet I hope everyone else
will turn their heads when an unrehearsed fish jumps
on the surface of Echo Lake;
when moonlight,
its bass note turned up loud,
hurts some building in Boston,
when the truly beautiful lie together.
I think of this, surely,
and would think of it far longer
if I were not . . . if I were not
at that old fire.

I could admit
that I am only a coward
crying *me me me*
and not mention the little gnats, the moths,
forced by circumstance
to suck on the electric bulb.
But surely you know that everyone has a death,
his own death,
waiting for him.
So I will go now
without old age or disease,
wildly but accurately,
knowing my best route,
carried by that toy donkey I rode all these years,
never asking, "Where are we going?"
We were riding (if I'd only known)
to this.

Dear friend,
please do not think
that I visualize guitars playing

or my father arching his bone.
I do not even expect my mother's mouth.
I know that I have died before —
once in November, once in June.
How strange to choose June again,
so concrete with its green breasts and bellies.
Of course guitars will not play!
The snakes will certainly not notice.
New York City will not mind.
At night the bats will beat on the trees,
knowing it all,
seeing what they sensed all day.

June 1965

IN THE BEACH HOUSE

The doors open
and the heat undoes itself,
everyone undoes himself,
everyone walks naked.
Two of them walk on the table.
They are not afraid of God's displeasure.
They will have no truck with the angel
who hoots from the fog horn
and throws the ocean into the rocks outside.
One of them covers the bedstead.
One of them winds round the bedpost
and both of them beat on the floor.

My little cot listens in
all night long —
even with the ocean turned up high,
even with every door boarded up,
they are allowed the lifting of the object,
the placing themselves upon the swing.

Inside my prison of pine and bedspring,
over my window sill, under my knob,
it is plain that they are at
the royal strapping.

Have mercy, little pillow,
stay mute and uncaring,
hear not one word of disaster!
Stay close, little sour feather,
little fellow full of salt.
My loves are oiling their bones
and then delivering them with unspeakable sounds
that carry them this way and that
while summer is hurrying its way in and out,
over and over,
in their room.

July 15, 1965

CRIPPLES AND OTHER STORIES

My doctor, the comedian
I called you every time
and made you laugh yourself
when I wrote this silly rhyme . . .

> *Each time I give lectures*
> *or gather in the grants*
> *you send me off to boarding school*
> *in training pants.*

God damn it, father-doctor.
I'm really thirty-six.
I see dead rats in the toilet.
I'm one of the lunatics.

Disgusted, mother put me
on the potty. She was good at this.
My father was fat on scotch.
It leaked from every orifice.

Oh the enemas of childhood,
reeking of outhouses and shame!
Yet you rock me in your arms
and whisper my nickname.

Or else you hold my hand
and teach me love too late.
And that's the hand of the arm
they tried to amputate.

Though I was almost seven
I was an awful brat.
I put it in the Easy Wringer.
It came out nice and flat.

I was an instant cripple
from my finger to my shoulder.
The laundress wept and swooned.
My mother had to hold her.

I knew I was a cripple.
Of course, I'd known it from the start.
My father took the crowbar
and broke that wringer's heart.

The surgeons shook their heads.
They really didn't know —
Would the cripple inside of me
be a cripple that would show?

My father was a perfect man,
clean and rich and fat.

My mother was a brilliant thing.
She was good at that.

You hold me in your arms.
How strange that you're so tender!
Child-woman that I am,
you think that you can mend her.

As for the arm,
unfortunately it grew.
Though mother said a withered arm
would put me in *Who's Who*.

For years she described it.
She sang it like a hymn.
By then she loved the shrunken thing,
my little withered limb.

My father's cells clicked each night,
intent on making money.
And as for my cells, they brooded,
little queens, on honey.

On boys too, as a matter of fact,
and cigarettes and cars.
Mother frowned at my wasted life.
My father smoked cigars.

My cheeks blossomed with maggots.
I picked at them like pearls.
I covered them with pancake.
I wound my hair in curls.

My father didn't know me
but you kiss me in my fever.
My mother knew me twice
and then I had to leave her.

But those are just two stories
and I have more to tell
from the outhouse, the greenhouse
where you draw me out of hell.

Father, I'm thirty-six,
yet I lie here in your crib.
I'm getting born again, Adam,
as you prod me with your rib.

October 1965

PAIN FOR A DAUGHTER

Blind with love, my daughter
has cried nightly for horses,
those long-necked marchers and churners
that she has mastered, any and all,
reigning them in like a circus hand —
the excitable muscles and the ripe neck;
tending this summer, a pony and a foal.
She who is too squeamish to pull
a thorn from the dog's paw,
watched her pony blossom with distemper,
the underside of the jaw swelling
like an enormous grape.
Gritting her teeth with love,
she drained the boil and scoured it
with hydrogen peroxide until pus
ran like milk on the barn floor.

Blind with loss all winter,
in dungarees, a ski jacket and a hard hat,
she visits the neighbors' stable,
our acreage not zoned for barns;

they who own the flaming horses
and the swan-whipped thoroughbred
that she tugs at and cajoles,
thinking it will burn like a furnace
under her small-hipped English seat.

Blind with pain she limps home.
The thoroughbred has stood on her foot.
He rested there like a building.
He grew into her foot until they were one.
The marks of the horseshoe printed
into her flesh, the tips of her toes
ripped off like pieces of leather,
three toenails swirled like shells
and left to float in blood in her riding boot.

Blind with fear, she sits on the toilet,
her foot balanced over the washbasin,
her father, hydrogen peroxide in hand,
performing the rites of the cleansing.
She bites on a towel, sucked in breath,
sucked in and arched against the pain,
her eyes glancing off me where
I stand at the door, eyes locked
on the ceiling, eyes of a stranger,
and then she cries . . .
Oh my God, help me!
Where a child would have cried *Mama!*
Where a child would have believed *Mama!*
she bit the towel and called on God
and I saw her life stretch out . . .
I saw her torn in childbirth,
and I saw her, at that moment,
in her own death and I knew that she
knew.

November 1965

THE ADDICT

Sleepmonger,
deathmonger,
with capsules in my palms each night,
eight at a time from sweet pharmaceutical bottles
I make arrangements for a pint-sized journey.
I'm the queen of this condition.
I'm an expert on making the trip
and now they say I'm an addict.
Now they ask why.
Why!

Don't they know
that I promised to die!
I'm keeping in practice.
I'm merely staying in shape.
The pills are a mother, but better,
every color and as good as sour balls.
I'm on a diet from death.

Yes, I admit
it has gotten to be a bit of a habit —
blows eight at a time, socked in the eye,
hauled away by the pink, the orange,
the green and the white goodnights.
I'm becoming something of a chemical
mixture.
That's it!

My supply
of tablets
has got to last for years and years.
I like them more than I like me.
Stubborn as hell, they won't let go.
It's a kind of marriage.
It's a kind of war

where I plant bombs inside
of myself.

Yes
I try
to kill myself in small amounts,
an innocuous occupation.
Actually I'm hung up on it.
But remember I don't make too much noise.
And frankly no one has to lug me out
and I don't stand there in my winding sheet.
I'm a little buttercup in my yellow nightie
eating my eight loaves in a row
and in a certain order as in
the laying on of hands
or the black sacrament.

It's a ceremony
but like any other sport
it's full of rules.
It's like a musical tennis match where
my mouth keeps catching the ball.
Then I lie on my altar
elevated by the eight chemical kisses.

What a lay me down this is
with two pink, two orange,
two green, two white goodnights.
Fee-fi-fo-fum —
Now I'm borrowed.
Now I'm numb.

First of February 1966

LIVE
Live or die, but don't poison everything . . .

Well, death's been here
for a long time —
it has a hell of a lot
to do with hell
and suspicion of the eye
and the religious objects
and how I mourned them
when they were made obscene
by my dwarf-heart's doodle.
The chief ingredient
is mutilation.
And mud, day after day,
mud like a ritual,
and the baby on the platter,
cooked but still human,
cooked also with little maggots,
sewn onto it maybe by somebody's mother,
the damn bitch!

Even so,
I kept right on going on,
a sort of human statement,
lugging myself as if
I were a sawed-off body
in the trunk, the steamer trunk.
This became a perjury of the soul.
It became an outright lie
and even though I dressed the body
it was still naked, still killed.
It was caught
in the first place at birth,
like a fish.
But I played it, dressed it up,
dressed it up like somebody's doll.

167

Is life something you play?
And all the time wanting to get rid of it?
And further, everyone yelling at you
to shut up. And no wonder!
People don't like to be told
that you're sick
and then be forced
to watch
you
come
down with the hammer.

Today life opened inside me like an egg
and there inside
after considerable digging
I found the answer.
What a bargain!
There was the sun,
her yolk moving feverishly,
tumbling her prize —
and you realize that she does this daily!
I'd known she was a purifier
but I hadn't thought
she was solid,
hadn't known she was an answer.
God! It's a dream,
lovers sprouting in the yard
like celery stalks
and better,
a husband straight as a redwood,
two daughters, two sea urchins,
picking roses off my hackles.
If I'm on fire they dance around it
and cook marshmallows.
And if I'm ice
they simply skate on me
in little ballet costumes.

Here,
all along,
thinking I was a killer,
anointing myself daily
with my little poisons.
But no.
I'm an empress.
I wear an apron.
My typewriter writes.
It didn't break the way it warned.
Even crazy, I'm as nice
as a chocolate bar.
Even with the witches' gymnastics
they trust my incalculable city,
my corruptible bed.

O dearest three,
I make a soft reply.
The witch comes on
and you paint her pink.
I come with kisses in my hood
and the sun, the smart one,
rolling in my arms.
So I say Live
and turn my shadow three times round
to feed our puppies as they come,
the eight Dalmatians we didn't drown,
despite the warnings: The abort! The destroy!
Despite the pails of water that waited
to drown them, to pull them down like stones,
they came, each one headfirst,
blowing bubbles the color of cataract-blue
and fumbling for the tiny tits.
Just last week, eight Dalmatians,
¾ of a lb., lined up like cord wood
each
like a

birch tree.
I promise to love more if they come,
because in spite of cruelty
and the stuffed railroad cars for the ovens,
I am not what I expected. Not an Eichmann.
The poison just didn't take.
So I won't hang around in my hospital shift,
repeating The Black Mass and all of it.
I say *Live, Live* because of the sun,
the dream, the excitable gift.

February the last, 1966

Love Poems

(1969)

One should say before sleeping, "I have lived many lives. I have been a slave and a prince. Many a beloved has sat upon my knees and I have sat upon the knees of many a beloved. Everything that has been shall be again."

From an essay by W. B. Yeats

THE TOUCH

For months my hand had been sealed off
in a tin box. Nothing was there but subway railings.
Perhaps it is bruised, I thought,
and that is why they have locked it up.
But when I looked in it lay there quietly.
You could tell time by this, I thought,
like a clock, by its five knuckles
and the thin underground veins.
It lay there like an unconscious woman
fed by tubes she knew not of.

The hand had collapsed,
a small wood pigeon
that had gone into seclusion.
I turned it over and the palm was old,
its lines traced like fine needlepoint
and stitched up into the fingers.
It was fat and soft and blind in places.
Nothing but vulnerable.

And all this is metaphor.
An ordinary hand — just lonely
for something to touch
that touches back.
The dog won't do it.
Her tail wags in the swamp for a frog.
I'm no better than a case of dog food.
She owns her own hunger.
My sisters won't do it.
They live in school except for buttons
and tears running down like lemonade.
My father won't do it.
He comes with the house and even at night
he lives in a machine made by my mother
and well oiled by his job, his job.

173

The trouble is
that I'd let my gestures freeze.
The trouble was not
in the kitchen or the tulips
but only in my head, my head.

Then all this became history.
Your hand found mine.
Life rushed to my fingers like a blood clot.
Oh, my carpenter,
the fingers are rebuilt.
They dance with yours.
They dance in the attic and in Vienna.
My hand is alive all over America.
Not even death will stop it,
death shedding her blood.
Nothing will stop it, for this is the kingdom
and the kingdom come.

THE KISS

My mouth blooms like a cut.
I've been wronged all year, tedious
nights, nothing but rough elbows in them
and delicate boxes of Kleenex calling *crybaby*
crybaby, you fool!

Before today my body was useless.
Now it's tearing at its square corners.
It's tearing old Mary's garments off, knot by knot
and see — Now it's shot full of these electric bolts.
Zing! A resurrection!

Once it was a boat, quite wooden
and with no business, no salt water under it
and in need of some paint. It was no more
than a group of boards. But you hoisted her, rigged her.
She's been elected.

My nerves are turned on. I hear them like
musical instruments. Where there was silence
the drums, the strings are incurably playing. You did this.
Pure genius at work. Darling, the composer has stepped
into fire.

THE BREAST

This is the key to it.
This is the key to everything.
Preciously.

I am worse than the gamekeeper's children,
picking for dust and bread.
Here I am drumming up perfume.

Let me go down on your carpet,
your straw mattress — whatever's at hand
because the child in me is dying, dying.

It is not that I am cattle to be eaten.
It is not that I am some sort of street.
But your hands found me like an architect.

Jugful of milk! It was yours years ago
when I lived in the valley of my bones,
bones dumb in the swamp. Little playthings.

A xylophone maybe with skin
stretched over it awkwardly.
Only later did it become something real.

Later I measured my size against movie stars.
I didn't measure up. Something between
my shoulders was there. But never enough.

Sure, there was a meadow,
but no young men singing the truth.
Nothing to tell truth by.

Ignorant of men I lay next to my sisters
and rising out of the ashes I cried
my sex will be transfixed!

Now I am your mother, your daughter,
your brand new thing — a snail, a nest.
I am alive when your fingers are.

I wear silk — the cover to uncover —
because silk is what I want you to think of.
But I dislike the cloth. It is too stern.

So tell me anything but track me like a climber
for here is the eye, here is the jewel,
here is the excitement the nipple learns.

I am unbalanced — but I am not mad with snow.
I am mad the way young girls are mad,
with an offering, an offering . . .

I burn the way money burns.

THE INTERROGATION OF
THE MAN OF MANY HEARTS

Who's she,
that one in your arms?

She's the one I carried my bones to
and built a house that was just a cot
and built a life that was over an hour
and built a castle where no one lives

and built, in the end, a song
to go with the ceremony.

Why have you brought her here?
Why do you knock on my door
with your little stories and songs?

I had joined her the way a man joins
a woman and yet there was no place
for festivities or formalities
and these things matter to a woman
and, you see, we live in a cold climate
and are not permitted to kiss on the street
so I made up a song that wasn't true.
I made up a song called *Marriage*.

You come to me out of wedlock
and kick your foot on my stoop
and ask me to measure such things?

Never. Never. Not my real wife.
She's my real witch, my fork, my mare,
my mother of tears, my skirtful of hell,
the stamp of my sorrows, the stamp of my bruises
and also the children she might bear
and also a private place, a body of bones
that I would honestly buy, if I could buy,
that I would marry, if I could marry.

And should I torment you for that?
Each man has a small fate allotted to him
and yours is a passionate one.

But I am in torment. We have no place.
The cot we share is almost a prison
where I can't say buttercup, bobolink,
sugarduck, pumpkin, love ribbon, locket,

valentine, summergirl, funnygirl and all
those nonsense things one says in bed.
To say I have bedded with her is not enough.
I have not only bedded her down.
I have tied her down with a knot.

*Then why do you stick your fists
into your pockets? Why do you shuffle
your feet like a schoolboy?*

For years I have tied this knot in my dreams.
I have walked through a door in my dreams
and she was standing there in my mother's apron.
Once she crawled through a window that was shaped
like a keyhole and she was wearing my daughter's
pink corduroys and each time I tied these women
in a knot. Once a queen came. I tied her too.
But this is something I have actually tied
and now I have made her fast.
I sang her out. I caught her down.
I stamped her out with a song.
There was no other apartment for it.
There was no other chamber for it.
Only the knot. The bedded-down knot.
Thus I have laid my hands upon her
and have called her eyes and her mouth
as mine, and also her tongue.

*Why do you ask me to make choices?
I am not a judge or a psychologist.
You own your bedded-down knot.*

And yet I have real daytimes and nighttimes
with children and balconies and a good wife.
Thus I have tied these other knots,
yet I would rather not think of them
when I speak to you of her. Not now.

If she were a room to rent I would pay.
If she were a life to save I would save.
Maybe I am a man of many hearts.

A man of many hearts?
Why then do you tremble at my doorway?
A man of many hearts does not need me.

I'm caught deep in the dye of her.
I have allowed you to catch me red-handed,
catch me with my wild oats in a wild clock
for my mare, my dove and my own clean body.
People might say I have snakes in my boots
but I tell you that just once am I in the stirrups,
just once, this once, in the cup.
The love of the woman is in the song.
I called her the woman in red.
I called her the girl in pink
but she was ten colors
and ten women.
I could hardly name her.

I know who she is.
You have named her enough.

Maybe I shouldn't have put it in words.
Frankly, I think I'm worse for this kissing,
drunk as a piper, kicking the traces
and determined to tie her up forever.
You see the song is the life,
the life I can't live.
God, even as he passes,
hands down monogamy like slang.
I wanted to write her into the law.
But, you know, there is no law for this.

Man of many hearts, you are a fool!
The clover has grown thorns this year

and robbed the cattle of their fruit
and the stones of the river
have sucked men's eyes dry,
season after season,
and every bed has been condemned,
not by morality or law,
but by time.

THAT DAY

This is the desk I sit at
and this is the desk where I love you too much
and this is the typewriter that sits before me
where yesterday only your body sat before me
with its shoulders gathered in like a Greek chorus,
with its tongue like a king making up rules as he goes,
with its tongue quite openly like a cat lapping milk,
with its tongue — both of us coiled in its slippery life.
That was yesterday, that day.

That was the day of your tongue,
your tongue that came from your lips,
two openers, half animals, half birds
caught in the doorway of your heart.
That was the day I followed the king's rules,
passing by your red veins and your blue veins,
my hands down the backbone, down quick like a firepole,
hands between legs where you display your inner knowledge,
where diamond mines are buried and come forth to bury,
come forth more sudden than some reconstructed city.
It is complete within seconds, that monument.
The blood runs underground yet brings forth a tower.
A multitude should gather for such an edifice.
For a miracle one stands in line and throws confetti.
Surely The Press is here looking for headlines.
Surely someone should carry a banner on the sidewalk.

If a bridge is constructed doesn't the mayor cut a ribbon?
If a phenomenon arrives shouldn't the Magi come bearing
  gifts?
Yesterday was the day I bore gifts for your gift
and came from the valley to meet you on the pavement.
That was yesterday, that day.

That was the day of your face,
your face after love, close to the pillow, a lullaby.
Half asleep beside me letting the old fashioned rocker stop,
our breath became one, became a child-breath together,
while my fingers drew little o's on your shut eyes,
while my fingers drew little smiles on your mouth,
while I drew I LOVE YOU on your chest and its drummer
and whispered, "Wake up!" and you mumbled in your sleep,
"Sh. We're driving to Cape Cod. We're heading for the Bourne
Bridge. We're circling around the Bourne Circle." Bourne!
Then I knew you in your dream and prayed of our time
that I would be pierced and you would take root in me
and that I might bring forth your born, might bear
the you or the ghost of you in my little household.
Yesterday I did not want to be borrowed
but this is the typewriter that sits before me
and love is where yesterday is at.

IN CELEBRATION OF MY UTERUS

Everyone in me is a bird.
I am beating all my wings.
They wanted to cut you out
but they will not.
They said you were immeasurably empty
but you are not.
They said you were sick unto dying
but they were wrong.

You are singing like a school girl.
You are not torn.

Sweet weight,
in celebration of the woman I am
and of the soul of the woman I am
and of the central creature and its delight
I sing for you. I dare to live.
Hello, spirit. Hello, cup.
Fasten, cover. Cover that does contain.
Hello to the soil of the fields.
Welcome, roots.

Each cell has a life.
There is enough here to please a nation.
It is enough that the populace own these goods.
Any person, any commonwealth would say of it,
"It is good this year that we may plant again
and think forward to a harvest.
A blight had been forecast and has been cast out."
Many women are singing together of this:
one is in a shoe factory cursing the machine,
one is at the aquarium tending a seal,
one is dull at the wheel of her Ford,
one is at the toll gate collecting,
one is tying the cord of a calf in Arizona,
one is straddling a cello in Russia,
one is shifting pots on the stove in Egypt,
one is painting her bedroom walls moon color,
one is dying but remembering a breakfast,
one is stretching on her mat in Thailand,
one is wiping the ass of her child,
one is staring out the window of a train
in the middle of Wyoming and one is
anywhere and some are everywhere and all
seem to be singing, although some can not
sing a note.

Sweet weight,
in celebration of the woman I am
let me carry a ten-foot scarf,
let me drum for the nineteen-year-olds,
let me carry bowls for the offering
(if that is my part).
Let me study the cardiovascular tissue,
let me examine the angular distance of meteors,
let me suck on the stems of flowers
(if that is my part).
Let me make certain tribal figures
(if that is my part).
For this thing the body needs
let me sing
for the supper,
for the kissing,
for the correct
yes.

THE NUDE SWIM

On the southwest side of Capri
we found a little unknown grotto
where no people were and we
entered it completely
and let our bodies lose all
their loneliness.

All the fish in us
had escaped for a minute.
The real fish did not mind.
We did not disturb their personal life.
We calmly trailed over them
and under them, shedding
air bubbles, little white

balloons that drifted up
into the sun by the boat
where the Italian boatman slept
with his hat over his face.

Water so clear you could
read a book through it.
Water so bouyant you could
float on your elbow.
I lay on it as on a divan.
I lay on it just like
Matisse's *Red Odalisque*.
Water was my strange flower.
One must picture a woman
without a toga or a scarf
on a couch as deep as a tomb.

The walls of that grotto
were everycolor blue and
you said, "Look! Your eyes
are seacolor. Look! Your eyes
are skycolor." And my eyes
shut down as if they were
suddenly ashamed.

SONG FOR A RED NIGHTGOWN

No. Not really red,
but the color of a rose when it bleeds.
It's a lost flamingo,
called somewhere Schiaparelli Pink
but not meaning pink, but blood and
those candy store cinnamon hearts.
It moves like capes in the unflawed
villages in Spain. Meaning a fire

layer and underneath, like a petal,
a sheath of pink, clean as a stone.

So I mean a nightgown of two colors
and of two layers that float from
the shoulders across every zone.
For years the moth has longed for them
but these colors are bounded by silence
and animals, half hidden but browsing.
One could think of feathers and
not know it at all. One could
think of whores and not imagine
the way of a swan. One could
imagine the cloth of a bee and
touch its hair and come close.

The bed is ravaged by such
sweet sights. The girl is.
The girl drifts up out of
her nightgown and its color.
Her wings are fastened onto
her shoulders like bandages.
The butterfly owns her now.
It covers her and her wounds.
She is not terrified of
begonias or telegrams but
surely this nightgown girl,
this awesome flyer, has not seen
how the moon floats through her
and in between.

LOVING THE KILLER

Today is the day they shipped
home our summer in two crates

and tonight is All Hallows Eve
and today you tell me the oak leaves
outside your office window will
outlast the New England winter.
But then, love is where our summer
was.

Though I never touched a rifle,
love was under the canvas,
deep in the bush of Tanzania.
Though I only carried a camera,
love came after the gun,
after the kill,
after the martinis and
the eating of the kill.
While Saedi, a former cannibal,
served from the left
in his white gown and red fez,
I vomited behind the dining tent.
Love where the hyena laughed
in the middle of nowhere
except the equator. Love!

Yet today our dog is full
of our dead dog's spirit
and limps on three legs,
holding up the dead dog's paw.
Though the house is full of
candy bars the wasted ghost
of my parents is poking
the keyhole, rubbing the bedpost.
Also the ghost of your father,
who was killed outright.
Tonight we will argue and shout,
"My loss is greater than yours!
My pain is more valuable!"

Today they shipped home our summer
in two crates wrapped in brown
waxed paper and sewn in burlap.
The first crate holds our personal
effects, sweaty jackets, 3 lb. boots
from the hold of the S.S. MORMACRIO
by way of Mombassa, Dar es Salaam,
Tanga, Lourence Marques and Zanzibar,
through customs along with the other
merchandise: ash blonde sisal like
horse's tails, and hairy strings,
bales of grease wool from the auctions
at Cape Town and something else. Bones!

Bones piled up like coal, animal bones
shaped like golf balls, school pencils,
fingers and noses. Oh my Nazi,
with your S.S. sky-blue eye —
I am no different from Emily Goering.
Emily Goering recently said she
thought the concentration camps
were for the re-education of Jews
and Communists. She thought!
So far the continents stay on the map
but there is always a new method.

The other crate we own is dead.
Bones and skins from Hold #1
going to New York for curing and
mounting. We have not touched these
skulls since a Friday in Arusha where
skulls lay humbly beside the Land Rover,
flies still sucking on eye pits,
all in a row, head by head,
beside the ivory that cost more
than your life. The wildebeest

skull, the eland skull, the Grant's
skull, the Thomson's skull, the impala
skull and the hartebeest skull,
on and on to New York along with
the skins of zebras and leopards.

And tonight our skins, our bones,
that have survived our fathers,
will meet, delicate in the hold,
fastened together in an intricate
lock. Then one of us will shout,
"My need is more desperate!" and
I will eat you slowly with kisses
even though the killer in you
has gotten out.

* FOR MY LOVER,
RETURNING TO HIS WIFE

She is all there.
She was melted carefully down for you
and cast up from your childhood,
cast up from your one hundred favorite aggies.

She has always been there, my darling.
She is, in fact, exquisite.
Fireworks in the dull middle of February
and as real as a cast-iron pot.

Let's face it, I have been momentary.
A luxury. A bright red sloop in the harbor.
My hair rising like smoke from the car window.
Littleneck clams out of season.

She is more than that. She is your have to have,
has grown you your practical your tropical growth.
This is not an experiment. She is all harmony.
She sees to oars and oarlocks for the dinghy,

has placed wild flowers at the window at breakfast,
sat by the potter's wheel at midday,
set forth three children under the moon,
three cherubs drawn by Michelangelo,

done this with her legs spread out
in the terrible months in the chapel.
If you glance up, the children are there
like delicate balloons resting on the ceiling.

She has also carried each one down the hall
after supper, their heads privately bent,
two legs protesting, person to person,
her face flushed with a song and their little sleep.

I give you back your heart.
I give you permission —

for the fuse inside her, throbbing
angrily in the dirt, for the bitch in her
and the burying of her wound —
for the burying of her small red wound alive —

for the pale flickering flare under her ribs,
for the drunken sailor who waits in her left pulse,
for the mother's knee, for the stockings,
for the garter belt, for the call —

the curious call
when you will burrow in arms and breasts

and tug at the orange ribbon in her hair
and answer the call, the curious call.

She is so naked and singular.
She is the sum of yourself and your dream.
Climb her like a monument, step after step.
She is solid.

As for me, I am a watercolor.
I wash off.

THE BREAK

It was also my violent heart that broke,
falling down the front hall stairs.
It was also a message I never spoke,
calling, riser after riser, *who cares*

about you, who cares, splintering up
the hip that was merely made of crystal,
the post of it and also the cup.
I exploded in the hallway like a pistol.

So I fell apart. So I came all undone.
Yes. I was like a box of dog bones.
But now they've wrapped me in like a nun.
Burst like firecrackers! Held like stones!

What a feat sailing queerly like Icarus
until the tempest undid me and I broke.
The ambulance drivers made such a fuss.
But when I cried, "Wait for my courage!" they smoked

and then they placed me, tied me up on their plate,
and wheeled me out to their coffin, my nest.

Slowly the siren, slowly the hearse, sedate
as a dowager. At the E.W. they cut off my dress.

I cried, "Oh Jesus, help me! Oh Jesus Christ!"
and the nurse replied, "Wrong name. My name
is Barbara," and hung me in an odd device,
a buck's extension and a Balkan overhead frame.

The orthopedic man declared,
"You'll be down for a year." His scoop. His news.
He opened the skin. He scraped. He pared
and drilled through bone for his four-inch screws.

That takes brute strength like pushing a cow
up hill. I tell you, it takes skill
and bedside charm and all that know how.
The body is a damn hard thing to kill.

But please don't touch or jiggle my bed.
I'm Ethan Frome's wife. I'll move when I'm able.
The T.V. hangs from the wall like a moose head.
I hide a pint of bourbon in my bedside table.

A bird full of bones, now I'm held by a sand bag.
The fracture was twice. The fracture was double.
The days are horizontal. The days are a drag.
All of the skeleton in me is in trouble.

Across the hall is the bedpan station.
The urine and stools pass hourly by my head
in silver bowls. They flush in unison
in the autoclave. My one dozen roses are dead.

They have ceased to menstruate. They hang
there like little dried up blood clots.

And the heart too, that cripple, how it sang
once. How it thought it could call the shots!

Understand what happened the day that I fell.
My heart had stammered and hungered at
a marriage feast until the angel of hell
turned me into the punisher, the acrobat.

My bones are loose as clothespins,
as abandoned as dolls in a toy shop
and my heart, old hunger motor, with its sins
revved up like an engine that would not stop.

And now I spend all day taking care
of my body, that baby. Its cargo is scarred.
I anoint the bedpan. I brush my hair,
waiting in the pain machine for my bones to get hard,

for the soft, soft bones that were laid apart
and were screwed together. They will knit.
And the other corpse, the fractured heart,
I feed it piecemeal, little chalice. I'm good to it.

Yet like a fire alarm it waits to be known.
It is wired. In it many colors are stored.
While my body's in prison, heart cells alone
have multiplied. My bones are merely bored

with all this waiting around. But the heart,
this child of myself that resides in the flesh,
this ultimate signature of the me, the start
of my blindness and sleep, builds a death crèche.

The figures are placed at the grave of my bones.
All figures knowing it is the other death
they came for. Each figure standing alone.
The heart burst with love and lost its breath.

This little town, this little country is real
and thus it is so of the post and the cup
and thus of the violent heart. The zeal
of my house doth eat me up.

IT IS A SPRING AFTERNOON

Everything here is yellow and green.
Listen to its throat, its earthskin,
the bone dry voices of the peepers
as they throb like advertisements.
The small animals of the woods
are carrying their deathmasks
into a narrow winter cave.
The scarecrow has plucked out
his two eyes like diamonds
and walked into the village.
The general and the postman
have taken off their packs.
This has all happened before
but nothing here is obsolete.
Everything here is possible.

Because of this
perhaps a young girl has laid down
her winter clothes and has casually
placed herself upon a tree limb
that hangs over a pool in the river.
She has been poured out onto the limb,
low above the houses of the fishes
as they swim in and out of her reflection
and up and down the stairs of her legs.
Her body carries clouds all the way home.
She is overlooking her watery face
in the river where blind men
come to bathe at midday.

Because of this
the ground, that winter nightmare,
has cured its sores and burst
with green birds and vitamins.
Because of this
the trees turn in their trenches
and hold up little rain cups
by their slender fingers.
Because of this
a woman stands by her stove
singing and cooking flowers.
Everything here is yellow and green.

Surely spring will allow
a girl without a stitch on
to turn softly in her sunlight
and not be afraid of her bed.
She has already counted seven
blossoms in her green green mirror.
Two rivers combine beneath her.
The face of the child wrinkles
in the water and is gone forever.
The woman is all that can be seen
in her animal loveliness.
Her cherished and obstinate skin
lies deeply under the watery tree.
Everything is altogether possible
and the blind men can also see.

JUST ONCE

Just once I knew what life was for.
In Boston, quite suddenly, I understood;
walked there along the Charles River,
watched the lights copying themselves,

all neoned and strobe-hearted, opening
their mouths as wide as opera singers;
counted the stars, my little campaigners,
my scar daisies, and knew that I walked my love
on the night green side of it and cried
my heart to the eastbound cars and cried
my heart to the westbound cars and took
my truth across a small humped bridge
and hurried my truth, the charm of it, home
and hoarded these constants into morning
only to find them gone.

AGAIN AND AGAIN AND AGAIN

You said the anger would come back
just as the love did.

I have a black look I do not
like. It is a mask I try on.
I migrate toward it and its frog
sits on my lips and defecates.
It is old. It is also a pauper.
I have tried to keep it on a diet.
I give it no unction.

There is a good look that I wear
like a blood clot. I have
sewn it over my left breast.
I have made a vocation of it.
Lust has taken plant in it
and I have placed you and your
child at its milk tip.

Oh the blackness is murderous
and the milk tip is brimming

and each machine is working
and I will kiss you when
I cut up one dozen new men
and you will die somewhat,
again and again.

YOU ALL KNOW THE STORY
OF THE OTHER WOMAN

It's a little Walden.
She is private in her breathbed
as his body takes off and flies,
flies straight as an arrow.
But it's a bad translation.
Daylight is nobody's friend.
God comes in like a landlord
and flashes on his brassy lamp.
Now she is just so-so.
He puts his bones back on,
turning the clock back an hour.
She knows flesh, that skin balloon,
the unbound limbs, the boards,
the roof, the removable roof.
She is his selection, part time.
You know the story too! Look,
when it is over he places her,
like a phone, back on the hook.

MOON SONG, WOMAN SONG

I am alive at night.
I am dead in the morning,
an old vessel who used up her oil,
bleak and pale boned.
No miracle. No dazzle.

I'm out of repair
but you are tall in your battle dress
and I must arrange for your journey.
I was always a virgin,
old and pitted.
Before the world was, I was.

I have been oranging and fat,
carrot colored, gaped at,
allowing my cracked o's to drop on the sea
near Venice and Mombasa.
Over Maine I have rested.
I have fallen like a jet into the Pacific.
I have committed perjury over Japan.
I have dangled my pendulum,
my fat bag, my gold, gold,
blinkedy light
over you all.

So if you must inquire, do so.
After all I am not artificial.
I looked long upon you,
love-bellied and empty,
flipping my endless display
for you, you my cold, cold
coverall man.

You need only request
and I will grant it.
It is virtually guaranteed
that you will walk into me like a barracks.
So come cruising, come cruising,
you of the blast off,
you of the bastion,
you of the scheme.
I will shut my fat eye down,
headquarters of an area,
house of a dream.

THE BALLAD OF
THE LONELY MASTURBATOR

The end of the affair is always death.
She's my workshop. Slippery eye,
out of the tribe of myself my breath
finds you gone. I horrify
those who stand by. I am fed.
At night, alone, I marry the bed.

Finger to finger, now she's mine.
She's not too far. She's my encounter.
I beat her like a bell. I recline
in the bower where you used to mount her.
You borrowed me on the flowered spread.
At night, alone, I marry the bed.

Take for instance this night, my love,
that every single couple puts together
with a joint overturning, beneath, above,
the abundant two on sponge and feather,
kneeling and pushing, head to head.
At night alone, I marry the bed.

I break out of my body this way,
an annoying miracle. Could I
put the dream market on display?
I am spread out. I crucify.
My little plum is what you said.
At night, alone, I marry the bed.

Then my black-eyed rival came.
The lady of water, rising on the beach,
a piano at her fingertips, shame
on her lips and a flute's speech.
And I was the knock-kneed broom instead.
At night, alone, I marry the bed.

She took you the way a woman takes
a bargain dress off the rack
and I broke the way a stone breaks.
I give back your books and fishing tack.
Today's paper says that you are wed.
At night, alone, I marry the bed.

The boys and girls are one tonight.
They unbutton blouses. They unzip flies.
They take off shoes. They turn off the light.
The glimmering creatures are full of lies.
They are eating each other. They are overfed.
At night, alone, I marry the bed.

BAREFOOT

Loving me with my shoes off
means loving my long brown legs,
sweet dears, as good as spoons;
and my feet, those two children
let out to play naked. Intricate nubs,
my toes. No longer bound.
And what's more, see toenails and
prehensile joints of joints and
all ten stages, root by root.
All spirited and wild, this little
piggy went to market and this little piggy
stayed. Long brown legs and long brown toes.
Further up, my darling, the woman
is calling her secrets, little houses,
little tongues that tell you.

The whole first stanza might be a metaphor for freedom, or honor in being a female [handwritten annotation]

There is no one else but us
in this house on the land spit.
The sea wears a bell in its navel.
And I'm your barefoot wench for a

whole week. Do you care for salami?
No. You'd rather not have a scotch?
No. You don't really drink. You do
drink me. The gulls kill fish,
crying out like three-year-olds.
The surf's a narcotic, calling out,
I am, I am, I am
all night long. Barefoot,
I drum up and down your back.
In the morning I run from door to door
of the cabin playing *chase me*.
Now you grab me by the ankles.
Now you work your way up the legs
and come to pierce me at my hunger mark.

*Talks about
the dominance of
male over female*
*how she's
helpless against
him.*

"Barefoot + Pregnant"

THE PAPA AND MAMA DANCE

Taking into consideration all your loveliness
why can't you burn your bootsoles and your
draft card? How can you sit there saying yes
to war? You'll be a pauper when you die, sore
boy. Dead, while I still live at our address.
Oh my brother, why do you keep making plans
when I am at seizures of hearts and hands?
Come dance the dance, the Papa-Mama dance;
bring costumes from the suitcase pasted *Ile de France,*
the S.S. *Gripsholm.* Papa's London Harness case
he took abroad and kept in our attic laced
with old leather straps for storage and his
scholar's robes, black licorice — that metamorphosis
with its crimson hood. Remember we played costume —
bride black and black, black, black the groom?

Taking into consideration all your loveliness,
the mad hours where once we danced on the sofa

200

screaming Papa, Papa, Papa, me in my dress,
my nun's habit and you black as a hammer, a bourgeois
priest who kept leaping and leaping and leaping,
Oh brother, Mr. Gunman, why were you weeping,
inventing curses for your sister's pink, pink ear?
Taking aim and then, as usual, being sincere,
saying something dangerous, something egg-spotted
like *I love you*, ignoring the room where we danced,
ignoring the gin that could get us honestly potted,
and crying Mama, Mama, Mama, that old romance:
I tell you the dances we had were really enough,
your hands on my breast and all that sort of stuff.

Remember the yellow leaves that October day
when we married the tree hut and I didn't go away?
Now I sit here burying the attic and all of your
loveliness. If I jump on the sofa you just sit
in the corner and then you just bang on the door.
YOU WON'T REMEMBER! Yes, Mr. Gunman, that's it!
Isn't the attic familiar? Doesn't the season
trample your mind? War, you say. War, you reason.
Please Mr. Gunman, dance one more, commenting
on costumes, holding them to your breast, lamenting
our black love and putting on that Papa dress.
Papa and Mama did so. Can we do less?

NOW

See. The lamp is adjusted. The ash tray
was carelessly broken by the maid.
Still, balloons saying *love me, love me*
float up over us on the ceiling.
Morning prayers were said as we sat
knee to knee. Four kisses for that!
And why in hell should we mind

the clock? Turn me over from twelve
to six. Then you taste of the ocean.
One day you huddled into a grief ball,
hurled into the corner like a schoolboy.
Oh come with your hammer, your leather
and your wheel. Come with your needle point.
Take my looking glass and my wounds
and undo them. Turn off the light and
then we are all over black paper.

Now it is time to call attention
to our bed, a forest of skin
where seeds burst like bullets.
We are in our room. We are in
a shoe box. We are in a blood box.
We are delicately bruised, yet we
are not old and not stillborn.
We are here on a raft, exiled from dust.
The earth smell is gone. The blood
smell is here and the blade and its bullet.
Time is here and you'll go his way.
Your lung is waiting in the death market.
Your face beside me will grow indifferent.
Darling, you will yield up your belly and be
cored like an apple. The leper will come
and take our names and change the calendar.
The shoemaker will come and he will rebuild
this room. He will lie on your bed
and urinate and nothing will exist.
Now it is time. Now!

US

I was wrapped in black
fur and white fur and

you undid me and then
you placed me in gold light
and then you crowned me,
while snow fell outside
the door in diagonal darts.
While a ten-inch snow
came down like stars
in small calcium fragments,
we were in our own bodies
(that room that will bury us)
and you were in my body
(that room that will outlive us)
and at first I rubbed your
feet dry with a towel
because I was your slave
and then you called me princess.
Princess!

Oh then
I stood up in my gold skin
and I beat down the psalms
and I beat down the clothes
and you undid the bridle
and you undid the reins
and I undid the buttons,
the bones, the confusions,
the New England postcards,
the January ten o'clock night,
and we rose up like wheat,
acre after acre of gold,
and we harvested,
we harvested.

MR. MINE

Notice how he has numbered the blue veins
in my breast. Moreover there are ten freckles.
Now he goes left. Now he goes right.
He is building a city, a city of flesh.
He's an industrialist. He has starved in cellars
and, ladies and gentlemen, he's been broken by iron,
by the blood, by the metal, by the triumphant
iron of his mother's death. But he begins again.
Now he constructs me. He is consumed by the city.
From the glory of boards he has built me up.
From the wonder of concrete he has molded me.
He has given me six hundred street signs.
The time I was dancing he built a museum.
He built ten blocks when I moved on the bed.
He constructed an overpass when I left.
I gave him flowers and he built an airport.
For traffic lights he handed out red and green
lollipops. Yet in my heart I am go children slow.

SONG FOR A LADY

On the day of breasts and small hips
the window pocked with bad rain,
rain coming on like a minister,
we coupled, so sane and insane.
We lay like spoons while the sinister
rain dropped like flies on our lips
and our glad eyes and our small hips.

"The room is so cold with rain," you said
and you, feminine you, with your flower
said novenas to my ankles and elbows.
You are a national product and power.

Oh my swan, my drudge, my dear wooly rose,
even a notary would notarize our bed
as you knead me and I rise like bread.

KNEE SONG

Being kissed on the back
of the knee is a moth
at the windowscreen and
yes my darling a dot
on the fathometer is
tinkerbelle with her cough
and twice I will give up my
honor and stars will stick
like tacks in the night
yes oh yes yes two
little snails at the back
of the knee building bon-
fires something like eye-
lashes something two zippos
striking yes yes yes small
and me maker.

EIGHTEEN DAYS WITHOUT YOU

December 1st

As we kissed good-bye
you made a little frown.
Now Christ's lights are
twinkling all over town.
The cornstalks are broken
in the field, broken and brown.
The pond at the year's end

turns her gray eyelid down.
Christ's lights are
twinkling all over town.

A cat-green ice spreads
out over the front lawn.
The hemlocks are the only
young thing left. You are gone.
I hibernated under the covers
last night, not sleeping until dawn
came up like twilight and the oak leaves
whispered like money, those hangers on.
The hemlocks are the only
young thing left. You are gone.

December 2nd

I slept last night
under a bird's shadow
dreaming of nuthatches at the feeder,
jailed to its spine, jailed right
down to the toes, waiting for slow
death in the hateful December snow.
Mother's death came in the spotlight
and mother slamming the door when I need her
and you at the door yesterday,
you at the loss, grown white,
saying what lovers say.

But in my dream
you were a weird stone man
who sleepwalked in, whose features did not change,
your mouth sewn like a seam,
a dressmaker's dummy who began
without legs and a caved-in waist, my old puritan.
You were all muslin, a faded cream

and I put you in six rooms to rearrange
your doors and your thread popped and spoke,
ripping out an uncovered scream
from which I awoke.

Then I took a pill to sleep again
and I was a criminal in solitary,
both cripple and crook
who had picked ruby eyes from men.
One-legged I became and then
you dragged me off by your Nazi hook.
I was the piece of bad meat they made you carry.
I was bruised. You could not miss.
Dreaming gives one such bad luck
and I had ordered this.

December 3rd

This is the mole-
gray mouth of the year.
Yesterday I stole
out to your hunter's cabin-studio,
surprising two woodchucks and a deer
outside our makeshift bungalow.

On the way to Groton
I saw a dead rabbit
in the road, rotten
with crows pecking at his green entrails.
It's nature, you would have said from habit
and continued on to cocktails.

The sun dogs were
in the sky overhead.
You, my voyager,
were dogging up the old globe going west

and I was at the feeder where juncos fed.
Alone in our place I was a guest.

December 4th

And where did we meet?
Was it in London on Carnaby Street?
Was it in Paris on the Left Bank?
That *there* that I can thank?

No. It was Harvard Square
at the kiosk with both of us crying.
I can thank that *there* —
the day Jack Kennedy was dying.

And one hour later he was dead.
The brains fell out of his dazzling head.
And we cried and drank our whiskey straight
and the world remembers the date, the date.

And we both wrote poems we couldn't write
and cried together the whole long night
and fell in love with a delicate breath
on the eve that great men call for death.

December 5th

That was Oswald's November
four long years ago.
I remember
meeting secretly once a week or oftener,
knowing it wrong, but having those reasons.
So I commute to your studio,
my smoothsmith, my softener.
We take love in all its seasons.

This is the last picture page
of the calendar.
Now I feel my age,
watching the feverish birds outside
pocketing grain in their beaks.
The wind is bizarre.
The wind goes *boo, boo, boo* at my side
and the kitchen faucet leaks.

This is the last leaf
in the year's book.
Now I come to grief
as the earth's breast goes hard and mean
and hay is packed for the manger.
Down by the brook
frogs freeze like chessmen and can't be seen
and you are gone, my stranger.

December 6th

A light rain, as tranquil as an apple, today . . .
mild and supple and fat and fullblown sweet
like the last February 2nd on Groundhog Day.
He wouldn't come out and we lay odds
that his Mickey Mouse nose would greet
us, that his coma wasn't part of the gods.

We thought he'd show at the Candlemass,
show his Chippewa shadow at eleven a.m.
We thought that coldblooded thing would pass
like a priest with his mouthful of beets
for the emerging mystic and the stratagem
that his wide awake shadow meets.

December 7th

Pearl Harbor Day.
The cruciform.
No rain last night, but an icestorm.
Jewels! Today each twig is important,
each ring, each infection, each form
is all that the gods must have meant.

Pearl Harbor Day
leaves scars.
Silver flies in the wind, little stars,
little eye pennies pock up and pock up
and the broken mirrors scatter far
and all the watch parts fill my cup.

Each rock is news.
Each has arrived.
The birds, those beggars, are hardly alive,
feathers like stone and the sealed in food.
Owls force mice into the open. Owls thrive.
The ice will do the birds in, or come unglued.

December 8th

In winter without you I send
a Florida postcard to myself
to somehow remind me of the week
after mid-July and towards the end
when scummy Dog Days were on the shelf
and we had a week of our own to spend.

Snakes snapped their venom
and leftover sparklers were lit
and Roman dogs sniffed the milkweed

210

from which fertile perfume had come.
Small blackcaps came bit by bit
and we came too, from our need.

The sumac had red heads on display
and the good blood moved into every lamb,
tomatoes and snap beans under Sirius,
field corn and field mice came to stay.
Mornings I washed our plates of egg and jam.
Our last light a whippoorwill spoke to us.

December 9th

Two years ago, Reservist,
you would have burned
your draft card or
else have gone A.W.O.L.
But you stayed to serve
the Air Force. Your head churned
with bad solutions, carrying
your heart like a football
to the goal, your good heart
that never quite ceases
to know its wrong. From
Frisco you made a phone call.
Next they manufactured you
into an Aero-medic
who placed together
shot off pieces
of men. Some were sent off
too dead to be sick.

But I wrote no diary
for that time then
and you say what you

do today is worse.
Today you unload the bodies of men
out at Travis Air Force
Base — that curse —
no trees, a crater
surrounded by hills.
The Starlifter from
Vietnam, the multi-hearse
jets in. One hundred
come day by day
just forty-eight hours
after death, filled
sometimes with as
many as sixty coffins in array.

Manual Minus Number
Sixteen Handbook
prefers to call this
the human remains.

This is the stand
that the world took
with the enemy's children
and the enemy's gains.
You unload them slipping
in their rubber sacks
within an aluminum coffin —
those human remains,
always the head higher
than the ten little toes.
They are priority when
they are shipped back
with four months pay
and a burial allotment
that they enclose.

All considerations
for these human remains!
They must have an escort!
They are classified!
Never jettisoned in
emergencies from any planes.
Stay aboard! More important
now that they've died.
You say, "You're treated like
shit until you're killed."

And then brought into The Cave,
those stamped human remains
on a Starlifter, a Cargomaster,
a packet, a Hercules
while napalm is in the frying pan,
while napalm is in the death nest.
And what was at home
was The Peace March —
this Washington we seize.

December 10th

I think today of the animal sounds,
how last night a rebellious fox
was barking out like Lucifer.
When the Beaver Moon lit up the ground
oak twigs scratched like mice in a box.
How in March we waited for the Hyla Crucifer,
those playbell peepers, those one-inch twinkletoes
that come with sticky pads into life when the ice goes.

Mostly it's soundless, the world sealed in,
life turned upside down and down the lock.
So I will remember, remember cicadas in August,

213

their high whine like a hi-fi, shrill and thin
and when you asked me if I were old enough to darn a sock
I cried and then you held me just as you must
and of course we're not married, we are a pair of scissors
who come together to cut, without towels saying His. Hers.

December 11th

Then I think of you in bed,
your tongue half chocolate, half ocean,
of the houses that you swing into,
of the steel wool hair on your head,
of your persistent hands and then
how we gnaw at the barrier because we are two.

How you come and take my blood cup
and link me together and take my brine.
We are bare. We are stripped to the bone
and we swim in tandem and go up and up
the river, the identical river called Mine
and we enter together. No one's alone.

December 12th

And what of me?
I work each day in my
leotards at the State School
where the retarded are
locked up with hospital techniques.
Always I walk past the hydro-
cephalic doorman on his stool,
a five-year-old who sits
all day and never speaks,
his head like a twenty-five

cent balloon, three times
the regular size. It's nature
but nature works such crimes.

I go to the large cement
day room where fifty kids
are locked up for what
they strangely call play.
The toys are not around,
not given to my invalids
because possessions might get
broken or in the way.
We can't go out. There are no
snowsuits, sometimes no shoes
so what I do for them is what
I bring for them to use.

The room stinks of urine.
Only the two-headed baby
is antiseptic in her crib.
Now I take the autoharp,
the drum, the triangle,
the tambourine and the keys
for locked doors and locked
sounds, blind and sharp.
We have clapping of hands
and stamping of feet, please.
I play my humming and lullaby
sounds for each disease.

I sing *The Fox Came Out
On a Chilly Night*
and Bobby, my favorite
Mongoloid sings Fox to me.
I bring out my silk scarfs
for a group of sprites.

Susan wants the blue scarf
and no one is orderly.
I sway with two red scarfs.
I'm in trance,
calling *love me, woo, woo*
and we all passionately dance.

December 13th

Remember that day last June
in the month of the Long-Day-Beauty
that is called Indians' *Wawe-Pesin?*
I tell you Summer came not one day too soon
and surely the calendar did its duty
and we stayed a weekend at the Provincetown Inn.

Remember that thunder storm in July
when the lightning came down the hill —
and I wore my sneakers to stay brave —
came rolling down like a beach ball to fry
and hang inside of the outdoor stone grill,
a toy fire that wouldn't behave?

Remember that barhopping hunt
for a good whiskey and a straight rye,
The Old Overholt with a picture of Washington
looking somewhat constipated on the front
or The Wild Turkey with the crossed eyes —
bourbon we tossed down until we were numb?

December 14th

The migratory birds
have flown the coop

but they'll be back
with their built-in compass.
They'll come back the way
the circus does each year —
with aerialists, our angular
birds that loop the loop.
Two years ago you bought
seats for the children in us.
Children of all ages
the ninety-sixth season is here!

La Toria held by her
wrist to a skyward rope
executed upwards of one
hundred body turns.
The lions in their cruel
cages marched up and down.
And FIREMAN SAVE MY CHILD
let midgets bring us hope,
scurrying to the scene, toy
engines while the toy fire burned.
On the outside, two days before
someone murdered a clown.

The ceiling was strung
up with tenement laundry.
A clown tied a bib on a lion
and fed him like a baby.
Ponies dressed like camels,
poodles dressed like whores
and Doval The Great with his
precious toes (I didn't want to see)
climbed up over the elephants
and the children into immortality.
And you had your pocket picked,
my boyish conspirator.

December 15th

The day of the lonely drunk
is here. No weather reports,
no fox, no birds, no sweet chipmunks,
no sofa game, no summer resorts.

No whatever it was we had,
no sky, no month — just booze.
The half moon is acid, bitter, sad
as I sing the Blended Whiskey Blues.

December 16th

Once upon a time
you grew up in a bedroom the size of a dime
and shared it with your sister. That was West End
Avenue in Manhattan. Longing for country you were penned
into city, peering across the Hudson at Palisades Park.
The boy in you played stickball until it was dark.

Once upon a time
I was the only child forbidden to climb
over the garden wall. I didn't dare to speak
up over the Victorian houseful of rare antiques.
My dolls were all proper, waiting in neat rows.
My room was high ceilinged, lonely and full of echoes.

Once upon a time
you said, "Now that the cabin is ours, I'm
going to run the power in." And we had a power party.
I made gingham curtains. We nailed up your Doctoral degree.
We turned the stove on twice. Oh my love, oh my louse,
we make our own electricity while we play house.

December 17th

Today I bought a Scotch Pine —
O Tannenbaum — a Christmas tree,
as green as a turtle, a forest
of gum and resin and turpentine.
My love, my louse, my absentee,
alone in our place I was not a guest.

With my box from the Five and Dime
I hung bells and balls and silver floss
and one intense strand of reds and greens.
At the end I topped off the ragged pine
with a flashy star, the five point cross
that twinkles for the Nazarene.

Doing this reminded me of the fall awards
we gave to different trees, *First Prize*
was tacked upon the rock maple
in Lincoln Center, then out towards
Weston we pinned *Best Birch at Sunrise*.
We took our census of colors not people.

The purple oaks, the quivering aspens,
those heavy popples the color of old coins;
the woodbine — each with an award on its trunk,
pinned by us with home-made ribbons
on Columbus Day. Prizes when acid joins
the pigment and the sap has been drunk.

Today I bought a sprig of mistletoe,
all warts and leaves and fruit
and stem — the angel of the kiss —
and hung it in our bungalow.
My love, we will take root
during the Christmas Armistice.

December 18th

Swift boomerang, come get!
I am delicate. You've been gone.
The losing has hurt me some, yet
I must bend for you. See me arch. I'm turned on.
My eyes are lawn-colored, my hair brunette.

Kiss the package, Mr. Bind!
Yes? Would you consider hurling yourself
upon me, rigorous but somehow kind?
I am laid out like paper on your cabin kitchen shelf.
So draw me a breast. I like to be underlined.

Look, lout! Say yes!
Draw me like a child. I shall need
merely two round eyes and a small kiss.
A small o. Two earrings would be nice. Then proceed
to the shoulder. You may pause at this.

Catch me. I'm your disease.
Please go slow all along the torso
drawing beads and mouths and trees
and o's, a little *graffiti* and a small *hello*
for I grab, I nibble, I lift, I please.

Draw me good, draw me warm.
Bring me your raw-boned wrist and your
strange, Mr. Bind, strange stubborn horn.
Darling, bring with this an hour of undulations, for
this is the music for which I was born.

Lock in! Be alert, my acrobat
and I will be soft wood and you the nail
and we will make fiery ovens for Jack Sprat
and you will hurl yourself into my tiny jail
and we will take a supper together and that
will be that.

Transformations

(1971)

*To Linda, who reads Hesse
and drinks clam chowder*

THE GOLD KEY

The speaker in this case
is a middle-aged witch, me —
tangled on my two great arms,
my face in a book
and my mouth wide,
ready to tell you a story or two.
I have come to remind you,
all of you:
Alice, Samuel, Kurt, Eleanor,
Jane, Brian, Maryel,
all of you draw near.
Alice,
at fifty-six do you remember?
Do you remember when you
were read to as a child?
Samuel,
at twenty-two have you forgotten?
Forgotten the ten P.M. dreams
where the wicked king
went up in smoke?
Are you comatose?
Are you undersea?

Attention,
my dears,
let me present to you this boy.
He is sixteen and he wants some answers.
He is each of us.
I mean you.
I mean me.
It is not enough to read Hesse
and drink clam chowder,
we must have the answers.
The boy has found a gold key

and he is looking for what it will open.
This boy!
Upon finding a nickel
he would look for a wallet.
This boy!
Upon finding a string
he would look for a harp.
Therefore he holds the key tightly.
Its secrets whimper
like a dog in heat.
He turns the key.
Presto!
It opens this book of odd tales
which transform the Brothers Grimm.
Transform?
As if an enlarged paper clip
could be a piece of sculpture.
(And it could.)

SNOW WHITE
AND THE SEVEN DWARFS

No matter what life you lead
the virgin is a lovely number:
cheeks as fragile as cigarette paper,
arms and legs made of Limoges,
lips like Vin Du Rhône,
rolling her china-blue doll eyes
open and shut.
Open to say,
Good Day Mama,
and shut for the thrust
of the unicorn.
She is unsoiled.
She is as white as a bonefish.

Once there was a lovely virgin
called Snow White.
Say she was thirteen.
Her stepmother,
a beauty in her own right,
though eaten, of course, by age,
would hear of no beauty surpassing her own.
Beauty is a simple passion,
but, oh my friends, in the end
you will dance the fire dance in iron shoes.
The stepmother had a mirror to which she referred —
something like the weather forecast —
a mirror that proclaimed
the one beauty of the land.
She would ask,
Looking glass upon the wall,
who is fairest of us all?
And the mirror would reply,
You are fairest of us all.
Pride pumped in her like poison.

Suddenly one day the mirror replied,
Queen, you are full fair, 'tis true,
but Snow White is fairer than you.
Until that moment Snow White
had been no more important
than a dust mouse under the bed.
But now the queen saw brown spots on her hand
and four whiskers over her lip
so she condemned Snow White
to be hacked to death.
Bring me her heart, she said to the hunter,
and I will salt it and eat it.
The hunter, however, let his prisoner go
and brought a boar's heart back to the castle.
The queen chewed it up like a cube steak.

225

Now I am fairest, she said,
lapping her slim white fingers.

Snow White walked in the wildwood
for weeks and weeks.
At each turn there were twenty doorways
and at each stood a hungry wolf,
his tongue lolling out like a worm.
The birds called out lewdly,
talking like pink parrots,
and the snakes hung down in loops,
each a noose for her sweet white neck.
On the seventh week
she came to the seventh mountain
and there she found the dwarf house.
It was as droll as a honeymoon cottage
and completely equipped with
seven beds, seven chairs, seven forks
and seven chamber pots.
Snow White ate seven chicken livers
and lay down, at last, to sleep.

The dwarfs, those little hot dogs,
walked three times around Snow White,
the sleeping virgin. They were wise
and wattled like small czars.
Yes. It's a good omen,
they said, and will bring us luck.
They stood on tiptoes to watch
Snow White wake up. She told them
about the mirror and the killer-queen
and they asked her to stay and keep house.
Beware of your stepmother,
they said.
Soon she will know you are here.
While we are away in the mines

during the day, you must not
open the door.

Looking glass upon the wall . . .
The mirror told
and so the queen dressed herself in rags
and went out like a peddler to trap Snow White.
She went across seven mountains.
She came to the dwarf house
and Snow White opened the door
and bought a bit of lacing.
The queen fastened it tightly
around her bodice,
as tight as an Ace bandage,
so tight that Snow White swooned.
She lay on the floor, a plucked daisy.
When the dwarfs came home they undid the lace
and she revived miraculously.
She was as full of life as soda pop.
Beware of your stepmother,
they said.
She will try once more.

Looking glass upon the wall . . .
Once more the mirror told
and once more the queen dressed in rags
and once more Snow White opened the door.
This time she bought a poison comb,
a curved eight-inch scorpion,
and put it in her hair and swooned again.
The dwarfs returned and took out the comb
and she revived miraculously.
She opened her eyes as wide as Orphan Annie.
Beware, beware, they said,
but the mirror told,
the queen came,

Snow White, the dumb bunny,
opened the door
and she bit into a poison apple
and fell down for the final time.
When the dwarfs returned
they undid her bodice,
they looked for a comb,
but it did no good.
Though they washed her with wine
and rubbed her with butter
it was to no avail.
She lay as still as a gold piece.

The seven dwarfs could not bring themselves
to bury her in the black ground
so they made a glass coffin
and set it upon the seventh mountain
so that all who passed by
could peek in upon her beauty.
A prince came one June day
and would not budge.
He stayed so long his hair turned green
and still he would not leave.
The dwarfs took pity upon him
and gave him the glass Snow White —
its doll's eyes shut forever —
to keep in his far-off castle.
As the prince's men carried the coffin
they stumbled and dropped it
and the chunk of apple flew out
of her throat and she woke up miraculously.

And thus Snow White became the prince's bride.
The wicked queen was invited to the wedding feast
and when she arrived there were
red-hot iron shoes,

in the manner of red-hot roller skates,
clamped upon her feet.
First your toes will smoke
and then your heels will turn black
and you will fry upward like a frog,
she was told.
And so she danced until she was dead,
a subterranean figure,
her tongue flicking in and out
like a gas jet.
Meanwhile Snow White held court,
rolling her china-blue doll eyes open and shut
and sometimes referring to her mirror
as women do.

THE WHITE SNAKE

There was a day
when all the animals talked to me.
Ten birds at my window saying,
Throw us some seeds,
Dame Sexton,
or we will shrink.
The worms in my son's fishing pail
said, It is chilly!
It is chilly on our way to the hook!
The dog in his innocence
commented in his clumsy voice,
Maybe you're wrong, good Mother,
maybe they're not *real* wars.
And then I knew that the voice
of the spirits had been let in —
as intense as an epileptic aura —
and that no longer would I sing
alone.

In an old time
there was a king as wise as a dictionary.
Each night at supper
a secret dish was brought to him,
a secret dish that kept him wise.
His servant,
who had won no roses before,
thought to lift the lid one night
and take a forbidden look.
There sat a white snake.
The servant thought, Why not?
and took a bite.
It was a furtive weed,
oiled and brooding
and desirably slim.
I have eaten the white snake!
Not a whisker on it! he cried.
Because of the white snake
he heard the animals
in all their voices speak.
Thus the aura came over him.
He was inside.
He had walked into a building
with no exit.
From all sides
the animals spoke up like puppets.
A cold sweat broke out on his upper lip
for now he was wise.

Because he was wise
he found the queen's lost ring
diddling around in a duck's belly
and was thus rewarded with a horse
and a little cash for traveling.
On his way
the fish in the weeds

were drowning on air
and he plunked them back in
and the fish covered him with promises.
On his way
the army ants in the road pleaded for mercy.
Step on us not!
And he rode around them
and the ants covered him with promises.
On his way
the gallow birds asked for food
so he killed his horse to give them lunch.
They sucked the blood up like whiskey
and covered him with promises.

At the next town
the local princess was having a contest.
A common way for princesses to marry.
Fifty men had perished,
gargling the sea like soup.
Still, the servant was stage-struck.
Nail me to the masthead, if you will,
and make a dance all around me.
Put on the gramophone and dance at my ankles.
But the princess smiled like warm milk
and merely dropped her ring into the sea.
If he could not find it, he would die;
die trapped in the sea machine.
The fish, however, remembered
and gave him the ring.
But the princess, ever woman,
said it wasn't enough.
She scattered ten bags of grain in the yard
and commanded him to pick them up by daybreak.
The ants remembered
and carried them in like mailmen.
The princess, ever Eve,

said it wasn't enough
and sent him out to find the apple of life.
He set forth into the forest for two years
where the monkeys jabbered, those trolls,
with their wine-colored underbellies.
They did not make a pathway for him.
The pheasants, those archbishops,
avoided him and the turtles
kept their expressive heads inside.
He was prepared for death
when the gallow birds remembered
and dropped that apple on his head.

He returned to the princess
saying, I am but a traveling man
but here is what you hunger for.
The apple was as smooth as oilskin
and when she took a bite
it was as sweet and crisp as the moon.
Their bodies met over such a dish.
His tongue lay in her mouth
as delicately as the white snake.
They played house, little charmers,
exceptionally well.
So, of course,
they were placed in a box
and painted identically blue
and thus passed their days
living happily ever after —
a kind of coffin,
a kind of blue funk.
Is it not?

RUMPELSTILTSKIN

Inside many of us
is a small old man
who wants to get out.
No bigger than a two-year-old
whom you'd call lamb chop
yet this one is old and malformed.
His head is okay
but the rest of him wasn't Sanforized.
He is a monster of despair.
He is all decay.
He speaks up as tiny as an earphone
with Truman's asexual voice:
I am your dwarf.
I am the enemy within.
I am the boss of your dreams.
No. I am not the law in your mind,
the grandfather of watchfulness.
I am the law of your members,
the kindred of blackness and impulse.
See. Your hand shakes.
It is not palsy or booze.
It is your Doppelgänger
trying to get out.
Beware . . . Beware . . .

There once was a miller
with a daughter as lovely as a grape.
He told the king that she could
spin gold out of common straw.
The king summoned the girl
and locked her in a room full of straw
and told her to spin it into gold
or she would die like a criminal.
Poor grape with no one to pick.

Luscious and round and sleek.
Poor thing.
To die and never see Brooklyn.

She wept,
of course, huge aquamarine tears.
The door opened and in popped a dwarf.
He was as ugly as a wart.
Little thing, what are you? she cried.
With his tiny no-sex voice he replied:
I am a dwarf.
I have been exhibited on Bond Street
and no child will ever call me Papa.
I have no private life.
If I'm in my cups
the whole town knows by breakfast
and no child will ever call me Papa.
I am eighteen inches high.
I am no bigger than a partridge.
I am your evil eye
and no child will ever call me Papa.
Stop this Papa foolishness,
she cried. Can you perhaps
spin straw into gold?
Yes indeed, he said,
that I can do.
He spun the straw into gold
and she gave him her necklace
as a small reward.
When the king saw what she had done
he put her in a bigger room of straw
and threatened death once more.
Again she cried.
Again the dwarf came.
Again he spun the straw into gold.
She gave him her ring

as a small reward.
The king put her in an even bigger room
but this time he promised
to marry her if she succeeded.
Again she cried.
Again the dwarf came.
But she had nothing to give him.
Without a reward the dwarf would not spin.
He was on the scent of something bigger.
He was a regular bird dog.
Give me your first-born
and I will spin.
She thought: Piffle!
He is a silly little man.
And so she agreed.
So he did the trick.
Gold as good as Fort Knox.

The king married her
and within a year
a son was born.
He was like most new babies,
as ugly as an artichoke
but the queen thought him a pearl.
She gave him her dumb lactation,
delicate, trembling, hidden,
warm, etc.
And then the dwarf appeared
to claim his prize.
Indeed! I have become a papa!
cried the little man.
She offered him all the kingdom
but he wanted only this —
a living thing
to call his own.

And being mortal
who can blame him?

The queen cried two pails of sea water.
She was as persistent
as a Jehovah's Witness.
And the dwarf took pity.
He said: I will give you
three days to guess my name
and if you cannot do it
I will collect your child.
The queen sent messengers
throughout the land to find names
of the most unusual sort.
When he appeared the next day
she asked: Melchior?
Balthazar?
But each time the dwarf replied:
No! No! That's not my name.
The next day she asked:
Spindleshanks? Spiderlegs?
But it was still no-no.
On the third day the messenger
came back with a strange story.
He told her:
As I came around the corner of the wood
where the fox says good night to the hare
I saw a little house with a fire
burning in front of it.
Around that fire a ridiculous little man
was leaping on one leg and singing:
Today I bake.
Tomorrow I brew my beer.
The next day the queen's only child will be mine.
Not even the census taker knows
that Rumpelstiltskin is my name . . .

The queen was delighted.
She had the name!
Her breath blew bubbles.

When the dwarf returned
she called out:
Is your name by any chance Rumpelstiltskin?
He cried: The devil told you that!
He stamped his right foot into the ground
and sank in up to his waist.
Then he tore himself in two.
Somewhat like a split broiler.
He laid his two sides down on the floor,
one part soft as a woman,
one part a barbed hook,
one part papa,
one part Doppelgänger.

THE LITTLE PEASANT

Oh how the women
grip and stretch
fainting on the horn.

The men and women
cry to each other.
Touch me,
my pancake,
and make me young.
And thus
like many of us,
the parson
and the miller's wife
lie down in sin.

The women cry,
Come, my fox,
heal me.
I am chalk white
with middle age
so wear me threadbare,
wear me down,
wear me out.
Lick me clean,
as clean as an almond.

The men cry,
Come, my lily,
my fringy queen,
my gaudy dear,
salt me a bird
and be its noose.
Bounce me off
like a shuttlecock.
Dance me dingo-sweet
for I am your lizard,
your sly thing.

Long ago
there was a peasant
who was poor but crafty.
He was not yet a voyeur.
He had yet to find
the miller's wife
at her game.
Now he had not enough
cabbage for supper
nor clover for his one cow.
So he slaughtered the cow
and took the skin
to town.

It was worth no more
than a dead fly
but he hoped for profit.

On his way
he came upon a raven
with damaged wings.
It lay as crumpled as
a wet washcloth.
He said, Come little fellow,
you're part of my booty.

On his way
there was a fierce storm.
Hail jabbed the little peasant's cheeks
like toothpicks.
So he sought shelter at the miller's house.
The miller's wife gave him only
a hunk of stale bread
and let him lie down on some straw.
The peasant wrapped himself and the raven
up in the cowhide
and pretended to fall asleep.

When he lay
as still as a sausage
the miller's wife
let in the parson, saying,
My husband is out
so we shall have a feast.
Roast meat, salad, cakes and wine.
The parson,
his eyes as black as caviar,
said, Come, my lily,
my fringy queen.
The miller's wife,
her lips as red as pimientos,

said, Touch me, my pancake,
and wake me up.
And thus they ate.
And thus
they dingoed-sweet.

Then the miller
was heard stomping on the doorstep
and the miller's wife
hid the food about the house
and the parson in the cupboard.

The miller asked, upon entering,
What is that dead cow doing in the corner?
The peasant spoke up.
It is mine.
I sought shelter from the storm.
You are welcome, said the miller,
but my stomach is as empty as a flour sack.
His wife told him she had no food
but bread and cheese.
So be it, the miller said,
and the three of them ate.

The miller looked once more
at the cowskin
and asked its purpose.
The peasant answered,
I hide my soothsayer in it.
He knows five things about you
but the fifth he keeps to himself.
The peasant pinched the raven's head
and it croaked, Krr. Krr.
That means, translated the peasant,
there is wine under the pillow.
And there it sat
as warm as a specimen.

240

Krr. Krr.
They found the roast meat under the stove.
It lay there like an old dog.
Krr. Krr.
They found the salad in the bed
and the cakes under it.
Krr. Krr.

Because of all this
the miller burned to know the fifth thing.
How much? he asked,
little caring he was being milked.
They settled on a large sum
and the soothsayer said,
The devil is in the cupboard.
And the miller unlocked it.
Krr. Krr.

There stood the parson,
rigid for a moment,
as real as a soup can
and then he took off like a fire
with the wind at its back.
I have tricked the devil,
cried the miller with delight,
and I have tweaked his chin whiskers.
I will be as famous as the king.

The miller's wife
smiled to herself.
Though never again to dingo-sweet
her secret was as safe
as a fly in an outhouse.

The sly little peasant
strode home the next morning,
a soothsayer over his shoulder

and gold pieces knocking like marbles
in his deep pants pocket.
Krr. Krr.

GODFATHER DEATH

Hurry, Godfather death,
Mister tyranny,
each message you give
has a dance to it,
a fish twitch,
a little crotch dance.

A man, say,
has twelve children
and damns the next
at the christening ceremony.
God will not be the godfather,
that skeleton wearing his bones like a broiler,
or his righteousness like a swastika.
The devil will not be the godfather
wearing his streets like a whore.
Only death with its finger on our back
will come to the ceremony.

Death, with a one-eyed jack in his hand,
makes a promise to the thirteenth child:
My Godchild, physician you will be,
the one wise one, the one never wrong,
taking your cue from me.
When I stand at the head of the dying man,
he will die indelicately and come to me.
When I stand at his feet,
he will run on the glitter of wet streets once more.
And so it came to be.

Thus this doctor was never a beginner.
He knew who would go.
He knew who would stay.
This doctor,
this thirteenth but chosen,
cured on straw or midocean.
He could not be elected.
He was not the mayor.
He was more famous than the king.
He peddled his fingernails for gold
while the lepers turned into princes.

His wisdom
outnumbered him
when the dying king called him forth.
Godfather death stood by the head
and the jig was up.
This doctor,
this thirteenth but chosen,
swiveled that king like a shoebox
from head to toe,
and so, my dears,
he lived.

Godfather death replied to this:
Just once I'll shut my eyelid,
you blundering cow.
Next time, Godchild,
I'll rap you under my ankle
and take you with me.
The doctor agreed to that.
He thought: A dog only laps lime once.

It came to pass,
however,
that the king's daughter was dying.

The king offered his daughter in marriage
if she were to be saved.
The day was as dark as the Führer's headquarters.
Godfather death stood once more at the head.
The princess was as ripe as a tangerine.
Her breasts purred up and down like a cat.
I've been bitten! I've been bitten!
cried the thirteenth but chosen
who had fallen in love
and thus turned her around like a shoebox.

Godfather death
turned him over like a camp chair
and fastened a rope to his neck
and led him into a cave.
In this cave, murmured Godfather death,
all men are assigned candles
that inch by inch number their days.
Your candle is here.
And there it sat,
no bigger than an eyelash.
The thirteenth but chosen
jumped like a wild rabbit on a hook
and begged it be relit.
His white head hung out like a carpet bag
and his crotch turned blue as a blood blister,
and Godfather death, as it is written,
put a finger on his back
for the big blackout,
the big no.

RAPUNZEL

   A woman
   who loves a woman

is forever young.
The mentor
and the student
feed off each other.
Many a girl
had an old aunt
who locked her in the study
to keep the boys away.
They would play rummy
or lie on the couch
and touch and touch.
Old breast against young breast . . .

Let your dress fall down your shoulder,
come touch a copy of you
for I am at the mercy of rain,
for I have left the three Christs of Ypsilanti,
for I have left the long naps of Ann Arbor
and the church spires have turned to stumps.
The sea bangs into my cloister
for the young politicians are dying,
are dying so hold me, my young dear,
hold me . . .

The yellow rose will turn to cinder
and New York City will fall in
before we are done so hold me,
my young dear, hold me.
Put your pale arms around my neck.
Let me hold your heart like a flower
lest it bloom and collapse.
Give me your skin
as sheer as a cobweb,
let me open it up
and listen in and scoop out the dark.
Give me your nether lips
all puffy with their art

and I will give you angel fire in return.
We are two clouds
glistening in the bottle glass.
We are two birds
washing in the same mirror.
We were fair game
but we have kept out of the cesspool.
We are strong.
We are the good ones.
Do not discover us
for we lie together all in green
like pond weeds.
Hold me, my young dear, hold me.

They touch their delicate watches
one at a time.
They dance to the lute
two at a time.
They are as tender as bog moss.
They play mother-me-do
all day.
A woman
who loves a woman
is forever young.

Once there was a witch's garden
more beautiful than Eve's
with carrots growing like little fish,
with many tomatoes rich as frogs,
onions as ingrown as hearts,
the squash singing like a dolphin
and one patch given over wholly to magic —
rampion, a kind of salad root,
a kind of harebell more potent than penicillin,
growing leaf by leaf, skin by skin,
as rapt and as fluid as Isadora Duncan.

246

However the witch's garden was kept locked
and each day a woman who was with child
looked upon the rampion wildly,
fancying that she would die
if she could not have it.
Her husband feared for her welfare
and thus climbed into the garden
to fetch the life-giving tubers.

Ah ha, cried the witch,
whose proper name was Mother Gothel,
you are a thief and now you will die.
However they made a trade,
typical enough in those times.
He promised his child to Mother Gothel
so of course when it was born
she took the child away with her.
She gave the child the name Rapunzel,
another name for the life-giving rampion.
Because Rapunzel was a beautiful girl
Mother Gothel treasured her beyond all things.
As she grew older Mother Gothel thought:
None but I will ever see her or touch her.
She locked her in a tower without a door
or a staircase. It had only a high window.
When the witch wanted to enter she cried:
Rapunzel, Rapunzel, let down your hair.
Rapunzel's hair fell to the ground like a rainbow.
It was as yellow as a dandelion
and as strong as a dog leash.
Hand over hand she shinnied up
the hair like a sailor
and there in the stone-cold room,
as cold as a museum,
Mother Gothel cried:

Hold me, my young dear, hold me,
and thus they played mother-me-do.

Years later a prince came by
and heard Rapunzel singing in her loneliness.
That song pierced his heart like a valentine
but he could find no way to get to her.
Like a chameleon he hid himself among the trees
and watched the witch ascend the swinging hair.
The next day he himself called out:
Rapunzel, Rapunzel, let down your hair,
and thus they met and he declared his love.
What is this beast, she thought,
with muscles on his arms
like a bag of snakes?
What is this moss on his legs?
What prickly plant grows on his cheeks?
What is this voice as deep as a dog?
Yet he dazzled her with his answers.
Yet he dazzled her with his dancing stick.
They lay together upon the yellowy threads,
swimming through them
like minnows through kelp
and they sang out benedictions like the Pope.

Each day he brought her a skein of silk
to fashion a ladder so they could both escape.
But Mother Gothel discovered the plot
and cut off Rapunzel's hair to her ears
and took her into the forest to repent.
When the prince came the witch fastened
the hair to a hook and let it down.
When he saw that Rapunzel had been banished
he flung himself out of the tower, a side of beef.
He was blinded by thorns that pricked him like tacks.
As blind as Oedipus he wandered for years

until he heard a song that pierced his heart
like that long-ago valentine.
As he kissed Rapunzel her tears fell on his eyes
and in the manner of such cure-alls
his sight was suddenly restored.

They lived happily as you might expect
proving that mother-me-do
can be outgrown,
just as the fish on Friday,
just as a tricycle.
The world, some say,
is made up of couples.
A rose must have a stem.

As for Mother Gothel,
her heart shrank to the size of a pin,
never again to say: Hold me, my young dear,
hold me,
and only as she dreamt of the yellow hair
did moonlight sift into her mouth.

IRON HANS

Take a lunatic
for instance,
with Saint Averton, the patron saint,
a lunatic wearing that strait jacket
like a sleeveless sweater,
singing to the wall like Muzak,
how he walks east to west,
west to east again
like a fish in an aquarium.
And if they stripped him bare
he would fasten his hands around your throat.

After that he would take your corpse
and deposit his sperm in three orifices.
You know, I know,
you'd run away.

I am mother of the insane.
Let me give you my children:

Take a girl sitting in a chair
like a china doll.
She doesn't say a word.
She doesn't even twitch.
She's as still as furniture.
And you'll move off.

Take a man who is crying
over and over,
his face like a sponge.
You'll move off.

Take a woman talking,
purging herself with rhymes,
drumming words out like a typewriter,
planting words in you like grass seed.
You'll move off.

Take a man full of suspicions
saying: Don't touch this,
you'll be electrocuted.
Wipe off this glass three times.
There is arsenic in it.
I hear messages from God
through the fillings in my teeth.

Take a boy on a bridge.
One hundred feet up. About to jump,
thinking: This is my last ball game.

This time it's a home run.
Wanting the good crack of the bat.
Wanting to throw his body away
like a corn cob.
And you'll move off.

Take an old lady in a cafeteria
staring at the meat loaf,
crying: Mama! Mama!
And you'll move off.

Take a man in a cage
wetting his pants,
beating on that crib,
breaking his iron hands in two.
And you'll move off.

Clifford, Vincent, Friedrich,
my scooter boys,
deep in books,
long before you were mad.
Zelda, Hannah, Renée.
Moon girls,
where did you go?

There once was a king
whose forest was bewitched.
All the huntsmen,
all the hounds,
disappeared in it like soap bubbles.
A brave huntsman and his dog
entered one day to test it.
The dog drank from a black brook;
as he lapped an arm reached out
and pulled him under.
The huntsman emptied the pool
pail by pail by pail
and at the bottom lay

a wild man,
his body rusty brown.
His hair covering his knees.
Perhaps he was no more dangerous
than a hummingbird;
perhaps he was Christ's boy-child;
perhaps he was only bruised like an apple
but he appeared to them to be a lunatic.
The king placed him in a large iron cage
in the courtyard of his palace.
The court gathered around the wild man
and munched peanuts and sold balloons
and not until he cried out:
Agony! Agony!
did they move off.

The king's son
was playing with his ball one day
and it rolled into the iron cage.
It appeared as suddenly as a gallstone.
The wild man did not complain.
He talked calmly to the boy
and convinced him to unlock the cage.
The wild man carried him and his ball
piggyback off into the woods
promising him good luck and gold for life.

The wild man set the boy at a golden spring
and asked him to guard it from a fox
or a feather that might pollute it.
The boy agreed and took up residence there.
The first night he dipped his finger in.
It turned to gold; as gold as a fountain pen,
but the wild man forgave him.
The second night he bent to take a drink
and his hair got wet, turning as gold

as Midas' daughter.
As stiff as the Medusa hair of a Greek statue.
This time the wild man could not forgive him.
He sent the boy out into the world.
But if you have great need, he said,
you may come into the forest and call *Iron Hans*
and I will come to help you for you
were the only one who was kind
to this accursed bull of a wild man.

The boy went out into the world,
his gold hair tucked under a cap.
He found work as a gardener's boy
at a far-off castle. All day set out
under the red ball to dig and weed.
One day he picked some wildflowers
for the princess and took them to her.
She demanded he take off his cap
in her presence. You look like a jester,
she taunted him, but he would not.
You look like a bird, she taunted him,
and snatched off the cap.
His hair fell down with a clang.
It fell down like a moon chain
and it delighted her.
The princess fell in love.

Next there was a war
that the king was due to lose.
The boy went into the forest
and called out: Iron Hans, Iron Hans,
and the wild man appeared.
He gave the boy a black charger,
a sword as sharp as a guillotine
and a great body of black knights.
They went forth and cut the enemy down

like a row of cabbage heads.
Then they vanished.
The court talked of nothing
but the unknown knight in a cap.
The princess thought of the boy
but the head gardener said:
Not he. He had only a three-legged horse.
He could have done better with a stork.
Three days in a row,
the princess, hoping to lure him back,
threw a gold ball.
Remember back,
the boy was good at losing balls
but was he good at catching them?
Three days running the boy,
thanks to Iron Hans,
performed like Joe Dimaggio.
And thus they were married.

At the wedding feast
the music stopped suddenly
and a door flew open
and a proud king walked in
and embraced the boy.
Of course
it was Iron Hans.
He had been bewitched
and the boy had broken the spell.
He who slays the warrior
and captures the maiden's heart
undoes the spell.
He who kills his father
and thrice wins his mother
undoes the spell.

Without Thorazine
or benefit of psychotherapy

Iron Hans was transformed.
No need for Master Medical;
no need for electroshock —
merely bewitched all along.
Just as the frog who was a prince.
Just as the madman his simple boyhood.

When I was a wild man,
Iron Hans said,
I tarnished all the world.
I was the infector.
I was the poison breather.
I was a professional,
but you have saved me
from the awful babble
of that calling.

CINDERELLA

You always read about it:
the plumber with twelve children
who wins the Irish Sweepstakes.
From toilets to riches.
That story.

Or the nursemaid,
some luscious sweet from Denmark
who captures the oldest son's heart.
From diapers to Dior.
That story.

Or a milkman who serves the wealthy,
eggs, cream, butter, yogurt, milk,
the white truck like an ambulance
who goes into real estate

and makes a pile.
From homogenized to martinis at lunch.

Or the charwoman
who is on the bus when it cracks up
and collects enough from the insurance.
From mops to Bonwit Teller.
That story.

Once
the wife of a rich man was on her deathbed
and she said to her daughter Cinderella:
Be devout. Be good. Then I will smile
down from heaven in the seam of a cloud.
The man took another wife who had
two daughters, pretty enough
but with hearts like blackjacks.
Cinderella was their maid.
She slept on the sooty hearth each night
and walked around looking like Al Jolson.
Her father brought presents home from town,
jewels and gowns for the other women
but the twig of a tree for Cinderella.
She planted that twig on her mother's grave
and it grew to a tree where a white dove sat.
Whenever she wished for anything the dove
would drop it like an egg upon the ground.
The bird is important, my dears, so heed him.

Next came the ball, as you all know.
It was a marriage market.
The prince was looking for a wife.
All but Cinderella were preparing
and gussying up for the big event.
Cinderella begged to go too.
Her stepmother threw a dish of lentils

into the cinders and said: Pick them
up in an hour and you shall go.
The white dove brought all his friends;
all the warm wings of the fatherland came,
and picked up the lentils in a jiffy.
No, Cinderella, said the stepmother,
you have no clothes and cannot dance.
That's the way with stepmothers.

Cinderella went to the tree at the grave
and cried forth like a gospel singer:
Mama! Mama! My turtledove,
send me to the prince's ball!
The bird dropped down a golden dress
and delicate little gold slippers.
Rather a large package for a simple bird.
So she went. Which is no surprise.
Her stepmother and sisters didn't
recognize her without her cinder face
and the prince took her hand on the spot
and danced with no other the whole day.

As nightfall came she thought she'd better
get home. The prince walked her home
and she disappeared into the pigeon house
and although the prince took an axe and broke
it open she was gone. Back to her cinders.
These events repeated themselves for three days.
However on the third day the prince
covered the palace steps with cobbler's wax
and Cinderella's gold shoe stuck upon it.
Now he would find whom the shoe fit
and find his strange dancing girl for keeps.
He went to their house and the two sisters
were delighted because they had lovely feet.
The eldest went into a room to try the slipper on
but her big toe got in the way so she simply

sliced it off and put on the slipper.
The prince rode away with her until the white dove
told him to look at the blood pouring forth.
That is the way with amputations.
They don't just heal up like a wish.
The other sister cut off her heel
but the blood told as blood will.
The prince was getting tired.
He began to feel like a shoe salesman.
But he gave it one last try.
This time Cinderella fit into the shoe
like a love letter into its envelope.

At the wedding ceremony
the two sisters came to curry favor
and the white dove pecked their eyes out.
Two hollow spots were left
like soup spoons.

Cinderella and the prince
lived, they say, happily ever after,
like two dolls in a museum case
never bothered by diapers or dust,
never arguing over the timing of an egg,
never telling the same story twice,
never getting a middle-aged spread,
their darling smiles pasted on for eternity.
Regular Bobbsey Twins.
That story.

ONE-EYE, TWO-EYES, THREE-EYES

Even in the pink crib
the somehow deficient,

the somehow maimed,
are thought to have
a special pipeline to the mystical,
the faint smell of the occult,
a large ear on the God-horn.

Still,
the parents have bizarre thoughts,
thoughts like a skill saw.
They accuse: Your grandfather,
your bad sperm, your evil ovary.
Thinking: The devil has put his finger upon us.
And yet in time
they consult their astrologer
and admire their trophy.
They turn a radish into a ruby.
They plan an elaborate celebration.
They warm to their roles.
They carry it off with a positive fervor.
The bird who cannot fly
is left like a cockroach.
A three-legged kitten is carried
by the scruff of the neck
and dropped into a blind cellar hole.
A malformed foal would not be nursed.
Nature takes care of nature.

I knew a child once
With the mind of a hen.
She was the favored one
for she was as innocent as a snowflake
and was a great lover of music.
She could have been a candidate
for the International Bach Society
but she was only a primitive.
A harmonica would do.

Love grew around her like crabgrass.
Even though she might live to the age of fifty
her mother planned a Mass of the Angels
and wore her martyrdom
like a string of pearls.

The unusual needs to be commented upon . . .
The Thalidomide babies
with flippers at their shoulders,
wearing their mechanical arms
like derricks.
The club-footed boy
wearing his shoe like a flat iron.
The idiot child,
a stuffed doll who can only masturbate.
The hunchback carrying his hump
like a bag of onions . . .
Oh how we treasure
their scenic value.

When a child stays needy until he is fifty —
oh mother-eye, oh mother-eye, crush me in —
the parent is as strong as a telephone pole.

Once upon a time
there were three sisters.
One with one eye
like a great blue aggie.
One with two eyes,
common as pennies.
One with three eyes,
the third like an intern.
Their mother loved only One-Eye and Three.
She loved them because they were God's lie.

And she liked to poke
at the unusual holes in their faces.
Two-Eyes was as ordinary
as an old man with a big belly
and she despised her.
Two-Eyes wore only rags
and ate only scraps from the dog's dish
and spent her days caring for their goat.

One day,
off in the fields with the goat,
Two-Eyes cried, her cheeks as wet as a trout
and an old woman appeared before her
and promised if she sang to her goat
a feast would always be provided.
Two-Eyes sang and there appeared a table
as rich as one at Le Pavillon
and each dish bloomed like floribunda.
Two-Eyes, her eyes as matched as a pen and pencil set,
ate all she could.
This went on in a secret manner
until the mother and sisters saw
that she was not lapping from the dog dish.
So One-Eye came with her and her goat
to see where and how she got the secret food.
However Two-Eyes sang to her as softly as milk
and soon she fell fast asleep.
In this way Two-Eyes enjoyed her usual magic meal.
Next the mother sent Three-Eyes to watch.
Again Two-Eyes sang and again her sister fell asleep.
However her third eye did not shut.
It stayed as open as a clam on a half shell
and thus she witnessed the magic meal,
thus the mother heard all of it
and thus they killed the goat.

Again Two-Eyes cried like a trout
and again the old woman came to her
and told her to take some of the insides
of the slaughtered goat and bury them
in front of the cottage.
She carried forth the green and glossy intestine
and buried it where she was told.
The next morning they all saw
a great tree with leaves of silver
glittering like tinfoil
and apples made of fourteen carat gold.
One-Eye tried to climb up and pick one
but the branches merely withdrew.
Three-Eyes tried and the branches withdrew.
The mother tried and the branches withdrew.
May I try, said Two-Eyes,
but they replied:
You with your two eyes,
what can you do?
Yet when she climbed up and reached out
an apple came into her hand
as simply as a chicken laying her daily egg.

They bade her come down from the tree to hide
as a handsome knight was riding their way.
He stopped
and admired the tree
as you knew he would.
They claimed the tree as theirs
and he said sadly:
He who owns a branch of that tree
would have all he wished for in this world.
The two sisters clipped around the tree
like a pair of miming clowns
but not a branch or an apple came their way.
The tree treated them like poison ivy.

At last Two-Eyes came forth
and easily broke off a branch for him.

Quite naturally the knight carried her off
and the sisters were overjoyed
as now the tree would belong to them.
It burned in their brains like radium
but the next morning the tree had vanished.
The tree had, in the way of such magic,
followed Two-Eyes to the castle.
The knight married her
and she wore gowns as lovely as kisses
and ate goose liver and peaches
whenever she wished.

Years later
two beggars came to the castle,
along with the fishermen and the peasants
and the whole mournful lot.
These beggars were none other than her sisters
wearing their special eyes,
one the Cyclops,
one the pawnshop.
Two-Eyes was kind to them
and took them in
for they were magical.
They were to become her Stonehenge,
her cosmic investment,
her seals, her rings, her urns
and she became as strong as Moses.
Two-Eyes was kind to them
and took them in
because they were needy.
They were to become her children,
her charmed cripples, her hybrids —
oh mother-eye, oh mother-eye, crush me in.

So they took root in her heart
with their religious hunger.

THE WONDERFUL MUSICIAN

My sisters,
do you remember the fiddlers
of your youth?
Those dances
so like a drunkard
lighting a fire in the belly?
That speech,
as piercing as a loon's,
exciting both mayors
and cab drivers?
Sometimes,
ear to the bedside radio,
frozen on your cot
like a humped hairpin,
or jolt upright in the wind
on alternating current
like a fish on the hook
dancing the death dance,
remember
the vibrato,
a wasp in the ear?
Remember dancing in
those electric shoes?
Remember?
Remember music
and beware.

Consider
the wonderful musician
who goes quite alone

through the forest
and plays his fiddle-me-roo
to bring forth a companion.
The fox
was a womanly sort,
his tongue lapping a mirror.
But when he heard the music
he danced forth
in those electric shoes
and promised his life
if he too could learn to play.
The musician despised the fox
but nevertheless he said,
You have only to do as I bid you.
The fox replied,
I will obey you as
a scholar obeys his master.
Thus the musician
took him to an oak tree
and bade him put his left paw
in its wooden slit.
Then he fixed him with a wedge
until he was caught.
The fox was left there
kneeling like Romeo.

The musician went on
playing his fiddle-me-roo
to bring forth a companion.
The wolf,
a greedy creature,
his eye on the soup kettle,
heard the music
and danced forth
in those electric shoes.
He came forth

and was bilked
by the same order.
The musician fastened
both his paws to a hazel bush
and he hung spread-eagle
on a miniature crucifix.

The musician went on
playing his fiddle-me-roo
to bring forth a companion.
The hare,
a child of the dark,
his tail twitching
over the cellar hole,
came forth and was had.
With a rope around his throat
he ran twenty times around the maypole
until he foamed up
like a rabid dog.

The fox
as clever as a martyr
freed himself
and coming upon the crucifixion
and the rabid dog,
undid them
and all three swept
through the forest
to tear off the musician's
ten wonderful fingers.

The musician had gone on
playing his fiddle-me-roo.
Old kiteskin,
the bird,
had seen the persecution

and lay as still
as a dollar bill.
Old drowse-belly,
the snake,
did not come forth —
He lay as still as a ruler.
But a poor woodcutter
came forth with his axe
promising his life
for that music.

The wolf, the fox,
and the hare
came in for the kill.
The woodcutter
held up his axe —
it glinted like a steak knife —
and forecast their death.
They scuttled back into the wood
and the musician played
fiddle-me-roo
once more.
Saved by his gift
like many of us —
little Eichmanns,
little mothers —
I'd say.

RED RIDING HOOD

Many are the deceivers:

The suburban matron,
proper in the supermarket,
list in hand so she won't suddenly fly,

buying her Duz and Chuck Wagon dog food,
meanwhile ascending from earth,
letting her stomach fill up with helium,
letting her arms go loose as kite tails,
getting ready to meet her lover
a mile down Apple Crest Road
in the Congregational Church parking lot.

Two seemingly respectable women
come up to an old Jenny
and show her an envelope
full of money
and promise to share the booty
if she'll give them ten thou
as an act of faith.
Her life savings are under the mattress
covered with rust stains
and counting.
They are as wrinkled as prunes
but negotiable.
The two women take the money and disappear.
Where is the moral?
Not all knives are for
stabbing the exposed belly.
Rock climbs on rock
and it only makes a seashore.
Old Jenny has lost her belief in mattresses
and now she has no wastebasket in which
to keep her youth.

The standup comic
on the "Tonight" show
who imitates the Vice President
and cracks up Johnny Carson
and delays sleep for millions
of bedfellows watching between their feet,

slits his wrist the next morning
in the Algonquin's old-fashioned bathroom,
the razor in his hand like a toothbrush,
wall as anonymous as a urinal,
the shower curtain his slack rubberman audience,
and then the slash
as simple as opening a letter
and the warm blood breaking out like a rose
upon the bathtub with its claw and ball feet.

And I. I too.
Quite collected at cocktail parties,
meanwhile in my head
I'm undergoing open-heart surgery.
The heart, poor fellow,
pounding on his little tin drum
with a faint death beat.
The heart, that eyeless beetle,
enormous that Kafka beetle,
running panicked through his maze,
never stopping one foot after the other
one hour after the other
until he gags on an apple
and it's all over.

And I. I too again.
I built a summer house on Cape Ann.
A simple A-frame and this too was
a deception — nothing haunts a new house.
When I moved in with a bathing suit and tea bags
the ocean rumbled like a train backing up
and at each window secrets came in
like gas. My mother, that departed soul,
sat in my Eames chair and reproached me
for losing her keys to the old cottage.
Even in the electric kitchen there was

the smell of a journey. The ocean
was seeping through its frontiers
and laying me out on its wet rails.
The bed was stale with my childhood
and I could not move to another city
where the worthy make a new life.

Long ago
there was a strange deception:
a wolf dressed in frills,
a kind of transvestite.
But I get ahead of my story.
In the beginning
there was just little Red Riding Hood,
so called because her grandmother
made her a red cape and she was never without it.
It was her Linus blanket, besides
it was red, as red as the Swiss flag,
yes it was red, as red as chicken blood.
But more than she loved her riding hood
she loved her grandmother who lived
far from the city in the big wood.

This one day her mother gave her
a basket of wine and cake
to take to her grandmother
because she was ill.
Wine and cake?
Where's the aspirin? The penicillin?
Where's the fruit juice?
Peter Rabbit got camomile tea.
But wine and cake it was.

On her way in the big wood
Red Riding Hood met the wolf.
Good day, Mr. Wolf, she said,

thinking him no more dangerous
than a streetcar or a panhandler.
He asked where she was going
and she obligingly told him.
There among the roots and trunks
with the mushrooms pulsing inside the moss
he planned how to eat them both,
the grandmother an old carrot
and the child a shy budkin
in a red red hood.
He bade her to look at the bloodroot,
the small bunchberry and the dogtooth
and pick some for her grandmother.
And this she did.
Meanwhile he scampered off
to Grandmother's house and ate her up
as quick as a slap.
Then he put on her nightdress and cap
and snuggled down into the bed.
A deceptive fellow.

Red Riding Hood
knocked on the door and entered
with her flowers, her cake, her wine.
Grandmother looked strange,
a dark and hairy disease it seemed.
Oh Grandmother, what big ears you have,
ears, eyes, hands and then the teeth.
The better to eat you with, my dear.
So the wolf gobbled Red Riding Hood down
like a gumdrop. Now he was fat.
He appeared to be in his ninth month
and Red Riding Hood and her grandmother
rode like two Jonahs up and down with
his every breath. One pigeon. One partridge.

He was fast asleep,
dreaming in his cap and gown,
wolfless.
Along came a huntsman who heard
the loud contented snores
and knew that was no grandmother.
He opened the door and said,
So it's you, old sinner.
He raised his gun to shoot him
when it occurred to him that maybe
the wolf had eaten up the old lady.
So he took a knife and began cutting open
the sleeping wolf, a kind of caesarian section.

It was a carnal knife that let
Red Riding Hood out like a poppy,
quite alive from the kingdom of the belly.
And grandmother too
still waiting for cakes and wine.
The wolf, they decided, was too mean
to be simply shot so they filled his belly
with large stones and sewed him up.
He was as heavy as a cemetery
and when he woke up and tried to run off
he fell over dead. Killed by his own weight.
Many a deception ends on such a note.

The huntsman and the grandmother and Red Riding
    Hood
sat down by his corpse and had a meal of wine and
    cake.
Those two remembering
nothing naked and brutal
from that little death,
that little birth,
from their going down
and their lifting up.

THE MAIDEN
WITHOUT HANDS

Is it possible
he marries a cripple
out of admiration?
A desire to own the maiming
so that not one of us butchers
will come to him with crowbars
or slim precise tweezers?
Lady, bring me your wooden leg
so I may stand on my own
two pink pig feet.
If someone burns out your eye
I will take your socket
and use it for an ashtray.
If they have cut out your uterus
I will give you a laurel wreath
to put in its place.
If you have cut off your ear
I will give you a crow
who will hear just as well.
My apple has no worm in it!
My apple is whole!

Once
there was a cruel father
who cut off his daughter's hands
to escape from the wizard.
The maiden held up her stumps
as helpless as dog's paws
and that made the wizard
want her. He wanted to lap
her up like strawberry preserve.
She cried on her stumps
as sweet as lotus water,

as strong as petroleum,
as sure-fire as castor oil.
Her tears lay around her like a moat.
Her tears so purified her
that the wizard could not approach.

She left her father's house
to wander in forbidden woods,
the good, kind king's woods.
She stretched her neck like an elastic,
up, up, to take a bite of a pear
hanging from the king's tree.
Picture her there for a moment,
a perfect still life.
After all,
she could not feed herself
or pull her pants down
or brush her teeth.

She was, I'd say,
without resources.
The king spied upon her at
that moment of stretching up, up
and he thought,
Eeny, Meeny, Miny, Mo —
There but for the grace of —
I will take her for my wife.

And thus they were married
and lived together on a sugar cube.
The king had silver hands made for her.
They were polished daily and kept in place,
little tin mittens.
The court bowed at the sight of them from a distance.
The leisurely passerby stopped and crossed himself.
What a fellow he is, they said of the king,
and kept their lips pursed as for a kiss.

But that was not the last word
for the king was called to war.
Naturally the queen was pregnant
so the king left her in care of his mother.
Buy her a perambulator, he said,
and send me a message when my son is born.
Let me hear no catcalls
or see a burned mattress.
He was superstitious.
You can see his point of view.

When the son was born
the mother sent a message
but the wizard intercepted it,
saying, instead, a changeling was born.
The king didn't mind.
He was used to this sort of thing by now.
He said: Take care,
but the wizard intercepted it,
saying: Kill both;
then cut out her eyes and send them,
also cut out his tongue and send it;
I will want my proof.

The mother,
now the grandmother —
a strange vocation to be a mother at all —
told them to run off in the woods.
The queen named her son
Painbringer
and fled to a safe cottage in the woods.
She and Painbringer were so good in the woods
that her hands grew back.
The ten fingers budding like asparagus,
the palms as whole as pancakes,
as soft and pink as face powder.

The king returned to the castle
and heard the news from his mother
and then he set out for seven years in the woods
never once eating a thing,
or so he said,
doing far better than Mahatma Gandhi.
He was good and kind as I have already said
so he found his beloved.
She brought forth the silver hands.
She brought forth Painbringer
and he realized they were his,
though both now unfortunately whole.
Now the butchers will come to *me*,
he thought, for I have lost my luck.
It put an insidious fear in him
like a tongue depressor held fast
at the back of your throat.
But he was good and kind
so he made the best of it
like a switch hitter.

They returned to the castle
and had a second wedding feast.
He put a ring on her finger this time
and they danced like dandies.
All their lives they kept the silver hands,
polished daily,
a kind of purple heart,
a talisman,
a yellow star.

THE TWELVE DANCING
PRINCESSES

   If you danced from midnight
   to six A.M. who would understand?

276

The runaway boy
who chucks it all
to live on the Boston Common
on speed and saltines,
pissing in the duck pond,
rapping with the street priest,
trading talk like blows,
another missing person,
would understand.

The paralytic's wife
who takes her love to town,
sitting on the bar stool,
downing stingers and peanuts,
singing "That ole Ace down in the hole,"
would understand.

The passengers
from Boston to Paris
watching the movie with dawn
coming up like statues of honey,
having partaken of champagne and steak
while the world turned like a toy globe,
those murderers of the nightgown
would understand.

The amnesiac
who tunes into a new neighborhood,
having misplaced the past,
having thrown out someone else's
credit cards and monogrammed watch,
would understand.

The drunken poet
(a genius by daylight)
who places long-distance calls
at three A.M. and then lets you sit

277

holding the phone while he vomits
(he calls it "The Night of the Long Knives")
getting his kicks out of the death call,
would understand.

The insomniac
listening to his heart
thumping like a June bug,
listening on his transistor
to Long John Nebel arguing from New York,
lying on his bed like a stone table,
would understand.

The night nurse
with her eyes slit like Venetian blinds,
she of the tubes and the plasma,
listening to the heart monitor,
the death cricket bleeping,
she who calls you "we"
and keeps vigil like a ballistic missile,
would understand.

Once
this king had twelve daughters,
each more beautiful than the other.
They slept together, bed by bed
in a kind of girls' dormitory.
At night the king locked and bolted the door.
How could they possibly escape?
Yet each morning their shoes
were danced to pieces.
Each was as worn as an old jockstrap.
The king sent out a proclamation
that anyone who could discover
where the princesses did their dancing
could take his pick of the litter.

However there was a catch.
If he failed, he would pay with his life.
Well, so it goes.

Many princes tried,
each sitting outside the dormitory,
the door ajar so he could observe
what enchantment came over the shoes.
But each time the twelve dancing princesses
gave the snoopy man a Mickey Finn
and so he was beheaded.
Poof! Like a basketball.

It so happened that a poor soldier
heard about these strange goings on
and decided to give it a try.
On his way to the castle
he met an old old woman.
Age, for a change, was of some use.
She wasn't stuffed in a nursing home.
She told him not to drink a drop of wine
and gave him a cloak that would make
him invisible when the right time came.
And thus he sat outside the dorm.
The oldest princess brought him some wine
but he fastened a sponge beneath his chin,
looking the opposite of Andy Gump.

The sponge soaked up the wine,
and thus he stayed awake.
He feigned sleep however
and the princesses sprang out of their beds
and fussed around like a Miss America Contest.
Then the eldest went to her bed
and knocked upon it and it sank into the earth.
They descended down the opening

one after the other. The crafty soldier
put on his invisible cloak and followed.
Yikes, said the youngest daughter,
something just stepped on my dress.
But the oldest thought it just a nail.

Next stood an avenue of trees,
each leaf made of sterling silver.
The soldier took a leaf for proof.
The youngest heard the branch break
and said, Oof! Who goes there?
But the oldest said, Those are
the royal trumpets playing triumphantly.
The next trees were made of diamonds.
He took one that flickered like Tinkerbell
and the youngest said: Wait up! He is here!
But the oldest said: Trumpets, my dear.

Next they came to a lake where lay
twelve boats with twelve enchanted princes
waiting to row them to the underground castle.
The soldier sat in the youngest's boat
and the boat was as heavy as if an icebox
had been added but the prince did not suspect.

Next came the ball where the shoes did duty.
The princesses danced like taxi girls at Roseland
as if those tickets would run right out.
They were painted in kisses with their secret hair
and though the soldier drank from their cups
they drank down their youth with nary a thought.
Cruets of champagne and cups full of rubies.
They danced until morning and the sun came up
naked and angry and so they returned
by the same strange route. The soldier
went forward through the dormitory and into

his waiting chair to feign his druggy sleep.
That morning the soldier, his eyes fiery
like blood in a wound, his purpose brutal
as if facing a battle, hurried with his answer
as if to the Sphinx. The shoes! The shoes!
The soldier told. He brought forth
the silver leaf, the diamond the size of a plum.

He had won. The dancing shoes would dance
no more. The princesses were torn from
their night life like a baby from its pacifier.
Because he was old he picked the eldest.
At the wedding the princesses averted their eyes
and sagged like old sweatshirts.
Now the runaways would run no more and never
again would their hair be tangled into diamonds,
never again their shoes worn down to a laugh,
never the bed falling down into purgatory
to let them climb in after
with their Lucifer kicking.

THE FROG PRINCE

Frau Doktor,
Mama Brundig,
take out your contacts,
remove your wig.

I write for you.
I entertain.
But frogs come out
of the sky like rain.

Frogs arrive
With an ugly fury.

You are my judge.
You are my jury.

My guilts are what
we catalogue.
I'll take a knife
and chop up frog.

Frog has no nerves.
Frog is as old as a cockroach.
Frog is my father's genitals.
Frog is a malformed doorknob.
Frog is a soft bag of green.

The moon will not have him.
The sun wants to shut off
like a light bulb.
At the sight of him
the stone washes itself in a tub.
The crow thinks he's an apple
and drops a worm in.
At the feel of frog
the touch-me-nots explode
like electric slugs.

Slime will have him.
Slime has made him a house.

Mr. Poison
is at my bed.
He wants my sausage.
He wants my bread.

Mama Brundig,
he wants my beer.
He wants my Christ
for a souvenir.

Frog has boil disease
and a bellyful of parasites.
He says: Kiss me. Kiss me.
And the ground soils itself.

Why
should a certain
quite adorable princess
be walking in her garden
at such a time
and toss her golden ball
up like a bubble
and drop it into the well?
It was ordained.
Just as the fates deal out
the plague with a tarot card.
Just as the Supreme Being drills
holes in our skulls to let
the Boston Symphony through.

But I digress.
A loss has taken place.
The ball has sunk like a cast-iron pot
into the bottom of the well.

Lost, she said,
my moon, my butter calf,
my yellow moth, my Hindu hare.
Obviously it was more than a ball.
Balls such as these are not
for sale in Au Bon Marché.
I took the moon, she said,
between my teeth
and now it is gone
and I am lost forever.
A thief had robbed by day.

Suddenly the well grew
thick and boiling
and a frog appeared.
His eyes bulged like two peas
and his body was trussed into place.
Do not be afraid, Princess,
he said, I am not a vagabond,
a cattle farmer, a shepherd,
a doorkeeper, a postman
or a laborer.
I come to you as a tradesman.
I have something to sell.
Your ball, he said,
for just three things.
Let me eat from your plate.
Let me drink from your cup.
Let me sleep in your bed.
She thought, Old Waddler,
those three you will never do,
but she made the promises
with hopes for her ball once more.
He brought it up in his mouth
like a tricky old dog
and she ran back to the castle
leaving the frog quite alone.

That evening at dinner time
a knock was heard at the castle door
and a voice demanded:
King's youngest daughter,
let me in. You promised;
now open to me.
I have left the skunk cabbage
and the eels to live with you.
The king then heard of her promise
and forced her to comply.

The frog first sat on her lap.
He was as awful as an undertaker.
Next he was at her plate
looking over her bacon
and calves' liver.
We will eat in tandem,
he said gleefully.
Her fork trembled
as if a small machine
had entered her.
He sat upon the liver
and partook like a gourmet.
The princess choked
as if she were eating a puppy.
From her cup he drank.
It wasn't exactly hygienic.
From her cup she drank
as if it were Socrates' hemlock.

Next came the bed.
The silky royal bed.
Ah! The penultimate hour!
There was the pillow
with the princess breathing
and there was the sinuous frog
riding up and down beside her.
I have been lost in a river
of shut doors, he said,
and I have made my way over
the wet stones to live with you.
She woke up aghast.
I suffer for birds and fireflies
but not frogs, she said,
and threw him across the room.
Kaboom!

Like a genie coming out of a samovar,
a handsome prince arose in the
corner of her royal bedroom.
He had kind eyes and hands
and was a friend of sorrow.
Thus they were married.
After all he had compromised her.

He hired a night watchman
so that no one could enter the chamber
and he had the well
boarded over so that
never again would she lose her ball,
that moon, that Krishna hair,
that blind poppy, that innocent globe,
that madonna womb.

HANSEL AND GRETEL

Little plum,
said the mother to her son,
I want to bite,
I want to chew,
I will eat you up.
Little child,
little nubkin,
sweet as fudge,
you are my blitz.
I will spit on you for luck
for you are better than money.
Your neck as smooth
as a hard-boiled egg;
soft cheeks, my pears,
let me buzz you on the neck
and take a bite.

I have a pan that will fit you.
Just pull up your knees like a game hen.
Let me take your pulse
and set the oven for 350.
Come, my pretender, my fritter,
my bubbler, my chicken biddy!
Oh succulent one,
it is but one turn in the road
and I would be a cannibal!

Hansel and Gretel
and their parents
had come upon evil times.
They had cooked the dog
and served him up like lamb chops.
There was only a loaf of bread left.
The final solution,
their mother told their father,
was to lose the children in the forest.
We have enough bread for ourselves
but none for them.
Hansel heard this
and took pebbles with him
into the forest.
He dropped a pebble every fifth step
and later, after their parents had left them,
they followed the pebbles home.
The next day their mother gave them
each a hunk of bread
like a page out of the Bible
and sent them out again.
This time Hansel dropped bits of bread.
The birds, however, ate the bread
and they were lost at last.
They were blind as worms.
They turned like ants in a glove

not knowing which direction to take.
The sun was in Leo
and water spouted from the lion's head
but still they did not know their way.

So they walked for twenty days
and twenty nights
and came upon a rococo house
made all of food from its windows
to its chocolate chimney.
A witch lived in that house
and she took them in.
She gave them a large supper
to fatten them up
and then they slept,
z's buzzing from their mouths like flies.
Then she took Hansel,
the smarter, the bigger,
the juicier, into the barn
and locked him up.
Each day she fed him goose liver
so that he would fatten,
so that he would be as larded
as a plump coachman,
that knight of the whip.
She was planning to cook him
and then gobble him up
as in a feast
after a holy war.

She spoke to Gretel
and told her how her brother
would be better than mutton;
how a thrill would go through her
as she smelled him cooking;
how she would lay the table

and sharpen the knives
and neglect none of the refinements.
Gretel
who had said nothing so far
nodded her head and wept.
She who neither dropped pebbles or bread
bided her time.

The witch looked upon her
with new eyes and thought:
Why not this saucy lass
for an hors d'oeuvre?
She explained to Gretel
that she must climb into the oven
to see if she would fit.
Gretel spoke at last:
Ja, Fräulein, show me how it can be done.
The witch thought this fair
and climbed in to show the way.
It was a matter of gymnastics.
Gretel,
seeing her moment in history,
shut fast the oven,
locked fast the door,
fast as Houdini,
and turned the oven on to bake.
The witch turned as red
as the Jap flag.
Her blood began to boil up
like Coca-Cola.
Her eyes began to melt.
She was done for.
Altogether a memorable incident.

As for Hansel and Gretel,
they escaped and went home to their father.

Their mother,
you'll be glad to hear, was dead.
Only at suppertime
while eating a chicken leg
did our children remember
the woe of the oven,
the smell of the cooking witch,
a little like mutton,
to be served only with burgundy
and fine white linen
like something religious.

BRIAR ROSE
(SLEEPING BEAUTY)

Consider
a girl who keeps slipping off,
arms limp as old carrots,
into the hypnotist's trance,
into a spirit world
speaking with the gift of tongues.
She is stuck in the time machine,
suddenly two years old sucking her thumb,
as inward as a snail,
learning to talk again.
She's on a voyage.
She is swimming further and further back,
up like a salmon,
struggling into her mother's pocketbook.
Little doll child,
come here to Papa.
Sit on my knee.
I have kisses for the back of your neck.
A penny for your thoughts, Princess.
I will hunt them like an emerald.

Come be my snooky
and I will give you a root.
That kind of voyage,
rank as honeysuckle.

Once
a king had a christening
for his daughter Briar Rose
and because he had only twelve gold plates
he asked only twelve fairies
to the grand event.
The thirteenth fairy,
her fingers as long and thin as straws,
her eyes burnt by cigarettes,
her uterus an empty teacup,
arrived with an evil gift.
She made this prophecy:
The princess shall prick herself
on a spinning wheel in her fifteenth year
and then fall down dead.
Kaputt!
The court fell silent.
The king looked like Munch's *Scream*.
Fairies' prophecies,
in times like those,
held water.
However the twelfth fairy
had a certain kind of eraser
and thus she mitigated the curse
changing that death
into a hundred-year sleep.

The king ordered every spinning wheel
exterminated and exorcized.
Briar Rose grew to be a goddess
and each night the king

bit the hem of her gown
to keep her safe.
He fastened the moon up
with a safety pin
to give her perpetual light
He forced every male in the court
to scour his tongue with Bab-o
lest they poison the air she dwelt in.
Thus she dwelt in his odor.
Rank as honeysuckle.

On her fifteenth birthday
she pricked her finger
on a charred spinning wheel
and the clocks stopped.
Yes indeed. She went to sleep.
The king and queen went to sleep,
the courtiers, the flies on the wall.
The fire in the hearth grew still
and the roast meat stopped crackling.
The trees turned into metal
and the dog became china.
They all lay in a trance,
each a catatonic
stuck in the time machine.
Even the frogs were zombies.
Only a bunch of briar roses grew
forming a great wall of tacks
around the castle.
Many princes
tried to get through the brambles
for they had heard much of Briar Rose
but they had not scoured their tongues
so they were held by the thorns
and thus were crucified.
In due time

292

a hundred years passed
and a prince got through.
The briars parted as if for Moses
and the prince found the tableau intact.
He kissed Briar Rose
and she woke up crying:
Daddy! Daddy!
Presto! She's out of prison!
She married the prince
and all went well
except for the fear —
the fear of sleep.

Briar Rose
was an insomniac . . .
She could not nap
or lie in sleep
without the court chemist
mixing her some knock-out drops
and never in the prince's presence.
If it is to come, she said,
sleep must take me unawares
while I am laughing or dancing
so that I do not know that brutal place
where I lie down with cattle prods,
the hole in my cheek open.
Further, I must not dream
for when I do I see the table set
and a faltering crone at my place,
her eyes burnt by cigarettes
as she eats betrayal like a slice of meat.

I must not sleep
for while asleep I'm ninety
and think I'm dying.
Death rattles in my throat

like a marble.
I wear tubes like earrings.
I lie as still as a bar of iron.
You can stick a needle
through my kneecap and I won't flinch.
I'm all shot up with Novocain.
This trance girl
is yours to do with.
You could lay her in a grave,
an awful package,
and shovel dirt on her face
and she'd never call back: Hello there!
But if you kissed her on the mouth
her eyes would spring open
and she'd call out: Daddy! Daddy!
Presto!
She's out of prison.

There was a theft.
That much I am told.
I was abandoned.
That much I know.
I was forced backward.
I was forced forward.
I was passed hand to hand
like a bowl of fruit.
Each night I am nailed into place
and I forget who I am.
Daddy?
That's another kind of prison.
It's not the prince at all,
but my father
drunkenly bent over my bed,
circling the abyss like a shark,
my father thick upon me
like some sleeping jellyfish.

What voyage this, little girl?
This coming out of prison?
God help —
this life after death?

The Book
of Folly

(1972)

*For Joy, when she comes to
this business of words*

THIRTY POEMS

THE AMBITION BIRD

So it has come to this —
insomnia at 3:15 A.M.,
the clock tolling its engine

like a frog following
a sundial yet having an electric
seizure at the quarter hour.

The business of words keeps me awake.
I am drinking cocoa,
that warm brown mama.

I would like a simple life
yet all night I am laying
poems away in a long box.

It is my immortality box,
my lay-away plan,
my coffin.

All night dark wings
flopping in my heart.
Each an ambition bird.

The bird wants to be dropped
from a high place like Tallahatchie Bridge.

He wants to light a kitchen match
and immolate himself.

He wants to fly into the hand of Michelangelo
and come out painted on a ceiling.

He wants to pierce the hornet's nest
and come out with a long godhead.

He wants to take bread and wine
and bring forth a man happily floating in the Caribbean.

He wants to be pressed out like a key
so he can unlock the Magi.

He wants to take leave among strangers
passing out bits of his heart like hors d'oeuvres.

He wants to die changing his clothes
and bolt for the sun like a diamond.

He wants, I want.
Dear God, wouldn't it be
good enough to just drink cocoa?

I must get a new bird
and a new immortality box.
There is folly enough inside this one.

THE DOCTOR OF THE HEART

Take away your knowledge, Doktor.
It doesn't butter me up.

You say my heart is sick unto.
You ought to have more respect!

You with the goo on the suction cup.
You with your wires and electrodes

fastened at my ankle and wrist,
sucking up the biological breast.

You with your zigzag machine
playing like the stock market up and down.

Give me the Phi Beta key you always twirl
and I will make a gold crown for my molar.

I will take a slug if you please
and make myself a perfectly good appendix.

Give me a fingernail for an eyeglass.
The world was milky all along.

I will take an iron and press out
my slipped disk until it is flat.

But take away my mother's carcinoma
for I have only one cup of fetus tears.

Take away my father's cerebral hemorrhage
for I have only a jigger of blood in my hand.

Take away my sister's broken neck
for I have only my schoolroom ruler for a cure.

Is there such a device for my heart?
I have only a gimmick called magic fingers.

Let me dilate like a bad debt.
Here is a sponge. I can squeeze it myself.

O heart, tobacco red heart,
beat like a rock guitar.

I am at the ship's prow.
I am no longer the suicide

with her raft and paddle.
Herr Doktor! I'll no longer **die**

to spite you, you wallowing
seasick grounded man.

OH

It is snowing and death bugs me
as stubborn as insomnia.
The fierce bubbles of chalk,
the little white lesions
settle on the street outside.
It is snowing and the ninety
year old woman who was combing
out her long white wraith hair
is gone, embalmed even now,
even tonight her arms are smooth
muskets at her side and nothing
issues from her but her last word —
"Oh." Surprised by death.

It is snowing. Paper spots
are falling from the punch.
Hello? Mrs. Death is here!
She suffers according to the digits
of my hate. I hear the filaments
of alabaster. I would lie down
with them and lift my madness
off like a wig. I would lie
outside in a room of wool
and let the snow cover me.
Paris white or flake white
or argentine, all in the washbasin
of my mouth, calling, "Oh."
I am empty. I am witless.
Death is here. There is no
other settlement. Snow!
See the mark, the pock, the pock!

Meanwhile you pour tea
with your handsome gentle hands.
Then you deliberately take your
forefinger and point it at my temple,
saying, "You suicide bitch!
I'd like to take a corkscrew
and screw out all your brains
and you'd never be back ever."
And I close my eyes over the steaming
tea and see God opening His teeth.
"Oh," He says.
I see the child in me writing, "Oh."
Oh, my dear, not why.

SWEENEY

My Sweeney, Mr. Eliot,
is that Australian who came
to the U.S.A. with one thought —
My books in the satchel, my name

and one question at customs —
Is Anne Sexton still alive?
He was a big dollar man, a Monopoly player
who bought up BOARDWALK with a ten or a five

to see the pallid bellboy smile, or please
the maid who supplied nonallergic
pillows. Unlike my father, his mouth a liturgy
of praise. Like a gangster, his wallet a limerick.
Your words, Sexton, are the only

red queens, the only ministers, the only beasts.
You are the altar cup and from this
I do fill my mouth. Sexton, I am your priest.

Sweeney who brought up himself, gone
was his murmurous mother at nine, gone
was his soused-up father at seventeen.
But talkative Sweeney at forty-five lives on.

Lord. Lord. How You leave off. How You eat up men —
leave them walking on the gummy pavements,
sucking in the tamed-up, used-up air,
fearing death and what death invents.

Sweeney from nine to five with a carnation
in his buttonhole introduces the rider
to the cabby; Sweeney who flies through bookshops
not like a turbojet but a Zurich glider.

Ersatz press agent man, buying up my books
by the dozen from Scribner's, Doubleday,
that Italian bookshop or wherever. Fan, fan,
drinking only Dom Perignon, my gray Aussie gourmet.

Yes. Yes. Sweeney gave me all of New York,
caviar at La Côte Basque, a pink shower cap
and death. Yes. That day my sister was killed
and the untimely weapons were unwrapped.

That unnatural death by car, her slim neck
snapped like a piece of celery. A one-week bride,
her dead blue eyes flapping into their solitude
while I drank with Sweeney and her death lied.

Now Sweeney phones from London, W. 2,
saying Martyr, my religion is love, is you.
Be seated, my Sweeney, my invisible fan.
Surely the words will continue, for that's
what's left that's true.

MOTHER AND DAUGHTER

Linda, you are leaving
your old body now.
It lies flat, an old butterfly,
all arm, all leg, all wing,
loose as an old dress.
I reach out toward it but
my fingers turn to cankers
and I am motherwarm and used,
just as your childhood is used.
Question you about this
and you hold up pearls.
Question you about this

and you pass by armies.
Question you about this —
you with your big clock going,
its hands wider than jackstraws —
and you'll sew up a continent.

Now that you are eighteen
I give you my booty, my spoils,
my Mother & Co. and my ailments.
Question you about this
and you'll not know the answer —
the muzzle at the mouth,
the hopeful tent of oxygen,
the tubes, the pathways,
the war and the war's vomit.
Keep on, keep on, keep on,
carrying keepsakes to the boys,
carrying powders to the boys,
carrying, my Linda, blood to
the bloodletter.

Linda, you are leaving
your old body now.
You've picked my pocket clean
and you've racked up all my
poker chips and left me empty
and, as the river between us
narrows, you do calisthenics,
that womanly leggy semaphore.
Question you about this
and you will sew me a shroud
and hold up Monday's broiler
and thumb out the chicken gut.
Question you about this
and you will see my death
drooling at these gray lips

while you, my burglar, will eat
fruit and pass the time of day.

THE WIFEBEATER

There will be mud on the carpet tonight
and blood in the gravy as well.
The wifebeater is out,
the childbeater is out
eating soil and drinking bullets from a cup.
He strides back and forth
in front of my study window
chewing little red pieces of my heart.
His eyes flash like a birthday cake
and he makes bread out of rock.

Yesterday he was walking
like a man in the world.
He was upright and conservative
but somehow evasive, somehow contagious.
Yesterday he built me a country
and laid out a shadow where I could sleep
but today a coffin for the madonna and child,
today two women in baby clothes will be hamburg.

With a tongue like a razor he will kiss,
the mother, the child,
and we three will color the stars black
in memory of his mother
who kept him chained to the food tree
or turned him on and off like a water faucet
and made *women* through all these hazy years
the enemy with a heart of lies.

Tonight all the red dogs lie down in fear
and the wife and daughter knit into each other
until they are killed.

THE FIREBOMBERS

We are America.
We are the coffin fillers.
We are the grocers of death.
We pack them in crates like cauliflowers.

The bomb opens like a shoebox.
And the child?
The child is certainly not yawning.
And the woman?
The woman is bathing her heart.
It has been torn out of her
and because it is burnt
and as a last act
she is rinsing it off in the river.
This is the death market.

America,
where are your credentials?

THE ONE-LEGGED MAN

Once there was blood
as in a murder
but now there is nothing.

Once there was a shoe,
brown cordovan,
which I tied
and it did me well.

Now
I have given away my leg
to be brought up beside orphans.
I have planted my leg beside the drowned mole
with his fifth pink hand sewn onto his mouth.
I have shipped off my leg so that
it may sink slowly like grit into the Atlantic.
I have jettisoned my leg so that it may
fall out of the sky like immense lumber.
I have eaten my leg so that
it may be spit out like a fingernail.

Yet all along . . .
Yes, all along,
I keep thinking that what I need
to do is buy my leg back.
Surely it is for sale somewhere,
poor broken tool, poor ornament.
It might be in a store somewhere beside a lady's scarf.
I want to write it letters.
I want to feed it supper.
I want to carve a bowstring out of it.
I want to hold it at noon in my bed
and stroke it slowly like a perfect woman.

Lady, lady,
why have you left me?

I did not mean to frighten her.
I wanted only to watch her quietly
as she worked.

THE ASSASSIN

The correct death is written in.
I will fill the need.
My bow is stiff.
My bow is in readiness.
I am the bullet and the hook.
I am cocked and held ready.
In my sights I carve him
like a sculptor. I mold out
his last look at everyone.
I carry his eyes and his
brain bone at every position.
I know his male sex and I do
march over him with my index finger.
His mouth and his anus are one.
I am at the center of feeling.

A subway train is
traveling across my crossbow.
I have a blood bolt
and I have made it mine.
With this man I take in hand
his destiny and with this gun
I take in hand the newspapers and
with my heat I will take him.
He will bend down toward me
and his veins will tumble out
like children . . . Give me
his flag and his eye.
Give me his hard shell and his lip.
He is my evil and my apple and
I will see him home.

GOING GONE

Over stone walls and barns,
miles from the black-eyed Susans,
over circus tents and moon rockets
you are going, going.
You who have inhabited me
in the deepest and most broken place,
are going, going.
An old woman calls up to you
from her deathbed deep in sores,
asking, "What do you keep of her?"
She is the crone in the fables.
She is the fool at the supper
and you, sir, are the traveler.
Although you are in a hurry
you stop to open a small basket
and under layers of petticoats
you show her the tiger-striped eyes
that you have lately plucked,
you show her your specialty, the lips,
those two small bundles,
you show her the two hands
that grip each other fiercely,
one being mine, one being yours.
Torn right off at the wrist bone
when you started in your
impossible going, gone.
Then you place the basket
in the old woman's hollow lap
and as a last act she fondles
these artifacts like a child's head
and murmurs, "Precious. Precious."
And you are glad you have given
them to this one for she too
is making a trip.

ANNA WHO WAS MAD

Anna who was mad,
I have a knife in my armpit.
When I stand on tiptoe I tap out messages.
Am I some sort of infection?
Did I make you go insane?
Did I make the sounds go sour?
Did I tell you to climb out the window?
Forgive. Forgive.
Say not I did.
Say not.
Say.

Speak Mary-words into our pillow.
Take me the gangling twelve-year-old
into your sunken lap.
Whisper like a buttercup.
Eat me. Eat me up like cream pudding.
Take me in.
Take me.
Take.

Give me a report on the condition of my soul.
Give me a complete statement of my actions.
Hand me a jack-in-the-pulpit and let me listen in.
Put me in the stirrups and bring a tour group through.
Number my sins on the grocery list and let me buy.
Did I make you go insane?
Did I turn up your earphone and let a siren drive through?
Did I open the door for the mustached psychiatrist
who dragged you out like a golf cart?
Did I make you go insane?
From the grave write me, Anna!
You are nothing but ashes but nevertheless
pick up the Parker Pen I gave you.

Write me.
Write.

THE HEX

Every time I get happy
the Nana-hex comes through.
Birds turn into plumber's tools,
a sonnet turns into a dirty joke,
a wind turns into a tracheotomy,
a boat turns into a corpse,
a ribbon turns into a noose,
all for the Nana-song,
sour notes calling out in her madness:
You did it. You are the evil.
I was thirteen,
her awkward namesake,
our eyes an identical green.
There is no news in it
except every time I say:
I feel great or
Life is marvelous or
I just wrote a poem,
the heartbeat,
the numb hand,
the eyes going black
from the outer edges,
the xylophone in the ears
and the voice, the voice,
the Nana-hex.
My eyes stutter. I am blind.

Sitting on the stairs at thirteen,
hands fixed over my ears,
the Hitler-mouth psychiatrist climbing

past me like an undertaker,
and the old woman's shriek of fear:
You did it. You are the evil.
It was the day meant for me.
Thirteen for your whole life,
just the masks keep changing.
Blood in my mouth,
a fish flopping in my chest
and doom stamping its little feet.
You did it. You are the evil.
She's long gone.
She went out on the death train.
But someone is in the shooting gallery
biding her time.
The dead take aim.
I feel great!
Life is marvelous!
and yet bull's eye,
the hex.

It's all a matter of history.
Brandy is no solace.
Librium only lies me down
like a dead snow queen.
Yes! I am still the criminal.
Yes! Take me to the station house.
But book my double.

DREAMING THE BREASTS

Mother,
strange goddess face
above my milk home,
that delicate asylum,
I ate you up.

All my need took
you down like a meal.

What you gave
I remember in a dream:
the freckled arms binding me,
the laugh somewhere over my woolly hat,
the blood fingers tying my shoe,
the breasts hanging like two bats
and then darting at me,
bending me down.

The breasts I knew at midnight
beat like the sea in me now.
Mother, I put bees in my mouth
to keep from eating
yet it did you no good.
In the end they cut off your breasts
and milk poured from them
into the surgeon's hand
and he embraced them.
I took them from him
and planted them.

I have put a padlock
on you, Mother, dear dead human,
so that your great bells,
those dear white ponies,
can go galloping, galloping,
wherever you are.

THE RED SHOES

I stand in the ring
in the dead city

and tie on the red shoes.
Everything that was calm
is mine, the watch with an ant walking,
the toes, lined up like dogs,
the stove long before it boils toads,
the parlor, white in winter, long before flies,
the doe lying down on moss, long before the bullet.
I tie on the red shoes.

They are not mine.
They are my mother's.
Her mother's before.
Handed down like an heirloom
but hidden like shameful letters.
The house and the street where they belong
are hidden and all the women, too,
are hidden.

All those girls
who wore the red shoes,
each boarded a train that would not stop.
Stations flew by like suitors and would not stop.
They all danced like trout on the hook.
They were played with.
They tore off their ears like safety pins.
Their arms fell off them and became hats.
Their heads rolled off and sang down the street.
And their feet — oh God, their feet in the market place —
their feet, those two beetles, ran for the corner
and then danced forth as if they were proud.
Surely, people exclaimed,
surely they are mechanical. Otherwise . . .

But the feet went on.
The feet could not stop.
They were wound up like a cobra that sees you.

They were elastic pulling itself in two.
They were islands during an earthquake.
They were ships colliding and going down.
Never mind you and me.
They could not listen.
They could not stop.
What they did was the death dance.

What they did would do them in.

THE OTHER

Under my bowels, yellow with smoke,
it waits.
Under my eyes, those milk bunnies,
it waits.
It is waiting.
It is waiting.
Mr. Doppelgänger. My brother. My spouse.
Mr. Doppelgänger. My enemy. My lover.
When truth comes spilling out like peas
it hangs up the phone.
When the child is soothed and resting on the breast
it is my other who swallows Lysol.
When someone kisses someone or flushes the toilet
it is my other who sits in a ball and cries.
My other beats a tin drum in my heart.
My other hangs up laundry as I try to sleep.
My other cries and cries and cries
when I put on a cocktail dress.
It cries when I prick a potato.
It cries when I kiss someone hello.
It cries and cries and cries
until I put on a painted mask
and leer at Jesus in His passion.

Then it giggles.
It is a thumbscrew.
Its hatred makes it clairvoyant.
I can only sign over everything,
the house, the dog, the ladders, the jewels,
the soul, the family tree, the mailbox.

Then I can sleep.

Maybe.

THE SILENCE

The more I write, the more the silence seems
to be eating away at me. C. K. Williams

My room is whitewashed,
as white as a rural station house
and just as silent;
whiter than chicken bones
bleaching in the moonlight,
pure garbage,
and just as silent.
There is a white statue behind me
and white plants
growing like obscene virgins,
pushing out their rubbery tongues
but saying nothing.

My hair is the one dark.
It has been burnt in the white fire
and is just a char.
My beads too are black,
twenty eyes heaved up
from the volcano,
quite contorted.

I am filling the room
with the words from my pen.
Words leak out of it like a miscarriage.
I am zinging words out into the air
and they come back like squash balls.
Yet there is silence.
Always silence.
Like an enormous baby mouth.

The silence is death.
It comes each day with its shock
to sit on my shoulder, a white bird,
and peck at the black eyes
and the vibrating red muscle
of my mouth.

THE HOARDER

*An idler is like a lump of dung; whoever picks
it up shakes it off his hand. Ecclesiasticus*

There is something there
I've got to get and I dig
down and people pop off and
muskrats float up backward
and open at my touch like
cereal flakes and still I've
got to dig because there is
something down there in my
Nana's clock I broke it I was
wrong I was digging even then
I had to find out and snap
and crack the hand broke like
a toothpick and I didn't learn
I keep digging for something
down there is my sister's five

dollar bill that I tore because
it wasn't mine was stage money
wasn't mine something down there
I am digging I am digging I will
win something like my first bike
teetering my first balancing act
a grasshopper who can fly she
of the damp smelling passageway
it was earlier much earlier it
was my first doll that water went
into and water came out of much
earlier it was the diaper I wore
and the dirt thereof and my
mother hating me for it and me
loving me for it but the hate
won didn't it yes the distaste
won the disgust won and because
of this I am a hoarder of words
I hold them in though they are
dung oh God I am a digger
I am not an idler
am I?

KILLING THE SPRING

*When the cold rains kept on and killed the
spring, it was as though a young person had died
for no reason. Ernest Hemingway, A Moveable Feast*

Spring had been bulldozed under.
She would not, would not, would not.
Late April, late May
and the metallic rains kept on.
From my gun-metal window I watched
how the dreadful tulips
swung on their hinges,
beaten down like pigeons.

Then I ignored spring.
I put on blinders and rode on a donkey
in a circle, a warm circle.
I tried to ride for eternity
but I came back.
I swallowed my sour meat
but it came back.
I struck out memory with an X
but it came back.
I tied down time with a rope
but it came back.

Then
I put my head in a death bowl
and my eyes shut up like clams.
They didn't come back.
I was declared legally blind
by my books and papers.
My eyes, those two blue gods,
would not come back.
My eyes, those sluts, those whores,
would play no more.

Next I nailed my hands
onto a pine box.
I followed the blue veins
like a neon road map.
My hands, those touchers, those bears,
would not reach out and speak.
They could no longer get in the act.
They were fastened down to oblivion.
They did not come back.
They were through with their abominable habits.
They were in training for a crucifixion.
They could not reply.

Next I took my ears,
those two cold moons,
and drowned them in the Atlantic.
They were not wearing a mask.
They were not deceived by laughter.
They were not luminous like the clock.
They sank like oiled birds.
They did not come back.
I waited with my bones on the cliff
to see if they'd float in like slick
but they did not come back.

I could not see the spring.
I could not hear the spring.
I could not touch the spring.
Once upon a time a young person
died for no reason.
I was the same.

THE DEATH OF THE FATHERS

1. *Oysters*

Oysters we ate,
sweet blue babies,
twelve eyes looked up at me,
running with lemon and Tabasco.
I was afraid to eat this father-food
and Father laughed
and drank down his martini,
clear as tears.
It was a soft medicine
that came from the sea into my mouth,
moist and plump.
I swallowed.

It went down like a large pudding.
Then I ate one o'clock and two o'clock.
Then I laughed and then we laughed
and let me take note —
there was a death,
the death of childhood
there at the Union Oyster House
for I was fifteen
and eating oysters
and the child was defeated.
The woman won.

2. *How We Danced*

The night of my cousin's wedding
I wore blue.
I was nineteen
and we danced, Father, we orbited.
We moved like angels washing themselves.
We moved like two birds on fire.
Then we moved like the sea in a jar,
slower and slower.
The orchestra played
"Oh how we danced on the night we were wed."
And you waltzed me like a lazy Susan
and we were dear,
very dear.
Now that you are laid out,
useless as a blind dog,
now that you no longer lurk,
the song rings in my head.
Pure oxygen was the champagne we drank
and clicked our glasses, one to one.
The champagne breathed like a skin diver
and the glasses were crystal and the bride

and groom gripped each other in sleep
like nineteen-thirty marathon dancers.
Mother was a belle and danced with twenty men.
You danced with me never saying a word.
Instead the serpent spoke as you held me close.
The serpent, that mocker, woke up and pressed against me
like a great god and we bent together
like two lonely swans.

3. *The Boat*

Father
(he calls himself
"old sea dog"),
in his yachting cap
at the wheel of the Chris-Craft,
a mahogany speedboat
named *Go Too III*,
speeds out past Cuckold's Light
over the dark brainy blue.
I in the very back
with an orange life jacket on.
I in the dare seat.
Mother up front.
Her kerchief flapping.
The waves deep as whales.
(Whales in fact have been sighted.
A school two miles out of Boothbay Harbor.)
It is bumpy and we are going too fast.
The waves are boulders that we ride upon.
I am seven and we are riding
to Pemaquid or Spain.
Now the waves are higher;
they are round buildings.
We start to go through them

and the boat shudders.
Father is going faster.
I am wet.
I am tumbling on my seat
like a loose kumquat.
Suddenly
a wave that we go under.
Under. Under. Under.
We are daring the sea.
We have parted it.
We are scissors.
Here in the green room
the dead are very close.
Here in the pitiless green
where there are no keepsakes
or cathedrals an angel spoke:
You *have no business.*
No business here.
Give me a sign,
cries Father,
and the sky breaks over us.
There is air to have.
There are gulls kissing the boat.
There is the sun as big as a nose.
And here are the three of us
dividing our deaths,
bailing the boat
and closing out
the cold wing that has clasped us
this bright August day.

4. *Santa*

Father,
the Santa Claus suit

you bought from Wolff Fording Theatrical Supplies,
back before I was born,
is dead.
The white beard you fooled me with
and the hair like Moses,
the thick crimpy wool
that used to buzz me on the neck,
is dead.
Yes, my busting rosy Santa,
ringing your bronze cowbell.
You with real soot on your nose
and snow (taken from the refrigerator some years)
on your big shoulder.
The room was like Florida.
You took so many oranges out of your bag
and threw them around the living room,
all the time laughing that North Pole laugh.
Mother would kiss you
for she was that tall.
Mother could hug you
for she was not afraid.
The reindeer pounded on the roof.
(It was my Nana with a hammer in the attic.
For my children it was my husband
with a crowbar breaking things up.)
The year I ceased to believe in you
is the year you were drunk.
My boozy red man,
your voice all slithery like soap,
you were a long way from Saint Nick
with Daddy's cocktail smell.
I cried and ran from the room
and you said, "Well, thank God that's over!"
And it was, until the grandchildren came.
Then I tied up your pillows
in the five A.M. Christ morning

and I adjusted the beard,
all yellow with age,
and applied rouge to your cheeks
and Chalk White to your eyebrows.
We were conspirators,
secret actors,
and I kissed you
because I was tall enough.
But that is over.
The era closes
and large children hang their stockings
and build a black memorial to you.
And you, you fade out of sight
like a lost signalman
wagging his lantern
for the train that comes no more.

5. *Friends*

Father,
who were all those friends,
that one in particular,
an oily creature,
who kept my picture in his wallet
and would show it to me
in secret like something dirty?
He used to sing to me,
I saw a little fly
and he buzzed me on the cheek.
I'd like to see that little fly
kiss our Annie every week.
And then he'd buzz,
on the cheek,
on the buttocks.
Or else he'd take a car

and run it up my back.
Or else he'd blow some whiskey
in my mouth, all dark and suede.
Who was he, Father?
What right, Father?
To pick me up like Charlie McCarthy
and place me on his lap?
He was as bald as a hump.
His ears stuck out like teacups
and his tongue, my God, his tongue,
like a red worm and when he kissed
it crawled right in.

Oh Father, Father,
who was that stranger
who knew Mother too well?
And he made me jump rope
five hundred times,
calling out,
Little one, jump higher, higher,
dragging me up and pushing me down
when it was you, Father,
who had the right
and ought.
He was beating me on the buttocks
with a jump rope.
I was stained with his red fingers
and I cried out for you
and Mother said you were gone on a trip.
You had sunk like the cat in the snow,
not a paw left to clasp for luck.
My heart cracked like a doll-dish,
my heart seized like a bee sting,
my eyes filled up like an owl,
and my legs crossed themselves like Christ's.
He was a stranger, Father.

Oh God,
he was a stranger,
was he not?

6. *Begat*

Father me not
for you are not my father.
Today there is that doubt.
Today there is that monster between us,
that monster of doubt.
Today someone else lurks in the wings
with your dear lines in his mouth
and your crown on his head.
Oh Father, Father-sorrow,
where has time brought us?

Today someone called.
"Merry Christmas," said the stranger.
"I am your real father."
That was a knife.
That was a grave.
That was a ship sailing through my heart.
From the galley I heard the slaves
calling out, *Fall* away, *fall* away.
And again I heard the stranger's
"I am your real father."

Was I transplanted?
Father, Father,
where is your tendril?
Where was the soil?
Who was the bee?
Where was the moment?

A courtesy uncle called —
that stranger —
and claimed me in my forty-second year.
Now I am a true blue,
as sure as a buffalo
and as mad as a salmon.
Illegitimate at last.
Father,
adored every night but one,
cuckolded that once,
the night of my conception
in that flapper way,
tell me, old dead thing,
where were you when Mother
swallowed me down whole?
Where were you, old fox,
two brown eyes, two moles,
hiding under your liquor
soft as oil?

Where was I begat?
In what room did
those definitive juices come?
A hotel in Boston
gilt and dim?
Was it a February night
all wrapped in fur
that knew me not?
I ask this.
I sicken.

Father,
you died once,
salted down at fifty-nine,
packed down like a big snow angel,
wasn't that enough?

To appear again and die out of me.
To take away your manic talking,
your broomstick legs, all those
familial resemblances we shared.
To take the *you* out of the *me.*
To send me into the genes
of this explorer.
He will hold me at knife point
and like a knife blade I will say:
Stranger,
bone to my bone man,
go your way.
I say take your sperm,
it is old,
it has turned to acid,
it will do you no good.

Stranger,
stranger,
take away your riddle.
Give it to a medical school
for I sicken.
My loss knocks.

For here stands my father,
a rosy Santa,
telling the old Rumpelstiltskin to me,
larger than God or the Devil.
He is my history.
I see him standing on the snowbank
on Christmas Eve
singing "Good King Wenceslas"
to the white, glowering houses
or giving Mother rubies to put in her eyes,
red, red, Mother, you are blood red.
He scoops her up in his arms

all red shivers and silks.
He cries to her:
How dare I hold this princess?
A mere man such as I
with a shark's nose and ten tar-fingers?
Princess of the artichokes,
my dickeybird,
my dolly mop,
my kiddley wink,
my jill of the jacks,
my rabbit pie!
And they kissed until I turned away.
Sometimes even I came into the royal ring
and those times he ate my heart in half
and I was glad.
Those times I smelled the Vitalis on his pajamas.
Those times I mussed his curly black hair
and touched his ten tar-fingers
and swallowed down his whiskey breath.
Red. Red. Father, you are blood red.
Father,
we are two birds on fire.

ANGELS OF THE LOVE AFFAIR

"Angels of the love affair, do you know that other,
the dark one, that other me?"

1. *Angel of Fire and Genitals*

Angel of fire and genitals, do you know slime,
that green mama who first forced me to sing,
who put me first in the latrine, that pantomime
of brown where I was beggar and she was king?
I said, "The devil is down that festering hole."
Then he bit me in the buttocks and took over my soul.

Fire woman, you of the ancient flame, you
of the Bunsen burner, you of the candle,
you of the blast furnace, you of the barbecue,
you of the fierce solar energy, Mademoiselle,
take some ice, take some snow, take a month of rain
and you would gutter in the dark, cracking up your brain.

Mother of fire, let me stand at your devouring gate
as the sun dies in your arms and you loosen its terrible
     weight.

2. Angel of Clean Sheets

Angel of clean sheets, do you know bedbugs?
Once in a madhouse they came like specks of cinnamon
as I lay in a chloral cave of drugs,
as old as a dog, as quiet as a skeleton.
Little bits of dried blood. One hundred marks
upon the sheet. One hundred kisses in the dark.

White sheets smelling of soap and Clorox
have nothing to do with this night of soil,
nothing to do with barred windows and multiple locks
and all the webbing in the bed, the ultimate recoil.
I have slept in silk and in red and in black.
I have slept on sand and, one fall night, a haystack.

I have known a crib. I have known the tuck-in of a child
but inside my hair waits the night I was defiled.

3. Angel of Flight and Sleigh Bells

Angel of flight and sleigh bells, do you know paralysis,
that ether house where your arms and legs are cement?

You are as still as a yardstick. You have a doll's kiss.
The brain whirls in a fit. The brain is not evident.
I have gone to that same place without a germ or a stroke.
A little solo act — that lady with the brain that broke.

In this fashion I have become a tree.
I have become a vase you can pick up or drop at will,
inanimate at last. What unusual luck! My body
passively resisting. Part of the leftovers. Part of the kill.
Angel of flight, you soarer, you flapper, you floater,
you gull that grows out of my back in the dreams I prefer,

stay near. But give me the totem. Give me the shut eye
where I stand in stone shoes as the world's bicycle goes by.

4. *Angel of Hope and Calendars*

Angel of hope and calendars, do you know despair?
That hole I crawl into with a box of Kleenex,
that hole where the fire woman is tied to her chair,
that hole where leather men are wringing their necks,
where the sea has turned into a pond of urine.
There is no place to wash and no marine beings to stir in.

In this hole your mother is crying out each day.
Your father is eating cake and digging her grave.
In this hole your baby is strangling. Your mouth is clay.
Your eyes are made of glass. They break. You are not brave.
You are alone like a dog in a kennel. Your hands
break out in boils. Your arms are cut and bound by bands

of wire. Your voice is out there. Your voice is strange.
There are no prayers here. Here there is no change.

5. Angel of Blizzards and Blackouts

Angel of blizzards and blackouts, do you know raspberries,
those rubies that sat in the green of my grandfather's
    garden?
You of the snow tires, you of the sugary wings, you freeze
me out. Let me crawl through the patch. Let me be ten.
Let me pick those sweet kisses, thief that I was,
as the sea on my left slapped its applause.

Only my grandfather was allowed there. Or the maid
who came with a scullery pan to pick for breakfast.
She of the rolls that floated in the air, she of the inlaid
woodwork all greasy with lemon, she of the feather and
    dust,
not I. Nonetheless I came sneaking across the salt lawn
in bare feet and jumping-jack pajamas in the spongy dawn.

Oh Angel of the blizzard and blackout, Madam white face,
take me back to that red mouth, that July 21st place.

6. Angel of Beach Houses and Picnics

Angel of beach houses and picnics, do you know solitaire?
Fifty-two reds and blacks and only myself to blame.
My blood buzzes like a hornet's nest. I sit in a kitchen chair
at a table set for one. The silverware is the same
and the glass and the sugar bowl. I hear my lungs fill and
    expel
as in an operation. But I have no one left to tell.

Once I was a couple. I was my own king and queen
with cheese and bread and rosé on the rocks of Rockport.
Once I sunbathed in the buff, all brown and lean,
watching the toy sloops go by, holding court

for busloads of tourists. Once I called breakfast the sexiest
meal of the day. Once I invited arrest

at the peace march in Washington. Once I was young and
    bold
and left hundreds of unmatched people out in the cold.

II

THE JESUS PAPERS

"And would you mock God?"
"God is not mocked except by believers."

JESUS SUCKLES

Mary, your great
white apples make me glad.
I feel your heart work its
machine and I doze like a fly.
I cough like a bird on its worm.
I'm a jelly-baby and you're my wife.
You're a rock and I the fringy algae.
You're a lily and I'm the bee that gets inside.
I close my eyes and suck you in like a fire.
I grow. I grow. I'm fattening out.
I'm a kid in a rowboat and you're the sea,
the salt, you're every fish of importance.

No. No.
All lies.
I am small
and you hold me.
You give me milk
and we are the same
and I am glad.

No. No.
All lies.
I am a truck. I run everything.
I own you.

JESUS AWAKE

It was the year
of the How To Sex Book,
the Sensuous Man and Woman were frolicking
but Jesus was fasting.
He ate His celibate life.
The ground shuddered like an ocean,
a great sexual swell under His feet.
His scrolls bit each other.
He was shrouded in gold like nausea.
Outdoors the kitties hung from their mother's tits
like sausages in a smokehouse.
Roosters cried all day, hammering for love.
Blood flowed from the kitchen pump
but He was fasting.
His sex was sewn onto Him like a medal
and His penis no longer arched with sorrow over Him.
He was fasting.
He was like a great house
with no people,
no plans.

JESUS ASLEEP

Jesus slept as still as a toy
and in His dream
He desired Mary.
His penis sang like a dog,

but He turned sharply away from that play
like a door slamming.
That door broke His heart
for He had a sore need.
He made a statue out of His need.
With His penis like a chisel
He carved the Pietà.
At this death it was important to have only one desire.
He carved this death.
He was persistent.
He died over and over again.
He swam up and up a pipe toward it,
breathing water through His gills.
He swam through stone.
He swam through the godhead
and because He had not known Mary
they were united at His death,
the cross to the woman,
in a final embrace,
poised forever
like a centerpiece.

JESUS RAISES UP THE HARLOT

The harlot squatted
with her hands over her red hair.
She was not looking for customers.
She was in a deep fear.
A delicate body clothed in red,
as red as a smashed fist
and she was bloody as well
for the townspeople were trying
to stone her to death.
Stones came at her like bees to candy
and sweet redheaded harlot that she was

she screamed out, *I never, I never.*
Rocks flew out of her mouth like pigeons
and Jesus saw this and thought to
exhume her like a mortician.

Jesus knew that a terrible sickness
dwelt in the harlot and He could lance it
with His two small thumbs.
He held up His hand and the stones
dropped to the ground like doughnuts.
Again He held up His hand
and the harlot came and kissed Him.
He lanced her twice. On the spot.
He lanced her twice on each breast,
pushing His thumbs in until the milk ran out,
those two boils of whoredom.
The harlot followed Jesus around like a puppy
for He had raised her up.
Now she forsook her fornications
and became His pet.
His raising her up made her feel
like a little girl again when she had a father
who brushed the dirt from her eye.
Indeed, she took hold of herself,
knowing she owed Jesus a life,
as sure-fire as a trump card.

JESUS COOKS

Jesus saw the multitudes were hungry
and He said, Oh Lord,
send down a short-order cook.
And the Lord said, Abracadabra.
Jesus took the fish,
a slim green baby,

in His right hand and said, Oh Lord,
and the Lord said,
Work on the sly
opening boxes of sardine cans.
And He did.
Fisherman, fisherman,
you make it look easy.
And lo, there were many fish.
Next Jesus held up a loaf
and said, Oh Lord,
and the Lord instructed Him
like an assembly-line baker man,
a Pied Piper of yeast,
and lo, there were many.

Jesus passed among the people
in a chef's hat
and they kissed His spoons and forks
and ate well from invisible dishes.

JESUS SUMMONS FORTH

Jesus saw Lazarus.
Lazarus was likely in heaven,
as dead as a pear
and the very same light green color.
Jesus thought to summon him
forth from his grave.
Oh hooded one, He cried,
come unto Me.
Lazarus smiled the smile of the dead
like a fool sucking on a dry stone.
Oh hooded one,
cried Jesus,
and it did no good.

The Lord spoke to Jesus
and gave Him instructions.
First Jesus put on the wrists,
then He inserted the hip bone,
He tapped in the vertebral column,
He fastened the skull down.
Lazarus was whole.
Jesus put His mouth to Lazarus's
and a current shot between them for a moment.
Then came tenderness.
Jesus rubbed all the flesh of Lazarus
and at last the heart, poor old wound,
started up in spite of itself.
Lazarus opened one eye. It was watchful.
And then Jesus picked him up
and set him upon his two sad feet.

His soul dropped down from heaven.
Thank you, said Lazarus,
for in heaven it had been no different.
In heaven there had been no change.

JESUS DIES

From up here in the crow's nest
I see a small crowd gather.
Why do you gather, my townsmen?
There is no news here.
I am not a trapeze artist.
I am busy with My dying.
Three heads lolling,
bobbing like bladders.
No news.
The soldiers down below
laughing as soldiers have done for centuries.

No news.
We are the same men,
you and I,
the same sort of nostrils,
the same sort of feet.
My bones are oiled with blood
and so are yours.
My heart pumps like a jack rabbit in a trap
and so does yours.
I want to kiss God on His nose and watch Him sneeze
and so do you.
Not out of disrespect.
Out of pique.
Out of a man-to-man thing.
I want heaven to descend and sit on My dinner plate
and so do you.
I want God to put His steaming arms around Me
and so do you.
Because we need.
Because we are sore creatures.
My townsmen,
go home now.
I will do nothing extraordinary.
I will not divide in two.
I will not pick out My white eyes.
Go now,
this is a personal matter,
a private affair and God knows
none of your business.

JESUS UNBORN

The gallowstree drops
one hundred heads upon the ground
and in Judea Jesus is unborn.

Mary is not yet with child.
Mary sits in a grove of olive trees
with the small pulse in her neck
beating. Beating the drumbeat.
The well that she dipped her pitcher into
has made her as instinctive as an animal.
Now she would like to lower herself down
like a camel and settle into the soil.
Although she is at the penultimate moment
she would like to doze fitfully like a dog.
She would like to be flattened out like the sea
when it lies down, a field of moles.
Instead a strange being leans over her
and lifts her chin firmly
and gazes at her with executioner's eyes.
Nine clocks spring open
and smash themselves against the sun.
The calendars of the world
burn if you touch them.
All this will be remembered.
Now we will have a Christ.
He covers her like a heavy door
and shuts her lifetime up
into this dump-faced day.

THE AUTHOR OF THE JESUS PAPERS SPEAKS

In my dream
I milked a cow,
the terrible udder
like a great rubber lily
sweated in my fingers
and as I yanked,
waiting for the moon juice,

waiting for the white mother,
blood spurted from it
and covered me with shame.
Then God spoke to me and said:
People say only good things about Christmas.
If they want to say something bad,
they whisper.
So I went to the well and drew a baby
out of the hollow water.
Then God spoke to me and said:
Here. Take this gingerbread lady
and put her in your oven.
When the cow gives blood
and the Christ is born
we must all eat sacrifices.
We must all eat beautiful women.

The Death Notebooks

(1974)

Because of mirrors
And mashed potatoes
for
Louise and Loring

Look, you con man, make a living out of your death.

Ernest Hemingway,
A Moveable Feast

GODS

Mrs. Sexton went out looking for the gods.
She began looking in the sky —
expecting a large white angel with a blue crotch.

No one.

She looked next in all the learned books
and the print spat back at her.

No one.

She made a pilgrimage to the great poet
and he belched in her face.

No one.

She prayed in all the churches of the world
and learned a great deal about culture.

No one.

She went to the Atlantic, the Pacific, for surely God . . .
No one.

She went to the Buddha, the Brahma, the Pyramids
and found immense postcards.

No one.

Then she journeyed back to her own house
and the gods of the world were shut in the lavatory.

At last!
she cried out,
and locked the door.

MAKING A LIVING

Jonah made his living
inside the belly.
Mine comes from the exact same place.
Jonah opened the door of his stateroom
and said, "Here I am!" and the whale liked this
and thought to take him in.

At the mouth Jonah cried out.
At the stomach he was humbled.
He did not beat on the walls.
Nor did he suck his thumb.
He cocked his head attentively
like a defendant at his own trial.

Jonah took out the wallet of his father
and tried to count the money
and it was all washed away.
Jonah took out the picture of his mother
and tried to kiss the eyes
and it was all washed away.
Jonah took off his coat and his trousers,
his tie, his watch fob, his cuff links
and gave them up.
He sat like an old-fashioned bather
in his undershirt and drawers.

This is my death,
Jonah said out loud,
and it will profit me to understand it.
I will make a mental note of each detail.
Little fish swam by his nose
and he noted them and touched their slime.
Plankton came and he held them in his palm
like God's littlest light bulbs.
His whole past was there with him
and he ate that.

At this point the whale
vomited him back out into the sea.
The shocking blue sky.
The shocking white boats.
The sun like a crazed eyeball.
Then he told the news media
the strange details of his death
and they hammered him up in the marketplace
and sold him and sold him and sold him.
My death the same.

FOR MR. DEATH WHO STANDS WITH
HIS DOOR OPEN

Time grows dim. Time that was so long
grows short, time, all goggle-eyed,
wiggling her skirts, singing her torch song,
giving the boys a buzz and a ride,
that Nazi Mama with her beer and sauerkraut.
Time, old gal of mine, will soon dim out.

May I say how young she was back then,
playing piggley-witch and hoola-hoop,
dancing the jango with six awful men,
letting the chickens out of the coop,
promising to marry Jack and Jerome,
and never bothering, never, never,
to come back home.

Time was when time had time enough
and the sea washed me daily in its delicate brine.
There is no terror when you swim in the buff
or speed up the boat and hang out a line.
Time was when I could hiccup and hold my breath
and not in that instant meet Mr. Death.

Mr. Death, you actor, you have many masks.
Once you were sleek, a kind of Valentino
with my father's bathtub gin in your flask.
With my cinched-in waist and my dumb vertigo
at the crook of your long white arm
and yet you never bent me back, never, never,
into your blackguard charm.

Next, Mr. Death, you held out the bait
during my first decline, as they say,
telling that suicide baby to celebrate
her own going in her own puppet play.
I went out popping pills and crying adieu
in my own death camp with my own little Jew.

Now your beer belly hangs out like Fatso.
You are popping your buttons and expelling gas.
How can I lie down with you, my comical beau
when you are so middle-aged and lower-class.
Yet you'll press me down in your envelope;
pressed as neat as a butterfly, forever, forever,
beside Mussolini and the Pope.

Mr. Death, when you came to the ovens it was short
and to the drowning man you were likewise kind,
and the nicest of all to the baby I had to abort
and middling you were to all the crucified combined.
But when it comes to my death let it be slow,
let it be pantomime, this last peep show,
so that I may squat at the edge trying on
my black necessary trousseau.

FAUSTUS AND I

I went to the opera and God was not there.
I was, at the time, in my apprenticeship.
The voices were as full as goblets; in mid-air
I caught them and threw them back. A form of worship.
In those vacant moments when our Lord sleeps
I have the voices. A cry that is mine for keeps.

I went to the galleries and God was not there,
only Mother Roulin and her baby, an old man infant,
his face lined in black and with a strange stare
in his black, black eyes. They seemed to hunt
me down. At the gallery van Gogh was violent
as the crows in the wheat field began their last ascent.

Three roads led to that death. All of them blind.
The sky had the presence of a thousand blue eyes
and the wheat beat itself. The wheat was not kind.
The crows go up immediately like an old man's lies.
The crimes, my Dutchman, that wait within us all
crawled out of that sea long before the fall.

I went to the bookstore and God was not there.
Doctor Faustus was baby blue with a Knopf dog
on his spine. He was frayed and threadbare
with needing. The arch-deceiver and I had a dialogue.
The Debble and I, the Father of Lies himself,
communed, as it were, from the bookshelf.

I have made a pact and a half in my day
and stolen Godes Boke during a love affair,
the Gideon itself for all devout salesmen who pray.
The Song of Solomon was underlined by some earlier pair.
The rest of the words turned to wood in my hands.
I am not immortal. Faustus and I are the also-ran.

THE DEATH BABY

1. *Dreams*

I was an ice baby.
I turned to sky blue.
My tears became two glass beads.
My mouth stiffened into a dumb howl.
They say it was a dream
but I remember that hardening.

My sister at six
dreamt nightly of my death:
"The baby turned to ice.
Someone put her in the refrigerator
and she turned as hard as a Popsicle."

I remember the stink of the liverwurst.
How I was put on a platter and laid
between the mayonnaise and the bacon.
The rhythm of the refrigerator
had been disturbed.
The milk bottle hissed like a snake.
The tomatoes vomited up their stomachs.
The caviar turned to lava.
The pimentos kissed like cupids.
I moved like a lobster,
slower and slower.
The air was tiny.
The air would not do.

*

I was at the dogs' party.
I was their bone.
I had been laid out in their kennel
like a fresh turkey.

354

This was my sister's dream
but I remember that quartering;
I remember the sickbed smell
of the sawdust floor, the pink eyes,
the pink tongues and the teeth, those nails.
I had been carried out like Moses
and hidden by the paws
of ten Boston bull terriers,
ten angry bulls
jumping like enormous roaches.
At first I was lapped,
rough as sandpaper.
I became very clean.
Then my arm was missing.
I was coming apart.
They loved me until
I was gone.

2. *The Dy-dee Doll*

My Dy-dee doll
died twice.
Once when I snapped
her head off
and let it float in the toilet
and once under the sun lamp
trying to get warm
she melted.
She was a gloom,
her face embracing
her little bent arms.
She died in all her rubber wisdom.

3. *Seven Times*

I died seven times
in seven ways
letting death give me a sign,
letting death place his mark on my forehead,
crossed over, crossed over.

And death took root in that sleep.
In that sleep I held an ice baby
and I rocked it
and was rocked by it.
Oh Madonna, hold me.
I am a small handful.

4. *Madonna*

My mother died
unrocked, unrocked.
Weeks at her deathbed
seeing her thrust herself against the metal bars,
thrashing like a fish on the hook
and me low at her high stage,
letting the priestess dance alone,
wanting to place my head in her lap
or even take her in my arms somehow
and fondle her twisted gray hair.
But her rocking horse was pain
with vomit steaming from her mouth.
Her belly was big with another child,
cancer's baby, big as a football.
I could not soothe.
With every hump and crack
there was less Madonna
until that strange labor took her.

Then the room was bankrupt.
That was the end of her paying.

5. *Max*

Max and I
two immoderate sisters,
two immoderate writers,
two burdeners,
made a pact.
To beat death down with a stick.
To take over.
To build our death like carpenters.
When she had a broken back,
each night we built her sleep.
Talking on the hot line
until her eyes pulled down like shades.
And we agreed in those long hushed phone calls
that when the moment comes
we'll talk turkey,
we'll shoot words straight from the hip,
we'll play it as it lays.
Yes,
when death comes with its hood
we won't be polite.

6. *Baby*

Death,
you lie in my arms like a cherub,
as heavy as bread dough.
Your milky wings are as still as plastic.
Hair as soft as music.
Hair the color of a harp.

And eyes made of glass,
as brittle as crystal.
Each time I rock you
I think you will break.
I rock. I rock.
Glass eye, ice eye,
primordial eye,
lava eye,
pin eye,
break eye,
how you stare back!

Like the gaze of small children
you know all about me.
You have worn my underwear.
You have read my newspaper.
You have seen my father whip me.
You have seen me stroke my father's whip.

I rock. I rock.
We plunge back and forth
comforting each other.
We are stone.
We are carved, a pietà
that swings and swings.
Outside, the world is a chilly army.
Outside, the sea is brought to its knees.
Outside, Pakistan is swallowed in a mouthful.

I rock. I rock.
You are my stone child
with still eyes like marbles.
There is a death baby
for each of us.
We own him.
His smell is our smell.

Beware. Beware.
There is a tenderness.
There is a love
for this dumb traveler
waiting in his pink covers.
Someday,
heavy with cancer or disaster
I will look up at Max
and say: It is time.
Hand me the death baby
and there will be
that final rocking.

RATS LIVE ON NO EVIL STAR
A palindrome seen on the side of a barn in Ireland

After Adam broke his rib in two
and ate it for supper,
after Adam, from the waist up,
an old mother,
had begun to question the wonder
Eve was brought forth.
Eve came out of that rib like an angry bird.
She came forth like a bird that got loose
suddenly from its cage.
Out of the cage came Eve,
escaping, escaping.
She was clothed in her skin like the sun
and her ankles were not for sale.

God looked out through his tunnel
and was pleased.

Adam sat like a lawyer
and read the book of life.

Only his eyes were alive.
They did the work of a blast furnace.

Only later did Adam and Eve go galloping,
galloping into the apple.
They made the noise of the moon-chew
and let the juice fall down like tears.

Because of this same apple
Eve gave birth to the evilest of creatures
with its bellyful of dirt
and its hair seven inches long.
It had two eyes full of poison
and routine pointed teeth.
Thus Eve gave birth.
In this unnatural act
she gave birth to a rat.
It slid from her like a pearl.
It was ugly, of course,
but Eve did not know that
and when it died before its time
she placed its tiny body
on that piece of kindergarten called STAR.

Now all us cursed ones falling out after
with our evil mouths and our worried eyes
die before our time
but do not go to some heaven, some hell
but are put on the RAT'S STAR
which is as wide as Asia
and as happy as a barbershop quartet.
We are put there beside the three thieves
for the lowest of us all
deserve to smile in eternity
like a watermelon.

GRANDFATHER, YOUR WOUND

The wound is open,
Grandfather, where you died,
where you sit inside it
as shy as a robin.
I am an ocean-going vessel
but you are a ceiling made of wood
and the island you were the man of,
is shaped like a squirrel and named thereof.
On this island, Grandfather, made of your stuff,
a rubber squirrel sits on the kitchen table
coughing up mica like phlegm.

I stand in your writing room
with the Atlantic painting its way toward us
and ask why am I left with stuffed fish on the wall,
why am I left with rubber squirrels with mica eyes,
when you were Mr. Funnyman, Mr. Nativeman,
when you were Mr. Lectureman, Mr. Editor,
the small town big shot who, although very short,
who although with a cigarette-stained mustache,
who although famous for lobster on the rocks,
left me here, nubkin, sucking in my vodka
and emphysema cigarettes, unable to walk
your walks, unable to write your writes.

Grandfather,
you blow your bone like a horn
and I hear it inside my pink facecloth.
I hear you, Mr. Iodineman,
and the sun goes down
just as it did in your life,
like a campaign ribbon,
an ingot from the iron works,

an eyelash,
and a dot and a dash.
Now it comes bright again —
my God, Grandfather,
you are here,
you are laughing,
you hold me and rock me
and we watch the lighthouse come on,
blinking its dry wings over us all,
over my wound
and yours.

BABY PICTURE

It's in the heart of the grape
where that smile lies.
It's in the good-bye-bow in the hair
where that smile lies.
It's in the clerical collar of the dress
where that smile lies.
What smile?
The smile of my seventh year,
caught here in the painted photograph.

It's peeling now, age has got it,
a kind of cancer of the background
and also in the assorted features.
It's like a rotten flag
or a vegetable from the refrigerator,
pocked with mold.
I am aging without sound,
into darkness, darkness.

Anne,
who were you?

I open the vein
and my blood rings like roller skates.
I open the mouth
and my teeth are an angry army.
I open the eyes
and they go sick like dogs
with what they have seen.
I open the hair
and it falls apart like dust balls.
I open the dress
and I see a child bent on a toilet seat.
I crouch there, sitting dumbly
pushing the enemas out like ice cream,
letting the whole brown world
turn into sweets.

Anne,
who were you?

Merely a kid keeping alive.

THE FURIES

The Fury of Beautiful Bones

Sing me a thrush, bone.
Sing me a nest of cup and pestle.
Sing me a sweetbread for an old grandfather.
Sing me a foot and a doorknob, for you are my love.
Oh sing, bone bag man, sing.
Your head is what I remember that August,
you were in love with another woman but
that didn't matter. I was the fury of your
bones, your fingers long and nubby, your
forehead a beacon, bare as marble and I worried

you like an odor because you had not quite forgotten,
bone bag man, garlic in the North End,
the book you dedicated, naked as a fish,
naked as someone drowning into his own mouth.
I wonder, Mr. Bone man, what you're thinking
of your fury now, gone sour as a sinking whale,
crawling up the alphabet on her own bones.
Am I in your ear still singing songs in the rain,
me of the death rattle, me of the magnolias,
me of the sawdust tavern at the city's edge.
Women have lovely bones, arms, neck, thigh
and I admire them also, but your bones
supersede loveliness. They are the tough
ones that get broken and reset. I just can't
answer for you, only for your bones,
round rulers, round nudgers, round poles,
numb nubkins, the sword of sugar.
I feel the skull, Mr. Skeleton, living its
own life in its own skin.

The Fury of Hating Eyes

I would like to bury
all the hating eyes
under the sand somewhere off
the North Atlantic and suffocate
them with the awful sand
and put all their colors to sleep
in that soft smother.
Take the brown eyes of my father,
those gun shots, those mean muds.
Bury them.
Take the blue eyes of my mother,
naked as the sea,
waiting to pull you down

where there is no air, no God.
Bury them.
Take the black eyes of my lover,
coal eyes like a cruel hog,
wanting to whip you and laugh.
Bury them.
Take the hating eyes of martyrs,
presidents, bus collectors,
bank managers, soldiers.
Bury them.
Take my eyes, half blind
and falling into the air.
Bury them.
Take your eyes.
I come to the center,
where a shark looks up at death
and thinks of my death.
They'd like to take my heart
and squeeze it like a doughnut.
They'd like to take my eyes
and poke a hatpin through
their pupils. Not just to bury
but to stab. As for your eyes,
I fold up in front of them
in a baby ball and you send
them to the State Asylum.
Look! Look! Both those
mice are watching you
from behind the kind bars.

The Fury of Guitars and Sopranos

This singing
is a kind of dying,
a kind of birth,

a votive candle.
I have a dream-mother
who sings with her guitar,
nursing the bedroom
with moonlight and beautiful olives.
A flute came too,
joining the five strings,
a God finger over the holes.
I knew a beautiful woman once
who sang with her fingertips
and her eyes were brown
like small birds.
At the cup of her breasts
I drew wine.
At the mound of her legs
I drew figs.
She sang for my thirst,
mysterious songs of God
that would have laid an army down.
It was as if a morning-glory
had bloomed in her throat
and all that blue
and small pollen
ate into my heart
violent and religious.

The Fury of Earth

The day of fire is coming, the thrush
will fly ablaze like a little sky rocket,
the beetle will sink like a giant bulldozer,
and at the breaking of the morning the houses
will turn into oil and will in their tides
of fire be a becoming and an ending, a red fan.

What then, man in your easy chair,
of the anointment of the sick,
of the New Jerusalem?
You will have to polish up the stars
with Bab-o and find a new God
as the earth empties out
into the gnarled hands of the old redeemer.

The Fury of Jewels and Coal

Many a miner has gone
into the deep pit
to receive the dust of a kiss,
an ore-cell.
He has gone with his lamp
full of mole eyes
deep deep and has brought forth
Jesus at Gethsemane.
Body of moss, body of glass,
body of peat, how sharp
you lie, emerald as heavy
as a golf course, ruby as dark
as an afterbirth,
diamond as white as sun
on the sea, coal, dark mother,
brood mother, let the sea birds
bring you into our lives
as from a distant island,
heavy as death.

The Fury of Cooks

Herbs, garlic,
cheese, please let me in!

Souffles, salads,
Parker House rolls,
please let me in!
Cook Helen,
why are you so cross,
why is your kitchen verboten?
Couldn't you just teach me
to bake a potato,
that charm,
that young prince?
No! No!
This is my country!
You shout silently.
Couldn't you just show me
the gravy. How you drill it out
of the stomach of that bird?
Helen, Helen,
let me in,
let me feel the flour,
is it blind and frightening,
this stuff that makes cakes?
Helen, Helen,
the kitchen is your dog
and you pat it
and love it
and keep it clean.
But all these things,
all these dishes of things
come through the swinging door
and I don't know from where?
Give me some tomato aspic, Helen!
I don't want to be alone.

The Fury of Cocks

There they are
drooping over the breakfast plates,
angel-like,
folding in their sad wing,
animal sad,
and only the night before
there they were
playing the banjo.
Once more the day's light comes
with its immense sun,
its mother trucks,
its engines of amputation.
Whereas last night
the cock knew its way home,
as stiff as a hammer,
battering in with all
its awful power.
That theater.
Today it is tender,
a small bird,
as soft as a baby's hand.
She is the house.
He is the steeple.
When they fuck they are God.
When they break away they are God.
When they snore they are God.
In the morning they butter the toast.
They don't say much.
They are still God.
All the cocks of the world are God,
blooming, blooming, blooming
into the sweet blood of woman.

The Fury of Abandonment

Someone lives in a cave
eating his toes,
I know that much.
Someone little lives under a bush
pressing an empty Coca-Cola can against
his starving bloated stomach,
I know that much.
A monkey had his hands cut off
for a medical experiment
and his claws wept.
I know that much.

I know that it is all
a matter of hands.
Out of the mournful sweetness of touching
comes love
like breakfast.
Out of the many houses come the hands
before the abandonment of the city,
out of the bars and shops,
a thin file of ants.

I've been abandoned out here
under the dry stars
with no shoes, no belt
and I've called Rescue Inc. —
that old-fashioned hot line —
no voice.
Left to my own lips, touch them,
my own dumb eyes, touch them,
the progression of my parts, touch them,
my own nostrils, shoulders, breasts,
navel, stomach, mound, kneebone, ankle,
touch them.

It makes me laugh
to see a woman in this condition.
It makes me laugh for America and New York City
when your hands are cut off
and no one answers the phone.

The Fury of Overshoes

They sit in a row
outside the kindergarten,
black, red, brown, all
with those brass buckles.
Remember when you couldn't
buckle your own
overshoe
or tie your own
shoe
or cut your own meat
and the tears
running down like mud
because you fell off your
tricycle?
Remember, big fish,
when you couldn't swim
and simply slipped under
like a stone frog?
The world wasn't
yours.
It belonged to
the big people.
Under your bed
sat the wolf
and he made a shadow
when cars passed by
at night.

They made you give up
your nightlight
and your teddy
and your thumb.
Oh overshoes,
don't you
remember me,
pushing you up and down
in the winter snow?
Oh thumb,
I want a drink,
it is dark,
where are the big people,
when will I get there,
taking giant steps
all day,
each day
and thinking
nothing of it?

The Fury of Rain Storms

The rain drums down like red ants,
each bouncing off my window.
These ants are in great pain
and they cry out as they hit,
as if their little legs were only
stitched on and their heads pasted.
And oh they bring to mind the grave,
so humble, so willing to be beat upon
with its awful lettering and
the body lying underneath
without an umbrella.

Depression is boring, I think,
and I would do better to make
some soup and light up the cave.

The Fury of Flowers and Worms

Let the flowers make a journey
on Monday so that I can see
ten daisies in a blue vase
with perhaps one red ant
crawling to the gold center.
A bit of the field on my table,
close to the worms
who struggle blindly,
moving deep into their slime,
moving deep into God's abdomen,
moving like oil through water,
sliding through the good brown.

The daisies grow wild
like popcorn.
They are God's promise to the field.
How happy I am, daisies, to love you.
How happy you are to be loved
and found magical, like a secret
from the sluggish field.
If all the world picked daisies
wars would end, the common cold would stop,
unemployment would end, the monetary market
would hold steady and no money would float.

Listen world,
if you'd just take the time to pick
the white fingers, the penny heart,
all would be well.
They are so unexpected.

They are as good as salt.
If someone had brought them
to van Gogh's room daily
his ear would have stayed on.
I would like to think that no one would die anymore
if we all believed in daisies
but the worms know better, don't they?
They slide into the ear of a corpse
and listen to his great sigh.

The Fury of God's Good-bye

One day He
tipped His top hat
and walked
out of the room,
ending the argument.
He stomped off
saying:
I don't give guarantees.
I was left
quite alone
using up the darkness.
I rolled up
my sweater,
up into a ball,
and took it
to bed with me,
a kind of stand-in
for God,
that washerwoman
who walks out
when you're clean
but not ironed.

When I woke up
the sweater
had turned to
bricks of gold.
I'd won the world
but like a
forsaken explorer,
I'd lost
my map.

The Fury of Sundays

Moist, moist,
the heat leaking through the hinges,
sun baking the roof like a pie
and I and thou and she
eating, working, sweating,
droned up on the heat.
The sun as red as the cop car siren.
The sun as red as the algebra marks.
The sun as red as two electric eyeballs.
She wanting to take a bath in jello.
You and me sipping vodka and soda,
ice cubes melting like the Virgin Mary.
You cutting the lawn, fixing the machines,
all this leprous day and then more vodka,
more soda and the pond forgiving our bodies,
the pond sucking out the throb.
Our bodies were trash.
We leave them on the shore.
I and thou and she
swim like minnows,
losing all our queens and kings,
losing our heels and our tongues,

cool, cool, all day that Sunday in July
when we were young and did not look
into the abyss,
that God spot.

The Fury of Sunsets

Something
cold is in the air,
an aura of ice
and phlegm.
All day I've built
a lifetime and now
the sun sinks to
undo it.
The horizon bleeds
and sucks its thumb.
The little red thumb
goes out of sight.
And I wonder about
this lifetime with myself,
this dream I'm living.
I could eat the sky
like an apple
but I'd rather
ask the first star:
why am I here?
why do I live in this house?
who's responsible?
eh?

The Fury of Sunrises

Darkness
as black as your eyelid,
poketricks of stars,
the yellow mouth,
the smell of a stranger,
dawn coming up,
dark blue,
no stars,
the smell of a lover,
warmer now
as authentic as soap,
wave after wave
of lightness
and the birds in their chains
going mad with throat noises,
the birds in their tracks
yelling into their cheeks like clowns,
lighter, lighter,
the stars gone,
the trees appearing in their green hoods,
the house appearing across the way,
the road and its sad macadam,
the rock walls losing their cotton,
lighter, lighter,
letting the dog out and seeing
fog lift by her legs,
a gauze dance,
lighter, lighter,
yellow, blue at the tops of trees,
more God, more God everywhere,
lighter, lighter,
more world everywhere,
sheets bent back for people,
the strange heads of love

and breakfast,
that sacrament,
lighter, yellower,
like the yolk of eggs,
the flies gathering at the windowpane,
the dog inside whining for food
and the day commencing,
not to die, not to die,
as in the last day breaking,
a final day digesting itself,
lighter, lighter,
the endless colors,
the same old trees stepping toward me,
the rock unpacking its crevices,
breakfast like a dream
and the whole day to live through,
steadfast, deep, interior.
After the death,
after the black of black,
this lightness —
not to die, not to die —
that God begot.

PRAYING ON A 707

Mother,
each time I talk to God
you interfere.
You of the bla-bla set,
carrying on about the state of letters.
If I write a poem
you give a treasurer's report.
If I make love
you give me the funniest lines.

Mrs. Sarcasm,
why are there any children left?

They hold up their bows.
They curtsy in just your style.
They shake hands how-do-you-do
in the same inimitable manner.
They pass over the soup with parsley
as you never could.
They take their children into their arms
like cups of warm cocoa
as you never could
and yet and yet
with your smile, your dimple we ape you,
we ape you further . . .
the great pine of summer,
the beach that oiled you,
the garden made of noses,
the moon tied down over the sea,
the great warm-blooded dogs . . .
the doll you gave me, Mary Gray,
or your mother gave me
or the maid gave me.
Perhaps the maid.
She had soul,
being Italian.

Mother,
each time I talk to God
you interfere.
Up there in the jet,
below the clouds as small as puppies,
the sun standing fire,
I talk to God and ask Him
to speak of my failures, my successes,

ask Him to morally make an assessment.
He does.

He says,
you haven't,
you haven't.

Mother,
you and God
float with the same belly
up.

CLOTHES

Put on a clean shirt
before you die, some Russian said.
Nothing with drool, please,
no egg spots, no blood,
no sweat, no sperm.
You want me clean, God,
so I'll try to comply.

The hat I was married in,
will it do?
White, broad, fake flowers in a tiny array.
It's old-fashioned, as stylish as a bedbug,
but it suits to die in something nostalgic.

And I'll take
my painting shirt
washed over and over of course
spotted with every yellow kitchen I've painted.
God, you don't mind if I bring all my kitchens?
They hold the family laughter and the soup.

For a bra
(need we mention it?),
the padded black one that my lover demeaned
when I took it off.
He said, "Where'd it all go?"

And I'll take
the maternity skirt of my ninth month,
a window for the love-belly
that let each baby pop out like an apple,
the water breaking in the restaurant,
making a noisy house I'd like to die in.

For underpants I'll pick white cotton,
the briefs of my childhood,
for it was my mother's dictum
that nice girls wore only white cotton.
If my mother had lived to see it
she would have put a WANTED sign up in the post office
for the black, the red, the blue I've worn.
Still, it would be perfectly fine with me
to die like a nice girl
smelling of Clorox and Duz.
Being sixteen-in-the-pants
I would die full of questions.

MARY'S SONG

Out of Egypt
with its pearls and honey,
out of Abraham, Isaac, Jacob,
out of the God I AM,
out of the diseased snakes,
out of the droppings of flies,

out of the sand dry as paper,
out of the deaf blackness,
I come here to give birth.

Write these words down.
Keep them on the tablet of miracles.
Withdraw from fine linen and goat's hair
and be prepared to anoint yourself with oil.
My time has come.
There are twenty people in my belly,
there is a magnitude of wings,
there are forty eyes shooting like arrows,
and they will all be born.
All be born in the yellow wind.

I will give suck to all
but they will go hungry,
they will go forth into suffering.
I will fondle each
but it will come to nothing.
They will not nest
for they are the Christs
and each will wave good-bye.

GOD'S BACKSIDE

Cold
like Grandfather's icehouse,
ice forming like a vein
and the trees,
rocks of frozen blood,
and me asking questions of the weather.
And me stupidly observing.
Me swallowing the stone of winter.
Three miles away cars push

by on the highway.
Across the world
bombs drop
in their awful labor.
Ten miles away
the city faints on its lights.
But here
there are only a few houses,
trees, rocks, telephone wires
and the cold punching the earth.
Cold slicing the windowpane
like a razor blade
for God, it seems,
has turned his backside to us,
giving us the dark negative,
the death wing,
until such time
as a flower breaks down the front door
and we cry "Father! Mother!"
and plan their wedding.

JESUS WALKING

When Jesus walked into the wilderness
he carried a man on his back,
at least it had the form of a man,
a fisherman perhaps with a wet nose,
a baker perhaps with flour in his eyes.
The man was dead it seems
and yet he was unkillable.
Jesus carried many men
yet there was only one man —
if indeed it was a man.
There in the wilderness all the leaves
reached out their hands

but Jesus went on by.
The bees beckoned him to their honey
but Jesus went on by.
The boar cut out its heart and offered it
but Jesus went on by
with his heavy burden.
The devil approached and slapped him on the jaw
and Jesus walked on.
The devil made the earth move like an elevator
and Jesus walked on.
The devil built a city of whores,
each in little angel beds,
and Jesus walked on with his burden.
For forty days, for forty nights
Jesus put one foot in front of the other
and the man he carried,
if it was a man,
became heavier and heavier.
He was carrying all the trees of the world
which are one tree.
He was carrying forty moons
which are one moon.
He was carrying all the boots
of all the men in the world
which are one boot.
He was carrying our blood.
One blood.

To pray, Jesus knew,
is to be a man carrying a man.

HURRY UP PLEASE IT'S TIME

What is death, I ask.
What is life, you ask.

I give them both my buttocks,
my two wheels rolling off toward Nirvana.
They are as neat as a wallet,
opening and closing on their coins,
the quarters, the nickels,
straight into the crapper.
Why shouldn't I pull down my pants
and moon at the executioner
as well as paste raisins on my breasts?
Why shouldn't I pull down my pants
and show my little cunny to Tom
and Albert? They wee-wee funny.
I wee-wee like a squaw.
I have ink but no pen, still
I dream that I can piss in God's eye.
I dream I'm a boy with a zipper.
It's so practical, la de dah.
The trouble with being a woman, Skeezix,
is being a little girl in the first place.
Not all the books of the world will change that.
I have swallowed an orange, being woman.
You have swallowed a ruler, being man.
Yet waiting to die we are the same thing.
Jehovah pleasures himself with his axe
before we are both overthrown.
Skeezix, you are me. La de dah.
You grow a beard but our drool is identical.

Forgive us, Father, for we know not.

Today is November 14th, 1972.
I live in Weston, Mass., Middlesex County,
U.S.A., and it rains steadily
in the pond like white puppy eyes.
The pond is waiting for its skin.

The pond is watching for its leather.
The pond is waiting for December and its Novocain.

It begins:

Interrogator:
What can you say of your last seven days?

Anne:
They were tired.

Interrogator:
One day is enough to perfect a man.

Anne:
I watered and fed the plant.

*

My undertaker waits for me.
He is probably twenty-three now,
learning his trade.
He'll stitch up the green,
he'll fasten the bones down
lest they fly away.
I am flying today.
I am not tired today.
I am a motor.
I am cramming in the sugar.
I am running up the hallways.
I am squeezing out the milk.
I am dissecting the dictionary.
I am God, la de dah.
Peanut butter is the American food.
We all eat it, being patriotic.

Ms. Dog is out fighting the dollars,
rolling in a field of bucks.

You've got it made if
you take the wafer,
take some wine,
take some bucks,
the green papery song of the office.
What a jello she could make with it,
the fives, the tens, the twenties,
all in a goo to feed to baby.
Andrew Jackson as an hors d'oeuvre,
la de dah.
I wish I were the U.S. Mint,
turning it all out,
turtle green
and monk black.
Who's that at the podium
in black and white,
blurting into the mike?
Ms. Dog.
Is she spilling her guts?
You bet.
Otherwise they cough . . .
The day is slipping away, why am I
out here, what do they want?
I am sorrowful in November . . .
(no they don't want that,
they want bee stings).
Toot, toot, tootsy don't cry.
Toot, toot, tootsy good-bye.
If you don't get a letter then
you'll know I'm in jail . . .
Remember that, Skeezix,
our first song?

Who's thinking those things?
Ms. Dog! She's out fighting the dollars.

Milk is the American drink.
Oh queen of sorrows,
oh water lady,
place me in your cup
and pull over the clouds
so no one can see.
She don't want no dollars.
She done want a mama.
The white of the white.

Anne says:
This is the rainy season.
I am sorrowful in November.
The kettle is whistling.
I must butter the toast.
And give it jam too.
My kitchen is a heart.
I must feed it oxygen once in a while
and mother the mother.

*

Say the woman is forty-four.
Say she is five seven-and-a-half.
Say her hair is stick color.
Say her eyes are chameleon.
Would you put her in a sack and bury her,
suck her down into the dumb dirt?
Some would.
If not, time will.
Ms. Dog, how much time you got left?
Ms. Dog, when you gonna feel that cold nose?
You better get straight with the Maker
cuz it's a coming, it's a coming!
The cup of coffee is growing and growing

and they're gonna stick your little doll's head
into it and your lungs a gonna get paid
and your clothes a gonna melt.
Hear that, Ms. Dog!
You of the songs,
you of the classroom,
you of the pocketa-pocketa,
you hungry mother,
you spleen baby!
Them angels gonna be cut down like wheat.
Them songs gonna be sliced with a razor.
Them kitchens gonna get a boulder in the belly.
Them phones gonna be torn out at the root.
There's power in the Lord, baby,
and he's gonna turn off the moon.
He's gonna nail you up in a closet
and there'll be no more Atlantic,
no more dreams, no more seeds.
One noon as you walk out to the mailbox
He'll snatch you up —
a woman beside the road like a red mitten.

There's a sack over my head.
I can't see. I'm blind.
The sea collapses. The sun is a bone.
Hi-ho the derry-o,
we all fall down.
If I were a fisherman I could comprehend.
They fish right through the door
and pull eyes from the fire.
They rock upon the daybreak
and amputate the waters.
They are beating the sea,
they are hurting it,
delving down into the inscrutable salt.

When mother left the room
and left me in the big black
and sent away my kitty
to be fried in the camps
and took away my blanket
to wash the me out of it
I lay in the soiled cold and prayed.
It was a little jail in which
I was never slapped with kisses.
I was the engine that couldn't.
Cold wigs blew on the trees outside
and car lights flew like roosters
on the ceiling.
Cradle, you are a grave place.

Interrogator:
What color is the devil?

Anne:
Black and blue.

Interrogator:
What goes up the chimney?

Anne:
Fat Lazarus in his red suit.

Forgive us, Father, for we know not.

Ms. Dog prefers to sunbathe nude.
Let the indifferent sky look on.
So what!
Let Mrs. Sewal pull the curtain back,
from her second story.
So what!

Let United Parcel Service see my parcel.
La de dah.
Sun, you hammer of yellow,
you hat on fire,
you honeysuckle mama,
pour your blonde on me!
Let me laugh for an entire hour
at your supreme being, your Cadillac stuff,
because I've come a long way
from Brussels sprouts.
I've come a long way to peel off my clothes
and lay me down in the grass.
Once only my palms showed.
Once I hung around in my woolly tank suit,
drying my hair in those little meatball curls.
Now I am clothed in gold air with
one dozen halos glistening on my skin.
I am a fortunate lady.
I've gotten out of my pouch
and my teeth are glad
and my heart, that witness,
beats well at the thought.

Oh body, be glad.
You are good goods.

*

Middle-class lady,
you make me smile.
You dig a hole
and come out with a sunburn.
If someone hands you a glass of water
you start constructing a sailboat.
If someone hands you a candy wrapper,

you take it to the book binder.
Pocketa-pocketa.

Once upon a time Ms. Dog was sixty-six.
She had white hair and wrinkles deep as splinters.
Her portrait was nailed up like Christ
and she said of it:
That's when I was forty-two,
down in Rockport with a hat on for the sun,
and Barbara drew a line drawing.
We were, at that moment, drinking vodka
and ginger beer and there was a chill in the air,
although it was July, and she gave me her sweater
to bundle up in. The next summer Skeezix tied
strings in that hat when we were fishing in Maine.
(It had gone into the lake twice.)
Of such moments is happiness made.

Forgive us, Father, for we know not.

Once upon a time we were all born,
popped out like jelly rolls
forgetting our fishdom,
the pleasuring seas,
the country of comfort,
spanked into the oxygens of death,
Good morning life, we say when we wake,
hail mary coffee toast
and we Americans take juice,
a liquid sun going down.
Good morning life.
To wake up is to be born.
To brush your teeth is to be alive.
To make a bowel movement is also desirable.
La de dah,
it's all routine.

Often there are wars
yet the shops keep open
and sausages are still fried.
People rub someone.
People copulate
entering each other's blood,
tying each other's tendons in knots,
transplanting their lives into the bed.
It doesn't matter if there are wars,
the business of life continues
unless you're the one that gets it.
Mama, they say, as their intestines
leak out. Even without wars
life is dangerous.
Boats spring leaks.
Cigarettes explode.
The snow could be radioactive.
Cancer could ooze out of the radio.
Who knows?
Ms. Dog stands on the shore
and the sea keeps rocking in
and she wants to talk to God.

Interrogator:
Why talk to God?

Anne:
It's better than playing bridge.

    *

Learning to talk is a complex business.
My daughter's first word was *utta*,
meaning button.
Before there are words
do you dream?

In utero
do you dream?
Who taught you to suck?
And how come?
You don't need to be taught to cry.
The soul presses a button.
Is the cry saying something?
Does it mean *help?*
Or hello?
The cry of a gull is beautiful
and the cry of a crow is ugly
but what I want to know
is whether they mean the same thing.
Somewhere a man sits with indigestion
and he doesn't care.
A woman is in a store buying bracelets
and earrings and she doesn't care.
La de dah.

Forgive us, Father, for we know not.

There are stars and faces.
There is ketchup and guitars.
There is the hand of a small child
when you're crossing the street.
There is the old man's last words:
More light! More light!
Ms. Dog wouldn't give them her buttocks.
She wouldn't moon at *them.*
Just at the killers of the dream.
The bus boys of the soul.
Or at death
who wants to make her a mummy.
And you too!
Wants to stuff her in a cold shoe
and then amputate the foot.

And you too!
La de dah.
What's the point of fighting the dollars
when all you need is a warm bed?
When the dog barks you let him in.
All we need is someone to let us in.
And one other thing:
to consider the lilies in the field.
Of course earth is a stranger,
we pull at its arms
and still it won't speak.
The sea is worse.
It comes in, falling to its knees
but we can't translate the language.
It is only known that they are here to worship,
to worship the terror of the rain,
the mud and all its people,
the body itself,
working like a city,
the night and its slow blood,
the autumn sky, Mary blue.
But more than that,
to worship the question itself,
though the buildings burn
and the big people topple over in a faint.
Bring a flashlight, Ms. Dog,
and look in every corner of the brain
and ask and ask and ask
until the kingdom,
however queer,
will come.

O YE TONGUES

First Psalm

Let there be a God as large as a sunlamp to laugh his heat at you.

Let there be an earth with a form like a jigsaw and let it fit for all of ye.

Let there be the darkness of a darkroom out of the deep. A worm room.

Let there be a God who sees light at the end of a long thin pipe and lets it in.

Let God divide them in half.

Let God share his Hoodsie.

Let the waters divide so that God may wash his face in first light.

Let there be pin holes in the sky in which God puts his little finger.

Let the stars be a heaven of jelly rolls and babies laughing.

Let the light be called Day so that men may grow corn or take busses.

Let there be on the second day dry land so that all men may dry their toes with Cannon towels.

Let God call this earth and feel the grasses rise up like angel hair.

Let there be bananas, cucumbers, prunes, mangoes, beans, rice and candy canes.

Let them seed and reseed.

Let there be seasons so that we may learn the architecture of the sky with eagles, finches, flickers, seagulls.

Let there be seasons so that we may put on twelve coats and shovel snow or take off our skins and bathe in the Carribean.

Let there be seasons so the sky dogs will jump across the sun in December.

Let there be seasons so that the eel may come out of her green cave.

Let there be seasons so that the raccoon may raise his blood level.

Let there be seasons so that the wind may be hoisted for an orange leaf.

Let there be seasons so that the rain will bury many ships.

Let there be seasons so that the miracles will fill our drinking glass with runny gold.

Let there be seasons so that our tongues will be rich in asparagus and limes.

Let there be seasons so that our fires will not forsake us and turn to metal.

Let there be seasons so that a man may close his palm on a woman's breast and bring forth a sweet nipple, a starberry.

Let there be a heaven so that man may outlive his grasses.

Second Psalm

For I pray there is an Almighty to bless the Piss Oak that surrounds me.

For I pray that there is an Almighty to bless the Dalmations that jump like sun spots.

For I pray that Emily King, whom I do not know except to say *good morning*, will observe my legs and fanny with good will.

For I pray that John F. Kennedy will forgive me for stealing his free-from-the-Senate Manila envelope.

For I pray that my honorary degree from Tufts is not making John Holmes stick out his tongue from the brackish grave in Medford.

For I pray that J. Brussel who writes that he is four score and more will prosper over his morning cock.

For I pray that Joy will unbend from her stone back and that the snakes will heat up her vertebrae.

For I pray that Mama Brundig, good doctor, will find rest at night after my yelling her name on the corner of Beacon and Dartmouth.

For I pray that this red wool suit that itches will come off for a nylon nighty.

For I pray that man, through the awful fog, will find my daughter proud although in Hawaii.

For I pray that my daughters will touch the faces of their daughters with bunny fur.

For I pray that my typewriter, ever faithful, will not break even though I threw it across the hospital room six years ago.

For I pray that Kayo who smiles from the photo above me from his lawn chair in Bermuda will smile at his name among tongues.

For I pray that the wooden room I live in will faithfully hold more books as the years pass.

For I pray that my apparel, my socks and my coats will not shrink any longer.

For I pray my two cats will enter heaven carrying their eyes in little tin sand pails.

For I pray that my wine will fatten.

For she prays that her touch will be milk.

For she prays that her night will be a small closed path.

For I pray that I may continue to stuff cheese potatoes in my mouth.

For I pray that Jack Daniels will go down as easily as a kiss.

For she prays that she will not cringe at the loneliness of the exile in Hamilton.

For she prays that she will not cringe at the death hole.

For I pray that God will digest me.

Third Psalm

Let Noah build an ark out of the old lady's shoe and fill it with the creatures of the Lord.

Let the ark of salvation have many windows so the creatures of the Lord will marry mouthfuls of oxygen.

Let the ark of salvation do homage to the Lord and notch his belt repeatedly.

Let Anne and Christopher kneel with a buzzard whose mouth will bite her toe so that she may offer it up.

Let Anne and Christopher appear with two robins whose worms are sweet and pink as lipstick.

Let them present a bee, cupped in their palms, zinging the electricity of the Lord out into little yellow Z's.

Let them give praise with a bull whose horns are yellow with history.

Praise the Lord with an ox who grows sweet in heaven and ties the hair ribbons of little girls.

Humble themselves with the fly buzzing like the mother of the engine.

Serve with the ape who tore down the Empire State Building and won the maid.

Dedicate an ant who will crawl toward the Lord like the print of this page.

Bless with a sable who bleeds ink across the dresses of ladies of the court.

Bless with a rabbit who comes with a whole sackful of sperm.

Bless with the locust who dances a curtain over the sky and makes the field blind.

Bless with the kingfish who melts down dimes into slim silver beside Frisco.

Rejoice with the day lily for it is born for a day to live by the mailbox and glorify the roadside.

Rejoice with the olive for it gives forth a faithful oil and eaten alone it will grease the mouth and bury the teeth.

Rejoice with a French angelfish which floats by like a jewel glowing like a blue iceberg in the Carribean.

Rejoice with a cottonbush which grows stars and seeds to clothe the multitudes of America.

Rejoice with the sea horse who lives in amusement parks and poems.

Let Anne and Christopher rejoice with the worm who moves into the light like a doll's penis.

Fourth Psalm

For I am an orphan with two death masks on the mantel and came from the grave of my mama's belly into the commerce of Boston.

For there were only two windows on the city and the buildings ate me.

For I was swaddled in grease wool from my father's company and could not move or ask the time.

For Anne and Christopher were born in my head as I howled at the grave of the roses, the ninety-four rose crèches of my bedroom.

For Christopher, my imaginary brother, my twin holding his baby cock like a minnow.

For I became a *we* and this imaginary *we* became a kind company when the big balloons did not bend over us.

For I could not read or speak and on the long nights I could not turn the moon off or count the lights of cars across the ceiling.

For I lay as pale as flour and drank moon juice from a rubber tip.

For I wet my pants and Christopher told the clock and it ticked like a July cricket and silently moved its spoons.

For I shat and Christopher smiled and said let the air be sweet with your soil.

For I listened to Christopher unless the balloon came and changed my bandage.

For my crotch itched and hands oiled it.

For I lay as single as death. Christopher lay beside me. He was living.

For I lay as stiff as the paper roses and Christopher took a tin basin and bathed me.

For I spoke not but the magician played me tricks of the blood.

For I heard not but for the magician lying beside me playing like a radio.

For I cried then and my little box wiggled with melancholy.

For I was in a boundary of wool and painted boards. Where are we Christopher? Jail, he said.

For the room itself was a box. Four thick walls of roses. A ceiling Christopher found low and menacing.

For I smiled and there was no one to notice. Christopher was asleep. He was making a sea sound.

For I wiggled my fingers but they would not stay. I could not put them in place. They broke out of my mouth.

For I was prodding myself out of my sleep, out the green room. The sleep of the desperate who travel backwards into darkness.

For birth was a disease and Christopher and I invented the cure.

For we swallow magic and we deliver Anne.

Fifth Psalm

Let Christopher and Anne come forth with a pig as bold as an assistant professor. He who comes forth from soil and the subway makes poison sweet.

Let them come forth with a mole who has come from the artificial anus into the light to swallow the sun.

Come forth with a daisy who opens like a hand and wants to be counted for *he loves me.*

Come forth with an orange who will turn its flashlight on and glow in the dark like something holy.

Come forth with a snail who ties and unties his brain within a hard skull. No one sends a letter to the snail.

Let Christopher and Anne come forth with a squid who will come bringing his poison to wash over the Lord like melted licorice.

Come forth with a cauliflower who will plunk herself down beside Him and worry like a white brain.

Come forth with a rose who unfolds like nether lips and is a languid delight.

Come forth with a daffodil who is got up as a ballerina and who dances out into the ancient spring.

Come forth with a dog who is spotted and smiling and holds up his paw for the awful stars.

Come forth with a cockroach large enough to be Franz Kafka (may he rest in peace though locked in his room). Surely all who are locked in boxes of different sizes should have their hands held. Trains and planes should not be locked. One should be allowed to fly out of them and into the Lord's mouth. The Lord is my shepherd, He will swallow me. The Lord is my shepherd, He will allow me back out.

Let Christopher and Anne come forth with a carp who is two-thirds too large to fit anywhere happy.

Come with a leopard who seeps like oil across the branch and has cotton batten for paws.

Come with the Mediterranean on a sunny day where the stars sleep one inch below the surface.

Come with a tree-frog who is more important to the field than Big Ben. He should not be locked in.

Sixth Psalm

For America is a lady rocking on a porch in an unpainted house on an unused road but Anne does not see it.

For America is a librarian in Wichita coughing dust and sharing sourballs with the postman.

For America is Dr. Abraham passing out penicillin and sugar pills to the town of Woolrich, Pennsylvania.

For America is an old man washing his feet in Albion, Michigan. Drying them carefully and then applying Dr. Scholl's foot powder. But Anne does not see it. Anne is locked in.

For America is a reformed burglar turned locksmith who pulls up the shades of his shop at nine A.M. daily (except Sunday when he leaves his phone number on the shop door).

For America is a fat woman dusting a grand piano in English Creek, New Jersey.

For America is a suede glove manufacturer sitting in his large swivel chair feeling the goods and assessing his assets and debits.

For America is a bus driver in Embarrass, Minnesota, clocking the miles and watching the little cardboard suitcases file by.

For America is a land of Commies and Prohibitionists but Anne does not see it. Anne is locked in. The Trotskyites don't see her. The Republicans have never tweaked her chin for she is not there. Anne hides inside folding and unfolding rose after rose. She has no one. She has Christopher. They sit in their room pinching the dolls' noses, poking the dolls' eyes. One time they gave a doll a ride in a fuzzy slipper but that was too far, too far wasn't it. Anne did not dare. She put the slipper with the doll inside it as in a car right into the closet and pushed the door shut.

For America is the headlight man at the Ford plant in Detroit, Michigan, he of the wires, he of the white globe, all day, all day, all year, all his year's headlights, seventy a day, improved by automation but Anne does not.

For America is a miner in Ohio, slipping into the dark hole and bringing forth cat's eyes each night.

For America is only this room . . . there is no useful activity.

For America only your dolls are cheerful.

Seventh Psalm

Let all rejoice with a boa whose twenty feet loosen the tree and the rock and coil like a rubber rope.

Rejoice with the Postmaster General who sits at his desk in Washington and draws faces on the stamps.

Bring forth the vulture who is a meat watcher from the clouds.

Give praise with the spider who builds a city out of her toes.

Rejoice with the Japanese beetle who feasts on rose petals, those mouths of honey.

Rejoice with Peter Pan who flies gold to the crocodile.

Rejoice with the sea otter who floats on her back and carries her young on her tummy.

Give praise with the lobster who is the almighty picker-upper and is still fine to the tongue.

Rejoice with the oyster who lies safely in his hard-nosed shell and who can be eaten alive.

Rejoice with the panda bear who hugs himself.

Rejoice with the roach who is despised among creatures and yet allowed his ugly place.

Rejoice with the anchovy who darts in and out of salads.

Give praise with the barnacle who cements himself to the rock and lets the waves feed him green stuff.

Give praise with the whale who will make a big warm home for Jonah and let him hang his very own pictures up.

Give praise with the grape for lovers will wear them on their toes.

Rejoice with the potato which is a sweet lover and made of angel-mattresses.

Rejoice with broccoli for it is a good bush-of-a-face and goes nicely in the mouth.

Let Christopher and Anne rejoice with Winston Churchill and his hot and cold Blitz.

Let them rejoice with the speedboat that skims by, leaving white lines behind it, making the sea a tennis court for a minute.

Eighth Psalm

No. No. The woman is cheerful, she smiles at her stomach. She has swallowed a bagful of oranges and she is well pleased.

For she has come through the voyage fit and her room carries the little people.

For she has outlived the dates in the back of Fords, she has outlived the penises of her teens to come here, to the married harbor.

For she is the forbidden one, telling time by her ten long fingers.

For she is the dangerous hills and many a climber will be lost on such a passage.

For she is lost from mankind; she is knitting her own hair into a baby shawl.

For she is stuffed by Christopher into a neat package that will not undo until the weeks pass.

For she is a magnitude, she is many. She is each of us patting ourselves dry with a towel.

For she is nourished by darkness.

For she is in the dark room putting bones into place.

For she is clustering the gold and the silver, the minerals and chemicals.

For she is a hoarder, she puts away silks and wools and lips and small white eyes.

For she is seeing the end of her confinement now and is waiting like a stone for the waters.

For the baby crowns and there is a people-dawn in the world.

For the baby lies in its water and blood and there is a people-cry in the world.

For the baby suckles and there is a people made of milk for her to use. There are milk trees to hiss her on. There are milk beds in which to lie and dream of a warm room. There are milk fingers to fold and unfold. There are milk bottoms that are wet and caressed and put into their cotton.

For there are many worlds of milk to walk through under the moon.

For the baby grows and the mother places her giggle-jog on her knee and sings a song of Christopher and Anne.

For the mother sings songs of the baby that knew.

For the mother remembers the baby she was and never locks and twists or puts lonely into a foreign place.

For the baby lives. The mother will die and when she does Christopher will go with her. Christopher who stabbed his kisses and cried up to make two out of one.

Ninth Psalm

Let the chipmunk praise the Lord as he bounds up Jacob's Ladder.

Let the airplane praise the Lord as she flirts with the kingdom.

Let the Good Fairy praise with her heavy bagful of dimes.

Let them praise with a garbage can for all who are cast out.

Praise with a basketball as it enters God's mouth.

Praise with a lemon peel as it floats in the president's drink.

Praise with an ice cube for it will hold up miniature polar bears for a second.

Serve with a sheep for it will crimp the Lord's beard with a curling iron.

Serve with a donkey to carry the worrying angel into Jerusalem.

Rejoice with a Mustang for it will dance down the highway and bump no one.

Appear with a flashlight so the stars will not get tired.

Bring forth a wheel to cart the dead into paradise.

Praise with a fork so that the angels may eat scrambled eggs on Sunday nights.

Come forth with an exit sign so that all those entering will know the way out.

Come forth with a homebody so that she may humble her mops on God's feet.

Come forth with an opera singer so that each concert she may let the moon out of her mouth.

Rejoice with the goldfish for it swallows the sunset from its little glass bowl.

Rejoice with a priest who swallows his collar like a tongue depressor.

Rejoice with a rabbi who combs his beard out like eel grass.

Bring forth a pigeon who will eat popcorn or toenail parings.

Tenth Psalm

For as the baby springs out like a starfish into her million light years Anne sees that she must climb her own mountain.

For as she eats wisdom like the halves of a pear she puts one foot in front of the other. She climbs the dark wing.

For as her child grows Anne grows and there is salt and cantaloupe and molasses for all.

For as Anne walks, the music walks and the family lies down in milk.

For I am not locked up.

For I am placing fist over fist on rock and plunging into the altitude of words. The silence of words.

For the husband sells his rain to God and God is well pleased with His family.

For they fling together against hardness and somewhere, in another room, a light is clicked on by gentle fingers.

For death comes to friends, to parents, to sisters. Death comes with its bagful of pain yet they do not curse the key they were given to hold.

For they open each door and it gives them a new day at the yellow window.

For the child grows to a woman, her breasts coming up like the moon while Anne rubs the peace stone.

For the child starts up her own mountain (not being locked in) and reaches the coastline of grapes.

For Anne and her daughter master the mountain and again and again. Then the child finds a man who opens like the sea.

For that daughter must build her own city and fill it with her own oranges, her own words.

For Anne walked up and up and finally over the years until she was old as the moon and with its naggy voice.

For Anne had climbed over eight mountains and saw the children washing the tiny statues in the square.

For Anne sat down with the blood of a hammer and built a tombstone for herself and Christopher sat beside her and was well pleased with their red shadow.

For they hung up a picture of a rat and the rat smiled and held out his hand.

For the rat was blessed on that mountain. He was given a white bath.

For the milk in the skies sank down upon them and tucked them in.

For God did not forsake them but put the blood angel to look after them until such time as they would enter their star.

For the sky dogs jumped out and shoveled snow upon us and we lay in our quiet blood.

For God was as large as a sunlamp and laughed his heat at us and therefore we did not cringe at the death hole.

The Awful
Rowing Toward God

(1975)

For Brother Dennis, wherever he is,
and for James Wright, who would know.

When the heavens are obscured to us, and nothing noble or heroic appears, but we are oppressed by imperfection and shortcoming on all hands, we are apt to suck our thumbs and decry our fates. As if nothing were to be done in cloudy weather, or, if heaven were not accessible by the upper road, men would not find out a lower . . . There are two ways to victory, —- to strive bravely, or to yield. How much pain the last will save we have not yet learned.

Henry David Thoreau

Sören Kierkegaard says, "But above all do not make yourself important by doubting."

The days, like great black oxen tread the world;
God the herdsman goads them from behind,
And I am broken by their passing feet.

A poet quoting a poet to a poet

ROWING

A story, a story!
(Let it go. Let it come.)
I was stamped out like a Plymouth fender
into this world.
First came the crib
with its glacial bars.
Then dolls
and the devotion to their plastic mouths.
Then there was school,
the little straight rows of chairs,
blotting my name over and over,
but undersea all the time,
a stranger whose elbows wouldn't work.
Then there was life
with its cruel houses
and people who seldom touched —
though touch is all —
but I grew,
like a pig in a trenchcoat I grew,
and then there were many strange apparitions,
the nagging rain, the sun turning into poison
and all of that, saws working through my heart,
but I grew, I grew,
and God was there like an island I had not rowed to,
still ignorant of Him, my arms and my legs worked,
and I grew, I grew,
I wore rubies and bought tomatoes
and now, in my middle age,
about nineteen in the head I'd say,
I am rowing, I am rowing
though the oarlocks stick and are rusty
and the sea blinks and rolls
like a worried eyeball,
but I am rowing, I am rowing,

417

though the wind pushes me back
and I know that that island will not be perfect,
it will have the flaws of life,
the absurdities of the dinner table,
but there will be a door
and I will open it
and I will get rid of the rat inside of me,
the gnawing pestilential rat.
God will take it with his two hands
and embrace it.

As the African says:
This is my tale which I have told,
if it be sweet, if it be not sweet,
take somewhere else and let some return to me.
This story ends with me still rowing.

THE CIVIL WAR

I am torn in two
but I will conquer myself.
I will dig up the pride.
I will take scissors
and cut out the beggar.
I will take a crowbar
and pry out the broken
pieces of God in me.
Just like a jigsaw puzzle,
I will put Him together again
with the patience of a chess player.

How many pieces?

It feels like thousands,
God dressed up like a whore
in a slime of green algae.

God dressed up like an old man
staggering out of His shoes.
God dressed up like a child,
all naked,
even without skin,
soft as an avocado when you peel it.
And others, others, others.

But I will conquer them all
and build a whole nation of God
in me — but united,
build a new soul,
dress it with skin
and then put on my shirt
and sing an anthem,
a song of myself.

THE CHILDREN

The children are all crying in their pens
and the surf carries their cries away.
They are old men who have seen too much,
their mouths are full of dirty clothes,
the tongues poverty, tears like pus.
The surf pushes their cries back.
Listen.
They are bewitched.
They are writing down their life
on the wings of an elf
who then dissolves.
They are writing down their life
on a century fallen to ruin.
They are writing down their life
on the bomb of an alien God.
I am too.

We must get help.
The children are dying in their pens.
Their bodies are crumbling.
Their tongues are twisting backwards.
There is a certain ritual to it.
There is a dance they do in their pens.
Their mouths are immense.
They are swallowing monster hearts.
So is my mouth.

Listen.
We must all stop dying in the little ways,
in the craters of hate,
in the potholes of indifference —
a murder in the temple.
The place I live in
is a kind of maze
and I keep seeking
the exit or the home.
Yet if I could listen
to the bulldog courage of those children
and turn inward into the plague of my soul
with more eyes than the stars
I could melt the darkness —
as suddenly as that time
when an awful headache goes away
or someone puts out the fire —
and stop the darkness and its amputations
and find the real McCoy
in the private holiness
of my hands.

TWO HANDS

From the sea came a hand,
ignorant as a penny,
troubled with the salt of its mother,
mute with the silence of the fishes,
quick with the altars of the tides,
and God reached out of His mouth
and called it man.
Up came the other hand
and God called it woman.
The hands applauded.
And this was no sin.
It was as it was meant to be.

I see them roaming the streets:
Levi complaining about his mattress,
Sarah studying a beetle,
Mandrake holding his coffee mug,
Sally playing the drum at a football game,
John closing the eyes of the dying woman,
and some who are in prison,
even the prison of their bodies,
as Christ was prisoned in His body
until the triumph came.

Unwind, hands,
you angel webs,
unwind like the coil of a jumping jack,
cup together and let yourselves fill up with sun
and applaud, world,
applaud.

THE ROOM OF MY LIFE

Here,
in the room of my life
the objects keep changing.
Ashtrays to cry into,
the suffering brother of the wood walls,
the forty-eight keys of the typewriter
each an eyeball that is never shut,
the books, each a contestant in a beauty contest,
the black chair, a dog coffin made of Naugahyde,
the sockets on the wall
waiting like a cave of bees,
the gold rug
a conversation of heels and toes,
the fireplace
a knife waiting for someone to pick it up,
the sofa, exhausted with the exertion of a whore,
the phone
two flowers taking root in its crotch,
the doors
opening and closing like sea clams,
the lights
poking at me,
lighting up both the soil and the laugh.
The windows,
the starving windows
that drive the trees like nails into my heart.
Each day I feed the world out there
although birds explode
right and left.
I feed the world in here too,
offering the desk puppy biscuits.
However, nothing is just what it seems to be.
My objects dream and wear new costumes,
compelled to, it seems, by all the words in my hands
and the sea that bangs in my throat.

422

THE WITCH'S LIFE

When I was a child
there was an old woman in our neighborhood
whom we called The Witch.
All day she peered from her second story window
from behind the wrinkled curtains
and sometimes she would open the window
and yell: Get out of my life!
She had hair like kelp
and a voice like a boulder.

I think of her sometimes now
and wonder if I am becoming her.
My shoes turn up like a jester's.
Clumps of my hair, as I write this,
curl up individually like toes.
I am shoveling the children out,
scoop after scoop.
Only my books anoint me,
and a few friends,
those who reach into my veins.
Maybe I am becoming a hermit,
opening the door for only
a few special animals?
Maybe my skull is too crowded
and it has no opening through which
to feed it soup?
Maybe I have plugged up my sockets
to keep the gods in?
Maybe, although my heart
is a kitten of butter,
I am blowing it up like a zeppelin.
Yes. It is the witch's life,
climbing the primordial climb,
a dream within a dream,

then sitting here
holding a basket of fire.

THE EARTH FALLS DOWN

If I could blame it all on the weather,
the snow like the cadaver's table,
the trees turned into knitting needles,
the ground as hard as a frozen haddock,
the pond wearing its mustache of frost.
If I could blame conditions on *that*,
if I could blame the hearts of strangers
striding muffled down the street,
or blame the dogs, every color,
sniffing each other
and pissing on the doorstep . . .
If I could blame the war on the war
where its fire Brillos my hair . . .
If I could blame the bosses
and the presidents for
their unpardonable songs . . .
If I could blame it on all
the mothers and fathers of the world,
they of the lessons, the pellets of power,
they of the love surrounding you like batter . . .
Blame it on God perhaps?
He of the first opening
that pushed us all into our first mistakes?
No, I'll blame it on Man
For Man is God
and man is eating the earth up
like a candy bar
and not one of them can be left alone with the ocean
for it is known he will gulp it all down.
The stars (possibly) are safe.

At least for the moment.
The stars are pears
that no one can reach,
even for a wedding.

Perhaps for a death.

COURAGE

It is in the small things we see it.
The child's first step,
as awesome as an earthquake.
The first time you rode a bike,
wallowing up the sidewalk.
The first spanking when your heart
went on a journey all alone.
When they called you crybaby
or poor or fatty or crazy
and made you into an alien,
you drank their acid
and concealed it.

Later,
if you faced the death of bombs and bullets
you did not do it with a banner,
you did it with only a hat to
cover your heart.
You did not fondle the weakness inside you
though it was there.
Your courage was a small coal
that you kept swallowing.
If your buddy saved you
and died himself in so doing,
then his courage was not courage,
it was love; love as simple as shaving soap.

Later,
if you have endured a great despair,
then you did it alone,
getting a transfusion from the fire,
picking the scabs off your heart,
then wringing it out like a sock.
Next, my kinsman, you powdered your sorrow,
you gave it a back rub
and then you covered it with a blanket
and after it had slept a while
it woke to the wings of the roses
and was transformed.

Later,
when you face old age and its natural conclusion
your courage will still be shown in the little ways,
each spring will be a sword you'll sharpen,
those you love will live in a fever of love,
and you'll bargain with the calendar
and at the last moment
when death opens the back door
you'll put on your carpet slippers
and stride out.

RIDING THE ELEVATOR INTO THE SKY

As the fireman said:
Don't book a room over the fifth floor
in any hotel in New York.
They have ladders that will reach further
but no one will climb them.
As the New York *Times* said:
The elevator always seeks out
the floor of the fire

and automatically opens
and won't shut.
These are the warnings
that you must forget
if you're climbing out of yourself.
If you're going to smash into the sky.

Many times I've gone past
the fifth floor,
cranking upward,
but only once
have I gone all the way up.
Sixtieth floor:
small plants and swans bending
into their grave.
Floor two hundred:
mountains with the patience of a cat,
silence wearing its sneakers.
Floor five hundred:
messages and letters centuries old,
birds to drink,
a kitchen of clouds.
Floor six thousand:
the stars,
skeletons on fire,
their arms singing.
And a key,
a very large key,
that opens something —
some useful door —
somewhere —
up there.

WHEN MAN ENTERS WOMAN

When man
enters woman,
like the surf biting the shore,
again and again,
and the woman opens her mouth in pleasure
and her teeth gleam
like the alphabet,
Logos appears milking a star,
and the man
inside of woman
ties a knot
so that they will
never again be separate
and the woman
climbs into a flower
and swallows its stem
and Logos appears
and unleashes their rivers.

This man,
this woman
with their double hunger,
have tried to reach through
the curtain of God
and briefly they have,
though God
in His perversity
unties the knot.

THE FISH THAT WALKED

Up from oysters
and the confused weeds,

428

out from the tears of God,
the wounding tides,
he came.
He became a hunter of roots
and breathed like a man.
He ruffled through the grasses
and became known to the sky.
I stood close and watched it all.
Beg pardon, he said
but you have skin divers,
you have hooks and nets,
so why shouldn't I
enter your element for a moment?
Though it is curious here,
unusually awkward to walk.
It is without grace.
There is no rhythm
in this country of dirt.

And I said to him:
From some country
that I have misplaced
I can recall a few things . . .
but the light of the kitchen
gets in the way.
Yet there was a dance
when I kneaded the bread
there was a song my mother
used to sing . . .
And the salt of God's belly
where I floated in a cup of darkness.
I long for your country, fish.

The fish replied:
You must be a poet,
a lady of evil luck

desiring to be what you are not,
longing to be
what you can only visit.

THE FALLEN ANGELS

"Who are they"
"Fallen angels who were not good enough to be saved,
nor bad enough to be lost" say the peasantry.

They come on to my clean
sheet of paper and leave a Rorschach blot.
They do not do this to be mean,
they do it to give me a sign
they want me, as Aubrey Beardsley once said,
to shove it around till something comes.
Clumsy as I am,
I do it.
For I am like them —
both saved and lost,
tumbling downward like Humpty Dumpty
off the alphabet.

Each morning I push them off my bed
and when they get in the salad
rolling in it like a dog,
I pick each one out
just the way my daughter
picks out the anchovies.
In May they dance on the jonquils,
wearing out their toes,
laughing like fish.
In November,
the dread month,
they suck the childhood out of the berries
and turn them sour and inedible.

Yet they keep me company.
They wiggle up life.
They pass out their magic
like Assorted Lifesavers.
They go with me to the dentist
and protect me from the drill.
At the same time,
they go to class with me
and lie to my students.

O fallen angel,
the companion within me,
whisper something holy
before you pinch me
into the grave.

THE EARTH

God loafs around heaven,
without a shape
but He would like to smoke His cigar
or bite His fingernails
and so forth.

God owns heaven
but He craves the earth,
the earth with its little sleepy caves,
its bird resting at the kitchen window,
even its murders lined up like broken chairs,
even its writers digging into their souls
with jackhammers,
even its hucksters selling their animals
for gold,
even its babies sniffing for their music,

the farm house, white as a bone,
sitting in the lap of its corn,
even the statue holding up its widowed life,
even the ocean with its cupful of students,
but most of all He envies the bodies,
He who has no body.

The eyes, opening and shutting like keyholes
and never forgetting, recording by thousands,
the skull with its brains like eels —
the tablet of the world —
the bones and their joints
that build and break for any trick,
the genitals,
the ballast of the eternal,
and the heart, of course,
that swallows the tides
and spits them out cleansed.

He does not envy the soul so much.
He is all soul
but He would like to house it in a body
and come down
and give it a bath
now and then.

AFTER AUSCHWITZ

Anger,
as black as a hook,
overtakes me.
Each day,
each Nazi
took, at 8:00 A.M., a baby
and sautéed him for breakfast
in his frying pan.

And death looks on with a casual eye
and picks at the dirt under his fingernail.

Man is evil,
I say aloud.
Man is a flower
that should be burnt,
I say aloud.
Man
is a bird full of mud,
I say aloud.

And death looks on with a casual eye
and scratches his anus.

Man with his small pink toes,
with his miraculous fingers
is not a temple
but an outhouse,
I say aloud.
Let man never again raise his teacup.
Let man never again write a book.
Let man never again put on his shoe.
Let man never again raise his eyes,
on a soft July night.
Never. Never. Never. Never. Never.
I say these things aloud.

I beg the Lord not to hear.

THE POET OF IGNORANCE

Perhaps the earth is floating,
I do not know.
Perhaps the stars are little paper cutups
made by some giant scissors,

433

I do not know.
Perhaps the moon is a frozen tear,
I do not know.
Perhaps God is only a deep voice
heard by the deaf,
I do not know.

Perhaps I am no one.
True, I have a body
and I cannot escape from it.
I would like to fly out of my head,
but that is out of the question.
It is written on the tablet of destiny
that I am stuck here in this human form.
That being the case
I would like to call attention to my problem.

There is an animal inside me,
clutching fast to my heart,
a huge crab.
The doctors of Boston
have thrown up their hands.
They have tried scalpels,
needles, poison gasses and the like.
The crab remains.
It is a great weight.
I try to forget it, go about my business,
cook the broccoli, open and shut books,
brush my teeth and tie my shoes.
I have tried prayer
but as I pray the crab grips harder
and the pain enlarges.

I had a dream once,
perhaps it was a dream,
that the crab was my ignorance of God.
But who am I to believe in dreams?

THE SERMON OF THE TWELVE
ACKNOWLEDGMENTS

January?
The month is dumb.
It is fraudulent.
It does not cleanse itself.
The hens lay blood-stained eggs.
Do not lend your bread to anyone
lest it nevermore rise.
Do not eat lentils or your hair will fall out.

Do not rely on February
except when your cat has kittens,
throbbing into the snow.
Do not use knives and forks
unless there is a thaw,
like the yawn of a baby.
The sun in this month
begets a headache
like an angel slapping you in the face.

Earthquakes mean March.
The dragon will move,
and the earth will open like a wound.
There will be great rain or snow
so save some coal for your uncle.
The sun of this month cures all.
Therefore, old women say:
Let the sun of March shine on my daughter,
but let the sun of February shine on my daughter-in-law.
However, if you go to a party
dressed as the anti-Christ
you will be frozen to death by morning.

During the rainstorms of April
the oyster rises from the sea

and opens its shell —
rain enters it —
when it sinks the raindrops
become the pearl.
So take a picnic,
open your body,
and give birth to pearls.

June and July?
These are the months
we call Boiling Water.
There is sweat on the cat but the grape
marries herself to the sun.

Hesitate in August.
Be shy.
Let your toes tremble in their sandals.
However, pick the grape
and eat with confidence.
The grape is the blood of God.
Watch out when holding a knife
or you will behead St. John the Baptist.

Touch the Cross in September,
knock on it three times
and say aloud the name of the Lord.
Put seven bowls of salt on the roof overnight
and the next morning the damp one
will foretell the month of rain.
Do not faint in September
or you will wake up in a dead city.

If someone dies in October
do not sweep the house for three days
or the rest of you will go.
Also do not step on a boy's head
for the devil will enter your ears
like music.

November?
Shave,
whether you have hair or not.
Hair is not good,
nothing is allowed to grow,
all is allowed to die.
Because nothing grows
you may be tempted to count the stars
but beware,
in November counting the stars
gives you boils.
Beware of tall people,
they will go mad.
Don't harm the turtle dove
because he is a great shoe
that has swallowed Christ's blood.

December?
On December fourth
water spurts out of the mouse.
Put herbs in its eyes and boil corn
and put the corn away for the night
so that the Lord may trample on it
and bring you luck.
For many days the Lord has been
shut up in the oven.
After that He is boiled,
but He never dies, never dies.

THE EVIL EYE

It comes oozing
out of flowers at night,
it comes out of the rain
if a snake looks skyward,
it comes out of chairs and tables
if you don't point at them and say their names.

It comes into your mouth while you sleep,
pressing in like a washcloth.
Beware. Beware.

If you meet a cross-eyed person
you must plunge into the grass,
alongside the chilly ants,
fish through the green fingernails
and come up with the four-leaf clover
or your blood will congeal
like cold gravy.

If you run across a horseshoe,
passerby,
stop, take your hands out of your pockets
and count the nails
as you count your children
or your money.
Otherwise a sand flea will crawl in your ear
and fly into your brain
and the only way you'll keep from going mad
is to be hit with a hammer every hour.

If a hunchback is in the elevator with you
don't turn away,
immediately touch his hump
for his child will be born from his back tomorrow
and if he promptly bites the baby's nails off
(so it won't become a thief)
that child will be holy
and you, simple bird that you are,
may go on flying.

When you knock on wood,
and you do,
you knock on the Cross

and Jesus gives you a fragment of His body
and breaks an egg in your toilet,
giving up one life
for one life.

THE DEAD HEART

After I wrote this, a friend scrawled on this page, "Yes."

And I said, merely to myself, "I wish it could be for a different seizure — as with Molly Bloom with her 'and yes I said yes I will Yes.' "

It is not a turtle
hiding in its little green shell.
It is not a stone
to pick up and put under your black wing.
It is not a subway car that is obsolete.
It is not a lump of coal that you could light.
It is a dead heart.
It is inside of me.
It is a stranger
yet once it was agreeable,
opening and closing like a clam.

What it has cost me you can't imagine,
shrinks, priests, lovers, children, husbands,
friends and all the lot.
An expensive thing it was to keep going.
It gave back too.
Don't deny it!
I half wonder if April would bring it back to life?
A tulip? The first bud?
But those are just musings on my part,
the pity one has when one looks at a cadaver.

How did it die?
I called it EVIL.
I said to it, your poems stink like vomit.
I didn't stay to hear the last sentence.
It died on the word EVIL.
I did it with my tongue.
The tongue, the Chinese say,
is like a sharp knife:
it kills
without drawing blood.

THE PLAY

I am the only actor.
It is difficult for one woman
to act out a whole play.
The play is my life,
my solo act.
My running after the hands
and never catching up.
(The hands are out of sight —
that is, offstage.)
All I am doing onstage is running,
running to keep up,
but never making it.

Suddenly I stop running.
(This moves the plot along a bit.)
I give speeches, hundreds,
all prayers, all soliloquies.
I say absurd things like:
eggs must not quarrel with stones
or, keep your broken arm inside your sleeve
or, I am standing upright
but my shadow is crooked.

And such and such.
Many boos. Many boos.

Despite that I go on to the last lines:
To be without God is to be a snake
who wants to swallow an elephant.
The curtain falls.
The audience rushes out.
It was a bad performance.
That's because I'm the only actor
and there are few humans whose lives
will make an interesting play.
Don't you agree?

THE SICKNESS UNTO DEATH

God went out of me
as if the sea dried up like sandpaper,
as if the sun became a latrine.
God went out of my fingers.
They became stone.
My body became a side of mutton
and despair roamed the slaughterhouse.

Someone brought me oranges in my despair
but I could not eat a one
for God was in that orange.
I could not touch what did not belong to me.
The priest came,
he said God was even in Hitler.
I did not believe him
for if God were in Hitler
then God would be in me.
I did not hear the bird sounds.
They had left.

I did not see the speechless clouds,
I saw only the little white dish of my faith
breaking in the crater.
I kept saying:
I've got to have something to hold on to.
People gave me Bibles, crucifixes,
a yellow daisy,
but I could not touch them,
I who was a house full of bowel movement,
I who was a defaced altar,
I who wanted to crawl toward God
could not move nor eat bread.

So I ate myself,
bite by bite,
and the tears washed me,
wave after cowardly wave,
swallowing canker after canker
and Jesus stood over me looking down
and He laughed to find me gone,
and put His mouth to mine
and gave me His air.

My kindred, my brother, I said
and gave the yellow daisy
to the crazy woman in the next bed.

LOCKED DOORS

For the angels who inhabit this town,
although their shape constantly changes,
each night we leave some cold potatoes
and a bowl of milk on the windowsill.
Usually they inhabit heaven where,
by the way, no tears are allowed.

They push the moon around like
a boiled yam.
The Milky Way is their hen
with her many children.
When it is night the cows lie down
but the moon, that big bull,
stands up.

However, there is a locked room up there
with an iron door that can't be opened.
It has all your bad dreams in it.
It is hell.
Some say the devil locks the door
from the inside.
Some say the angels lock it from
the outside.
The people inside have no water
and are never allowed to touch.
They crack like macadam.
They are mute.
They do not cry help
except inside
where their hearts are covered with grubs.

I would like to unlock that door,
turn the rusty key
and hold each fallen one in my arms
but I cannot, I cannot.
I can only sit here on earth
at my place at the table.

THE EVIL SEEKERS

We are born with luck
which is to say with gold in our mouth.

As new and smooth as a grape,
as pure as a pond in Alaska,
as good as the stem of a green bean —
we are born and that ought to be enough,
we ought to be able to carry on from that
but one must learn about evil,
learn what is subhuman,
learn how the blood pops out like a scream,
one must see the night
before one can realize the day,
one must listen hard to the animal within,
one must walk like a sleepwalker
on the edge of the roof,
one must throw some part of her body
into the devil's mouth.
Odd stuff, you'd say.
But I'd say
you must die a little,
have a book of matches go off in your hand,
see your best friend copying your exam,
visit an Indian reservation and see
their plastic feathers,
the dead dream.
One must be a prisoner just once to hear
the lock twist into his gut.
After all that
one is free to grasp at the trees, the stones,
the sky, the birds that make sense out of air.
But even in a telephone booth
evil can seep out of the receiver
and we must cover it with a mattress,
and then tear it from its roots
and bury it,
bury it.

THE WALL

Nature is full of teeth
that come in one by one, then
decay,
fall out.
In nature nothing is stable,
all is change, bears, dogs, peas, the willow,
all disappear. Only to be reborn.
Rocks crumble, make new forms,
oceans move the continents,
mountains rise up and down like ghosts
yet all is natural, all is change.

As I write this sentence
about one hundred and four generations
since Christ, nothing has changed
except knowledge, the test tube.
Man still falls into the dirt
and is covered.
As I write this sentence one thousand are going
and one thousand are coming.
It is like the well that never dries up.
It is like the sea which is the kitchen of God.

We are all earthworms,
digging into our wrinkles.
We live beneath the ground
and if Christ should come in the form of a plow
and dig a furrow and push us up into the day
we earthworms would be blinded by the sudden light
and writhe in our distress.
As I write this sentence I too writhe.

For all you who are going,
and there are many who are climbing their pain,

many who will be painted out with a black ink
suddenly and before it is time,
for those many I say,
awkwardly. clumsily,
take off your life like trousers,
your shoes, your underwear,
then take off your flesh,
unpick the lock of your bones.
In other words
take off the wall
that separates you from God.

IS IT TRUE?

Once more
the sun roaming on the carpenter's back
as he puts joist to sill
and then occasionally he looks to the sky
as even the hen when it drinks
looks toward heaven.
Once in Rome I knelt in front of the Pope
as he waved from his high window.
It was because of a pain in my bowels.
Occasionally the devil has crawled
in and out of me,
through my cigarettes I suppose,
my passionate habit.

Now even the promised land of
Israel has a Hilton
and many tall buildings.
Perhaps it is true,
just as the sun passes over filth
and is not defiled.
For this reason I can book a room in a Hilton

or its terrible playfellow The Holiday Inn
though I never know what city I'm in when I wake up.
I have lost my map
and Jesus has squeezed out of the Gideon,
down to the bar for pretzels and a beer.

Today the Supreme Court made abortion legal.
Bless them.
Bless all women
who want to remake their own likeness
but not every day.
Bless the woman who took the cop's gun.
Bless also the woman who gave it back.
Bless woman for the apple she married.
Bless woman for her brain cells, little cell-computers.
Is it true?
Is it true?

Hare krishna, hare krishna,
krishna, krishna, hare hare
hare rama hare rama
rama rama hare,
they sing on the streets of Harvard Square,
tinkling their little thumb cymbals
and reed pipes, dancing with their joy.
They know what they know.

When I tell the priest I am evil
he asks for a definition of the word.
Do you mean sin? he asks.
Sin, hell! I reply.
I've committed every one.
What I mean is evil,
(not meaning to be, you understand,
just something I ate).

Evil is maybe lying to God.
Or better, lying to love.
The priest shakes his head.
He doesn't comprehend.

But the priest understands
when I tell him that I want to
pour gasoline over my evil body
and light it,
He says, "That's more like it!
That kind of evil!"
(Evil it seems comes in brands,
like soup or detergent.)

Ms. Dog,
why is you evil?
It climbed into me.
It didn't mean to.

Maybe my mother cut the God out of me
when I was two in my playpen.
Is it too late, too late
to open the incision and plant Him there again?
All is wilderness.
All is hay that died from too much rain,
my stinky tears.
Whose God are you looking for? asked the priest.
I replied:
a starving man doesn't ask what the meal is.
I would eat a tomato, or a fire bird or music.
I would eat a moth soaked in vinegar.
But is there any food anywhere,
in the wind's hat?
in the sea's olive?
Is it true?
Is it true?

I wouldn't mind if God were wooden,
I'd wear Him like a house,
praise His knot holes,
shine Him like a shoe.
I would not let Him burn.
I would not burn myself
for I would be wearing Him.
Oh wood, my father, my shelter,
bless you.

Bless all useful objects,
the spoons made of bone,
the mattress I cook my dreams upon,
the typewriter that is my church
with an altar of keys always waiting,
the ladders that let us climb,
both fireman and roofer.
Bless also the skillet,
black and oil-soaked,
that fries eggs like the eyes of saints.
Bless the shoe for holding my foot
and letting me walk with the omnipotence
of a cat over glass or dog shit.
Bless the lights for going on
giving me eyes like two small cameras.
Is it true?

If all this can be
then why am I in this country of black mud?

> *and the land shall become blazing pitch, which night
> and day shall never be quenched, and its smoke shall
> go up forever. From generation to generation it shall
> lie waste and no man shall pass through it ever again.*

Yet I pass through.
I pass through.
On the northern shore of Lake Galilee
Jesus and John preached to the local fishermen.

Yet I am not a fisherman.
I pass through.
I pass through.
The sun is black mud.
The moon becomes a blood ball.
If religion were a dream, someone said,
then it were still a dream worth dreaming.
True! True!
I whisper to my wood walls.

The state Capitol of Boston
has a gold dome.
During the War,
the one I grew up in,
they painted out the gold.
What did they think the Nazis
would do with it,
make it into teeth?
Peel it off and buy whores?
Wrap the Mayor up in it like a mummy
and put him on display in the Public Gardens?
In heaven,
there will be a secret door,
there will be flowers with eyes that wink,
there will be light flowing from a bronze bell,
there will be as much love as there
are cunners off the coast of Maine,
there will be gold that no one hides
from the Nazis,
there will be statues that the angel
inside of Michelangelo's hand fashioned.

450

I will lay open my soul
and hear an answer.
Hello. Hello. It will call back,
"Here's a butter knife," it will say.
"So scrape off your hunger and the mud."
But is it true?
Is it true?

My tongue is slit.
It cannot eat.
Even if I were a king,
with a whole tongue,
I would be put to death with a shovel.
True, I have friends,
a few,
each one is a soul in two bodies.
Each one is a man or a woman.

Let me now praise
the male of our species,
let me praise men,
and their eggs of courage,
their fine lives of the cock,
their awful lives in the office.
Let me praise men for eating the apple
and finding woman
like a big brain of coral.

Let me praise humans,
praise the men of God.
The men of God are God.

From the Tamil, I read,
"The rock that resists the crowbar
gives way to the roots of the tender plant."
I read this and go to sleep

and when I wake
Nixon will have declared the Vietnam war
is over. No more deaths, body by body.
(But this will be such old news
before you read my words.
Old and senile.)
Still I will hear this and will be happy,
happy kind of,
for I know there will be more wars
and more deaths
and then the headlines will be no more than a petal
upon a crater.
Deep earth,
redeem us from our redeemers.
Keep us, God, far from our politicians
and keep us near to the grape that wakes us up.
Keep us near to the wolf of death.
Keep us near to the wife of the sun.
Is it true?
Is it true?

Never mind.
I'll do my own wash.

I have,
for some time,
called myself,
Ms. Dog.
Why?
Because I am almost animal
and yet the animal I lost most —
that animal is near to God,
but lost from Him.
Do you understand?
Can you read my hieroglyphics?
No language is perfect.

I only know English.
English is not perfect.
When I tell the priest I am full
of bowel movement, right into the fingers,
he shrugs. To him shit is good.
To me, to my mother, it was poison
and the poison was all of me
in the nose, in the ears, in the lungs.
That's why language fails.
Because to one, shit is a feeder of plants,
to another the evil that permeates them
and although they try,
day after day of childhood,
they can't push the poison out.
So much for language.
So much for psychology.
God lives in shit — I have been told.
I believe both.
Is it true?
Is it true?

> Do you not know, have you not heard, were you not told
> long ago, have you not perceived ever since the world
> began that God sits throned on the vaulted roof of
> earth, whose inhabitants are like grasshoppers?

Grasshoppers
and me one of them,
my eight legs like crutches.
Bless the animals of this earth,
the wolf in its hiding spoon,
the fly in its tiny life,
the fish in its fragrance I lost,
The Genghis dog of the Serengeti
that kills its baby
because it was born to kill,

born to pound out life like flour,
the mouse and the rat for the vermin
and disease that they must put up with,
all, all, bless them,
bless them,
lest they die without God.

Bless also, vegetable,
trees, the sea without which there is no mother,
the earth without which there is no father,
no flowers that grow out of rock.
Is it true?
Is it true?
I can only imagine it is true
that Jesus comes with his eggful of miracles,
his awful death, his blackboard full of graffiti.
Maybe I'm dead now
and have found Him.
Maybe my evil body is done with.
For I look up,
and in a blaze of butter is
Christ,
soiled with my sour tears,
Christ,
a lamb that has been slain,
his guts drooping like a sea worm,
but who lives on, lives on
like the wings of an Atlantic seagull.
Though he has stopped flying,
the wings go on flapping
despite it all,
despite it all.

WELCOME MORNING

There is joy
in all:
in the hair I brush each morning,
in the Cannon towel, newly washed,
that I rub my body with each morning,
in the chapel of eggs I cook
each morning,
in the outcry from the kettle
that heats my coffee
each morning,
in the spoon and the chair
that cry "hello there, Anne"
each morning,
in the godhead of the table
that I set my silver, plate, cup upon
each morning.

All this is God,
right here in my pea-green house
each morning
and I mean,
though often forget,
to give thanks,
to faint down by the kitchen table
in a prayer of rejoicing
as the holy birds at the kitchen window
peck into their marriage of seeds.

So while I think of it,
let me paint a thank-you on my palm
for this God, this laughter of the morning,
lest it go unspoken.

The Joy that isn't shared, I've heard,
dies young.

JESUS, THE ACTOR, PLAYS THE HOLY GHOST

Oh, Mother,
Virgin Mother,
before the gulls take me out the door,
marry me.
Marry me not to a goat
but to a goddess.
What?
You say it can not be done!

Then I will do it!
I wash the crows
but they do not whiten.
I push out the desk,
pulling it from its roots.
I shave the caterpillar
but he is only a worm.
I take the yellow papers
and I write on them
but they crumble like men's ashes.
I take the daisy
and blow my heart into it
but it will not speak.

Oh, mother,
marry me,
before the gulls take me out the door.
Will I marry the dark earth,
the thief of the daylight?
Will I marry a tree
and only wave my hands at you
from your front yard?
Oh, mother,
oh, mother,

you marry me,
save me from the cockroach,
weave me into the sun.
There will be bread.
There will be water.
My elbows will be salt.

Oh, Mary,
Gentle Mother,
open the door and let me in.
A bee has stung your belly with faith.
Let me float in it like a fish.
Let me in! Let me in!
I have been born many times, a false Messiah,
but let me be born again
into something true.

THE GOD-MONGER

With all my questions,
all the nihilistic words in my head,
I went in search of an answer,
I went in search of the other world
which I reached by digging underground,
past the stones as solemn as preachers,
past the roots, throbbing like veins
and went in search of some animal of wisdom,
and went in search, it could be said,
of my husband (i.e. the one who carries you through).

Down.
Down.
Down.
There I found a mouse
with trees growing out of his belly.

He was all wise.
He was my husband.
Yet he was silent.

He did three things.
He extruded a gourd of water.
Then I hit him on the head,
gently, a hit more like a knock.
Then he extruded a gourd of beer.
I knocked once more
and finally a dish of gravy.

Those were my answers.
Water. Beer. Food.
I was not satisfied.

Though the mouse
had not licked my leprous skin
that was my final answer.

The soul was not cured,
it was as full as a clothes closet
of dresses that did not fit.
Water. Beer. Gravy.
It simply had to be enough.
Husband,
who am I to reject the naming of foods
in a time of famine?

WHAT THE BIRD WITH THE HUMAN HEAD KNEW

I went to the bird
with the human head,
and asked,

Please Sir,
where is God?

God is too busy
to be here on earth,
His angels are like
one thousand geese assembled
and always flapping.
But I can tell you where the well of God is.

Is it on earth?
I asked.
He replied,
Yes. It was dragged down
from paradise by one of the geese.

I walked many days,
past witches that eat grandmothers knitting booties
as if they were collecting a debt.
Then, in the middle of the desert
I found the well,
it bubbled up and down like a litter of cats
and there was water,
and I drank,
and there was water,
and I drank.

Then the well spoke to me.
It said: Abundance is scooped from abundance,
yet abundance remains.

Then I knew.

THE FIRE THIEF

It began with begging.
In the beginning it was all God's icebox
and everyone ate raw fish or animals
and there was no fire at night to dance to,
no fire at day to cook by.

Everyone was two years old.
Yet they tried,
how they tried,
to get the fire:
the vultures tried, the coyote tried, the rabbit
tried; the spider tried
and almost made it back with a balloon
of fire on his back.

First the crow had it,
then a wren stole it,
then a hawk stole it,
and set the whole land on fire,
making the land as treeless as a dinner plate.
Nevertheless, it went out.
Maybe the bee went out of it?
Maybe it was killed by the tears of God?

Next a water rat and a codfish had it,
cooking their mussels every day,
but it went out.
Maybe the mussels were cross.

Next a human killed a snake with a yam-stick
and fire bloomed like a scar from its mouth.
But it went out.
The snake in it died.

460

A woman came
with six fingers
and in the extra finger was fire
and she gave it away like a kiss.
But it went out.
Maybe the skin of the finger undressed.

Next another woman had it,
she could take fire from between her legs
and she gave it to one man.
But it went out.
Maybe he thought touching was an act of war,
and he pissed on it in disgust.

Next it was stolen from God while He was sleeping
by the soldiers of the sun.
But it went out.
The soldiers of the sun now hide in volcanoes.

Next crafty Prometheus stole it from heaven
and for this deed his liver and heart were eaten each day.
So in due course it went out.
With each liver, each heart,
it grew fainter.
Maybe it could not bloom in the death house.

Then a dog went up to God,
he swam through the sky,
and when he got there he pleaded
and God said, *Take it! Take it!*
But keep it sacred.
and the dog came down and gave it to many men
saying:
Hide the fire!
Hide the fire!

They did not listen forever
for they burned Joan
and many, and many,
burned at the stake,
peeling their skin off,
boiling their good red blood,
their hearts like eggs,
and the great house of God was wrong
to give the fire to the dog,
and the great house of God will never forget it,
and each day, asks the sea,
its mother,
to forgive,
to forgive.

THE BIG HEART

*Too many things are occurring for even
a big heart to hold.* From an essay by W. B. Yeats

Big heart,
wide as a watermelon,
but wise as birth,
there is so much abundance
in the people I have:
Max, Lois, Joe, Louise,
Joan, Marie, Dawn,
Arlene, Father Dunne,
and all in their short lives
give to me repeatedly,
in the way the sea
places its many fingers on the shore,
again and again
and they know me,
they help me unravel,
they listen with ears made of conch shells,

they speak back with the wine of the best region.
They are my staff.
They comfort me.

They hear how
the artery of my soul has been severed
and soul is spurting out upon them,
bleeding on them,
messing up their clothes,
dirtying their shoes.
And God is filling me,
though there are times of doubt
as hollow as the Grand Canyon,
still God is filling me.
He is giving me the thoughts of dogs,
the spider in its intricate web,
the sun
in all its amazement,
and a slain ram
that is the glory,
the mystery of great cost,
and my heart,
which is very big,
I promise it is very large,
a monster of sorts,
takes it all in —
all in comes the fury of love.

WORDS

Be careful of words,
even the miraculous ones.
For the miraculous we do our best,
sometimes they swarm like insects

and leave not a sting but a kiss.
They can be as good as fingers.
They can be as trusty as the rock
you stick your bottom on.
But they can be both daisies and bruises.

Yet I am in love with words.
They are doves falling out of the ceiling.
They are six holy oranges sitting in my lap.
They are the trees, the legs of summer,
and the sun, its passionate face.

Yet often they fail me.
I have so much I want to say,
so many stories, images, proverbs, etc.
But the words aren't good enough,
the wrong ones kiss me.
Sometimes I fly like an eagle
but with the wings of a wren.

But I try to take care
and be gentle to them.
Words and eggs must be handled with care.
Once broken they are impossible
things to repair.

MOTHERS
for J.B.

Oh mother,
here in your lap,
as good as a bowlful of clouds,
I your greedy child
am given your breast,
the sea wrapped in skin,

and your arms,
roots covered with moss
and with new shoots sticking out
to tickle the laugh out of me.
Yes, I am wedded to my teddy
but he has the smell of you
as well as the smell of me.
Your necklace that I finger
is all angel eyes.
Your rings that sparkle
are like the moon on the pond.
Your legs that bounce me up and down,
your dear nylon-covered legs,
are the horses I will ride
into eternity.

Oh mother,
after this lap of childhood
I will never go forth
into the big people's world
as an alien,
a fabrication,
or falter
when someone else
is as empty as a shoe.

DOCTORS

They work with herbs
and penicillin.
They work with gentleness
and the scalpel.
They dig out the cancer,
close an incision

and say a prayer
to the poverty of the skin.
They are not Gods
though they would like to be;
they are only a human
trying to fix up a human.
Many humans die.
They die like the tender,
palpitating berries
in November.
But all along the doctors remember:
First do no harm.
They would kiss if it would heal.
It would not heal.

If the doctors cure
then the sun sees it.
If the doctors kill
then the earth hides it.
The doctors should fear arrogance
more than cardiac arrest.
If they are too proud,
and some are,
then they leave home on horseback
but God returns them on foot.

FRENZY

I am not lazy.
I am on the amphetamine of the soul.
I am, each day,
typing out the God
my typewriter believes in.
Very quick. Very intense,
like a wolf at a live heart.

Not lazy.
When a lazy man, they say,
looks toward heaven,
the angels close the windows.

Oh angels,
keep the windows open
so that I may reach in
and steal each object,
objects that tell me the sea is not dying,
objects that tell me the dirt has a life-wish,
that the Christ who walked for me,
walked on true ground
and that this frenzy,
like bees stinging the heart all morning,
will keep the angels
with their windows open,
wide as an English bathtub.

SNOW

Snow,
blessed snow,
comes out of the sky
like bleached flies.
The ground is no longer naked.
The ground has on its clothes.
The trees poke out of sheets
and each branch wears the sock of God.

There is hope.
There is hope everywhere.
I bite it.
Someone once said:
Don't bite till you know

if it's bread or stone.
What I bite is all bread,
rising, yeasty as a cloud.

There is hope.
There is hope everywhere.
Today God gives milk
and I have the pail.

SMALL WIRE

My faith
is a great weight
hung on a small wire,
as doth the spider
hang her baby on a thin web,
as doth the vine,
twiggy and wooden,
hold up grapes
like eyeballs,
as many angels
dance on the head of a pin.

God does not need
too much wire to keep Him there,
just a thin vein,
with blood pushing back and forth in it,
and some love.
As it has been said:
Love and a cough
cannot be concealed.
Even a small cough.
Even a small love.
So if you have only a thin wire,
God does not mind.

He will enter your hands
as easily as ten cents used to
bring forth a Coke.

THE SAINTS COME MARCHING IN
*(With thanks and gratitude to Phyllis McGinley
for her book of the lives of the Saints.)*

The Saints come,
as human as a mouth,
with a bag of God in their backs,
like a hunchback,
they come,
they come marching in.
They come
crowding together
like the devout baseball fans
at a game.
Their game is taking God literally,
taking Him at His word,
though often He be mute.

Catherine of Sienna,
the illiterate girl who lectured to Popes,
each word a flower,
yet hung out cold in its loneliness.

Saint Augustine said:
God, make me chaste,
but not yet.
The party had not begun.
The food was there, the drinks were there
but the people were waiting at the door
to be let in,
waiting as Augustine was waiting

with their open mouths
like the beaks of nestlings.

Teresa of Ávila said:
I have no defense against affection.
I could be bribed with a sardine.
Oh dear Teresa,
I could be bribed likewise.
The hand in mine,
or the chapel inside a bean.

Elisha,
an early Desert Father,
who caroled like a thrush
three hundred thousand songs.
I am not a saint
but I carol with what the typewriter gives,
with what God gives,
as even He gives the hair on our heads.

Nicholas the Pilgrim,
a shepherd
who kept his sheep calm
by singing to them
Kyrie eleison.
The sheep or the horse,
numb as the moon,
need God to be sung unto them.
The dog needs it too.
He is sick of dead bodies.

Saints have no moderation,
nor do poets,
just exuberance.

Ávilan of Teresa
who taught her nuns
to dance for joy
in the cloister,
a dance of Joy,
unto God,
as the birds fling
themselves into the air,
as the human face moves
knowing it will be kissed.

Blessed Bertilla Boscardin,
called "the goose"
in the Italian village of Brendola.
"I am a goose," she said,
"but teach me to be a saint."
There among the pots and pans
of potato peelings
she arrived at her goal.

Vincent Pallotti
who many times came home
half naked
because he had parted with his clothes.
When one gives one's clothes
one says "good morning."
When one gives one's clothes
one gives the suit of Jehovah.

Saint Paul said to the Galatians:
There is neither Jew nor Greek,
there is neither male nor female,
for ye are all . . . heirs according
to the promise.
He knew that each fish
was given paradise

in its slimy skin,
in its little gasping kiss of the sea.

And I who have visited many beds
and never belonged in one
speak of
Saint Dominic who in his happy poverty
had to die in Brother Moneta's bed
because he had none of his own.

No matter whose bed you die in
the bed will be yours
for your voyage
onto the surgical andiron
of God.

NOT SO. NOT SO.

I cannot walk an inch
without trying to walk to God.
I cannot move a finger
without trying to touch God.
Perhaps it is this way:
He is in the graves of the horses.
He is in the swarm, the frenzy of the bees.
He is in the tailor mending my pantsuit.
He is in Boston, raised up by the skyscrapers.
He is in the bird, that shameless flyer.
He is in the potter who makes clay into a kiss.

Heaven replies:
Not so! Not so!

I say thus and thus
and heaven smashes my words.

Is not God in the hiss of the river?

Not so! Not so!

Is not God in the ant heap,
stepping, clutching, dying, being born?

Not so! Not so!

Where then?
I cannot move an inch.

Look to your heart
that flutters in and out like a moth.
God is not indifferent to your need.
You have a thousand prayers
but God has one.

THE ROWING ENDETH

I'm mooring my rowboat
at the dock of the island called God.
This dock is made in the shape of a fish
and there are many boats moored
at many different docks.
"It's okay," I say to myself,
with blisters that broke and healed
and broke and healed —
saving themselves over and over.
And salt sticking to my face and arms like
a glue-skin pocked with grains of tapioca.
I empty myself from my wooden boat
and onto the flesh of The Island.

"On with it!" He says and thus
we squat on the rocks by the sea
and play —— can it be true ——
a game of poker.
He calls me.
I win because I hold a royal straight flush.
He wins because He holds five aces.
A wild card had been announced
but I had not heard it
being in such a state of awe
when He took out the cards and dealt.
As he plunks down His five aces
and I sit grinning at my royal flush,
He starts to laugh,
the laughter rolling like a hoop out of His mouth
and into mine,
and such laughter that He doubles right over me
laughing a Rejoice-Chorus at our two triumphs.
Then I laugh, the fishy dock laughs
the sea laughs. The Island laughs.
The Absurd laughs.

Dearest dealer,
I with my royal straight flush,
love you so for your wild card,
that untamable, eternal, gut-driven *ha-ha*
and lucky love.

POSTHUMOUSLY
PUBLISHED WORK

45 Mercy Street

(1976)

*For Barbara and the wrecked house
she reconstructs even though it
fell upon her very private beach.*

Editor's Note

Anne Sexton's voice did not cease with her death. She left two unpublished manuscripts: *45 Mercy Street* and an untitled binder full of new poems. Although she considered the first collection "complete," she was still revising it at the time of her death. In June of 1974, she wrote to her literary agent: "I have actually finished another book, *45 Mercy Street*, but am glad to have the time to reform the poems, rewrite and delete." Ordinarily, Anne Sexton reworked her poems again and again, often changing a line or a word while the "finished" manuscript was in its final stages at the publisher's. Although she was often obdurate — sticking by any aspect of her work that she believed in — she also knew how to use others' criticism to advantage. She relied heavily on her editors, friends, and fellow poets, watching and listening to their reactions. So it began with *45 Mercy Street*, although ultimately she did not find time enough for that final perfection.

45 Mercy Street charts Anne Sexton's poetic growth and the events of her life from 1971 through 1974. The manuscript has been edited but changes are few. All those concerned with the production of the book felt that the basic text must be preserved. As her literary executor, I have altered the placement of a few poems. Having placed them in order in her black binder, she had not yet arrived at a final arrangement, and her trial organization has proved somewhat confusing. The new arrangement allows the poems to build to a clear progression of thought and emotion. The first section has also been retitled, and I am indebted to Lois Ames for my introduction to the word "hegira."

In preparing *45 Mercy Street* for press, I have strugged to decipher her handwriting, those crooked black scars which she herself referred to as "a terrible scribble." There are probable alternative readings for a few words, but, apart from these minor uncertainties, the poems themselves have not been edited. Each line appears exactly as she wrote it. Certain poems have been omitted, however, because of their intensely personal content, and the pain their publication would bring to individuals still living. As she commented in February of 1974, "part of *45 Mercy Street* is still too personal to publish for some time." The complete manuscript, in its original order, has been preserved with all her worksheets, private papers and letters in the Anne Sexton Archive, presently at Boston University.

I thank all those who have supported me during my startling and sometimes painful initiation into "this business of words."

Linda Gray Sexton
September, 1975

I

BEGINNING THE HEGIRA

hegira (hĭ-jĭ′rə). noun. A journey or trip especially when undertaken as a means of escaping from an undesirable or dangerous environment; or as a means of arriving at a highly desirable destination.

---

45 MERCY STREET

In my dream,
drilling into the marrow
of my entire bone,
my real dream,
I'm walking up and down Beacon Hill
searching for a street sign —
namely MERCY STREET.
Not there.

I try the Back Bay.
Not there.
Not there.
And yet I know the number.
45 Mercy Street.
I know the stained-glass window
of the foyer,
the three flights of the house
with its parquet floors.
I know the furniture and
mother, grandmother, great-grandmother,

the servants.
I know the cupboard of Spode,
the boat of ice, solid silver,
where the butter sits in neat squares
like strange giant's teeth
on the big mahogany table.
I know it well.
Not there.

Where did you go?
45 Mercy Street,
with great-grandmother
kneeling in her whale-bone corset
and praying gently but fiercely
to the wash basin,
at five A.M.
at noon
dozing in her wiggy rocker,
grandfather taking a nip in the pantry,
grandmother pushing the bell for the downstairs maid,
and Nana rocking Mother with an oversized flower
on her forehead to cover the curl
of when she was good and when she was . . .
And where she was begat
and in a generation
the third she will beget,
me,
with the stranger's seed blooming
into the flower called *Horrid*.

I walk in a yellow dress
and a white pocketbook stuffed with cigarettes,
enough pills, my wallet, my keys,
and being twenty-eight, or is it forty-five?
I walk. I walk.
I hold matches at the street signs

for it is dark,
as dark as the leathery dead
and I have lost my green Ford,
my house in the suburbs,
two little kids
sucked up like pollen by the bee in me
and a husband
who has wiped off his eyes
in order not to see my inside out
and I am walking and looking
and this is no dream
just my oily life
where the people are alibis
and the street is unfindable for an
entire lifetime.

Pull the shades down —
I don't care!
Bolt the door, mercy,
erase the number,
rip down my street sign,
what can it matter,
what can it matter to this cheapskate
who wants to own the past
that went out on a dead ship
and left me only with paper?

Not there.

I open my pocketbook,
as women do,
and fish swim back and forth
between the dollars and the lipstick.
I pick them out,
one by one
and throw them at the street signs,
and shoot my pocketbook

into the Charles River.
Next I pull the dream off
and slam into the cement wall
of the clumsy calendar
I live in,
my life,
and its hauled up
notebooks.

TALKING TO SHEEP

My life
has appeared unclothed in court,
detail by detail,
death-bone witness by death-bone witness,
and I was shamed at the verdict
and given a cut penny
and the entrails of a cat.
But nevertheless I went on
to the invisible priests,
confessing, confessing
through the wire of hell
and they wet upon me in that phone booth.

Then I accosted winos,
the derelicts of the region,
winning them over into the latrine of my details.
Yes. It was a compulsion
but I denied it, called it fiction
and then the populace screamed *Me too, Me too*
and I swallowed it like my fate.

Now,
in my middle age,
I'm well aware

I keep making statues
of my acts, carving them with my sleep —
or if it is not my life I depict
then someone's close enough to wear my nose —
My nose, my patrician nose,
sniffing at me or following theirs down the street.

Yet even five centuries ago this smelled queer,
confession, confession,
and your devil was thought to push out their eyes
and all the eyes had seen (too much! too much!).
It was proof that you were a needle
to push into their pupils.
And the only cure for such confessions overheard
was to sit in a cold bath for six days,
a bath full of leeches, drawing out your blood
into which confessors had heated the devil in them,
inhabited them with their madness.

It was wise, the wise medical men said,
wise to cry *Baa* and be smiling into your mongoloid hood,
while you simply tended the sheep.
Or else to sew your lips shut
and not let a word or a deadstone sneak out.

I too have my silence,
where I enter another room
and am not only blind,
but speech has flown out of me
and I call it dead
though the respiration be okay.
Perhaps it is a sheep call?
I feel I must learn to speak the *Baa*
of the simple-minded, while my mind
dives into the multi-colored,
crowded voices,

cries for help, *My breasts are off me.*
The transvestite whispering to me,
over and over, *My legs are disappearing.*
My mother, her voice like water,
saying *Fish are cut out of me.*
My father,
his voice thrown into a cigar,
A marble of blood rolls into my heart.
My great aunt,
her voice,
thrown into a lost child at the freaks' circus,
I am the flame swallower
but turn me over in bed
and I am the fat lady.

Yes! While my mind plays simple-minded,
plays dead-woman in neon,
I must recall to say
Baa
to the black sheep I am.

Baa. Baa. Baa.

THE FALLING DOLLS

Dolls,
by the thousands,
are falling out of the sky
and I look up in fear
and wonder who will catch them?
The leaves, holding them like green dishes?
The ponds, open as wine glasses to drink them down?
The tops of buildings to smash in their stomachs
and leave them there to get sooty?
The highways with their hard skins

so that they may be run over like muskrats?
The seas, looking for something to shock the fish?
The electric fences to burn their hair off?
The cornfields where they can lie unpicked?
The national parks where centuries later
they'll be found petrified like stone babies?

I hold open my arms
and catch
one,
two,
three . . . ten in all,
running back and forth like a badminton player,
catching the dolls, the babies I practice upon,
but others crack on the roof
and I dream, awake, I dream of falling dolls
who need cribs and blankets and pajamas
with real feet in them.
Why is there no mother?
Why are all these dolls falling out of the sky?
Was there a father?
Or have the planets cut holes in their nets
and let our childhood out,
or are we the dolls themselves,
born but never fed?

THE MONEY SWING
After "Babylon Revisited" *by F. Scott Fitzgerald*

Mother, Father,
I hold this snapshot of you,
taken, it says, in 1929
on the deck of the yawl.
Mother, Father,
so young, so hot, so jazzy,

so like Zelda and Scott
with drinks and cigarettes and turbans
and designer slacks and frizzy permanents
and all that dough,
what do you say to me now,
here at my sweaty desk in 1971?

I know the ice in your drink is senile.
I know your smile will develop a boil.
You know only that you are on top,
swinging like children on the money swing
up and over, up and over,
until even New York City lies down small.
You know that when winter comes
and the snow comes
that it won't be real snow.
If you don't want it to be snow
you just pay money.

FOOD

I want mother's milk,
that good sour soup.
I want breasts singing like eggplants,
and a mouth above making kisses.
I want nipples like shy strawberries
for I need to suck the sky.
I need to bite also
as in a carrot stick.
I need arms that rock,
two clean clam shells singing *ocean*.
Further I need weeds to eat
for they are the spinach of the soul.
I am hungry and you give me
a dictionary to decipher.

I am a baby all wrapped up in its red howl
and you pour salt into my mouth.
Your nipples are stitched up like sutures
and although I suck
I suck air
and even the big fat sugar moves away.
Tell me! Tell me! Why is it?
I need food
and you walk away reading the paper.

THE CHILD BEARERS

Jean, death comes close to us all,
flapping its awful wings at us
and the gluey wings crawl up our nose.
Our children tremble in their teen-age cribs,
whirling off on a thumb or a motorcycle,
mine pushed into gnawing a stilbestrol cancer
I passed on like hemophilia,
or yours in the seventh grade, with her spleen
smacked in by the balance beam.
And we, mothers, crumpled, and flyspotted
with bringing them this far
can do nothing now but pray.

Let us put your three children
and my two children,
ages ranging from eleven to twenty-one,
and send them in a large air net up to God,
with many stamps, *real* air mail,
and huge signs attached:
SPECIAL HANDLING.
DO NOT STAPLE, FOLD OR MUTILATE!
And perhaps He will notice
and pass a psalm over them

for keeping safe for a whole,
for a whole God-damned life-span.

And not even a muddled angel will
peek down at us in our foxhole.
And He will not have time
to send down an eyedropper of prayer for us,
the mothering thing of us,
as we drop into the soup
and drown
in the worry festering inside us,
lest our children
go so fast
they go.

THE TAKER

While the house was away
and the curtains were baby-sitting,
you made your crossing over.
The pitiless rugs had nothing to say,
the grandfather clock went on with its knitting,
the disposal vomited up chives and clover.
The house became a stage where you played
on the night, my string bean, that you were made.

Our song, *Melancholy Baby*, could not
be heard. *Goodnight Moon* was outgrown,
and two fireflies died unnoticed.
A moth lay down in the jelly pot.
The driveway waited. The grass was mown.
And string bean lay down in her wedding bed.
Her heart went out on a train to meet him
and her mother blessed her,
as best she could,
limb to limb.

THE RISK

When a daughter tries suicide
and the chimney falls down like a drunk
and the dog chews her tail off
and the kitchen blows up its shiny kettle
and the vacuum cleaner swallows its bag
and the toilet washes itself in tears
and the bathroom scales weigh in the ghost
of the grandmother and the windows,
those sky pieces, ride out like boats
and the grass rolls down the driveway
and the mother lies down on her marriage bed
and eats up her heart like two eggs.

PRAYING TO BIG JACK
for Ruthie, my God-child

God, Jack of all trades,
I've got Ruthie's life to trade for today.
She's six. She's got her union card
and a brain tumor, that apple gone sick.
Take in mind, Jack, that her dimple
would erase a daisy. She's one of yours,
small walker of dogs and ice cream.
And she being one of yours
hears the saw lift off her skull
like a baseball cap. Cap off
and then what? The brains as
helpless as oysters in a pint container,
the nerves like phone wires.
God, take care, take infinite care
with the tumor lest it spread like grease.
Ruthie, somewhere in Toledo, has a twin,
mirror girl who plays marbles

491

and wonders: _Where is the other me?_
The girl of the same dress and my smile?
Today they sing together, they sing for alms.
God have you lapsed?
Are you so bitter with the world
you would put us down the drainpipe at six?

You of the top hat,
Mr. God,
you of the Cross made of lamb bones,
you of the camps, sacking the rejoice out of Germany,
I tell you this . . .
it will not do.
I will run up into the sky and chop wood.
I will run to sea and find a thousand-year servant.
I will run to the cave and bring home a Captain
if you will only, will only,
dear inquisitor.

Banish Ruth, plump Jack,
and you banish all the world.

RED ROSES

Oral Dreip?

Tommy is three and when he's bad
his mother dances with him.
She puts on the record,
"Red Roses for a Blue Lady"
and throws him across the room.
Mind you,
she never laid a hand on him,
only the wall laid a hand on him.
He gets red roses in different places,
the head, that time he was as sleepy as a river,
the back, that time he was a broken scarecrow,

the arm like a diamond had bitten it,
the leg, twisted like a licorice stick,
all the dance they did together,
Blue Lady and Tommy.
You fell, she said, just remember you fell.
I fell, is all he told the doctors
in the big hospital. A nice lady came
and asked him questions but because
he didn't want to be sent away he said, I fell.
He never said anything else although he could talk fine.
He never told about the music
or how she'd sing and shout
holding him up and throwing him.

He pretends he is her ball.
He tries to fold up and bounce
but he squashes like fruit.
For he loves Blue Lady and the spots
of red red roses he gives her.

THE SHOUT

Are you in Eden again, America?
Haggling it out with Adam and his rib?
If so forget them like hamburg!
Look inward, America.
Move our own furniture into the house.
Take little Joe, for instance,
he was as small as a nail
but he shouted the sky down.
The clouds fell down like water-wings.
The stars fell down like slivers of glass.
The trees turned to rubber
and their leaves sat on the ground like shoes.
All the people of America,

those out on the town and
those snugging to their beds,
heard the shout.

A sound like *that*
out of a child's mouth
not to announce the Magi,
not to ward off a beating,
but to show the infernal sleepers
his gift.

They did not know where the sound came from.
Only that it was hungry.

KEEPING THE CITY

*Unless the Lord keepeth the city, the watchman
guardeth in vain.*—John F. Kennedy's unspoken words
in Dallas on November 23, 1963.

Once,
in August,
head on your chest,
I heard wings
battering up the place,
something inside trying to fly out
and I was silent
and attentive,
the watchman.
I was your small public,
your small audience
but it was you that was clapping,
it was you untying the snarls and knots,
the webs, all bloody and gluey;
you with your twelve tongues and twelve wings
beating, wresting, beating, beating

494

your way out of childhood,
that airless net that fastened you down.

Since then I was more silent
though you had gone miles away,
tearing down, rebuilding the fortress.
I was there
but could do nothing
but guard the city
lest it break.
I was silent.
I had a strange idea I could overhear
but that your voice, tongue, wing
belonged solely to you.
The Lord was silent too.
I did not know if he could keep you whole,
where I, miles away, yet head on your chest,
could do nothing. Not a single thing.

The wings of the watchman,
if I spoke, would hurt the bird of your soul
as he nested, bit, sucked, flapped.
I wanted him to fly, burst like a missile from your throat,
burst from the spidery-mother-web,
burst from *Woman* herself
where too many had laid out lights
that stuck to you and left a burn
that smarted into your middle age.

The city
of my choice
that I guard
like a butterfly, useless, useless
in her yellow costume, swirling
swirling around the gates.
The city shifts, falls, rebuilds,

and I can do nothing.
A watchman
should be on the alert,
but never cocksure.
And The Lord —
who knows what he keepeth?

II

BESTIARY U.S.A.

I look at the strangeness in them and the naturalness they cannot help, in order to find some virtue in the beast in me.

BAT

His awful skin
stretched out by some tradesman
is like my skin, here between my fingers,
a kind of webbing, a kind of frog.
Surely when first born my face was this tiny
and before I was born surely I could fly.
Not well, mind you, only a veil of skin
from my arms to my waist.
I flew at night, too. Not to be seen
for if I were I'd be taken down.
In August perhaps as the trees rose to the stars
I have flown from leaf to leaf in the thick dark.
If you had caught me with your flashlight
you would have seen a pink corpse with wings,
out, out, from her mother's belly, all furry
and hoarse skimming over the houses, the armies.
That's why the dogs of your house sniff me.
They know I'm something to be caught
somewhere in the cemetery hanging upside down
like a misshapen udder.

HOG

Oh you brown bacon machine,
how sweet you lie,
gaining a pound and a half a day,
you rolled-up pair of socks,
you dog's nightmare,
your snout pushed in
but leaking out the ears,
your eyes as soft as eggs,
hog, big as a cannon,
how sweet you lie.

I lie in my bed at night
in the closet of my mind
and count hogs in a pen,
brown, spotted, white, pink, black,
moving on the shuttle toward death
just as my mind moves over
for its own little death.

PORCUPINE

Spine hog,
how do you grow?
Little steel wings
that stick into me.
Knitting needles
that stick into me.
Long steel bullets
that stick into me,
so like the four-inch
screws that hold me
in place, an iron
maiden the doctors
devised.

498

Well then,
I'm taking them out,
spine by spine,
somebody else's nails,
not Jesus', not Anne's,
but nails. They
don't belong to the
Brooklyn Bridge,
they don't fit into
the holes of the
White House, they
don't (any longer)
fit into Martin
Luther King, they
won't do in a Kennedy,
they can't make it
with the governors
or the senators,
they push, push,
push into the earth,
bringing forth some
old diamonds we'd never thought of.
And why not, old
Spine Hog U.S.A.?

HORNET

A red-hot needle
hangs out of him, he steers by it
as if it were a rudder, he
would get in the house any way he could
and then he would bounce from window
to ceiling, buzzing and looking for you.
Do not sleep for he is there wrapped in the curtain.
Do not sleep for he is there under the shelf.
Do not sleep for he wants to sew up your skin,

499

he wants to leap into your body like a hammer
with a nail, do not sleep he wants to get into
your nose and make a transplant, he wants do not
sleep he wants to bury your fur and make
a nest of knives, he wants to slide under your
fingernail and push in a splinter, do not sleep
he wants to climb out of the toilet when you sit on it
and make a home in the embarrassed hair do not sleep
he wants you to walk into him as into a dark fire.

STAR-NOSED MOLE

Mole, angel-dog of the pit,
digging six miles a night,
what's up with you in your sooty suit,
where's your kitchen at?

I find you at the edge of our pond,
drowned, numb drainer of weeds,
insects floating in your belly,
grubs like little fetuses bobbing

and your dear face with its fifth hand,
doesn't it know it's the end of the war?
It's all over, no need to go deep into ponds,
no fires, no cripples left.

                    Mole dog,
I wish your mother would wake you up
and you wouldn't lie there like the Pietà
wearing your cross on your nose.

SNAIL

The snail in his museum
wears his mother all day,
he hides his mysterious bottom
as if it were rotten fruit.
He desires not the kiss.
He desires not the radio.
He desires not directions to Paris.
He desires to lie in his fragile doorway
scratching his back all day.

All this is very well
until hands come like a backhoe
to bring him to the kitchen.
They keep his house.
They swallow the rest.

LOBSTER

A shoe with legs,
a stone dropped from heaven,
he does his mournful work alone,
he is like the old prospector for gold,
with secret dreams of God-heads and fish heads.
Until suddenly a cradle fastens round him
and he is trapped as the U.S.A. sleeps.
Somewhere far off a woman lights a cigarette;
somewhere far off a car goes over a bridge;
somewhere far off a bank is held up.
This is the world the lobster knows not of.
He is the old hunting dog of the sea
who in the morning will rise from it
and be undrowned
and they will take his perfect green body
and paint it red.

SNAKE

Made of old rags of tongues,
of flesh slipped through the abortionist's knife —
you snake thing, made of an army of grapes,
how cleverly you pick your way in and out
of the grass and overhead in the tree.
What can I make of you with my halting footsteps?
Do we go together?
Only by way of Eve's snake
whom I've held up to my man,
time after time, and said,
Let us put him to some use,
let us swallow this snake like a cigar
and allow all our body hair to turn green
with envy.

MOOSE

American Archangel you are going —
your body as big as a moving van —
the houses, the highways are turning you in.
Before my house was, you stood there grazing
and before that my grandfather's home with you
on the wall. Antlers for hat racks
and I felt the rest of your body somewhere outside
the wall merely asking for an invitation.
You stand now in a field in Maine,
hopelessly alive,
your antlers like seaweed,
your face like a wolf's death mask,
your mouth a virgin, your nose a nipple,
your legs muscled up like knitting balls,
your neck mournful as an axe,
and I would like to ask you into my garden

502

so that I might pack you quickly in salt
and keep your proud body past your mystery
and mine.

SHEEP

Little oily fuzzbear,
wearing your wool full of wood,
Mr. Ba-Ba, you yellow man,
you grease ball of thistles,
you yes sir, yes sir three bags full,
have been the work of the men of my life
for all of my life and the mention of you
turns my hands into green money. No longer.
Now the sheep in Australia and Cape Town
are cheaper and boss the world-wide market.
May they turn sour. May many mean things
happen upon them, no shepherds, no dogs,
a blight of the skin, a mange of the wool,
and they will die eating foreign money,
choking on its green alphabet.

COCKROACH

Roach, foulest of creatures,
who attacks with yellow teeth
and an army of cousins big as shoes,
you are lumps of coal that are mechanized
and when I turn on the light you scuttle
into the corners and there is this hiss upon the land.
Yet I know you are only the common angel
turned into, by way of enchantment, the ugliest.
Your uncle was made into an apple.
Your aunt was made into a Siamese cat,

all the rest were made into butterflies
but because you lied to God outrightly —
told him that all things on earth were in order —
He turned his wrath upon you and said,
I will make you the most loathsome,
I will make you into God's lie,
and never will a little girl fondle you
or hold your dark wings cupped in her palm.

But that was not true. Once in New Orleans
with a group of students a roach fled across
the floor and I shrieked and she picked it up
in her hands and held it from my fear for one hour.
And held it like a diamond ring that should not escape.
These days even the devil is getting overturned
and held up to the light like a glass of water.

RACCOON

Coon, why did you come to this dance
with a mask on? Why not the tin man
and his rainbow girl? Why not Racine,
his hair marcelled down to his chest?
Why not come as a stomach digesting
its worms? Why you little fellow
with your ears at attention and your
nose poking up like a microphone?
You whig emblem, you woman chaser,
why do you dance over the wide lawn tonight
clanging the garbage pail like great silver bells?

SEAL

I dreamt of a seal
with wide wings,
made of vinegar and little boys,
sailing past the star motes,
up over the city of Frisco,
saying forgive me lord
for I have lived so little
I have need of night people.
I have need to see the bum dozing
off on scag, the women in labor
pushing forth a pink head,
lord I need to fly I am sick of
rocks and sea water, I need to
see the moon,
old gyrator,
old butter ball,
and the stars pinching each other
like children.
I want the prairie, the city, the mountain,
I am sick and tired of the rock off Frisco
with its bleating and cowing.
Lord, let me see Jesus before it's all over,
crawling up some mountain, reckless and outrageous,
calling out poems
as he lets out his blood.

EARTHWORM

Slim inquirer, while the old fathers sleep
you are reworking their soil, you have
a grocery store there down under the earth
and it is well stocked with broken wine bottles,
old cigars, old door knobs and earth,

that great brown flour that you kiss each day.
There are dark stars in the cool evening and
you fondle them like killer birds' beaks.
But what I want to know is why when small boys
dig you up for curiosity and cut you in half
why each half lives and crawls away as if whole.
Have you no beginning and end? Which heart is
the real one? Which eye the seer? Why
is it in the infinite plan that you would
be severed and rise from the dead like a gargoyle
with two heads?

WHALE

Whale on the beach, you dinosaur,
what brought you smoothing into this dead harbor?
If you'd stayed inside you could have grown
as big as the Empire State. Still you are not a fish,
perhaps you like the land, you'd had enough of
holding your breath under water. What is it we want
of you? To take our warm blood into the great sea
and prove we are not the sufferers of God?
We are sick of babies crying and the birds flapping
loose in the air. We want the double to be big,
and ominous and we want to remember when you were
money in Massachusetts and yet were wild and rude
and killers. We want our killers dressed in black
like grease for we are sick of writing checks,
putting on our socks and working in the little boxes
we call the office.

HORSE

Horse, you flame thrower,
you shark-mouthed man,
you laughter at the end of poems,
you brown furry locomotive
whipping the snow, I am
a pale shadow beside you.
Your nostrils open like field glasses
and can smell all my fear. I am
a silver spoon. You are a four-footed
wing. If I am thirsty you feed me
through an eyedropper, for you are a
gallon drum. Beside you I feel
like a little girl with a papa
who is screaming.
                    And yet and yet,
field horse lapping the grass
like stars and then your droppings,
sweet melons, all brown and
good for gardens and carrots.
Your soft nose would nuzzle me
and my fear would go out singing
into its own body.

JUNE BUG

June bug came on the first of June,
plucking his guitar at the west window,
telling his whole green story, telling —
little buzzard who is all heart who
wants us to know how expensive it is
to keep the stars in their grainy places,
to keep the moles burning underground,
for the roots are stealing all the water,

and so he pulses at each window, a presence,
a huge hairy question who sees our light
and thinks of it:
                    You are the food,
you are the tooth, you are the husband,
light, light, sieving through the screen
whereon I bounce my big body at you
like shoes after a wedding car.

GULL

You with your wings like spatulas,
letting the blue turn into sugar kisses,
letting the fog slip through your fingertips,
informing the lighthouse like turning on the oven,
sobbing at the fish over the Atlantic,
crying out like young girls in fevers and chills,
crying out like friends who sing from the tavern
of fighting hands, crying out, like a goat with
its mouth full of pearls, snatching the bait
like blood from the coals. Oh Gull of my childhood,
cry over my window over and over, take me back,
oh harbors of oil and cunners, teach me to laugh
and cry again that way that was the good bargain
of youth, when the man following you was not a tail
but an uncle, when the death that came upon you
when you were thirsty was solved by a Coke,
but what can be done gull gull when you turn the sun
on again, a dead fruit
                    and all that flies today
is crooked and vain and has been cut from a book.

III

THE DIVORCE PAPERS

WHERE IT WAS AT BACK THEN

Husband,
last night I dreamt
they cut off your hands and feet.
Husband,
you whispered to me,
Now we are both incomplete.

Husband,
I held all four
in my arms like sons and daughters.
Husband,
I bent slowly down
and washed them in magical waters.

Husband,
I placed each one
where it belonged on you.
"A miracle,"
you said and we laughed
the laugh of the well-to-do.

THE WEDLOCK

My breast waited
shy as a clam
until you came,
Mr. Firecracker,
Mr. Panzer-man.
You with your pogo stick,
you with your bag full of jokes.
At the corner of your eyes,
little incisions,
smile wrinkles that tell and tell.
When I shout *help* in my dream
you do not fold me in like a slipper its foot.

Suppertime I float toward you
from the stewpot
holding poems you shrug off
and you kiss me like a mosquito.
No zing and zap
or ounce of gentleness
and when anger comes
like a finger in a light socket,
you of the karate chop,
you of the Tommy Gun,
force me downwards like a stone.

More often now I am your punching bag.
Most days I'm curled like a spotted dog
at your elbow, Panzer-man.
When I'm crazy a daughter buys
a single yellow rose to come home by.
Home is our spy pond pool in the backyard,
the willow with its spooky yellow fingers
and the great orange bed where we lie
like two frozen paintings in a field of poppies.

LANDSCAPE WINTER

Snow, out over the elephant's rump,
my rock outside my word-window,
where it lies in a doze on the front lawn.
Oak leaves, each separate and pink
in the setting sun, as good cows' tongues.
The snow far off on the pine
nesting into the needles
like addicts into their fix.
The mailbox as stiff as a soldier
but wearing a chef's hat.
The ground is full.
It will not eat any more.
Armies of angels have sunk onto it
with their soft parachutes.

And within the house
ashes are being stuffed into my marriage,
fury is lapping the walls,
dishes crack on the shelves,
a strangler needs my throat,
the daughter has ceased to eat anything,
the wife speaks of this
but only the ice cubes listen.

The sweat of fear pumps inside me.
In my sleep I wet the bed,
the marriage bed,
three nights in a row
and soon, soon I'd better run out
while there is time.

Yet, right now,
the outside world seems oblivious
and the snow is happy and all is quiet
as the night waits for its breakfast.

511

DESPAIR

Who is he?
A railroad track toward hell?
Breaking like a stick of furniture?
The hope that suddenly overflows the cesspool?
The love that goes down the drain like spit?
The love that said *forever, forever*
and then runs you over like a truck?
Are you a prayer that floats into a radio advertisement?
Despair,
I don't like you very well.
You don't suit my clothes or my cigarettes.
Why do you locate here
as large as a tank,
aiming at one half of a lifetime?
Couldn't you just go float into a tree
instead of locating here at my roots,
forcing me out of the life I've led
when it's been my belly so long?

All right!
I'll take you along on the trip
where for so many years
my arms have been speechless.

DIVORCE

I have killed our lives together,
axed off each head,
with their poor blue eyes stuck in a beach ball
rolling separately down the drive.
I have killed all the good things,
but they are too stubborn for me.
They hang on.

The little words of companionship
have crawled into their graves,
the thread of compassion,
dear as a strawberry,
the mingling of bodies
that bore two daughters within us,
the look of you dressing,
early,
all the separate clothes, neat and folded,
you sitting on the edge of the bed
polishing your shoes with boot black,
and I loved you then, so wise from the shower,
and I loved you many other times
and I have been, for months,
trying to drown it,
to push it under,
to keep its great red tongue
under like a fish,
but wherever I look they are on fire,
the bass, the bluefish, the wall-eyed flounder
blazing among the kelp and seaweed
like many suns battering up the waves
and my love stays bitterly glowing,
spasms of it will not sleep,
and I am helpless and thirsty and need shade
but there is no one to cover me —
not even God.

WAKING ALONE

Skull,
museum object,
I could squash you like a rotten melon,
but I would rather — no, I need
to hold you gently like a puppy,

to give you milk and berries for your dear mouth,
husband, husband.
I lust for your smile,
spread open like an old flower,
and your eyes, blue moons,
and your chin, ever Nazi, ever stubborn,
and what can I do with this memory?
Shake the bones out of it?
Defoliate the smile?
Stub out the chin with cigarettes?
Take the face of the man I love
and squeeze my foot into it
when all the while my heart is making a museum?
I love you the way the oboe plays.
I love you the way skinny dipping makes my body feel.
I love you the way a ripe artichoke tastes.
Yet I fear you,
as one in the desert fears the sun.
True.
True.
Yet love enters my blood like an I.V.,
dripping in its little white moments.
In drips the whiplash you delivered,
the Thomas collar I wore,
and then in comes you, ordering wine,
fixing my beach umbrella, mowing grass,
making my kitchen happy with a charcoal steak,
and I come back again to your skull,
the ruffly hair of the morning
that I wasn't allowed to touch,
and then I come back to you saying,
(as I was saying the truth)
my ears are turned off.
And I don't know,
don't know,
if we belong together or apart,

except that my soul lingers over the skin of you
and I wonder if I'm ruining all we had,
and had not,
by making this break,
this torn wedding ring,
this wrenched life
this God who is only half a God,
having separated the resurrection
from the glory,
having ripped the cross off Jesus
and left only the nails.
Husband,
Husband,
I hold up my hand and see
only nails.

BAYONET

What can I do with this bayonet?
Make a rose bush of it?
Poke it into the moon?
Shave my legs with its sliver?
Spear a goldfish?
No. No.

It was made
in my dream
for you.
My eyes were closed.
I was curled fetally
and yet I held a bayonet
that was for the earth of your stomach.
The belly button singing its puzzle.
The intestines winding like the alpine roads.
It was made to enter you

as you have entered me
and to cut the daylight into you
and let out your buried heartland,
to let out the spoon you have fed me with,
to let out the bird that said *fuck you,*
to carve him onto a sculpture until he is white
and I could put him on a shelf,
an object unthinking as a stone,
but with all the vibrations
of a crucifix.

THE WEDDING RING DANCE

I dance in circles holding
the moth of the marriage,
thin, sticky, fluttering
its skirts, its webs.
The moth oozing a tear,
or is it a drop of urine?
The moth, grinning like a pear,
or is it teeth
clamping the iron maiden shut?

The moth,
who is my mother,
who is my father,
who was my lover,
floats airily out of my hands
and I dance slower,
pulling off the fat diamond engagement ring,
pulling off the elopement wedding ring,
and holding them, clicking them
in thumb and forefinger,
the indent of twenty-five years,
like a tiny rip leaving its mark,

the tiny rip of a tiny earthquake.
Underneath the soil lies the violence,
the shift, the crack of continents,
the anger,
and above only a cut,
a half-inch space to stick a pencil in.

The finger is scared
but it keeps its long numb place.
And I keep dancing,
a sort of waltz,
clicking the two rings,
all of a life at its last cough,
as I swim through the air of the kitchen,
and the same radio plays its songs
and I make a small path through them
with my bare finger and my funny feet,
doing the undoing dance,
on April 14th, 1973,
letting my history rip itself off me
and stepping into
something unknown
and transparent,
but all ten fingers stretched outward,
flesh extended as metal
waiting for a magnet.

WHEN THE GLASS OF MY BODY BROKE

Oh mother of sex,
lady of the staggering cuddle,
where do these hands come from?
A man, a Moby Dick of a man,
a swimmer going up and down in his brain,
the gentleness of wine in his fingertips,

where do these hands come from?
I was born a glass baby and nobody picked me up
except to wash the dust off me.
He has picked me up and licked me alive.

Hands
growing like ivy over me,
hands growing out of me like hair,
yet turning into fire grass,
planting an iris in my mouth,
spinning and blue,
the nipples turning into wings,
the lips turning into days that would not give birth,
days that would not hold us in their house,
days that would not wrap us in their secret lap,
and yet hands, hands growing out of pictures,
hands crawling out of the walls,
hands that excite oblivion,
like a wind,
a strange wind
from somewhere tropic
making a storm between my blind legs,
letting me lift the mask of the child from my face,
while all the toy villages fall
and I sink softly into
the heartland.

THE BREAK AWAY

Your daisies have come
on the day of my divorce:
the courtroom a cement box,
a gas chamber for the infectious Jew in me
and a perhaps land, a possibly promised land
for the Jew in me,

but still a betrayal room for the till-death-do-us —
and yet a death, as in the unlocking of scissors
that makes the now separate parts useless,
even to cut each other up as we did yearly
under the crayoned-in sun.
The courtroom keeps squashing our lives as they break
into two cans ready for recycling,
flattened tin humans
and a tin law,
even for my twenty-five years of hanging on
by my teeth as I once saw at Ringling Brothers.
The gray room:
Judge, lawyer, witness
and me and invisible Skeezix,
and all the other torn
enduring the bewilderments
of their division.

Your daisies have come
on the day of my divorce.
They arrive like round yellow fish,
sucking with love at the coral of our love.
Yet they wait,
in their short time,
like little utero half-borns,
half killed, thin and bone soft.
They know they are about to die,
but breathe like premies, in and out,
upon my kitchen table.
They breathe the air that stands
for twenty-five illicit days,
the sun crawling inside the sheets,
the moon spinning like a tornado
in the washbowl,
and we orchestrated them both,
calling ourselves TWO CAMP DIRECTORS.

There was a song, our song on your cassette,
that played over and over
and baptised the prodigals.
It spoke the unspeakable,
as the rain will on an attic roof,
letting the animal join its soul
as we kneeled before a miracle —
forgetting its knife.

The daisies confer
in the old-married kitchen
papered with blue and green chefs
who call out *pies, cookies, yummy,*
at the charcoal and cigarette smoke
they wear like a yellow salve.
The daisies absorb it all —
the twenty-five-year-old sanctioned love
(If one could call such handfuls of fists
and immobile arms *that!*)
and on this day my world rips itself up
while the country unfastens along
with its perjuring king and his court.
It unfastens into an abortion of belief,
as in me —
the legal rift —
as one *might* do with the daisies
but does not
for they stand for a love
undergoing open heart surgery
that might take
if one prayed tough enough.
And yet I demand,
even in prayer,
that I am not a thief,
a mugger of need,
and that your heart survive

on its own,
belonging only to itself,
whole, entirely whole,
and workable
in its dark cavern under your ribs.

I pray it will know truth,
if truth catches in its cup
and yet I pray, as a child would,
that the surgery take.

I dream it is taking.
Next I dream the love is swallowing itself.
Next I dream the love is made of glass,
glass coming through the telephone
that is breaking slowly,
day by day, into my ear.
Next I dream that I put on the love
like a lifejacket and we float,
jacket and I,
we bounce on that priest-blue.
We are as light as a cat's ear
and it is safe,
safe far too long!
And I awaken quickly and go to the opposite window
and peer down at the moon in the pond
and know that beauty has walked over my head,
into this bedroom and out,
flowing out through the window screen,
dropping deep into the water
to hide.

I will observe the daisies
fade and dry up
until they become flour,
snowing themselves onto the table

beside the drone of the refrigerator,
beside the radio playing Frankie
(as often as FM will allow)
snowing lightly, a tremor sinking from the ceiling —
as twenty-five years split from my side
like a growth that I sliced off like a melanoma.

It is six P.M. as I water these tiny weeds
and their little half-life,
their numbered days
that raged like a secret radio,
recalling love that I picked up innocently,
yet guiltily,
as my five-year-old daughter
picked gum off the sidewalk
and it became suddenly an elastic miracle.

For me it was love found
like a diamond
where carrots grow —
the glint of diamond on a plane wing,
meaning: DANGER! THICK ICE!
but the good crunch of that orange,
the diamond, the carrot,
both with four million years of resurrecting dirt,
and the love,
although Adam did not know the word,
the love of Adam
obeying his sudden gift.

You, who sought me for nine years,
in stories made up in front of your naked mirror
or walking through rooms of fog women,
you trying to forget the mother
who built guilt with the lumber of a locked door
as she sobbed her soured milk and fed you loss

through the keyhole,
you who wrote out your own birth
and built it with your own poems,
your own lumber, your own keyhole,
into the trunk and leaves of your manhood,
you, who fell into my words, years
before you fell into me (the other,
both the Camp Director and the camper),
you who baited your hook with wide-awake dreams,
and calls and letters and once a luncheon,
and twice a reading by me for you.
But I wouldn't!

Yet this year,
yanking off all past years,
I took the bait
and was pulled upward, upward,
into the sky and was held by the sun —
the quick wonder of its yellow lap —
and became a woman who learned her own skin
and dug into her soul and found it full,
and you became a man who learned his own skin
and dug into his manhood, his humanhood
and found you were as real as a baker
or a seer
and we became a home,
up into the elbows of each other's soul,
without knowing —
an invisible purchase —
that inhabits our house forever.

We were
blessed by the House-Dic
by the altar of the color T.V.
and somehow managed to make a tiny marriage,
a tiny marriage

called belief,
as in the child's belief in the tooth fairy,
so close to absolute,
so daft within a year or two.
The daisies have come
for the last time.
And I who have,
each year of my life,
spoken to the tooth fairy,
believing in her,
even when I *was* her,
am helpless to stop your daisies from dying,
although your voice cries into the telephone:
Marry me! Marry me!
and my voice speaks onto these keys tonight:
The love is in dark trouble!
The love is starting to die,
right now —
we are in the process of it.
The empty process of it.

I see two deaths,
and the two men plod toward the mortuary of my heart,
and though I willed one away in court today
and I whisper dreams and birthdays into the other,
they both die like waves breaking over me
and I am drowning a little,
but always swimming
among the pillows and stones of the breakwater.
And though your daisies are an unwanted death,
I wade through the smell of their cancer
and recognize the prognosis,
its cartful of loss . . .

I say now,
you gave what you could.

It was quite a ferris wheel to spin on!
and the dead city of my marriage
seems less important
than the fact that the daisies came weekly,
over and over,
likes kisses that can't stop themselves.

There sit two deaths on November 5th, 1973.
Let one be forgotten —
Bury it! Wall it up!
But let me not forget the man
of my child-like flowers
though he sinks into the fog of Lake Superior,
he remains, his fingers the marvel
of fourth of July sparklers,
his furious ice cream cones of licking,
remains to cool my forehead with a washcloth
when I sweat into the bathtub of his being.

For the rest that is left:
name it gentle,
as gentle as radishes inhabiting
their short life in the earth,
name it gentle,
gentle as old friends waving *so long* at the window,
or in the drive,
name it gentle as maple wings singing
themselves upon the pond outside,
as sensuous as the mother-yellow in the pond,
that night that it was ours,
when our bodies floated and bumped
in moon water and the cicadas
called out like tongues.

Let such as this
be resurrected in all men

wherever they mold their days and nights
as when for twenty-five days and nights you molded mine
and planted the seed that dives into my God
and will do so forever
no matter how often I sweep the floor.

THE STAND-INS

In the dream
the swastika is neon
and flashes like a strobe light
into my eyes, all colors,
all vibrations
and I see the killer in him
and he turns on an oven,
an oven, an oven, an oven
and on a pie plate he sticks
in my Yellow Star
and then
then when it is ready for serving —
this dream goes off into the wings
and on stage The Cross appears,
with Jesus sticking to it
and He is breathing
and breathing
and He is breathing
and breathing
and then He speaks,
a kind of whisper,
and says . . .
This is the start.
This is the end.
This is a light.
This is a start.

I woke.
I did not know the hour,
an hour of night like thick scum
but I considered the dreams,
the two: Swastika, Crucifix,
and said: Oh well,
it doesn't belong to me,
if a cigar can be a cigar
then a dream can be a dream.
Right?
Right?
And went back to sleep
and another start.

THE LOVE PLANT

A freak but moist flower
tangles my lungs, knits into my heart,
crawls up my throat
and sucks like octopi on my tongue.
You planted it happily last summer
and I let it take root with my moon-hope,
not knowing it would come to crowd me out,
to explode inside me this March.
All winter trying to diminish it,
I felt it enlarge.
But of course never spoke to you of this,
for my sanity was awful enough,
and I felt compelled to think only of yours.
Now that you have gone for always
why does not the plant shrivel up?
I try to force it away.
I swallow stones.
Three times I swallow slender vials
with crossbones on them.

527

But it thrives on their liquid solution.
I light matches and put them in my mouth,
and my teeth melt but the greenery hisses on.
I drink blood from my wrists
and the green slips out like a bracelet.
Couldn't one of my keepers get a lawn mower
and chop it down if I turned inside out for an hour?
This flower, this pulp, the hay stuff
has got me, got me.
Apparently both of us are unkillable.

I am coughing. I am gagging. I feel it enter
the nasal passages, the sinus, lower, upper
and thus to the brain — spurting out of my eyes,
I must find a surgeon who will cut it out, burn it out
as they do sometimes with violent epileptics.
I will dial one quickly before I erupt!

Would you guess at it
if you looked at me swinging down Comm. Ave.
in my long black coat with its fur hood,
and my long pink skirt poking out step by step?
That under the coat, the pink, the bra, the pants,
in the recesses where love knelt
a coughing plant is smothering me?

Perhaps I am becoming unhuman
and should accept its natural order?
Perhaps I am becoming part of the green world
and maybe a rose will just pop out of my mouth?
Oh passerby, let me bite it off and spit it at you
so you can say "How nice!" and nod your thanks
and walk three blocks to your lady love
and she will stick it behind her ear
not knowing it will crawl into her ear, her brain
and drive her mad.

Then she will be like me —
a pink doll with her frantic green stuffing.

KILLING THE LOVE

I am the love killer,
I am murdering the music we thought so special,
that blazed between us, over and over.
I am murdering me, where I kneeled at your kiss.
I am pushing knives through the hands
that created two into one.
Our hands do not bleed at this,
they lie still in their dishonor.
I am taking the boats of our beds
and swamping them, letting them cough on the sea
and choke on it and go down into nothing.
I am stuffing your mouth with your
promises and watching
you vomit them out upon my face.
The Camp we directed?
I have gassed the campers.

Now I am alone with the dead,
flying off bridges,
hurling myself like a beer can into the wastebasket.
I am flying like a single red rose,
leaving a jet stream
of solitude
and yet I feel nothing,
though I fly and hurl,
my insides are empty
and my face is as blank as a wall.

Shall I call the funeral director?
He could put our two bodies into one pink casket,

those bodies from before,
and someone might send flowers,
and someone might come to mourn
and it would be in the obits,
and people would know that something died,
is no more, speaks no more, won't even
drive a car again and all of that.

When a life is over,
the one you were living for,
where do you go?

I'll work nights.
I'll dance in the city.
I'll wear red for a burning.
I'll look at the Charles very carefully,
wearing its long legs of neon.
And the cars will go by.
The cars will go by.
And there'll be no scream
from the lady in the red dress
dancing on her own Ellis Island,
who turns in circles,
dancing alone
as the cars go by.

THE RED DANCE

There was a girl
who danced in the city that night,
that April 22nd,
all along the Charles River.
It was as if one hundred men were watching
or do I mean the one hundred eyes of God?
The yellow patches in the sycamores

glowed like miniature flashlights.
The shadows, the skin of them
were ice cubes that flashed
from the red dress to the roof.
Mile by mile along the Charles she danced
past the benches of lovers,
past the dogs pissing on the benches.
She had on a red, red dress
and there was a small rain
and she lifted her face to it
and thought it part of the river.
And cars and trucks went by
on Memorial Drive.
And the Harvard students in the brick
hallowed houses studied Sappho in cement rooms.
And this Sappho danced on the grass
and danced and danced and danced.
It was a death dance.
The Larz Anderson bridge wore its lights
and many cars went by,
and a few students strolling under
their Coop umbrellas.
And a black man who asked this Sappho the time,
the time, as if her watch spoke.
Words were turning into grease,
and she said, "Why do you lie to me?"
And the waters of the Charles were beautiful,
sticking out in many colored tongues
and this strange Sappho knew she would enter the lights
and be lit by them and sink into them.
And how the end would come —
it had been foretold to her —
she would aspirate swallowing a fish,
going down with God's first creature
dancing all the way.

THE INVENTORY OF GOODBYE

I have a pack of letters.
I have a pack of memories.
I could cut out the eyes of both.
I could wear them like a patchwork apron.
I could stick them in the washer, the drier,
and maybe some of the pain would float off like dirt?
Perhaps down the disposal I could grind up the loss.
Besides — what a bargain — no expensive phone calls.
No lengthy trips on planes in the fog.
No manicky laughter or blessings from an odd-lot priest.
That priest is probably still floating on a fog pillow.
Blessing us. Blessing us.

Am I to bless the lost you,
sitting here with my clumsy soul?
Propaganda time is over.
I sit here on the spike of truth.
No one to hate except the slim fish of memory
that slides in and out of my brain.
No one to hate except the acute feel of my nightgown
brushing my body like a light that has gone out.
It recalls the kiss we invented, tongues like poems,
meeting, returning, inviting, causing a fever of need.
Laughter, maps, cassettes, touch singing its path —
all to be broken and laid away in a tight strongbox.
The monotonous dead clog me up and there is only
black done in black that oozes from the strongbox.
I must disembowel it and then set the heart, the legs,
of two who were one upon a large woodpile
and ignite, as I was once ignited, and let it whirl
into flame, reaching the sky
making it dangerous with its red.

THE LOST LIE

There is rust in my mouth,
the stain of an old kiss.
And my eyes are turning purple,
my mouth is glue
and my hands are two stones
and the heart,
is still there,
that place where love dwelt
but it is nailed into place.
Still I feel no pity for these oddities,
in fact the feeling is one of hatred.
For it is only the child in me bursting out
and I keep plotting how to kill her.

Once there was a woman,
full as a theater of moon
and love begot love
and the child, when she peeked out,
did not hate herself back then.
Funny, funny, love what you do.
But today I roam a dead house,
a frozen kitchen, a bedroom
like a gas chamber.
The bed itself is an operating table
where my dreams slice me into pieces.

Oh love,
the terror,
the fright wig,
that your dear curly head
was, was, was, was.

END, MIDDLE, BEGINNING

There was an unwanted child.
Aborted by three modern methods
she hung on to the womb,
hooked onto it
building her house into it
and it was to no avail,
to black her out.

At her birth
she did not cry,
spanked indeed,
but did not yell —
instead snow fell out of her mouth.

As she grew, year by year,
her hair turned like a rose in a vase,
and bled down her face.
Rocks were placed on her to keep
the growing silent,
and though they bruised,
they did not kill,
though kill was tangled into her beginning.

They locked her in a football
but she merely curled up
and pretended it was a warm doll's house.
They pushed insects in to bite her off
and she let them crawl into her eyes
pretending they were a puppet show.

Later, later,
grown fully, as they say,
they gave her a ring,
and she wore it like a root

and said to herself,
"To be not loved is the human condition,"
and lay like a statue in her bed.

Then once,
by terrible chance,
love took her in his big boat
and she shoveled the ocean
in a scalding joy.

Then,
slowly,
love seeped away,
the boat turned into paper
and she knew her fate,
at last.
Turn where you belong,
into a deaf mute
that metal house,
let him drill you into no one.

IV

EATING THE LEFTOVERS

CIGARETTES AND WHISKEY
AND WILD, WILD WOMEN
(*from a song*)

Perhaps I was born kneeling,
born coughing on the long winter,
born expecting the kiss of mercy,
born with a passion for quickness
and yet, as things progressed,
I learned early about the stockade
or taken out, the fume of the enema.
By two or three I learned not to kneel,
not to expect, to plant my fires underground
where none but the dolls, perfect and awful,
could be whispered to or laid down to die.

Now that I have written many words,
and let out so many loves, for so many,
and been altogether what I always was —
a woman of excess, of zeal and greed,
I find the effort useless.
Do I not look in the mirror,
these days,
and see a drunken rat avert her eyes?
Do I not feel the hunger so acutely
that I would rather die than look
into its face?

I kneel once more,
in case mercy should come
in the nick of time.

THE PASSION OF THE MAD RABBIT

While the carrots sang arias into the holy earth
and the snowmen turned into bronze weathervanes,
I underwent a removal, tearing my skin off me,
plucking out the eyes like Ping-Pong balls,
squashing the shriek of my heart like a phone off the hook —
and as these phenomena occurred, a fool walked straight into
    me.
He was named Mr. Rabbit. My own voice spoke to people,
anyone, friends, strangers on the street, saying,
"I am Mr. Rabbit." The flesh itself had become mad
and at three mirrors this was confirmed.

Next it was bad Friday and they nailed me up
like a scarecrow and many gathered eating popcorn, carrying
hymnals or balloons. There were three of us there,
though *they* appeared normal. My ears, so pink like powder,
were nailed. My paws, sweet as baby mittens, were nailed.
And my two fuzzy ankles. I said, "Pay no attention. I am
    crazy."
But some giggled and some knelt. My oxygen became tiny
and blood rang over and over in my head like a bell.
The others died, the luck of it blurting through them.
I could not. I was a silly broken umbrella
and oblivion would not kiss me. For three days it
was thus.

Then they took me down and had a conference.
It is Easter, they said, and you are the Easter Bunny.
Then they built a great pyre of kindling and laid me on top
and just before the match they handed me a pink basket

of eggs the color of the circus.
Fire lit, I tossed the eggs to them, *Hallelujah* I sang
    to the eggs,
singing as I burned to nothing in the tremor of the flames.
My blood came to a boil as I looked down the throat of
    madness,
but singing yellow egg, blue egg, pink egg, red egg, green
    egg,
Hallelujah, to each hard-boiled-colored egg.

In place of the Lord,
I whispered,
a fool has risen.

THE ANGEL FOOD DOGS

Leaping, leaping, leaping,
down, line by line,
growling at the cadavers,
filling the holy jugs with their piss,
falling into windows and mauling the parents,
but soft, kiss-soft,
and sobbing sobbing
into their awful dog dish.

No point? No twist for you
in my white tunnel?
Let me speak plainly,
let me whisper it from the podium —

Mother, may I use you as a pseudonym?
May I take the dove named Mary
and shove out Anne?
May I take my check book, my holographs,
my eight naked books,
and sign it Mary, Mary, Mary

full of grace?
I know my name is not offensive
but my feet hang in the noose.
I want to be white.
I want to be blue.
I want to be a bee digging into an onion heart,
as you did to me, dug and squatted
long after death and its fang.

Hail Mary, full of me,
Nibbling in the sitting room of my head.
Mary, Mary, virgin forever,
whore forever,
give me your name,
give me your mirror.
Boils fester in my soul,
so give me your name so I may kiss them,
and they will fly off,
nameless
but named,
and they will fly off like angel food dogs
with thee
and with thy spirit.
Let me climb the face of my kitchen dog
and fly off into my terrified years.

LEAVES THAT TALK

Yes.
It's May 20th and the leaves,
green, green, wearing their masks
and speaking, calling out their Sapphic loves,
are here — here — here —
calling out their death wish:

"Anne, Anne, come to us."

to die of course. Come when listening
to the voices of the doves
that burst in them and out of them.
I mean their veins, their hearts
who scare you and beguile you
with their woman apron lives,
their doves' arms flapping
from their cage, their brown stick branches.

I told someone once how they called to me,
sang to me, and that someone fled.
Now I will tell a priest
or is it a priestess?
Both, one and all and the same.
They call, though I sit here
sensibly behind my window screen.
They call, even if I'm pinned behind bars.
They call, they call their green death call.
They want me. They need me.
I belong lying down under them,
letting the green coffin fold and unfold
above me as I go out.

I flee. I flee.
I block my ears and eat salami.
I turn on THE song of THE LADY
but the leaves' song crawls through
and into it and mixes like a dream in a dream.
I confess. I confess.
They steam all summer,
calling dark and light and moonstone
and they do not shut up.
They do not.

It is bad for me, dear confessor,
and yet I am in love with it.
It has a body.

It has many bodies.
I do not believe in ghosts
(very much)
but I wonder if they aren't my whole past —
the generation of women, down the line,
the genealogical line right to the *Mayflower*,
and William Brewster and his woman
who rolled herself sick unto death
until she reached this promised land.
Oh well — whoever my green girls are —
they *are*.

I dream it's the fourth of July
and I'm having a love affair
with grandfather (his real birthday)
and that the leaves fall off,
clank, clank,
crashing down like stones, New England
stones, one by one,
and in my dream
grandfather touches my neck and breast
and says, "Do not be afraid!
It's only the leaves falling!"
There are one hundred thousand woman cries,
tree by tree, and I scream out in my fear
that my green ladies are leaving,
my lovely obsessions,
and I need them.
I sob.
I wake up.
Kleenex.
Grandfather.

And, dear God,
I am Rip van Winkle.
It is six A.M.

July 5th, 1974,
and the branches are bare.
The leaves lie in green mounds,
like fake green snow huts.
And from the window as I peer out,
I see they have left their cages forever —
those wiry, spidery branches —
for me to people
someday soon when I turn green
and faithless to the summer.

"DADDY" WARBUCKS

In Memoriam

What's missing is the eyeballs
in each of us, but it doesn't matter
because you've got the bucks, the bucks, the bucks.
You let me touch them, fondle the green faces
lick at their numbers and it lets you be
my "Daddy!" "Daddy!" and though I fought all alone
with molesters and crooks, I knew your money
would save me, your courage, your "I've had
considerable experience as a soldier . . .
fighting to win millions for myself, it's true.
But I *did* win," and me praying for "our men out there"
just made it okay to be an orphan whose blood was no one's,
whose curls were hung up on a wire machine and electrified,
while you built and unbuilt intrigues called nations,
and did in the bad ones, always, always,
and always came at my perils, the black Christs of childhood,
always came when my heart stood naked in the street
and they threw apples at it or twelve-day-old-dead-fish.

"Daddy!" "Daddy," we all won that war,
when you sang me the money songs

Annie, Annie you sang
and I knew you drove a pure gold car
and put diamonds in your coke
for the crunchy sound, the adorable sound
and the moon too was in your portfolio,
as well as the ocean with its sleepy dead.
And I was always brave, wasn't I?
I never bled?
I never saw a man expose himself.
No. No.
I never saw a drunkard in his blubber.
I never let lightning go in one ear and out the other.
And all the men out there were never to come.
Never, like a deluge, to swim over my breasts
and lay their lamps in my insides.
No. No.
Just me and my "Daddy"
and his tempestuous bucks
rolling in them like corn flakes
and only the bad ones died.

But I died yesterday,
"Daddy," I died,
swallowing the Nazi-Jap-animal
and it won't get out
it keeps knocking at my eyes,
my big orphan eyes,
kicking! Until eyeballs pop out
and even my dog puts up his four feet
and lets go
of his military secret
with his big red tongue
flying up and down
like yours should have

as we board our velvet train.

544

DIVORCE, THY NAME IS WOMAN

I am divorcing daddy — Dybbuk! Dybbuk!
I have been doing it daily all my life
since his sperm left him
drilling upwards and stuck to an egg.
Fetus, fetus — glows and glows in that home
and bursts out, electric, demanding moths.

For years it was woman to woman,
breast, crib, toilet, dolls, dress-ups.
WOMAN! WOMAN!
Daddy of the whiskies, daddy of the rooster breath,
would visit and then dash away
as if I were a disease.

Later,
when blood and eggs and breasts
dropped onto me,
Daddy and his whiskey breath
made a long midnight visit
in a dream that is not a dream
and then called his lawyer quickly.
Daddy divorcing me.

I have been divorcing him ever since,
going into court with Mother as my witness
and both long dead or not
I am still divorcing him,
adding up the crimes
of how he came to me,
how he left me.

I am pacing the bedroom.
Opening and shutting the windows.
Making the bed and pulling it apart.

I am tearing the feathers out of the pillows,
waiting, waiting for Daddy to come home
and stuff me so full of our infected child
that I turn invisible, but married,
at last.

THE FIERCENESS OF FEMALE

I am spinning,
I am spinning on the lips,
they remove my shadow,
my phantom from my past,
they invented a timetable of tongues,
that take up all my attention.
Wherein there is no room.
No bed.
The clock does not tick
except where it vibrates my 4000 pulses,
and where all was absent,
all is two,
touching like a choir of butterflies,
and like the ocean,
pushing toward land
and receding
and pushing
with a need that gallops
all over my skin,
yelling at the reefs.

I unknit.
Words fly out of place
and I, long into the desert,
drink and drink
and bow my head to that meadow
the breast, the melon in it,

and then the intoxicating flower of it.
Our hands that stroke each other
the nipples like baby starfish —
to make our lips sucking into lunatic rings
until they are bubbles,
our fingers naked as petals
and the world pulses on a swing.
I raise my pelvis to God
so that it may know the truth of how
flowers smash through the long winter.

THE BIG BOOTS OF PAIN

There can be certain potions
needled in by the clock
for the body's fall from grace,
to untorture and to plead for.
These I have known
and would sell all my furniture
and books and assorted goods
to avoid, and more, more.

But the other pain . . .
I would sell my life to avoid
the pain that begins in the crib
with its bars or perhaps
with your first breath
when the planets drill
your future into you
for better or worse
as you marry life
and the love that gets doled out
or doesn't.

I find now, swallowing one teaspoon
of pain, that it drops downward

to the past where it mixes
with last year's cupful
and downward into a decade's quart
and downward into a lifetime's ocean.
I alternate treading water
and deadman's float.

The teaspoon ought to be bearable
if it didn't mix into the reruns
and thus enlarge into what it is not,
a sea pest's sting turning promptly
into the shark's neat biting off
of a leg because the soul
wears a magnifying glass.
Kicking the heart
with pain's big boots running up and down
the intestines like a motorcycle racer.

Yet one does get out of bed
and start over, plunge into the day
and put on a hopeful look
and does not allow fear to build a wall
between you and an old friend
or a new friend and reach out your hand,
shutting down the thought that
an axe may cut it off unexpectedly.
One learns not to blab about all this
except to yourself or the typewriter keys
who tell no one until they get brave
and crawl off onto the printed page.

I'm getting bored with it,
I tell the typewriter,
this constantly walking around
in wet shoes and then, surprise!
Somehow DECEASED keeps getting

stamped in red over the word HOPE.
And I who keep falling thankfully
into each new pillow of belief,
finding my Mercy Street,
kissing it and tenderly gift-wrapping my love,
am beginning to wonder just what
the planets had in mind on November 9th, 1928.
The pillows are ripped away,
the hand guillotined,
dog shit thrown into the middle of a laugh,
a hornets' nest building into the hi-fi speaker
and leaving me in silence,
where, without music,
I become a cracked orphan.

Well,
one gets out of bed
and the planets don't always hiss
or muck up the day, each day.
As for the pain and its multiplying teaspoon,
perhaps it is a medicine
that will cure the soul
of its greed for love
next Thursday.

DEMON

A young man is afraid of his demon and puts his hand
over the demon's mouth sometimes . . . – D. H. Lawrence

I mentioned my demon to a friend
and the friend swam in oil and came forth to me
greasy and cryptic
and said,
"I'm thinking of taking him out of hock.
I pawned him years ago."

Who would buy?
The pawned demon,
Yellowing with forgetfulness
and hand at his throat?
Take him out of hock, my friend,
but beware of the grief
that will fly into your mouth like a bird.

My demon,
too often undressed,
too often a crucifix I bring forth,
too often a dead daisy I give water to
too often the child I give birth to
and then abort, nameless, nameless . . .
earthless.

Oh demon within,
I am afraid and seldom put my hand up
to my mouth and stitch it up
covering you, smothering you
from the public voyeury eyes
of my typewriter keys.
If I should pawn you,
what bullion would they give for you,
what pennies, swimming in their copper kisses
what bird on its way to perishing?

No.
No.
I accept you,
you come with the dead who people my dreams,
who walk all over my desk
(as in Mother, cancer blossoming on her
Best & Co. tits —
waltzing with her tissue paper ghost)
the dead, who give sweets to the diabetic in me,

who give bolts to the seizure of roses
that sometimes fly in and out of me.
Yes.
Yes.
I accept you, demon.
I will not cover your mouth.
If it be man I love, apple laden and foul
or if it be woman I love, sick unto her blood
and its sugary gasses and tumbling branches.

Demon come forth,
even if it be God I call forth
standing like a carrion,
wanting to eat me,
starting at the lips and tongue.
And me wanting to glide into His spoils,
I take bread and wine,
and the demon farts and giggles,
at my letting God out of my mouth
anonymous woman
at that anonymous altar.

THE SEA CORPSE

The beach was crowded,
people tossed like ripe corn,
buttering themselves as they went
and on the dunes thousands of crabs,
moved their yellowy eyes.
Up above the sea grass
flew like a woman's hair in labor.
And you were at the sea.
Perhaps you did not notice,
that it had gone out,
a permanent removal.

I was at the same sea but in a different locale
and saw only it had gone out like an awful visitor.
There was no suck and slump.
But that's the least of it.
Right out to the horizon
it had been removed surgically;
the blue, the green, the gray, the blood red,
had been sucked out of it
and the water of it, the brine of it
had gone somewhere else.
Not even a tide pool remained.
I think I cried
but perhaps I didn't.
I flew into my head and there
fifty tiny oceans lay in a coffin.
Their coffins were pink and embossed and gaudy
and after the rabbi had sung over them,
they were quickly buried.
I did not cry then.
I knew it was a natural order.
The centuries of our blue mothers came
and we spoke to them, adored their moods,
immersed in their holy waters
but one day they were dead.
And I threw a little earth
on the pink coffin
covered by the fake plastic grass
and said O.K., God,
if it's the end of the world,
it must be necessary.

THERE YOU WERE

There you were,
solitary, 7:00 A.M.

surveying your own unpeopled beach
and the sea, that day,
was as calm as an unplayed piano,
and the gulls popped in and out,
softly, softly and your eyes grew soft
with their unused power
and your defenses swept out into
the baby tongues of the tide,
that day, Barbara,
when an entire house broke out of the sea
and collapsed at your feet.
And you strode toward it
to see if it had a problem,
or if the sea-carpenter in you
could set it upright.

This was pure instinct
and though as you peeked in the ghosty windows,
and felt the nails growing the wrong way out
you had only a small fear
and the fear was not for yourself
but for her, lest she drift outward,
into the sea at war with itself.
You laughed at her doors,
and opened them with care,
lest a convulsion crush the structure.

The house waited on your private beach
each day,
when you had the time to return to her.
And you so often had the time,
even when fury blew out her chimney,
even when love lifted the shingles
even when loss after loss
cracked her cage
and the sea boiled at the edge of the structure.

Yet you battled for that house
with a small delight in your power
over the teeth that had bitten it in two.

The house of my body has spoken
often as you rebuild me like blocks,
and promise to come visit
when I'm finally adjusted on safe land,
and am livable, joist to joist
with storm windows and screens,
mattresses, fixtures,
sand dollars, cups —
inhabitable and all that.
But not for sale!
Perhaps when I'm an antique,
as a gift,
cranky but firm,
I'll take in boarders
who admire my ocean view.

THE CONSECRATING MOTHER

I stand before the sea
and it rolls and rolls in its green blood
saying, "Do not give up one god
for I have a handful."
The trade winds blew
in their twelve-fingered reversal
and I simply stood on the beach
while the ocean made a cross of salt
and hung up its drowned
and they cried *Deo Deo*.
The ocean offered them up in the vein of its might.
I wanted to share this
but I stood alone like a pink scarecrow.

The ocean steamed in and out,
the ocean gasped upon the shore
but I could not define her,
I could not name her mood, her locked-up faces.
Far off she rolled and rolled
like a woman in labor
and I thought of those who had crossed her,
in antiquity, in nautical trade, in slavery, in war.
I wondered how she had borne those bulwarks.
She should be entered skin to skin,
and put on like one's first or last cloth,
entered like kneeling your way into church,
descending into that ascension,
though she be slick as olive oil,
as she climbs each wave like an embezzler of white.
The big deep knows the law as it wears its gray hat,
though the ocean comes in its destiny,
with its one hundred lips,
and in moonlight she comes in *her* nudity,
flashing breasts made of milk-water,
flashing buttocks made of unkillable lust,
and at night when you enter her
you shine like a neon soprano.

I am that clumsy human
on the shore
loving you, coming, coming,
going,
and wish to put my thumb on you
like The Song of Solomon.

Words for Dr. Y.

(1978)

Editor's Note

Words for Dr. Y. is the first collection of Anne Sexton's poetry from which her editorial guidance was totally absent. *45 Mercy Street*, her first posthumous publication, was the last book she actively planned. In preparing *Anne Sexton: A Self-Portrait in Letters*, however, I realized that among her files and manuscripts in progress was a considerable body of valuable material that deserved to be published.

The first section of this book, "Letters to Dr. Y.," written from 1960 to 1970, was originally a series of poems Anne wanted to include in her sixth volume, *The Book of Folly*. When friends and editors convinced her it did not belong there, she specifically reserved it for publication after her death. As far as I know, this is the only time she ever set work aside for such a purpose.*

The second section is composed of poems written between July 1971 and July 1973; she had no chance to incorporate these into a book or to place them with magazines.

* Originally Anne had intended *The Death Notebooks* for posthumous publication. However, she had a change of heart and the collection appeared in February 1973.

Though she had put the series "Scorpio, Bad Spider, Die" in one of her file cabinets beside *45 Mercy Street* and other poems intended for publication, I believe she was actually quite uncertain about its final destination. Although written in the later years of her career, these poems often return to the stricter form, rhyme, and meter of her earlier work. Perhaps this return, coupled with the very personal content of these poems, made her initially uneasy about publishing them, particularly after the mythmaking and free stylistics she had used so successfully in *Transformations* (1971). Also, since the "Scorpio" poems never fit thematically into any book she worked on thereafter, she simply may have been waiting for an appropriate collection in which to include them.

Anne Sexton wrote many of the poems collected here at a time when her process of revision was still quite rigorous, and therefore this volume may seem more finished than *45 Mercy Street*. Still, it must be remembered that she honed her manuscripts right up until the last minute; as with *45 Mercy Street*, much that is included here might well have been rewritten had she been alive to edit the poems herself. In choosing what to publish, I could only try to approximate her hand.

Editing this collection involved only a process of selection; as in *45 Mercy Street*, everything in *Words for Dr. Y.* appears as originally written. However, I have deleted a few poems from Parts I and III that I felt would not add to the reader's understanding of Anne's poetry or life.

Anne Sexton's final poems were written between March and October of 1974. These last will be included in a forthcoming volume of her collected work.

Linda Gray Sexton
December 4, 1977

LETTERS TO DR. Y.

(1960–1970)

Dr. Y.
I need a thin hot wire,
your Rescue Inc. voice
to stretch me out,
to keep me from going underfoot
and growing stiff
as a yardstick.

Death,
I need your hot breath,
my index finger in the flame,
two cretins standing at my ears,
listening for the cop car.

Death,
I need a little cradle
to carry me out,
a boxcar for my books,
a nickel in my palm,
and no kiss
on my kiss.

Death,
I need my little addiction to you.
I need that tiny voice who,
even as I rise from the sea,
all woman, all there,

says kill me, kill me.
My manic eye
sees only the trapeze artist
who flies without a net.
Bravo, I cry,
swallowing the pills,
the do die pills.
Listen ducky,
death is as close to pleasure
as a toothpick.
To die whole,
riddled with nothing
but desire for it,
is like breakfast
after love.

February 16, 1960

I have words for you, Dr. Y.,
words for sale.
Words that have been hoarded up,
waiting for the pleasure act of coming out,
hugger-mugger, higgily-piggily
onto the stage.

And where is the order? you will ask.

A disorderly display of words,
one after the other.
It's a huge gathering ball of words,
not a snowball, but an old string ball,
one from the rag bag.

And where is the order? you will ask.

Words out through the lips like toads!
And if there is a pearl among them

562

she will surely get lost in the confusion.
Words, words, words,
piled up one on another,
making a kind of weight of themselves.
   1. each less than a pound
   2. each less than a stick of butter
   3. one the size of a roasted peanut, light and wrinkled
   4. another one, a slim precise girl, a sunflower seed
   5. one, as small as my thumb, a beach stone in the hand
   6. and there is always that one, the toad. The toad
has many brothers.

And where is the order? you will ask.

Words waiting, angry, masculine,
with their fists in a knot.
Words right now, alive in the head,
heavy and pressing as in a crowd.
Pushing for headroom, elbowing,
knowing their rights.

And where is the order? you will ask.

A word, a sunflower seed.
One we would surely overlook.
So easily lost, a dead bee.
So vulnerable.
She is already trampled, that one,
having traveled so far from the heart.
She weighs so little.
She is so light and vulnerable.
She is the dead bee called love.

June 6, 1960

My three poets!
John, Maxine, George.
We meet once a month
like the moon,
like the menses.

We weep together
and make a bed for rain.

None of them has
the sense of evil that I have,
evil that jaw breaker,
that word-wife.

January 1, 1961

I begin again, Dr. Y.,
this neverland journal,
full of my own sense of filth.
Why else keep a journal, if not
to examine your own filth?

January 1, 1962

I love the word warm.
It is almost unbearable —
so moist and breathlike.
I feel the earth like a nurse,
curing me of winter.
I feel the earth,
its worms oiling upward,
the ants ticking,
the oak leaf rotting like feces
and the oats rising like angels.

In the beginning,
summer is a sense

564

of this earth,
or of yourself.

June 3, 1962

This loneliness is just an exile from God.

April 1, 1963

I remember my mother dying . . .
a strange feeling to know that life is just
going out of you with every breath.
Strange walls and colors.
The nurses coming and going.
White, white, mother I am leaving.
Faces, suddenly suspended above you;
faces that you think it's your business to love
if only you could remember their names.
Pain and never knowing that you are getting ugly.
The fog of medication and old ether dreams.
White. White.
Perhaps the ugliness is that of a new baby —
growing back to your first skull.

And all this with a memory of attics
and dining room wallpaper, the A & P
and the superhighway and those small roads —
roadways where you've never been
and that you would like to speak of if
you could remember how to form the words.
White, white, mother I am leaving.

A baby just lies there
having come from its bath;
lies there getting used to being outside the bath,
lies there getting used to being outside of something,

while you, death-child, lie fitfully
waiting to go inside.

And surely the people clasp at your bedsheet
and your railing and peer at you through
your tubes and rustle the bedside flowers.
White, white.

Oh there is no use in loving the dying.
I have tried.
I have tried but you can't,
you just can't guard the dead.
You are the watchman and you
can't keep the gate shut.

March 14, 1964

I put some daisies in a bowl
with a weed that looks like babies'-breath.
I put them in that bowl to show
my husband I am here. I care.
They are steady in their sleep.
Daisies in water are the longest lasting
flower you can give to someone.
Fact.
Buy daisies.
Not roses.
Yes daisies.
Buy them for everyone, sick or well.
Buy them for well people especially.

Name your girl-child Daisy
or name your heroine Daisy
and watch her sun-heart with its inner urges
and her chalk petals stick straight up
like doll's thumbs.

But let her bend her head sadly
now and then for sometimes her palm
will read *He loves me not*.

But not always.

June 14, 1964

What has it come to, Dr. Y.
my needing you?
I work days,
stuffed into a pine-paneled box.
You work days
with your air conditioner gasping
like a tube-fed woman.
I move my thin legs into your office
and we work over the cadaver of my soul.
We make a stage set out of my past
and stuff painted puppets into it.
We make a bridge toward my future
and I cry to you: I will be steel!
I will build a steel bridge over my need!
I will build a bomb shelter over my heart!
But my future is a secret.
It is as shy as a mole.

What has it come to
my needing you . . .
I am the irritating pearl
and you are the necessary shell.
You are the twelve faces of the Atlantic
and I am the rowboat. I am the burden.

How dependent, the fox asks?
Why so needy, the snake sings?
It's this way . . .
Time after time I fall down into the well

567

and you dig a tunnel in the dangerous sand,
you take the altar from a church and shore it up.
With your own white hands you dig me out.
You give me hoses so I can breathe.
You make me a skull to hold the worms
of my brains. You give me hot chocolate
although I am known to have no belly.
The trees are whores yet you place
me under them. The sun is poison
yet you toss me under it like a rose.
I am out of practice at living.
You are as brave as a motorcycle.

What has it come to
that I should defy you?
I would be a copper wire
without electricity.
I would be a Beacon Hill dowager
without her hat.
I would be a surgeon
who cut with his own nails.
I would be a glutton
who threw away his spoon.
I would be God
without Jesus to speak for me.

I would be Jesus
without a cross to prove me.

August 24, 1964

Blue eyes wash off sometimes.
They have already torn up the sky
for they have torn off its color.
Also they have swallowed up the salt
and this, in turn, closes up the beaches.

Mr. God,
why are you that blue?

Blue eyes I'm married to.

But brown eyes where Father Inc. waits,
that little Freud shoveling dirt in the cellar,
that Mr. Man, Mr. Cellar Man, brown as
old blood.

February 23, 1965

I called him *Comfort*.
Dr. Y., I gave him the wrong name.
I should have called him *Preacher*
for all day there on the coastland
he read me the Bible.
He read me the Bible to prove I was sinful.
For in the night he was betrayed.
And then he let me give him a Judas-kiss,
that red lock that held us in place,
and then I gave him a drink from my cup
and he whispered, "Rape, rape."
And then I gave him my wrist
and he sucked on the blood,
hating himself for it,
murmuring, "God will see. God will see."

And I said,
"To hell with God!"

And he said,
"Would you mock God?"

And I said,
"God is only mocked by believers!"

And he said,
"I love only the truth."

And I said,
"This holy concern for the truth —
no one worries about it except liars."

And God was bored.
He turned on his side
like an opium eater
and slept.

March 28, 1965

Dr. Y., I have a complaint.
Why do you smile that liverish smile?
Why do you double over in a spaz and a swoon,
gurgling on my past, my grief, my bile?
Am I a joke?
Am I a gas?

Everything I say to you is awfully serious.
I don't make puns.
I have no slips of tongue.
I pay in cold hard cash.
I am prompt as you have noted.
I am among the few who make songs.
My sisters laughed at me always.
When I drew pictures they laughed.
When I danced they laughed.
When I wrote they laughed.
When I ate they laughed.

Ha-ha-ha.

Urine and tears pour out of me.
I'm the one you broke.

February 14, 1966

570

What do the voices say? Dr. Y. asks.

My voices are as real as books, I answer.

They say,
"We are your voices. When you look at your soup
one of us is here saying, '*You!* You're on trial
and if you tell, then Nana will choke you
and no sane man will believe you and your face
will grow as black as a German stump.' "

Voice number one says,
"I am the leaves. I am the martyred.
Come unto me with death for I am the siren.
I am forty young girls in green shells.
Come out of your house and come unto me
for I am silk and convalescent."

Voice number two says,
"Choke on me. I am the rock in front
of your window. I am a pit to gag on.
I am male and I will take my sword blade
and cut loose your children and your mate.
I am a large puppet. I am Mr. Gobblegook."

Voice number three says,
"I am the white clown. I am whitewashed.
I am nothing but salt and powder
and I spit on you for you are impure.
Your Nana had white powdery hair, eh?
My whisper goes crazy even in you."

Voice number four says,
"I am the razor. I am so humble
in your little white medicine chest.

I am alert. My language is a thin whine.
Have you ever thought, my single one,
that your hands are thorns to be cut to the quick?"

Voice number five says,
"I am a whip. Could you not find
someone to put me to a proper use?
I will cut. I will make blood into brine.
I will mark you all over with little red fish.
You will be almost killed, a delight.
You will suffer, child, and it will be kind."

June 6, 1967

It's music you've never heard
that I've heard,
that makes me think of you —
not Villa Lobos, my heart's media,
but pop songs on my kitchen radio
bleating like a goat.
I know a little bit
about a lot of things
but I don't know enough about you . . .
Songs like cherries in a bowl,
sweet and sour and small.
Suddenly I'm not half the girl
I used to be.
There's a shadow hanging over me . . .
From me to you out of my electric devil
but easy like the long skirts
in a Renoir picnic with clouds and parasols.

Fourteen boys in cars are parked
with fourteen girls in cars and they
are listening to our song with one blood.
No one is ruined. Everyone is in
a delight at this ardor.

I am in a delight with you, Music Man.
Your name is Dr. Y. My name is Anne.

November 18, 1967

I am no longer at war with sin,
working daily with my little shield and paddle
against those willful acts,
those small loaves,
those drops of angel sperm.

And yet and yet . . .
the old sense of evil remains,
evil that wife.
Evil who leaves me here,
most days,
dead broke.

She is a commercial woman.
She waits at the gate.
She dogs me on the street.
She shuts me in a lavatory.
She is my other face,
grunting as I sigh,
vomiting as I chew.

Take adultery or theft.
Merely sins.
It is evil who dines on the soul,
stretching out its long bone tongue.
It is evil who tweezers my heart,
picking out its atomic worms.

December 4, 1967

Remember *The Shadow Knows?*
And he did. He could see me
squatting there beside my sensible brown radio.
And it goes on. It goes on even now.
They all see you when you least suspect.
Out flat in your p.j.'s glowering at T.V.
or at the oven gassing the cat
or at the Hotel 69 head to knee.

Didn't you know it, Dr. Y.,
you're news to someone? Someone's
got a secret file in case you resist,
in case you light a fuse. Take,
for instance, the druggist.
Have you seen him eyeball and smile,
meanwhile keeping tabs on what you're taking?
He's the FBI of sleeping and the FBI of waking.

April Fools' Day 1968

What about all the psychotics
of the world?
Why do they keep eating?
Why do they keep making plans
and meeting people at the appointed time?
Don't they know there is nothing,
a void, an eyeless socket,
a grave with the corpse stolen?
Don't they know that God gave them
their miraculous sickness
like a shield, like armor
and if their eyes are in the wrong
part of their heads, they shouldn't complain?
What are they doing seeing their doctors
when the world's up for grabs.

January 12, 1969

As Ruth said, "Enlarge the place of thy tent."

July 4, 1969

I'm dreaming the My Lai soldier again,
I'm dreaming the My Lai soldier night after night.
He rings the doorbell like the Fuller Brush Man
and wants to shake hands with me
and I do because it would be rude to say no
and I look at my hand and it is green
with intestines.
And they won't come off,
they won't. He apologizes for this over and over.
The My Lai soldier lifts me up again and again
and lowers me down with the other dead women and babies
saying, *It's my job. It's my job.*

Then he gives me a bullet to swallow
like a sleeping tablet.
I am lying in this belly of dead babies
each one belching up the yellow gasses of death
and their mothers tumble, eyeballs, knees, upon me,
each for the last time, each authentically dead.
The soldier stands on a stepladder above us
pointing his red penis right at me and saying,
Don't take this personally.

December 17, 1969

What are the leaves saying? you ask.

I am not allowed to repeat it.
There are rules about this.

What is it like? you ask.

575

Words for it crawl in and out of me
like worms. I do not like them.
And yet my heart thumps like applause.

There are warnings . . .

What are the leaves saying? you ask.

Orders. Demands.

What do the leaves remind you of? you ask.

Green. Green!

What does green remind you of? you ask.

Weed memories.
A fisherman with green fruit in his net . . .
The back lawn I danced on when I was eight . . .

The slime pool that the dog drowned in . . .
A drunk vomiting up a teaspoon of bile . . .
Washing the polio off the grapes when I was ten . . .
A Harvard book bag in Rome . . .
Night baseball games . . .
Lake Como . . .
But those are painted colors.
Only the leaves are human.

Human? you ask.

They are girls. Green girls.
Death and life is their daily work.
Death seams up and down the leaf.
I call the leaves my death girls.
The death girls turn at the raggedy edge

and swim another length down the veins
to the raggedy heart.

And these death girls sing to you? you ask.

Yes.

And does it excite you? you ask.

Yes.
It's a canker-suicide high.
It's a sisterhood.
I need to be laid out at last
under them, as straight as a pea pod.
To die whole. To die as soft and young as a leaf.
To lie down whole in that green god's belly.

Have the leaves always talked? Even when you were young?
    you ask.

When I was five.I played under pines.
Pines that were stiff and sturdy.
State of Maine pines sifting the air
like harps, sifting over that fifth me.
Dark green.
A different order.
A different sign.
I was safe there at five under that stiff crotch.

The leaves tell you to die? you ask.

Yes.

A strange theater.

                                        May 5, 1970

                                        577

My safe, safe psychosis is broken.
It was hard.
It was made of stone.
It covered my face like a mask.
But it has cracked.
Today I drove a train through it looking for my mouth.
And then I fed it.
With Dr. Y.'s hands I fed it.

My little illustrated armor,
my hard, hard shell has cracked
for Dr. Y. held my hand
and with that touch
my dead father rode on the Superchief
back to me with dollar bills in his fist
and my dead mother started to knit me a sweater
and told me, as usual, to sit up straight,
and my dead sister danced into the room
to borrow something and I said
yes, yes, yes.

My hand in his hand,
a family of fingers,
leaf to leaf.
Dread I have attended thee.
Death I have attended thee.
But now touch is here.
Touch is difficult.
Touch is the revolution.
Now tears run down me like Campbell's Soup.
Now the Lord hath given me my petition.

Your hand is the outrageous redeemer.

July 21, 1970

I begin to see. Today I am not all wood.

September 3, 1970

I am happy today with the sheets of life.
I washed out the bedsheets.
I hung out the bedsheets and watched them
slap and lift like gulls.
When they were dry I unfastened them
and buried my head in them.
All the oxygen of the world was in them.
All the feet of the babies of the world were in them.
All the crotches of the angels of the world were in them.
All the morning kisses of Philadelphia were in them.
All the hopscotch games on the sidewalks were in them.
All the ponies made of cloth were in them.

So this is happiness,
that journeyman.

November 9, 1970

POEMS 1971–1973

BUYING THE WHORE

You are a roast beef I have purchased
and I stuff you with my very own onion.

You are a boat I have rented by the hour
and I steer you with my rage until you run aground.

You are a glass that I have paid to shatter
and I swallow the pieces down with my spit.

You are the grate I warm my trembling hands on,
searing the flesh until it's nice and juicy.

You stink like my Mama under your bra
and I vomit into your hand like a jackpot
its cold hard quarters.

July 15, 1971

TO LIKE, TO LOVE

Aphrodite,
my Cape Town lady,
my mother, my daughter,
I of your same sex
goggling on your right side
have little to say about LIKE and LOVE.
I dream you Nordic and six foot tall,

I dream you masked and blood-mouthed,
yet here you are with kittens and puppies,
subscribing to five ecological magazines,
sifting all the blacks out of South Africa
onto a Free-Ship, kissing them all like candy,
liking them all, but love? Who knows?

I ask you to inspect my heart
and name its pictures.
I push open the door to your heart
and I see all your children sitting around a campfire.
They sit like fruit waiting to be picked.
I am one of them. The one sipping whiskey.
You nod to me as you pass by and I look up
at your great blond head and smile.
We are all singing as in a holiday
and then you start to cry,
you fall down into a huddle,
you are sick.

What do we do?
Do we kiss you to make it better?
No. No. We all walk softly away.
We would stay and be the nurse but
there are too many of us and we are too worried to help.
It is love that walks away
and yet we have terrible mouths
and soft milk hands.
We worry with *like*.
We walk away like *love*.

Daughter of us all,
Aphrodite,
we would stay and telegraph God,
we would mother like six kitchens,
we would give lessons to the doctors

but we leave, hands empty,
because you are no one.

Not ours.
You are someone soft who plays
the piano on Mondays and Fridays
and examines our murders for flaws.

Blond lady,
do you love us, love us, love us?
As I love America, you might mutter,
before you fall asleep.

May 17, 1972

THE SURGEON
for Jack McGinty

Jack, oh big Jack,
of the rack and the screw,
why in New York did you seem
tinier. Doctor Jack,
in your office, in the O.R.
last week unscrewing my hip,
you seemed as big as an island.
I stir my martinis with the screw,
four-inch and stainless steel,
and think of my hip where it lay
for four years like a darkness.
Jack, oh big Jack,
would you like an ear or a finger
to keep of me? From you I have
one of the tools of your carpentry.
But what do you keep of me?
The memory of my bones flying
up into your hands.

June 5, 1972

SPEAKING BITTERNESS

Born like a dwarf
in eighteen ninety-four, the last
of nine children, stuffed in my pram
in Louisburg Square or shortest
to line up at Boothbay Harbor's wharf
where the cunners sulked and no one ever swam.
Blurting through the lobsters and the kelp
we were off to Squirrel Island with five in help.

The cook would vomit
over the rail and the Scotties would bark
and the wind would whip out Old Glory
until the Stewarts, the lots of them, would disembark.
I loved that island like Jesus loves the Jesuit
even though I drowned past Cuckolds' light, another story.
When I was eight Infantile struck. I was the crippled one.
The whole world down the spout, except my skeleton.

They bought a nurse
to live my whole life through
but I've outlived all seventeen
with never a man to say *I do, I do.*
Mother, to be well-born is another curse.
Now I am just an elderly lady who is full of spleen,
who humps around greater Boston in a God-awful hat,
who never lived and yet outlived her time,
hating men and dogs and Democrats.

When I was thirty-two
the doctor kissed my withered limbs
and said he'd leave his wife and run
away with me. Oh, I remember the likes of him,
his hand over my boots, up my skirts like a corkscrew.
The next month he moved his practice to Washington.
Not one man is forgiven! East, West, North, South!

I bite off their dingbats. Christ rots in my mouth.
I curse the seed of my father that put me here
for when I die there'll be no one to say: *Oh No!*
Oh dear.

August 29, 1972

TELEPHONE

Take a red book called TELEPHONE,
size eight by four. There it sits.
My red book, name, address and number.
These are all people that I somehow own.
Yet some of these names are counterfeit.
There beside *Frigidaire* and *Dictaphone*,
there beside Max and Fred and Peggy and John,
beside Eric of Seattle and Snook of Saskatchewan
are all the dear dead names. The ink lies.
Hello! Hello! Goodbye. And then excise.

And thus I do a death dance, a dance
of the thumb. I lay a snake skin
over the name but it won't erase.
I ink my thumbprint. I drool in a trance
and take spit and blood and wine and aspirin
to make a sauce and wipe it on my face.
Then I bite the page, a strange lover of the dead
and my watch dial sings Hello and the name is fed.
Name, I will drown in you like the mother in vinegar
for I have inherited you, a raincheck, a transfer.

And you, witchman, who died without my approval,
you who never loved me although I offered up
every sugar at star-fall, you who blackened
my garden and my hipbone with your chronicle

of my flaws, you who put gum in my coffee cup
and worms in my Jell-O, you who let me pretend
you were daddy of the poets, witchman, you stand
for all, for all the bad dead, a Salvation Army Band
who plays for no one. I am cement. The bird in me is blind
as I knife out your name and all your dead kind.

September 11, 1972

YELLOW

When they turn the sun
on again I'll plant children
under it, I'll light up my soul
with a match and let it sing, I'll
take my mother and soap her up, I'll
take my bones and polish them, I'll
vacuum up my stale hair, I'll
pay all my neighbors' bad debts, I'll
write a poem called *Yellow* and put
my lips down to drink it up, I'll
feed myself spoonfuls of heat and
everyone will be home playing with
their wings and the planet will
shudder with all those smiles and
there will be no poison anywhere, no plague
in the sky and there will be a mother-broth
for all of the people and we will
never die, not one of us, we'll go on
won't we?

September 23, 1972

THE DEATH KING

I hired a carpenter
to build my coffin
and last night I lay in it,
braced by a pillow,
sniffing the wood,
letting the old king
breathe on me,
thinking of my poor murdered body,
murdered by time,
waiting to turn stiff as a field marshal,
letting the silence dishonor me,
remembering that I'll never cough again.

Death will be the end of fear
and the fear of dying,
fear like a dog stuffed in my mouth,
fear like dung stuffed up my nose,
fear where water turns into steel,
fear as my breast flies into the Disposall,
fear as flies tremble in my ear,
fear as the sun ignites in my lap,
fear as night can't be shut off,
and the dawn, my habitual dawn,
is locked up forever.

Fear and a coffin to lie in
like a dead potato.
Even then I will dance in my fire clothes,
a crematory flight,
blinding my hair and my fingers,
wounding God with his blue face,
his tyranny, his absolute kingdom,
with my aphrodisiac.

September 1972

THE ERRAND

I've been going right on, page by page,
since we last kissed, two long dolls in a cage,
two hunger-mongers throwing a myth in and out,
double-crossing our lives with doubt,
leaving us separate now, foggy with rage.

But then I've told my readers what I think
and scrubbed out the remainder with my shrink,
have placed my bones in a jar as if possessed,
have pasted a black wing over my left breast,
have washed the white out of the moon at my sink,

have eaten The Cross, have digested its lore,
indeed, have loved that eggless man once more,
have placed my own head in the kettle because
in the end death won't settle for my hypochondrias,
because this errand we're on goes to one store.

That shopkeeper may put up barricades,
and he may advertise cognac and razor blades,
he may let you dally at Nice or the Tuileries,
he may let the state of our bowels have ascendancy,
he may let such as we flaunt our escapades,

swallow down our portion of whiskey and dex,
salvage the day with some soup or some sex,
juggle our teabags as we inch down the hall,
let the blood out of our fires with phenobarbital,
lick the headlines for Starkweathers and Specks,

let us be folk of the literary set,
let us deceive with words the critics regret,
let us dog down the streets for each invitation,
typing out our lives like a Singer sewing sublimation,
letting our delicate bottoms settle and yet

they were spanked alive by some doctor of folly,
given a horn or a dish to get by with, by golly,
exploding with blood in this errand called life,
dumb with snow and elbows, rubber man, a mother wife,
tongues to waggle out the words, mistletoe and holly,

tables to place our stones on, decades of disguises,
until the shopkeeper plants his boot in our eyes,
and unties our bone and is finished with the case,
and turns to the next customer, forgetting our face
or how we knelt at the yellow bulb with sighs
like moth wings for a short while in a small place.

December 2, 1972

THE TWELVE-THOUSAND-DAY
HONEYMOON

The twelve-thousand-day honeymoon
is over.
Hands crumble like clay,
the mouth, its bewildered tongue,
turns yellow with pain,
the breasts with their doll teacups
lie in a grave of silence,
the arms fall down like boards,
the stomach,
so lightly danced over,
lies grumbling in its foul nausea,
the mound that lifted like the waves
again and again
at your touch
stops, lies helpless as a pinecone,
the vagina, where a daisy rooted,
where a river of sperm rushed home,
lies like a clumsy, unused puppet,
and the heart

slips backward,
remembering, remembering,
where the god had been
as he beat his furious wings.
And then the heart
grabs a prayer out of the newspaper
and lets it buzz through its ventricle, its auricle,
like a wasp
stinging where it will,
yet glowing furiously
in the little highways
where you remain.

July 20, 1973

SCORPIO, BAD SPIDER, DIE

THE HOROSCOPE POEMS

(1971)

And reading my own life with loathing, I tremble and curse.

Pushkin

MADAME ARRIVES IN THE MAIL

Dear Friend,
It may seem to you superstitious and childish to consult the Forecast in your daily activities, but the main object of reading your horoscope should be self-training and knowledge of yourself and your character traits.

Madame, I have a confusion,
will you take it away?
Madame, I have a sickness,
will you take it away?
Madame, I am the victim of an odor,
will you take it away?
Take! For God's sake take!
Mend everything!
The moon is always up there pulling and pulling.
Why not let you bring off some occult tricks?
I'd like to nail the moon up there, a sad crucifix,

and inspect its hair, its roots, its glands
and see if the agony dropped from me like sand.
Yes, indeed,
Madame,
you are a soft shape.
You hiss as you go.
I hear the death of me, the murderous weeds,
the stallion breathing sulphur, the hara-kiri rape,
the bludgeon, the bludgeon and the lowering below
into the deep thorax, the big legs of the ground
so I'll give you a year of me, a kind of iron cast
to assess. Take this Scorpio, this death-bitch me
and advise, advise. Madame, bring on your forecast
for I was only sitting here in my white study
with the awful black words pushing me around.

August 18–25, 1971

JANUARY 1st

Today is favorable for joint financial affairs but do not take any chances with speculation.

My daddy played the market.
My mother cut her coupons.
The children ran in circles.
The maid announced, the soup's on.

The guns were cleaned on Sunday.
The family went out to shoot.
We sat in the blind for hours.
The ducks fell down like fruit.

The big fat war was going on.
So profitable for daddy.

She drove a pea green Ford.
He drove a pearl gray Caddy.

In the end they used it up.
All that pale green dough.
The rest I spent on doctors
who took it like gigolos.

My financial affairs are small.
Indeed they seem to shrink.
My heart is on a budget.
It keeps me on the brink.

I tell it stories now and then
and feed it images like honey.
I will not speculate today
with poems that think they're money.

August 26, 1971

JANUARY 19th

*Your home can be helpful to your health through rest
and the care you get from family members.*

Home is my Bethlehem,
my succoring shelter,
my mental hospital,
my wife, my dam,
my husband, my sir,
my womb, my skull.
Never leave it.
Never leave it.

Home is my daughters
pouring cups of tea,
the dumb brown eyes
of my animals, a liqueur
on the rocks, each a guarantee
of the game and the prize.
Never leave it.
Never leave it.

I leave you, home,
when I'm ripped from the doorstep
by commerce or fate. Then I submit
to the awful subway of the world, the awful shop
of trousers and skirts. Oh animal bosom,
let me stay! Let me never quit
the sweet cereal, the sweet thumb!

August 27–September 8, 1971

JANUARY 24th

Originality is important.

I am alone here in my own mind.
There is no map
and there is no road.
It is one of a kind
just as yours is.
It's in a vapor. It's in a flap.
It makes jelly. It chews toads.
It's a dummy. It's a whiz.
Sometimes I have to hunt her down.
Sometimes I have to track her.
Sometimes I hold her still and use a nutcracker.

594

Such conceit! Such maggoty thoughts,
such an enormous con
just cracks me up.
My brown study will do me in
gushing out of me cold or hot.
Yet I'd risk my life
on that dilly dally buttercup
called dreams. She of the origin,
she of the primal crack, she of the boiling
beginning, she of the riddle, she keeps me here,
toiling and toiling.

[undated]

FEBRUARY 3rd

Your own ideas may be too fanciful to be practical.

My ideas are a curse.
They spring from a radical discontent
with the awful order of things.
I play clown. I play carpenter. I play nurse.
I play witch. Each like an advertisement
for change. My husband always plays King
and is continually shopping in his head for a queen
when only clown, carpenter, nurse, witch can be seen.

Take my LIBRARY CAPER.
I took thirty experts from our town
and each bought thirty expert books.
On an October night when witchery can occur
we each stole thirty books, we took them down
from the town library shelves, each of us a crook,
and placed them in the town dump, all that lovely paper.
We left our expert books upon the shelves. My library caper.

One night we crashed a wedding dinner,
but not the guests. We crashed the chef.
We put dollar bills in the salad, right beside
the lettuce and tomatoes. Our salad was a winner.
The guests kept picking out the bucks, such tiny thefts,
and cawing and laughing like seagulls at their landslide.
There was a strange power to it. Power in that lovely paper.
The bride and groom were proud. I call it my Buck Wedding
    Caper.

My own ideas are a curse for a king and a queen.
I'm a wound without blood, a car without gasoline
unless I can shake myself free of my dog, my flag,
of my desk, my mind, I find life a bit of a drag.
Not always, mind you. Usually I'm like my frying pan —
useful, graceful, sturdy and with no caper, no plan.

                                        August 28, 1971

FEBRUARY 4th

*The day is good for attempts to advance a secret hope
or dream.*

It's a room I dream about.
I had it twice. Two years out of forty-two.
Once at nine. Once more at thirty-six.
There I was dragging the ocean, that knock-out,
in and out by its bottle-green neck, letting it chew
the rocks, letting it haul beach glass and furniture sticks
in and out. From my room I controlled the woman-of-war,
that Mary who came in and in opening and closing the door.

Both times it was an island
in a room with a wide window, a spy hole,

on the sea scrubbing away like an old woman
her wash. A lobsterman hunting for a refund,
gulls like flying babies come by for their dole.
My grandfather typing, He is my little Superman,
he rocks me when the lighthouse flattens her eyes out.
All from the room I pray to when I am dreaming and devout.

August 29, 1971

FEBRUARY 11th

The day is favorable for real-estate affairs.

Houses haunt me.
That last house!
How it sat like a square box!
No closets.
No family room.
Old Oaks bent over city sidewalks.

Still I yearn.
A first home.
A place to take a first baby to.
Railroad tracks
outside the kitchen
window and the good-morning choo-choo.

Tricycles hanging
from the chandeliers.
Kitties like blackboard sharks
nosing their dish.
Buttons and eggs
leaving their little round marks.

A fight
the children called

The Bloody Mary Fight, that worried red
splashed through
the house in the Boston
Strangler way. As if I were dead,

as if I had kissed
the walls in a circle,
hall, kitchen, dining room and back
again. Oh baby bunting,
a first house,
its small mouths, its Union Jack

flying for
our British name.
I'm part Indian I always said
and I was happy there,
part Venetian vase,
part Swiss watch, part Indian head.

August 30, 1971

FEBRUARY 17th

Take nothing for granted.

Yes, I know.
Wallace will be declared king.
For his queen, Shirley Temple Black.
Yes, I know.
The moon will wear garters.
The goldfish will wear a wedding ring.
The chipmunks will subscribe
to the *Old Farmer's Almanac*.
That's just for starters.
Next Queen Elizabeth will take a bribe.

Next the Atlantic will turn to solid ice.
Then the doctors will hand out cancer with their advice.

Yes, I know.
Death sits with his key in my lock.
Not one day is taken for granted.
Even nursery rhymes have put me in hock.
If I die before I wake. Each night in bed.
My husband sings *Baa Baa black sheep* and we pretend
that all's certain and good, that the marriage won't end.

September 1, 1971

FEBRUARY 20th

Concentration should be easier.

I concentrate.
My books hypnotize each other.
Jarrell tells Bishop to stare
at the spot. Tate
tells Plath she's going under.
Eliot remembers his long lost mother,
St. Louis and Sweeney who rise out of thin air,
Mr. Boiler Man, his mouth a mountain,
his tongue pure red, his tongue pure thunder,
Hurry up please it's time. Again. Again.

I concentrate.
My typewriter sinks deeper
and deeper. Dear Ruth, Dear John,
Dear Oscar. All dead now. It's late,
hurry up please it's time. Max, surely you're
still here for drinks. Max out, dinner's on.

Max, surely you'll meet me at the Ritz at five.
Hurry up somebody's dead we're still alive.

September 8th, 1971

FEBRUARY 21st

The day is favorable for teamwork.

The photograph where we smile
at each other, dark head to light head,
sits on my desk. It lay unkissed all week.
That photograph walked up the aisle
for the twenty three years we've been wed
on onward into Carolina, cheek to cheek.
Husband, mad hammer, man of force.
This last week has been our divorce.

I'm not a war baby. I'm a baby
at war. Thumbs grow into my throat.
I wear slaps like a spot of rouge.
Woodsman, who made me into your tree?
Drowner, who made me into your boat?
Lover, I feel a darkness, I feel a fugue
come over us. The photo sits over my desk
as we dance the karate, the mad burlesque.

October 30, 1971

MARCH 4th

Improve your finances.

The high ones, Berryman said, die, die, die.
You look up and who is there?
Daddy's not there shaking his money cane.
Mother's not there waving dollars good-bye
or coughing diamonds into her hanky. Not a forbear,
not an aunt or a chick to call me by name,
not the gardener with his candy dimes and tickles,
not grandpa with his bag full of nickels.

They are all embalmed with their cash
and there is no one here but us kids.
You and me lapping stamps and paying
the bills, shoveling up the beans and the hash.
Our checks are pale. Our wallets are invalids.
Past due, past due, is what our bills are saying
and yet we kiss in every corner, scuffing the dust
and the cat. Love rises like bread as we go bust.

November 22, 1971

MARCH 7th

The day is favorable for creative work.

The big toad sits in my writing room
preventing me from writing. I am a flower
who drys out under her hot breath. She is blowing grass
through her hands! She is knitting up a womb,
knitting up a baby's foot. Her breath is sour.
Her breath is tarnishing up my silver and my brass.

Toad! Are you someone's grunting left-over squaw,
a fat asthmatic Asia, a mother-in-law?

November 22, 1971

MAY 30th

Don't look now, God, we're all right.
All the suicides are eating Black Bean Soup;
the Dalmatian, our turnip, our spotted parasite
snoozles in her chair. The trees, that group
of green girls wiggle at every window;
a sea bird, all nude and intimate, comes in low.

The house sinks in its fill, heavy with books;
in the kitchen the big fat sugar sits in a chamber pot;
in the freezer the Blue Fish vomit up their hooks;
the marriage twists, holds firm, a sailor's knot.
Last night he blamed the economy on Roosevelt and Truman.
I countered with Ike and Nixon. Both wrong. Both human.

Please God, we're all right here. Please leave us alone.
Don't send death in his fat red suit and his ho-ho baritone.

May 30, 1971

AUGUST 8th

*And do not be indiscreet or unconventional. Play it
safe.*

Listen here. I've never played it safe
in spite of what the critics say.
Ask my imaginary brother, that waif,
that childhood best friend who comes to play

dress-up and stick-up and jacks and Pick-Up-Sticks,
bike downtown, stick out tongues at the Catholics.

Or form a Piss Club where we all go
in the bushes and peek at each other's sex.
Pop-gunning the street lights like crows.
Not knowing what to do with funny Kotex
so wearing it in our school shoes. Friend, friend,
spooking my lonely hours, you were there, but pretend.

[undated]

AUGUST 17th

Good for visiting hospitals or charitable work. Take
some time to attend to your health.

Surely I will be disquieted
by the hospital, that body zone —
bodies wrapped in elastic bands,
bodies cased in wood or used like telephones,
bodies crucified up onto their crutches,
bodies wearing rubber bags between their legs,
bodies vomiting up their juice like detergent,
bodies smooth and bare as darning eggs.

Here in this house
there are other bodies.
Whenever I see a six-year-old
swimming in our aqua pool
a voice inside me says what can't be told . . .
Ha, someday you'll be old and withered
and tubes will be in your nose
drinking up your dinner.
Someday you'll go backward. You'll close

603

up like a shoebox and you'll be cursed
as you push into death feet first.

Here in the hospital, I say,
that is not my body, not my body.
I am not here for the doctors
to read like a recipe.
No. I am a daisy girl
blowing in the wind like a piece of sun.
On ward 7 there are daisies, all butter and pearl
but beside a blind man who can only
eat up the petals and count to ten.
The nurses skip rope around him and shiver
as his eyes wiggle like mercury and then
they dance from patient to patient to patient
throwing up little paper medicine cups and playing
catch with vials of dope as they wait for new accidents.
Bodies made of synthetics. Bodies swaddled like dolls
whom I visit and cajole and all they do is hum
like computers doing up our taxes, dollar by dollar.
Each body is in its bunker. The surgeon applies his gum.
Each body is fitted quickly into its ice-cream pack
and then stitched up again for the long voyage
back.

August 17–25, 1971

Last Poems

ADMONITIONS TO A SPECIAL PERSON

Watch out for power,
for its avalanche can bury you,
snow, snow, snow, smothering your mountain.

Watch out for hate,
it can open its mouth and you'll fling yourself out
to eat off your leg, an instant leper.

Watch out for friends,
because when you betray them,
as you will,
they will bury their heads in the toilet
and flush themselves away.

Watch out for intellect,
because it knows so much it knows nothing
and leaves you hanging upside down,
mouthing knowledge as your heart
falls out of your mouth.

Watch out for games, the actor's part,
the speech planned, known, given,
for they will give you away
and you will stand like a naked little boy,
pissing on your own child-bed.

Watch out for love
(unless it is true,
and every part of you says yes including the toes),
it will wrap you up like a mummy,
and your scream won't be heard
and none of your running will run.

Love? Be it man. Be it woman.
It must be a wave you want to glide in on,

give your body to it, give your laugh to it,
give, when the gravelly sand takes you,
your tears to the land. To love another is something
like prayer and can't be planned, you just fall
into its arms because your belief undoes your disbelief.

Special person,
if I were you I'd pay no attention
to admonitions from me,
made somewhat out of your words
and somewhat out of mine.
A collaboration.
I do not believe a word I have said,
except some, except I think of you like a young tree
with pasted-on leaves and know you'll root
and the real green thing will come.

Let go. Let go.
Oh special person,
possible leaves,
this typewriter likes you on the way to them,
but wants to break crystal glasses
in celebration,
for you,
when the dark crust is thrown off
and you float all around
like a happened balloon.

March 24, 1974

IN EXCELSIS

It is half winter, half spring,
and Barbara and I are standing
confronting the ocean.
Its mouth is open very wide,

and it has dug up its green,
throwing it, throwing it at the shore.
You say it is angry.
I say it is like a kicked Madonna.
Its womb collapses, drunk with its fever.
We breathe in its fury.

I, the inlander,
am here with you for just a small space.
I am almost afraid,
so long gone from the sea.
I have seen her smooth as a cheek.
I have seen her easy,
doing her business,
lapping in.
I have seen her rolling her hoops of blue.
I have seen her tear the land off.
I have seen her drown me twice,
and yet not take me.
You tell me that as the green drains backward
it covers Britain,
but have you never stood on *that* shore
and seen it cover you?

We have come to worship,
the tongues of the surf are prayers,
and we vow,
the unspeakable vow.
Both silently.
Both differently.
I wish to enter her like a dream,
leaving my roots here on the beach
like a pan of knives.
And my past to unravel, with its knots and snarls,
and walk into ocean,
letting it explode over me

and outward, where I would drink the moon
and my clothes would slip away,
and I would sink into the great mother arms
I never had,
except here where the abyss
throws itself on the sand
blow by blow,
over and over,
and we stand on the shore
loving its pulse
as it swallows the stars,
and has since it all began
and will continue into oblivion,
past our knowing
and the wild toppling green that enters us today,
for a small time
in half winter, half spring.

April 1, 1974

USES

Papa died in the gas chamber,
slipping blue as an undressed minnow,
gulping in the shower to wash the Jew off him.
Mama died in the medical experiments,
they had stuffed a pig into her womb
and the pig died, and after she lost her vision,
she lost her heart stuffing.

I, alone, came through,
starved but making it by eating
a body or two.

Then came the Americans with peanut butter.
I gobbled it up like a vacation.
I loved them all, even the GI who said "Jew pig"

and put it into me, into me,
though I was only eleven.

Later I joined a convent,
to fall in love with a Jesus home,
but I had to leave,
for I was turning gray — hair, eyes, nose, mouth, face.
I was a mouse
searching for its cheddar trap.

I never cried.
Remember that!
I never cried.

Then the U.S.
and its funny cities of butter
buildings without bullet holes
or bombed-out towns.
But it had jails
and I flew into one
and stood in the cell with the whores
and hung onto the bars,
saying nothing except
"I am a Jew.
Can't you do something with it?"

May 1, 1974

AS IT WAS WRITTEN

Earth, earth,
riding your merry-go-round
toward extinction,
right to the roots,
thickening the oceans like gravy,
festering in your caves,
you are becoming a latrine.

Your trees are twisted chairs.
Your flowers moan at their mirrors,
and cry for a sun that doesn't wear a mask.

Your clouds wear white,
trying to become nuns
and say novenas to the sky.
The sky is yellow with its jaundice,
and its veins spill into the rivers
where the fish kneel down
to swallow hair and goat's eyes.

All in all, I'd say,
the world is strangling.
And I, in my bed each night,
listen to my twenty shoes
converse about it.
And the moon,
under its dark hood,
falls out of the sky each night,
with its hungry red mouth
to suck at my scars.

August 4, 1974

LESSONS IN HUNGER

"Do you like me?"
I asked the blue blazer.
No answer.
Silence bounced out of his books.
Silence fell off his tongue
and sat between us
and clogged my throat.
It slaughtered my trust.
It tore cigarettes out of my mouth.
We exchanged blind words,

612

and I did not cry,
and I did not beg,
but blackness filled my ears,
blackness lunged in my heart,
and something that had been good,
a sort of kindly oxygen,
turned into a gas oven.

Do you like me?
How absurd!
What's a question like that?
What's a silence like that?
And what am I hanging around for,
riddled with what his silence said?

August 7, 1974

LOVE LETTER WRITTEN IN
A BURNING BUILDING

Dearest Foxxy,

I am in a crate,
the crate that was ours,
full of white shirts and salad greens,
the icebox knocking at our delectable knocks,
and I wore movies in my eyes,
and you wore eggs in your tunnel,
and we played sheets, sheets, sheets
all day, even in the bathtub like lunatics.
But today I set the bed afire
and smoke is filling the room,
it is getting hot enough for the walls to melt,
and the icebox, a gluey white tooth.

I have on a mask in order to write my last words,
and they are just for you, and I will place them

in the icebox saved for vodka and tomatoes,
and perhaps they will last.
The dog will not. Her spots will fall off.
The old letters will melt into a black bee.
The nightgowns are already shredding
into paper, the yellow, the red, the purple.
The bed — well, the sheets have turned to gold —
hard, hard gold, and the mattress
is being kissed into a stone.

As for me, my dearest Foxxy,
my poems to you may or may not reach the icebox
and its hopeful eternity,
for isn't yours enough?
The one where you name
my name right out in P. R.?
If my toes weren't yielding to pitch
I'd tell the whole story —
not just the sheet story
but the belly-button story,
the pried-eyelid story,
the whiskey-sour-of-the-nipple story —
and shovel back our love where it belonged.

Despite my asbestos gloves,
the cough is filling me with black,
and a red powder seeps through my veins,
our little crate goes down so publicly
and without meaning it, you see,
meaning a solo act,
a cremation of the love,
but instead we seem to be going down
right in the middle of a Russian street,
the flames making the sound of
the horse being beaten and beaten,
the whip is adoring its human triumph

while the flies wait, blow by blow,
straight from United Fruit, Inc.

September 27, 1974

Index of Titles

617

621